CRIME, PRISONS, AND JAILS

ISSN 1938-890X

CRIME, PRISONS, AND JAILS

Kim Masters Evans

INFORMATION PLUS® REFERENCE SERIES
Formerly Published by Information Plus, Wylie, Texas

GALE
CENGAGE Learning·

Farmington Hills, Mich • San Francisco • New York • Waterville, Maine
Meriden, Conn • Mason, Ohio • Chicago

Crime, Prisons, and Jails

Kim Masters Evans

Kepos Media, Inc.: Steven Long and
Janice Jorgensen, Series Editors

Project Editors: Tracie Moy, Laura Avery

Rights Acquisition and Management: Ashley
Maynard, Amanda Kopczynski

Composition: Evi Abou-El-Seoud, Mary Beth
Trimper

Manufacturing: Rita Wimberley

Product Design: Kristine Julien

For product information and technology assistance, contact us at
Gale Customer Support, 1-800-877-4253.
For permission to use material from this text or product,
submit all requests online at **www.cengage.com/permissions.**
Further permissions questions can be e-mailed to
permissionrequest@cengage.com

Cover photograph: © txking/Shutterstock.com.

While every effort has been made to ensure the reliability of the information presented in this publication, Gale, a part of Cengage Learning, does not guarantee the accuracy of the data contained herein. Gale accepts no payment for listing; and inclusion in the publication of any organization, agency, institution, publication, service, or individual does not imply endorsement of the editors or publisher. Errors brought to the attention of the publisher and verified to the satisfaction of the publisher will be corrected in future editions.

Gale
27500 Drake Rd.
Farmington Hills, MI 48331-3535

ISBN-13: 978-0-7876-5103-9 (set)
ISBN-13: 978-1-57302-649-9

ISSN 1938-890X

This title is also available as an e-book.
ISBN-13: 978-1-57302-675-8 (set)
Contact your Gale sales representative for ordering information.

Printed in the United States of America
1 2 3 4 5   19 18 17 16 15

TABLE OF CONTENTS

PREFACE

Crime, Prisons, and Jails is part of the *Information Plus Reference Series*. The purpose of each volume of the series is to present the latest facts on a topic of pressing concern in modern American life. These topics include the most controversial and studied social issues of the 21st century: abortion, capital punishment, care of senior citizens, education, the environment, health care, immigration, national security, social welfare, water, women, youth, and many more. Although this series is written especially for high school and undergraduate students, it is an excellent resource for anyone in need of factual information on current affairs.

By presenting the facts, it is the intention of Gale, Cengage Learning, to provide its readers with everything they need to reach an informed opinion on current issues. To that end, there is a particular emphasis in this series on the presentation of scientific studies, surveys, and statistics. These data are generally presented in the form of tables, charts, and other graphics placed within the text of each book. Every graphic is directly referred to and carefully explained in the text. The source of each graphic is presented within the graphic itself. The data used in these graphics are drawn from the most reputable and reliable sources, such as from the various branches of the U.S. government and from private organizations and associations. Every effort has been made to secure the most recent information available. Readers should bear in mind that many major studies take years to conduct and that additional years often pass before the data from these studies are made available to the public. Therefore, in many cases the most recent information available in 2015 is dated from 2012 or 2013. Older statistics are sometimes presented as well if they are landmark studies or of particular interest and no more-recent information exists.

Although statistics are a major focus of the *Information Plus Reference Series*, they are by no means its only content. Each book also presents the widely held positions and important ideas that shape how the book's subject is discussed in the United States. These positions are explained in detail and, where possible, in the words of their proponents. Some of the other material to be found in these books includes historical background, descriptions of major events related to the subject, relevant laws and court cases, and examples of how these issues play out in American life. Some books also feature primary documents or have pro and con debate sections that provide the words and opinions of prominent Americans on both sides of a controversial topic. All material is presented in an evenhanded and unbiased manner; readers will never be encouraged to accept one view of an issue over another.

HOW TO USE THIS BOOK

In general, crime has been on the decline in recent years. Some crimes, however, are increasing in number among different segments of the population. For example, violent crime has decreased since the 1990s, whereas identity theft has increased. Besides exploring crime in the United States, this volume examines the U.S. penal system as well as its inmates. Prisons and jails are an important and controversial part of the effort to control crime in the United States. Much public funding is spent on the construction of new prisons and jails and on the maintenance of old facilities, but many people question the effectiveness of prisons and jails as a deterrent to crime. Who is locked up in U.S. prisons, what crimes have they committed, and how effective is the prison system? These and other basic questions are discussed in this volume.

Crime, Prisons, and Jails consists of 10 chapters and three appendixes. Each chapter is devoted to a particular aspect of crime, prisons, and jails in the United States. For a summary of the information that is covered in each chapter, please see the synopses that are provided in the Table of Contents. Chapters generally begin with an overview of the basic facts and background information on the chapter's topic, then proceed to examine subtopics of particular interest. For example, Chapter 5, White-Collar Crime, describes many different types of white-collar crimes, which are crimes in which deception and trickery, rather than violent means, are used against victims. Statistics from federal and state law enforcement agencies are presented on the number of arrests for these types of crimes. One of the most pervasive white-collar crimes is identity theft. The chapter examines the ways in which identity theft is perpetrated, and the financial consequences to victims. Cybercrime (the conduct of crime via the Internet) is also discussed in detail with focus on online deception, malware (such as computer viruses), and computer hacking. Other white-collar crimes addressed include intellectual property crimes, currency counterfeiting, corporate and securities fraud, and public official corruption. The chapter ends with a discussion of the various victimization surveys and complaint centers that provide data about white-collar crime victims. Readers can find their way through a chapter by looking for the section and subsection headings, which are clearly set off from the text. They can also refer to the book's extensive Index, if they already know what they are looking for.

Statistical Information

The tables and figures featured throughout *Crime, Prisons, and Jails* will be of particular use to readers in learning about this topic. These tables and figures represent an extensive collection of the most recent and valuable statistics on prisons and jails, as well as related issues—for example, graphics cover the number of people in jail or prison in the United States, the characteristics of those on probation, and the amount of money the government spends on the criminal justice system. Gale, Cengage Learning, believes that making this information available to readers is the most important way to fulfill the goal of this book: to help readers understand the issues and controversies surrounding crime, prisons, and jails in the United States and to reach their own conclusions.

Each table or figure has a unique identifier appearing above it for ease of identification and reference. Titles for the tables and figures explain their purpose. At the end of each table or figure, the original source of the data is provided.

To help readers understand these often complicated statistics, all tables and figures are explained in the text. References in the text direct readers to the relevant statistics. Furthermore, the contents of all tables and figures are fully indexed. Please see the opening section of the Index at the back of this volume for a description of how to find tables and figures within it.

Appendixes

Besides the main body text and images, *Crime, Prisons, and Jails* has three appendixes. The first is the Important Names and Addresses directory. Here, readers will find contact information for a number of government and private organizations that can provide further information on aspects of crime and the U.S. prison and jail systems. The second appendix is the Resources section, which can also assist readers in conducting their own research. In this section, the author and editors of *Crime, Prisons, and Jails* describe some of the sources that were most useful during the compilation of this book. The final appendix is the detailed Index. It has been greatly expanded from previous editions and should make it even easier to find specific topics in this book.

COMMENTS AND SUGGESTIONS

The editors of the *Information Plus Reference Series* welcome your feedback on *Crime, Prisons, and Jails*. Please direct all correspondence to:

Editors
Information Plus Reference Series
27500 Drake Rd.
Farmington Hills, MI 48331-3535

CHAPTER 1
AN OVERVIEW OF CRIME

A crime occurs when a person commits an act that is prohibited by law or fails to act where there is a legal responsibility to do so. Crime has both legal and moral components. Federal, state, and local laws define criminal behavior and specify corresponding punishments. These laws are designed to protect the public good and are based, in some part, on the moral beliefs that are held by U.S. society about the relative rightness and wrongness of various human actions. Americans consider crime to be a serious problem. They worry about the level of criminal behavior in their neighborhoods and in the country as a whole.

CATEGORIZING CRIME
Etymology, Morality, and Mental State

Etymology is the study of the origins and evolving meanings of words. Many English words have their roots in ancient Latin or Greek. In "The Conceptualisation of 'Crime' in Classical Greek Antiquity" (*ERCES Online Quarterly Review*, vol. 2, no. 2, 2005), Michael Bakaoukas notes that neither ancient language had a word encompassing the many activities now lumped under the word "crime." Instead, he indicates there was "a variety of words for 'wrongdoing,' 'injustice' or 'judgment and conviction,'" including "krima" in classical Greek and "crimen" in Republican Latin. The rise of Christianity led to changing uses for these words, and they became associated with violating "God's will." For example, the Online Etymology Dictionary (2014, http://www.etymonline.com/index.php?term=crime) notes that the 13th-century French word "crimne" translates as "sinfulness." Over time a broader, less religious meaning evolved. Bakaoukas points out that the modern notion of crime "involves the idea of an offence not just against an individual, but against the community, against society, against the state, or against the peace. It also suggests that the apprehended offender will be punished."

The criminal codes for western societies evolved from the Judeo-Christian bible. This is evident in the criminal justice system of the early American colonies, which was deeply influenced by the Christian church. People could be prosecuted for witchcraft, gossiping, and blasphemy (insulting or showing contempt for God or anyone or anything considered sacred). Numerous sexual activities outside of those approved by the church were defined as crimes. So-called "blue laws" dictated what people could and could not do on Sundays; for example, church attendance was mandatory in some communities. Working, traveling, engaging in commerce or recreation, and many other activities were forbidden on Sundays, and violators faced severe penalties, including execution. Over time U.S. legal codes evolved to reflect greater separation between the church and the state. Behaviors that had been deemed criminal because they violated church dictates slowly became decriminalized. Nevertheless some "blue laws" lingered into the 21st century, particularly those regarding alcohol sales on Sundays.

The Latin term *mala in se* means "morally wrong" or "inherently wrong." *Mala in se* crimes are those condemned universally as wrong or evil because the criminal action is inherently bad. Crimes such as murder and stealing have been considered wrong since ancient times. They remain morally unacceptable in the 21st century. However, other behaviors have been alternatively accepted and rejected as crimes based on changing public attitudes. Slavery was once considered a legal practice in the United States. Eventually, it became so morally repugnant that it was deemed a crime. American attitudes about the criminality of alcohol and drug usage and certain sexual activities have varied over time as will be explained later in this chapter.

Some minor crimes are considered *mala prohibita* (wrongs prohibited). These are behaviors that are not inherently bad in themselves but are prohibited by government policy. Many traffic laws are *mala prohibita*. For example, speeding is criminal not because it is morally evil but because it is deemed criminal by government authorities.

An important element in how crimes are categorized and punished is called *mens rea*, which translates from Latin as "guilty mind," or more commonly, "criminal intent." The U.S. justice system seeks to determine the mental state of a perpetrator at the time the criminal act was committed and to assign punishment accordingly. Intentional criminal acts that are planned in advance are considered much more serious than unintentional criminal acts or crimes committed in the "heat of passion."

Punishment Categories

Governments' decisions about how to punish certain crimes are based, in part, on the moral beliefs of the society in which the crimes occur. Although *mala in se* behaviors are universally condemned as wrong, punishments for these crimes can vary significantly between societies and between governments. During the colonial period in U.S. history, the death penalty was commonly meted out for crimes such as horse stealing and robbery. Over time, societal morals demanded less harsh punishments for these crimes. The evolution in U.S. attitudes about appropriate punishments for criminal behavior is discussed in more detail in chapter 7.

Under U.S. law, crimes are divided into three broad categories: felonies, misdemeanors, and infractions. Felonies are considered the most serious crimes and are punished the most severely. The word *felony* is believed to be derived from a Latin word meaning "evil doer." Crimes that inflict death or serious injury or the threat of death or serious injury are considered felonies. Many property crimes that involve large economic losses to the victim are also classified as felonies. In general, people convicted of felonies are punished with prison terms at least a year in length and are sometimes assessed a fine of many thousands of dollars. Convicted felons may also lose some of their constitutional rights, such as the right to vote in elections. In some states the loss of rights only applies while a felon is incarcerated; in other states rights can be lost permanently. The most serious felony is the intentional murder of another human being. This crime is considered so heinous that capital punishment (execution) is sometimes the penalty for committing murder.

Misdemeanors are less serious crimes than felonies. They involve less personal harm and lower economic losses than felonies. These "lesser" crimes are typically punished with jail sentences of less than one year and fines of up to a few thousand dollars. People convicted of misdemeanors do not typically lose any of their constitutional rights once their sentences are served.

States divide felonies and misdemeanors into levels or classes to indicate their relative seriousness. For example, the Virginia Department of Alcoholic Beverage Control indicates in "Punishment for Criminal Offenses" (2015, http://www.abc.state.va.us/facts/punish.html) that Virginia has six classes of felonies and four classes of misdemeanors. In both categories Class 1 crimes are the most serious and punished the most severely. Other states use a letter system in which Class A felonies or misdemeanors are considered the most serious in their category.

Finally, the least serious crimes are called infractions (or petty offenses). These include minor traffic and parking violations and violations of local ordinances. The punishment for an infraction is usually only a fine of up to a few hundred dollars.

DEFINING THE TYPES OF CRIMES

Crimes are defined and punished differently by different jurisdictions within the United States. Sorting out all the various and complicated legal definitions for particular crimes can be challenging. This section will present some general and widely used definitions for the most common crimes.

Killing Crimes

Killing crimes are defined and punished at various levels depending on the mental state of the killer and the circumstances under which the killing took place. Criminal intent (or lack thereof) plays a major role in how these crimes are categorized. Killing with criminal intent is typically called murder. There are various degrees (or levels) of murder in criminal law. First-degree murder is the most serious charge and means the killer planned the crime and deliberately carried it out. First-degree murder is often described as deliberate killing with "malice aforethought." Malice is the desire or intent to cause great harm. Aforethought means "previously in mind." In other words, murder committed with aforethought is premeditated (considered and thought through before being committed).

Second-degree murder is a lesser charge that is applied to a killing that may or may not be intentional but is not premeditated. A person who gets into a fistfight and ultimately kills his or her opponent might be charged with second-degree murder. This crime might also be called manslaughter. There are two levels of manslaughter: voluntary manslaughter and involuntary manslaughter. Voluntary manslaughter is a killing believed to be intentional but not premeditated. It occurs on a sudden impulse, as in the fistfight example. Involuntary manslaughter is an unintentional killing that occurs as a consequence of reckless behavior or extreme negligence. The reckless behavior is typically some minor unlawful action that is not ordinarily expected to result in a death.

An example is a driver who runs a red light and inadvertently strikes and kills a pedestrian crossing the street. Ordinarily, running a red light is a minor crime. The accidental taking of life elevates the crime to the level of manslaughter. Involuntary manslaughter involving extreme negligence may also be called criminally negligent homicide. Involuntary manslaughter involving recklessness, rather than negligence, is often called nonnegligent homicide.

An accidental killing that occurs as a result of a felony is a much more serious crime in the eyes of the law. Some states define a crime called felony murder. It can be charged against any willing participant in a serious felony (such as a bank robbery) if a person is inadvertently killed as a result of the felonious act. These laws apply even to criminals who are not actually in the victim's presence at the time of the accidental death (e.g., getaway drivers at bank robberies). As a result, these laws are highly controversial.

Some homicides are not considered criminal. These include killings performed in self-defense and accidental killings that occur during noncriminal actions. Intent and circumstances are the primary elements that influence whether criminal charges are filed and the extent of any resulting punishments.

Bodily Harm Crimes

Bodily harm crimes are crimes that are intended to cause or do cause personal injury to another person. The primary example is assault, which is an attempted or completed attack on a victim by a perpetrator who intends to inflict or recklessly inflicts bodily harm.

AGGRAVATED AND SIMPLE ASSAULT. In general, there are two levels of assault: aggravated assault and simple assault. Aggravated assault charges are typically filed if the attacker uses a deadly weapon and/or intends to inflict or does inflict serious injury to the victim. Aggravated assault can also result from reckless behavior. Simple assault is a lesser crime that does not include the more serious circumstances or consequences to the victim. Simple assault can also be charged when a person's extreme negligence causes bodily harm to another person. Some state laws define a crime called assault and battery that includes both threat (assault) and bodily attack (battery).

In most jurisdictions the penalties for assault (or assault and battery) are more severe when the victim is a public official, such as a law enforcement officer, firefighter, social worker, judge, or schoolteacher, who is attacked while on duty.

Sex Crimes

Sexually based offenses involve some type of sexual activity that is deemed illegal. Changing moral views over time have slowly led to decriminalization of some activities that were once outlawed. In 2003 in *Lawrence et al. v. Texas* (539 U.S. 558) the U.S. Supreme Court struck down as unconstitutional a Texas law that prohibited people of the same sex from engaging in sexual conduct. The ruling invalidated similar laws across the country. According to Ethan Bronner, in "Adultery, an Ancient Crime That Remains on Many Books" (NYTimes.com, November 14, 2012), as of 2012, 23 U.S. states still had laws criminalizing adultery (i.e., consensual sexual acts by married people with partners other than their spouses). In light of the *Lawrence et al. v. Texas* ruling, the adultery laws would likely not survive court challenges and are not enforced; nevertheless, they remain on the books. Bronner notes that politicians are reluctant to eliminate the laws because "many like the idea of the criminal code serving as a kind of moral guide even if certain laws are almost never applied." Laws against fornication (consensual sexual acts between unmarried people) also lingered in some states as of January 2015, including Idaho, Massachusetts, and Virginia. The state supreme courts in Georgia and Virginia ruled their fornication laws unconstitutional in 2003 and 2005, respectively.

The most serious sexual offenses are those in which force or the threat of force is used by the perpetrator and those in which the victims are children. Rape, or sexual assault as it is called in some states, is a crime that has different definitions depending on the jurisdiction. In addition, state laws typically classify rapes at different felony levels depending on the circumstances of the crime. For example, the Office of Code Revision Indiana Legislative Services Agency (2014, http://www.in.gov/legislative/ic/code/title35/ar42/ch4.html) indicates that Indiana classifies rape as a Class A felony if the rape includes the threat or use of deadly force, the perpetrator has a deadly weapon (such as a firearm), the victim is seriously injured during the attack, or the victim is unknowingly drugged by the perpetrator. Otherwise, rape is a Class B felony in Indiana.

Use (or threat) of force and lack of consent are common elements that define rape when the victim is an adult with full mental and physical capacities. Statutory rape is a separately defined crime in which the victim is either younger than a legally set age of consent or the victim is an adult with a debilitating mental or physical condition. In these cases a crime occurs even if the victim consents to the sexual activity and no force or threat of force is used.

Many other offenses besides rape may be considered sexually based crimes under the law. Typical examples include offenses related to prostitution or pornography. Depending on the circumstances, these crimes might be deemed felonies or less serious misdemeanors.

Theft Crimes

Theft crimes cover a broad spectrum of offenses. The most serious theft crime is called robbery. An important distinction between robbery and other theft crimes is that robbery involves an element of personal force or the threat of personal force and harm to the victim. Thus, robberies are typically face-to-face crimes in which the victim is personally menaced by the perpetrator. This can occur on the street (e.g., a mugging or carjacking) or in a business or residence (e.g., a bank robbery or home invasion). Because of the danger to the victims posed by these personal encounters, the penalties for robbery are severe.

Burglary is a theft crime that includes unlawful entry, such as into a house. Burglary is sometimes also known as breaking and entering, although the actual act of "breaking in" is not always required. In general, any entry made without the owner's permission (for example, through an unlocked door) may legally be considered burglary.

Theft (or larceny) is a broad category that includes many different offenses. For example, California's penal code Section 484(a) (March 17, 2014, http://law.onecle .com/california/penal/484.html) defines theft as:

> Every person who shall feloniously steal, take, carry, lead, or drive away the personal property of another, or who shall fraudulently appropriate property which has been entrusted to him or her, or who shall knowingly and designedly, by any false or fraudulent representation or pretense, defraud any other person of money, labor or real or personal property, or who causes or procures others to report falsely of his or her wealth or mercantile character and by thus imposing upon any person, obtains credit and thereby fraudulently gets or obtains possession of money, or property or obtains the labor or service of another, is guilty of theft.

Many other theft-type offenses are also defined by law. Examples include forgery, counterfeiting, fraud, identity theft, confidence games, writing bad checks, and embezzlement. In all these cases, the intent of the perpetrator is to obtain something of value through illegal means.

Theft crimes are generally classified into levels or degrees of seriousness based on the particular circumstances of the crime. These classifications often take into account the economic losses to the victim. In other words, a large-value theft is treated more severely than a low-value theft.

WHITE-COLLAR CRIMES. White-collar crimes are a subset of theft crimes. They differ from crimes such as burglary and robbery in that white-collar crimes are typically conducted without the threat or use of violence and without physical labor (e.g., breaking into a building) on the part of the perpetrator. Examples include fraud, counterfeiting, and embezzlement. White-collar crimes are discussed in detail in Chapter 5.

Alcohol and Drug Crimes

Alcohol and drugs are substances that can impair judgment and inflame passions. People under the influence of these substances may engage in reckless or violent behavior that seriously harms others. Societal concerns about alcohol and drug use have varied dramatically throughout U.S. history.

ALCOHOL CRIMES. During the late 1800s and early 1900s, a Progressive movement swept the nation in which many people believed that laws could "socially engineer" Americans out of immoral and destructive behaviors—such as drinking alcohol. Some states passed laws that were intended to restrict its consumption. By 1918 alcohol was considered such a menace to the public good that its manufacture and sale were outlawed by Congress via the 18th Amendment to the U.S. Constitution. Prohibition, as it was called, proved to be unworkable and was abandoned at the federal level in 1933. Nevertheless, states and local jurisdictions have passed laws that criminalize certain alcohol-related actions, particularly public drunkenness and driving under the influence of alcohol.

DRUG CRIMES. The history of drug criminalization has also been checkered. Drugs such as cocaine and heroin were once common ingredients in popular products that Americans bought and consumed. Over time, growing awareness about the physical, psychological, and social harms associated with the use of these drugs spurred laws against them. Modern drug laws are complex and sometimes controversial as Americans continue to debate how best to control human behaviors that are considered undesirable to the public good. A detailed discussion of drug crimes is presented in Chapter 4.

Hate Crimes

Hate crimes are criminal offenses that are motivated by the offender's personal prejudice or bias against the victim. The first federal legislation against hate crimes was passed in 1969. Since that time additional laws have expanded the types of offenses that are considered hate crimes. Chapter 2 presents hate crime statistics and discusses the legislation and constitutional issues associated with hate crimes.

Terrorism

Terrorism is difficult to define legally. In fact, there are many different definitions under federal and state laws. In 22 USC Section 2656f(d)(2) (2015, http://www .law.cornell.edu/uscode/text/22/2656f), which focuses on foreign relations, the federal government defines terrorism as "premeditated, politically motivated violence perpetrated against noncombatant targets by subnational groups or clandestine agents."

Generally, the term *terrorism* is associated with violent actions that are perpetrated by people with a certain mind-set against other people. The perpetrators of terrorist acts typically justify their behavior as appropriate because it is waged against people they consider to be enemies for various political, social, and/or religious reasons. Thus, terrorism is the ultimate hate crime and is motivated by bias. Much modern terrorism is international in nature, meaning that it involves perpetrators and victims of different nationalities. Some horrifying acts of international terrorism have taken place, including the September 11, 2001, attacks on the United States. Such acts are criminal under U.S. law, and the perpetrators can be tried and convicted of criminal offenses. The scope of international terrorism places it squarely under the jurisdiction of federal authorities. However, capturing and trying foreign nationals can be difficult, particularly when they are in countries unfriendly to the United States. In some cases, the U.S. armed forces may become involved, as they did in the war in Afghanistan (2001–2014), to capture alleged terrorists for prosecution under U.S. law.

The U.S. government has numerous agencies and offices that are devoted to protecting U.S. national security, including preventing, investigating, and responding to terrorist attacks. The FBI, which is a law enforcement agency within the U.S. Department of Justice, takes a lead role in domestic terrorism cases.

Domestic Terrorism

Terrorism is domestic when the perpetrators and the victims are citizens or residents of the same country, such as a terrorist attack that is carried out on U.S. soil by U.S. citizens or residents. The perpetrators would actually be charged with legally defined crimes, such as murder, assault, arson, and so on. The main distinction between acts of domestic terrorism and other domestic crimes hinges on motive.

It can be difficult to determine whether a particular crime is committed for social/political reasons, personal reasons (e.g., revenge), or a mixture of these motives. For example, in October 2002 two men dubbed "the Beltway snipers" terrorized people in the District of Columbia area with a killing spree that left 10 people dead and three people wounded. One of the perpetrators, John Allen Muhammad (1960–2009), was described in the media as committing the killings for a mixture of personal and social/political reasons. He reportedly hoped to extract revenge on his former wife as well as extort money from the government to fund a terrorist training camp. Muhammad was ultimately convicted of a number of crimes, including murder and terrorism-related charges, and was executed in 2009.

In "Major Terrorism Cases" (2015, http://www.fbi.gov/about-us/investigate/terrorism/terrorism_cases), the FBI describes some of the major U.S. terrorism cases

the agency investigated from the 1920s through 2013, including many domestic cases. The vast majority of the cases in the 21st century have involved Islamist extremists. These perpetrators are often referred to as "homegrown" terrorists because they were either born in the United States or became U.S. citizens before committing their crimes.

Types of Domestic Terrorism

While cases involving homegrown jihadists (terrorists who use the cover of the Islamic religion to carry out violence against those who stand in the way of Muslims) elicit intense media attention, they are not the only types of domestic terrorism that take place. In "Major Terrorism Cases," the FBI refers readers to the Global Terrorism Database (http://www.start.umd.edu/gtd), a project of the U.S. Department of Homeland Security's National Consortium for the Study of Terrorism and Responses to Terrorism at the University of Maryland. The database contains information from 1970 through 2013 about more than 125,000 terrorist cases worldwide. Information about perpetrators is provided as known; however, many perpetrators remain unidentified. A search of the database as of January 2015 for incidents within the United States returned 2,381 incidents.

Many of the domestic attacks in the United States with known or suspected perpetrators are believed to have been carried out by ecoterrorist groups. These are extremist groups that support environmentalism, animal rights, or similar causes, but use criminal violence to promote their ideas and attack their perceived enemies. For example, radical animal rights activists are believed to be behind bombs that exploded outside the homes of two University of California, Santa Cruz, biomedical researchers in August 2008. One person was wounded in the attacks. The scientists were allegedly targeted because they use animals in their research (research that the university claims is being conducted using the highest humane standards). The remaining incidents of U.S. domestic terrorism in the database that are not examples of homegrown jihadism are attributed to perpetrators with a variety of political, religious, and social biases, for example, white supremacists and antiabortion activists.

Four domestic terrorist incidents that have occurred in recent decades are of particular note:

OKLAHOMA CITY BOMBING. On April 19, 1995, a 2-ton (1.8-t) truck bomb exploded outside the Alfred P. Murrah Federal Building in Oklahoma City, Oklahoma, killing 168 people and injuring more than 800. The attack was perpetrated by Timothy McVeigh (1968–2001), a 27-year-old military veteran with ties to antigovernment militia groups. McVeigh was executed by lethal injection in June 2001. Terry L. Nichols (1955–), an accomplice who helped McVeigh plan the attack and construct the bomb, was sentenced to life in prison without the possibility of parole.

OLYMPIC PARK BOMBING. On July 27, 1996, during the Olympic Games in Atlanta, Georgia, a nail-packed pipe bomb exploded in a large common area. One person was killed and more than 100 people were injured. Authorities had no leads at the time, but similar explosive devices were later used in bomb attacks on a nightclub that was favored by homosexuals and two abortion clinics. These incidents led investigators to Eric Robert Rudolph (1966–), a Christian extremist whose views combined antigovernment political sentiments with antihomosexual bigotry and opposition to abortion. Rudolph eluded capture for five years before he surrendered to authorities in May 2003. Confessing to the Olympic bombing, he said he was motivated by antigovernment and antisocialist beliefs. He was sentenced to life in prison without the possibility of parole.

ANTHRAX ATTACKS. On September 25, 2001, a letter containing a white powdery substance was handled by an assistant to the NBC News anchor Tom Brokaw (1940–). After complaining of a rash, the assistant consulted a physician and tested positive for exposure to the anthrax bacterium (*Bacillus anthracis*), an infectious agent that, if inhaled into the lungs, can lead to death. Over the next two months envelopes testing positive for anthrax were received by various U.S. news organizations and by government offices, including the offices of the U.S. Senate majority leader Tom Daschle (1947–; D-SD) and the New York governor George Pataki (1945–). As a result of exposure to anthrax that was sent via the U.S. mail system, five people died, including two postal workers who handled letters carrying the anthrax spores. Hundreds more who were exposed were placed on antibiotics as a preventive measure.

The FBI eventually traced the source of the anthrax to the U.S. Army Medical Research Institute of Infectious Diseases, a bioweapons laboratory at Fort Detrick, Maryland. At first, authorities focused on a civilian researcher at that facility who was later cleared of the attacks. In August 2008 Bruce Ivins (1946–2008), another researcher at the same laboratory, committed suicide before he could be arrested and charged with the crime. The FBI has expressed confidence that Ivins was the perpetrator of the 2001 anthrax attacks. However, because he will never stand trial, some doubts remain about the strength of the government's case against Ivins.

BOSTON MARATHON BOMBING. On April 15, 2013, two bombs exploded near the finish line of the Boston Marathon killing three people and injuring more than 200 others. The perpetrators are believed to have been two brothers: Tamerlan Tsarnaev (1986–2013), who was killed during the subsequent manhunt, and Dzhokhar Tsarnaev (1993–), who was captured by police. Their family has ties to Chechnya, a Russian republic that has been roiled by violent clashes between Islamist groups and government forces. In "Boston Suspects Are Seen as Self-Taught and Fueled by Web" (NYTimes.com, April 24, 2013), Michael Cooper, Michael S. Schmidt, and Eric Schmitt indicate that authorities believe the brothers "were motivated by extremist Islamic beliefs but were not acting with known terrorist groups." As of January 2015, Dzhokhar Tsarnaev, a naturalized U.S. citizen, faced the death penalty if convicted of the attack.

GOVERNMENT JURISDICTION AND SPENDING

As noted throughout this chapter, criminal legislation and law enforcement are carried out by federal, state, and local governments. Sometimes government entities have overlapping responsibilities. State and local governments have always played a central role in controlling crime. They operate police and law enforcement agencies, court systems, and correctional facilities, such as prisons and jails. The federal government enforces laws that fall within its jurisdiction. Examples include mail fraud, bank robbery, gun laws, counterfeiting, forgery, espionage, immigration violations, child pornography, drug trafficking, and money laundering. The federal government also operates the federal court system and has its own prisons for people convicted of federal crimes. In addition, the federal government provides funding for some state and local crime-control programs.

Table 1.1 shows criminal justice system expenditures by federal, state, and local governments in fiscal year (FY) 2011. A fiscal year is a 12-month period used for accounting and budgeting purposes and typically differs from a calendar year (i.e., January 1 to December 31). Different government entities define fiscal years differently. The federal government defines a fiscal year as beginning October 1 and ending September 30; thus, FY 2011 extended from October 1, 2010, through September 30, 2011. Table 1.1 includes both direct expenditures and intergovernmental expenditures. The latter are amounts transferred between levels of government, for example, in FY 2011 the federal government transferred nearly $3.8 billion to state and local governments to fund justice system activities.

Overall, the federal government spent $53.6 billion on the nation's justice system in FY 2011. (See Table 1.1.) Most of the money ($49.8 billion) was for direct expenditures. The breakdown of the federal total by activity was $30.5 billion for police protection, $14.6 billion for judicial and legal activities, and $8.5 billion for corrections. State governments spent $86 billion on their justice systems in FY 2011. Most of the money ($80.6 billion) was for direct expenditures. The breakdown of the state total by activity was $14.2 billion for police protection, $22.6 billion for judicial and legal activities, and $49.2 billion for corrections. Local governments spent $131.6 billion on their justice systems in FY 2011. Nearly all the money

TABLE 1.1

Government expenditures on criminal justice, by level of government, fiscal year 2011

[Amount (thousands of dollars)]

Activity	All governments*	Federal government	State governments	Local governments
Total justice system	**261,838,327**	**53,579,000**	**86,017,873**	**131,629,692**
Direct expenditure	261,838,327	49,826,000	80,613,651	131,398,676
Intergovernmental expenditure	—	3,753,000	5,404,222	231,016
Police protection	**124,689,979**	**30,517,642**	**14,248,537**	**83,458,015**
Direct expenditure	124,689,979	28,380,000	12,857,062	83,452,917
Intergovernmental expenditure	—	2,137,642	1,391,475	5,098
Judicial and legal	**56,470,162**	**14,569,539**	**22,602,337**	**21,904,581**
Direct expenditure	56,470,162	13,549,000	21,045,486	21,875,676
Intergovernmental expenditure	—	1,020,539	1,556,851	28,905
Corrections	**80,678,186**	**8,491,819**	**49,166,999**	**26,267,096**
Direct expenditure	80,678,186	7,897,000	46,711,103	26,070,083
Intergovernmental expenditure	—	594,819	2,455,896	197,013

*The total lines for each criminal justice activity, and for the total justice system, exclude duplicative intergovernmental amounts. The intergovernmental expenditure lines are not totaled for the same reason.
Notes: Local government data are estimates subject to sampling variability.
Federal government data are for the fiscal period beginning October 1, 2010 and ending September 30, 2011.

SOURCE: Adapted from "Table 1. Percent Distribution of Expenditure for the Justice System by Type of Government, Fiscal 2011 (Preliminary)," in *Justice Expenditure and Employment Extracts, 2011 – Preliminary*, U.S. Department of Justice, Bureau of Justice Statistics, July 1, 2014, http://www.bjs.gov/index.cfm?ty=pbdetail&iid=5050 (accessed October 31, 2014)

($131.4 billion) was for direct expenditures. The breakdown of the local total by activity was $83.5 billion for police protection, $21.9 billion for judicial and legal activities, and $26.3 billion for corrections.

Figure 1.1 categorizes direct justice system expenditures by government level. For the justice system as a whole, local governments accounted for about half (50.2%) of the total direct expenditures, state governments accounted for 30.8% of the total, and the federal government accounted for 19% of the total. As shown in Figure 1.1, local governments paid the largest share (66.9%) of the direct expenditures for police protection, whereas state governments paid the largest share (57.9%) of the direct expenditures for corrections. In regards to judicial and legal activities, local governments bore slightly more of the direct expenditures (38.7% versus 37.3%) than did state governments.

PUBLIC OPINION ABOUT CRIME
Crime and Its Control

Since 2001 the Gallup Organization has conducted annual polls asking Americans about their levels of worry regarding specific problems facing the country. Table 1.2 shows the breakdown of responses in regards to "crime and violence." In March 2014 more than a third (39%) of those asked said they personally worry "a great deal" about crime and violence. Another 31% said they worry "a fair amount" about it. Together these factions totaled 70%. By contrast, in 2001, a much higher percentage (88%) said they worry "a great deal" (62%) or "a fair amount" (26%) about crime and violence in the United States.

FIGURE 1.1

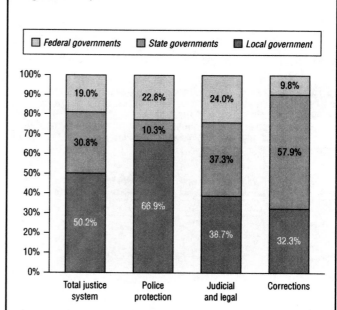

Direct government expenditures on criminal justice, by level of government, 2011

SOURCE: Adapted from "Table 1. Percent Distribution of Expenditure for the Justice System by Type of Government, Fiscal 2011 (Preliminary)," in *Justice Expenditure and Employment Extracts, 2011 – Preliminary*, U.S. Department of Justice, Bureau of Justice Statistics, July 1, 2014, http://www.bjs.gov/index.cfm?ty=pbdetail&iid=5050 (accessed October 31, 2014)

As shown in Table 1.3, just over half of the poll participants in March 2014 said they are "very satisfied" (10%) or "somewhat satisfied" (41%) with "the nation's

TABLE 1.2

Public worry about crime and violence, selected years, 2001–14

NEXT, I'M GOING TO READ A LIST OF PROBLEMS FACING THE COUNTRY. FOR EACH ONE, PLEASE TELL ME IF YOU PERSONALLY WORRY ABOUT THIS PROBLEM A GREAT DEAL, A FAIR AMOUNT, ONLY A LITTLE, OR NOT AT ALL? FIRST, HOW MUCH DO YOU PERSONALLY WORRY ABOUT CRIME AND VIOLENCE?

	Great deal	Fair amount	Only a little	Not at all	No opinion
	%	%	%	%	%
2014 Mar 6–9**	39	31	24	5	1
2013 Mar 7–10	47	28	20	5	*
2012 Mar 8–11	42	31	21	5	*
2011 Mar 3–6	44	30	19	6	*
2010 Mar 4–7	43	30	21	6	*
2008 Mar 6–9	49	31	16	3	*
2007 Mar 11–14	48	32	16	4	*
2006 Mar 13–16	45	36	15	4	*
2005 Mar 7–10	46	25	26	3	*
2004 Mar 8–11	46	26	24	4	*
2003 Mar 24–25	45	31	18	5	1
2002 Mar 4–7	49	27	20	4	0
2001 Mar 5–7	62	26	9	3	*

* = less than 0.5%.
**Asked of a half sample.

SOURCE: "Next, I'm going to read a list of problems facing the country. For each one, please tell me if you personally worry about this problem a great deal, a fair amount, only a little, or not at all? First, how much do you personally worry about crime and violence?" in *Crime*, The Gallup Organization, October 2014, http://www.gallup.com/poll/1603/Crime.aspx (accessed November 13, 2014).

TABLE 1.3

Public opinion on the nation's policies to reduce or control crime, 2001–14

NEXT, WE'D LIKE TO KNOW HOW YOU FEEL ABOUT THE STATE OF THE NATION IN EACH OF THE FOLLOWING AREAS. FOR EACH ONE, PLEASE SAY WHETHER YOU ARE—VERY SATISFIED, SOMEWHAT SATISFIED, SOMEWHAT DISSATISFIED, OR VERY DISSATISFIED. IF YOU DON'T HAVE ENOUGH INFORMATION ABOUT A PARTICULAR SUBJECT TO RATE IT, JUST SAY SO. HOW ABOUT THE NATION'S POLICIES TO REDUCE OR CONTROL CRIME?

	Very satisfied	Somewhat satisfied	Somewhat dissatisfied	Very dissatisfied	No opinion
	%	%	%	%	%
2014 Jan 5–8	10	41	23	19	7
2013 Jan 7–10	8	33	30	24	5
2012 Jan 5–8	7	43	25	20	6
2008 Jan 4–6	7	41	30	18	4
2007 Jan 15–18	9	38	31	18	4
2006 Jan 9–12	8	40	29	18	5
2005 Jan 3–5	11	46	23	16	4
2004 Jan 12–15	10	43	28	16	3
2003 Jan 13–16	8	43	28	18	3
2002 Jan 7–9	10	44	30	13	3
2001 Jan 10–14	6	39	32	20	3

SOURCE: "Next, we'd like to know how you feel about the state of the nation in each of the following areas. For each one, please say whether you are—very satisfied, somewhat satisfied, somewhat dissatisfied, or very dissatisfied. If you don't have enough information about a particular subject to rate it, just say so. How about the nation's policies to reduce or control crime?" in *Crime*, The Gallup Organization, October 2014, http://www.gallup.com/poll/1603/Crime.aspx (accessed November 13, 2014).

policies to reduce or control crime." The satisfied value has risen somewhat since 2001, when 6% of respondents were very satisfied and 39% were somewhat satisfied.

In another Gallup poll conducted in October 2014 Americans were asked how often they personally worry about being victimized by particular crimes. Table 1.4 shows the results for those people saying they frequently or occasionally worry about being victimized. The largest faction (69%) was concerned about having their credit card information stolen by computer hackers. Nearly as many (62%) worried that their computer or smartphone would be hacked and the information stolen by thieves. These two crimes are examples of white-collar crimes, which are described in detail in Chapter 5. More than 40% of the respondents said they frequently or occasionally worry about their home being burglarized while they are not there (45%) or their car being stolen or broken into by thieves (42%).

As shown in Figure 1.2, nearly two-thirds (63%) of respondents told Gallup in October 2014 that they believed crime had increased over the previous year. This value has risen dramatically since 2001, when 41% of those asked said that crime had increased from the previous year. However, older polling results show much more pessimism about the nation's crime rate. In 1989, 84% of respondents said they believed crime had increased since the previous year.

Gallup pollsters have also quizzed Americans about the seriousness of the nation's crime problem as a whole

TABLE 1.4

Poll respondents who frequently or occasionally worry about falling victim to particular crimes, October 2014

HOW OFTEN DO YOU, YOURSELF, WORRY ABOUT THE FOLLOWING THINGS—FREQUENTLY, OCCASIONALLY, RARELY OR NEVER? HOW ABOUT ...

	% Frequently or occasionally worry
Having the credit card information you have used at stores stolen by computer hackers	69
Having your computer or smartphone hacked and the information stolen by unauthorized persons	62
Your home being burglarized when you are not there	45
Having your car stolen or broken into	42
Having a school-aged child physically harmed attending school	31
Getting mugged	31
Your home being burglarized when you are there	30
Being the victim of terrorism	28
Being attacked while driving your car	20
Being a victim of a hate crime	18
Being sexually assaulted	18
Getting murdered	18
Being assaulted/killed by a coworker/employee where you work	7

SOURCE: Rebecca Riffkin, "Crime Worries in U.S.," in *Hacking Tops List of Crimes Americans Worry About Most*, The Gallup Organization, October 27, 2014, http://www.gallup.com/poll/178856/hacking-tops-list-crimes-americans-worry.aspx (accessed October 31, 2014).

FIGURE 1.2

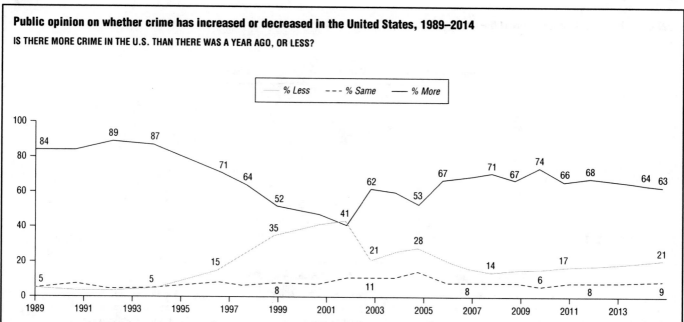

Public opinion on whether crime has increased or decreased in the United States, 1989–2014

IS THERE MORE CRIME IN THE U.S. THAN THERE WAS A YEAR AGO, OR LESS?

— % Less   - - - % Same   —— % More

FIGURE 1.3

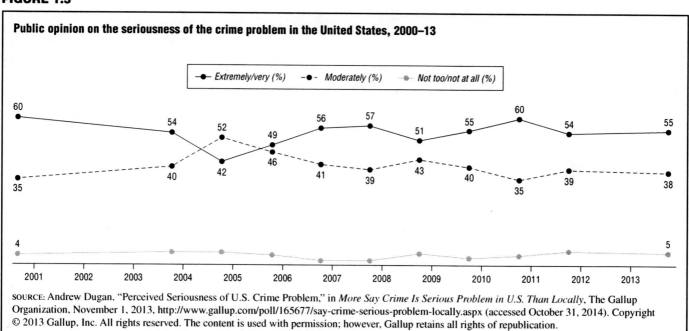

Public opinion on the seriousness of the crime problem in the United States, 2000–13

—●— Extremely/very (%)   -●- Moderately (%)   ⋯●⋯ Not too/not at all (%)

and in their local areas. In 2013 more than half (55%) of those asked said they are extremely worried about the crime problem in the United States. (See Figure 1.3.) Another 38% said crime is moderately serious nationwide, and 5% said it is either not too serious or not serious at all. This breakdown of opinions has been relatively consistent since 2000. The primary exception was in 2004, when a higher percentage perceived crime as moderately serious (52%) than extremely or very serious (42%).

As shown in Figure 1.4, in 2013 just over half of respondents (51%) said that crime was extremely or very serious in the area where they live. Just over a third (35%) considered it a moderately serious problem, and 13% said it was either not too serious or not serious at all. The breakdown has been fairly consistent dating back to 2000. Since 1972, Gallup pollsters have asked Americans whether there is more crime or less crime in their local area when compared to the previous year. (See Figure 1.5.)

FIGURE 1.4

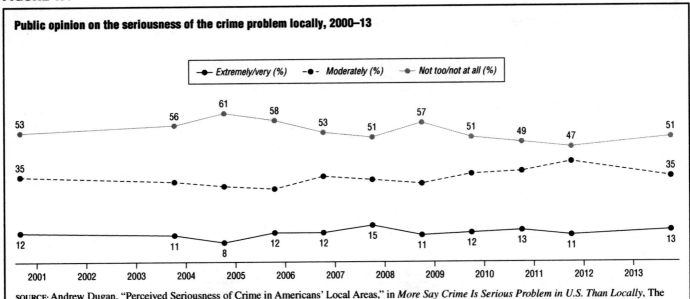

Public opinion on the seriousness of the crime problem locally, 2000–13

● Extremely/very (%) ● Moderately (%) ● Not too/not at all (%)

FIGURE 1.5

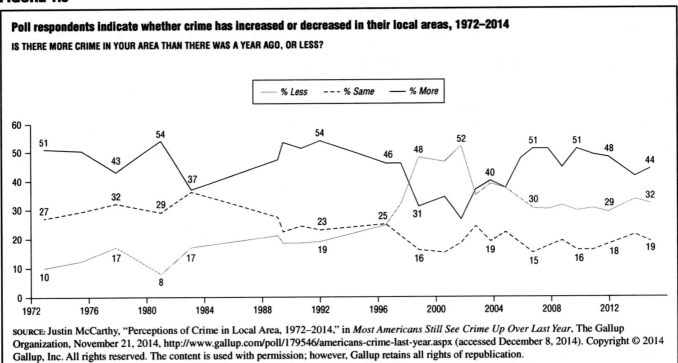

Poll respondents indicate whether crime has increased or decreased in their local areas, 1972–2014

IS THERE MORE CRIME IN YOUR AREA THAN THERE WAS A YEAR AGO, OR LESS?

···· % Less - - - % Same —— % More

Through the mid-1990s the percentage of respondents saying there was more crime in their area was generally much higher than the percentage saying there was less crime in their area. Since that time the difference between the two factions has narrowed considerably. In 2014, 44% of those asked said crime had increased over the past year in their area, compared with 32% who said it had decreased.

Figure 1.6 illustrates the results obtained by Gallup when poll participants were asked if there is an area near where they live (i.e., within a mile of their homes) where they "would be afraid to walk alone at night." Nearly two thirds (63%) said there was not such an area, whereas 37% said there was such an area.

Violent Crime: Perceptions versus Data

As will be explained in Chapter 2, the nation's violent crime rate rose dramatically between 1960 and the mid-1990s before beginning a sharp decline. However,

FIGURE 1.6

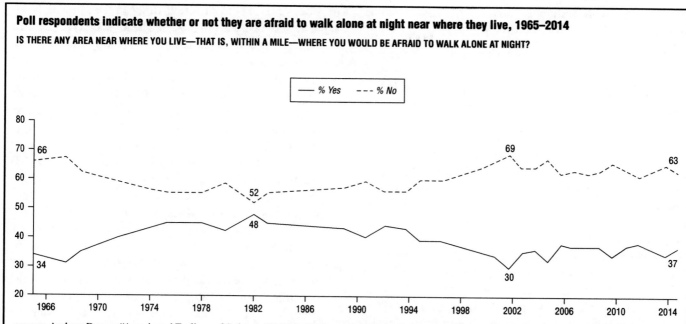

Poll respondents indicate whether or not they are afraid to walk alone at night near where they live, 1965–2014

IS THERE ANY AREA NEAR WHERE YOU LIVE—THAT IS, WITHIN A MILE—WHERE YOU WOULD BE AFRAID TO WALK ALONE AT NIGHT?

SOURCE: Andrew Dugan, "Americans' Feelings of Safety in Walking Alone at Night in Their Communities," in *In U.S., 37% Do Not Feel Safe Walking at Night Near Home*, The Gallup Organization, November 24, 2014, http://www.gallup.com/poll/179558/not-feel-safe-walking-night-near-home.aspx (accessed December 8, 2014). Copyright © 2014 Gallup, Inc. All rights reserved. The content is used with permission; however, Gallup retains all rights of republication.

FIGURE 1.7

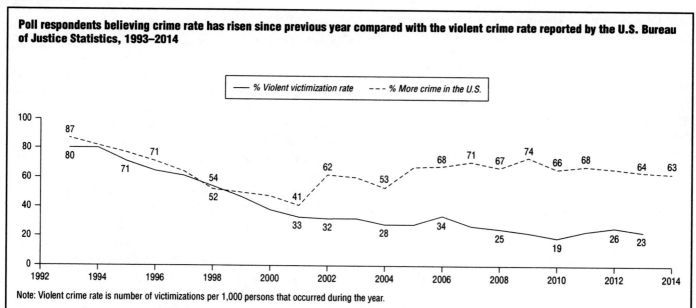

Poll respondents believing crime rate has risen since previous year compared with the violent crime rate reported by the U.S. Bureau of Justice Statistics, 1993–2014

Note: Violent crime rate is number of victimizations per 1,000 persons that occurred during the year.

SOURCE: Justin McCarthy, "U.S. Violent Crime Rate vs. Americans' Perception of Crime Rate vs. Year Ago," in *Most Americans Still See Crime Up Over Last Year*, The Gallup Organization, November 21, 2014, http://www.gallup.com/poll/179546/americans-crime-last-year.aspx (accessed December 8, 2014). Copyright © 2014 Gallup, Inc. All rights reserved. The content is used with permission; however, Gallup retains all rights of republication.

public opinion polls indicate a disconnection between the data and the perceptions of the American public on the issue. Figure 1.7 shows the violent victimization rate for 1993 through 2013 as reported by the U.S. Department of Justice's Bureau of Justice Statistics (BJS). The number of violent victimizations per 1,000 households decreased from 80 in 1993 to 23 in 2013. Despite the drop, high percentages of poll respondents continued to tell Gallup

that violent crime was increasing each year. For example, in 2014 nearly two-thirds (63%) of those asked said there was more crime nationally than in 2013.

CRIMINAL NOTORIETY

Criminal acts, especially those involving *mala in se* offenses, violate society's moral beliefs about appropriate behavior. Nevertheless there is a curious fascination in the United States with certain criminals who have become infamous (i.e., famous for bad deeds).

Some perpetrators gained notoriety because of the eras in which they lived. Billy the Kid (William H. Bonney, 1859–1881), Butch Cassidy (Robert Leroy Parker 1866–1908), and the Sundance Kid (Harry Alonzo Longabaugh, 1867–1908) are well-known outlaws of the Old West. Their criminal acts have been romanticized (depicted in an idealized and rather favorable manner) to highlight the adventuresome aspects of their exploits, rather than their victims. Some gangsters and bootleggers who operated criminal enterprises during Prohibition (1920–1933) became celebrities. Al Capone (1899–1947) headed a notorious mob of Chicago gangsters blamed for numerous killings, including the St. Valentine's Day massacre of February 14, 1929, which left seven people dead. The wealthy and sociable Capone reveled in the publicity he received. In "Al Capone: Chicago's Most Infamous Mob Boss" (undated, http://www.crimelibrary.com/gangsters _outlaws/mob_bosses/capone/day_8.html), Marilyn Bardsley describes Capone as having an image of "grisly glamour."

The Great Depression (1929–1941) also featured outlaws who captured the public imagination. John Dillinger (1903–1934), Charles "Pretty Boy" Floyd (1904–1934), Baby Face Nelson (Lester Gills, 1908–1934), and Bonnie and Clyde (Bonnie Parker, 1910–1934, and Clyde Barrow, 1909–1934) are infamous criminals of the era. They are primarily remembered as bank robbers, although they committed other violent acts, including murders. In "People & Events: John Dillinger, 1903–1934" (undated, http://www .pbs.org/wgbh/amex/dillinger/peopleevents/p_dillinger.html), PBS notes that Dillinger became "a folk hero to Americans disillusioned with failing banks and the ineffective federal government."

Murderers who kill multiple victims (especially strangers) are relatively rare in U.S. criminal history, but they garner much public attention. In "Serial Murder: Multi-disciplinary Perspectives for Investigators" (July 2008, http://www.fbi.gov/stats-services/publications/serial-murder/serial-murder-july-2008-pdf), the FBI defines serial killers as perpetrators who kill at least two victims in separate events at different times. Serial killing holds a particular fascination in American society. The FBI notes, "there is a macabre interest in the topic that far exceeds its scope and has generated countless articles, books, and movies." In *Why We Love Serial Killers: The Curious Appeal of the World's Most Savage Murderers* (2014), Scott Bonn states, "Serial killers tantalize, terrify, and entertain the public." Infamous examples include Ted Bundy (1946–1989), who raped and murdered dozens of girls and women, and John Wayne Gacy (1942–1994), who raped and murdered dozens of teenage boys and young men. Both killers were captured and executed for their crimes. Charles Manson (1934–) was found guilty in 1971 of ordering his cult members to gruesomely kill seven people. He was originally given the death penalty, but his sentence was changed to life in prison after California abolished capital punishment. Over the decades Manson has been the subject of much media attention and has received "fan" mail from devotees. In November 2014 the 80-year-old inmate obtained a marriage license to marry a 25-year-old woman who had become enamored with him. As of January 2015 the marriage had not taken place.

A mass murderer kills multiple victims during a single event, like the Boston Marathon bombing described earlier. Since 1999 several school massacres have been committed by mass murderers, including students. The incidents involving juvenile offenders (i.e., offenders under the age of 18 years) are described in Chapter 10. A particularly horrific school massacre was committed by an adult. On December 14, 2012, a lone gunman entered the Sandy Hook Elementary School in Newtown, Connecticut, and opened fire. Twenty young children and six faculty members were killed. The alleged shooter, 20-year-old Adam Lanza (1992–2012), committed suicide as police stormed the building. Prior to the school shooting, Lanza is believed to have murdered his mother at the home in which the two lived. As of January 2015, the motive in the shooting had not been ascertained with certainty; however, there were media reports that Lanza was emotionally disturbed.

CHAPTER 2
CRIME STATISTICS

The U.S. Department of Justice (DOJ) is the primary government source for national crime statistics. As noted in Chapter 1 criminal offenses are enforced by state or federal authorities depending on the crime. The DOJ's Bureau of Justice Statistics (BJS) compiles data on cases handled by the federal justice system, and the Federal Bureau of Investigation (FBI) compiles data related to crimes reported to local law enforcement agencies and prosecuted at the state level. The latter data set is far larger than the federal data set because most crimes fall under state or local jurisdiction.

In *Federal Justice Statistics, 2011–2012* (January 2015, http://www.bjs.gov/content/pub/pdf/fjs1112.pdf), Mark Motivans of the BJS presents data related to the federal justice system. Figure 2.1 shows the number of suspects and defendants (people charged with crimes) whose cases were processed at the federal level from fiscal year (FY) 1994 through 2012. A federal fiscal year extends from October 1 through September 30; thus, FY 2012 lasted from October 1, 2011, through September 30, 2012. In FY 2012 more than 172,000 people were arrested by federal authorities. As shown in Figure 2.2, federal cases overwhelmingly involve drug and immigration offenses. Drug crimes are discussed in detail in Chapter 4. Therefore, the remainder of this chapter will focus on statistics related to crimes falling under state or local jurisdiction.

The FBI's Uniform Crime Reporting (UCR) Program gathers crime data from law enforcement agencies throughout the country and publishes selected data annually in *Crime in the United States*. The most recent edition, *Crime in the United States, 2013* (http://www.fbi.gov/about-us/cjis/ucr/crime-in-the-u.s/2013/crime-in-the-u.s.-2013/cius-home), was published in November 2014. According to the FBI (http://www.fbi.gov/about-us/cjis/ucr/crime-in-the-u.s/2013/crime-in-the-u.s.-2013/about-ucr), in 2013 more than 18,000 agencies participated in the program, representing about 98% of the U.S. population. However, not every agency contributed data for every crime that was tracked by the UCR Program. In other words, the tables and figures in *Crime in the United States, 2013* provide crime statistics on only those crimes that were reported to the UCR Program and do not reflect the total number of crimes that were committed or processed by local agencies.

The FBI compiles two main sets of crime statistics: crimes reported to agencies and crimes cleared by agencies. Reported crimes do not necessarily result in arrests or convictions. Cleared offenses are of two types. The first type of cleared offenses consists of crimes for which agencies report that at least one person has been arrested, charged, and turned over to the court for prosecution. This does not necessarily mean the person arrested was guilty or convicted of the crime. The second type of cleared offenses includes those cleared by "extraordinary means," that is, offenses for which there can be no arrest. Such cases include, for example, a murder-suicide, when the perpetrator is known to be deceased.

The FBI collects data for dozens of specifically defined crimes. Some of these crimes are categorized as violent crimes or property crimes. In *Crime in the United States, 2013*, the FBI defines violent crimes as those that "involve force or threat of force." These crimes include murder and nonnegligent manslaughter, forcible rape, robbery, and aggravated assault. The FBI classifies four types of crimes as property crimes: burglary, larceny-theft, motor vehicle theft, and arson. The FBI explains that "the object of the theft-type offenses is the taking of money or property, but there is no force or threat of force against the victims."

REPORTED CRIMES

Table 2.1 lists the number of certain crimes that were reported by law enforcement agencies between 1994 and 2013 and the rates of these crimes per 100,000 inhabitants.

FIGURE 2.1

Suspects and defendants processed in the federal justice system, 1994–2012

— Defendants sentenced to prison[b] --- Defendants convicted[b] — Defendants charged[b] ···· Suspects arrested[a] —·— Suspects investigated

[a]Excludes D.C. superior court arrests.
[b]Represents defendants charged with a felony or Class A misdemeanor offense in U.S. district court.

SOURCE: Mark Motivans, "Figure 1. Suspects and Defendants Processed in the Federal Justice System, 1994–2012," in *Federal Justice Statistics, 2011–2012*, U.S. Department of Justice, Office of Justice Programs, Bureau of Justice Statistics, January 2015, http://www.bjs.gov/content/pub/pdf/fjs1112 .pdf (accessed January 26, 2015)

FIGURE 2.2

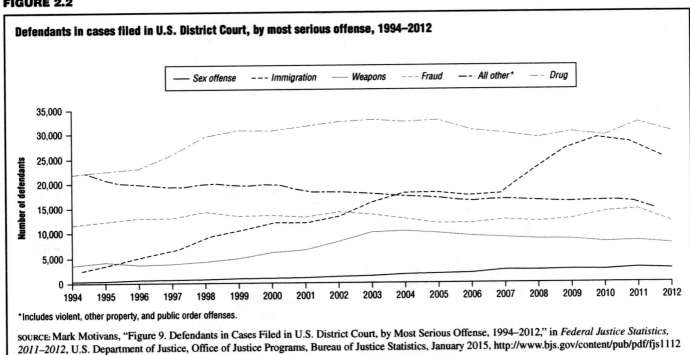

Defendants in cases filed in U.S. District Court, by most serious offense, 1994–2012

— Sex offense --- Immigration — Weapons ···· Fraud —·— All other* —— Drug

*Includes violent, other property, and public order offenses.

SOURCE: Mark Motivans, "Figure 9. Defendants in Cases Filed in U.S. District Court, by Most Serious Offense, 1994–2012," in *Federal Justice Statistics, 2011–2012*, U.S. Department of Justice, Office of Justice Programs, Bureau of Justice Statistics, January 2015, http://www.bjs.gov/content/pub/pdf/fjs1112 .pdf (accessed January 26, 2015)

In 2013 nearly 1.2 million violent crimes were reported, down from almost 1.9 million in 1994. The overall rate for violent crime in 2013 was 367.9 per 100,000 inhabitants. This compares to a rate of 713.6 per 100,000 inhabitants in 1994.

Murder and Nonnegligent Manslaughter

According to the FBI in *Crime in the United States, 2013*, murder and nonnegligent manslaughter is "the willful (nonnegligent) killing of one human being by another." The murder statistics do not include suicides, accidents, or justifiable homicides by either citizens or law enforcement officers.

The total number of reported murders and nonnegligent manslaughters in 2013 was 14,196 for a rate of 4.5 per 100,000 inhabitants. (See Table 2.1.) During the 1990s the murder rate was much higher; in 1994 it stood

TABLE 2.1

Violent crimes and property crimes by volume and rate per 100,000 inhabitants, 1994–2013

Year	Population[a]	Violent crime	Violent crime rate	Murder and non-negligent man-slaughter	Murder and non-negligent man-slaughter rate	Rape (legacy definition)[b]	Rape (legacy definition)[b] rate	Robbery	Robbery rate	Aggravated assault	Aggravated assault rate	Property crime	Property crime rate	Burglary	Burglary rate	Larceny-theft	Larceny-theft rate	Motor vehicle theft	Motor vehicle theft rate
1994	260,327,021	1,857,670	713.6	23,326	9.0	102,216	39.3	618,949	237.8	1,113,179	427.6	12,131,873	4,660.2	2,712,774	1,042.1	7,879,812	3,026.9	1,539,287	591.3
1995	262,803,276	1,798,792	684.5	21,606	8.2	97,470	37.1	580,509	220.9	1,099,207	418.3	12,063,935	4,590.5	2,593,784	987.0	7,997,710	3,043.2	1,472,441	560.3
1996	265,228,572	1,688,540	636.6	19,645	7.4	96,252	36.3	535,594	201.9	1,037,049	391.0	11,805,323	4,451.0	2,506,400	945.0	7,904,685	2,980.3	1,394,238	525.7
1997	267,783,607	1,636,096	611.0	18,208	6.8	96,153	35.9	498,534	186.2	1,023,201	382.1	11,558,475	4,316.3	2,460,526	918.8	7,743,760	2,891.8	1,354,189	505.7
1998	270,248,003	1,533,887	567.6	16,974	6.3	93,144	34.5	447,186	165.5	976,583	361.4	10,951,827	4,052.5	2,332,735	863.2	7,376,311	2,729.5	1,242,781	459.9
1999	272,690,813	1,426,044	523.0	15,522	5.7	89,411	32.8	409,371	150.1	911,740	334.3	10,208,334	3,743.6	2,100,739	770.4	6,955,520	2,550.7	1,152,075	422.5
2000	281,421,906	1,425,486	506.5	15,586	5.5	90,178	32.0	408,016	145.0	911,706	324.0	10,182,584	3,618.3	2,050,992	728.8	6,971,590	2,477.3	1,160,002	412.2
2001[c]	285,317,559	1,439,480	504.5	16,037	5.6	90,863	31.8	423,557	148.5	909,023	318.6	10,437,189	3,658.1	2,116,531	741.8	7,092,267	2,485.7	1,228,391	430.5
2002	287,973,924	1,423,677	494.4	16,229	5.6	95,235	33.1	420,806	146.1	891,407	309.5	10,455,277	3,630.6	2,151,252	747.0	7,057,379	2,450.7	1,246,646	432.9
2003	290,788,976	1,383,676	475.8	16,528	5.7	93,883	32.3	414,235	142.5	859,030	295.4	10,442,862	3,591.2	2,154,834	741.0	7,026,802	2,416.5	1,261,226	433.7
2004	293,656,842	1,360,088	463.2	16,148	5.5	95,089	32.4	401,470	136.7	847,381	288.6	10,319,386	3,514.1	2,144,446	730.3	6,937,089	2,362.3	1,237,851	421.5
2005	296,507,061	1,390,745	469.0	16,740	5.6	94,347	31.8	417,438	140.8	862,220	290.8	10,174,754	3,431.5	2,155,448	726.9	6,783,447	2,287.8	1,235,859	416.8
2006	299,398,484	1,435,123	479.3	17,309	5.8	94,472	31.6	449,246	150.0	874,096	292.0	10,019,601	3,346.6	2,194,993	733.1	6,626,363	2,213.2	1,198,245	400.2
2007	301,621,157	1,422,970	471.8	17,128	5.7	92,160	30.6	447,324	148.3	866,358	287.2	9,882,212	3,276.4	2,190,198	726.1	6,591,542	2,185.4	1,100,472	364.9
2008	304,059,724	1,394,461	458.6	16,465	5.4	90,750	29.8	443,563	145.9	843,683	277.5	9,774,152	3,214.6	2,228,887	733.0	6,586,206	2,166.1	959,059	315.4
2009	307,006,550	1,325,896	431.9	15,399	5.0	89,241	29.1	408,742	133.1	812,514	264.7	9,337,060	3,041.3	2,203,313	717.7	6,338,095	2,064.5	795,652	259.2
2010	309,330,219	1,251,248	404.5	14,722	4.8	85,593	27.7	369,089	119.3	781,844	252.8	9,112,625	2,945.9	2,168,459	701.0	6,204,601	2,005.8	739,565	239.1
2011	311,587,816	1,206,005	387.1	14,661	4.7	84,175	27.0	354,746	113.9	752,423	241.5	9,052,743	2,905.4	2,185,140	701.3	6,151,095	1,974.1	716,508	230.0
2012[d]	313,873,685	1,217,057	387.8	14,856	4.7	85,141	27.1	355,051	113.1	762,009	242.8	9,001,992	2,868.0	2,109,932	672.2	6,168,874	1,965.4	723,186	230.4
2013	316,128,839	1,163,146	367.9	14,196	4.5	79,770	25.2	345,031	109.1	724,149	229.1	8,632,512	2,730.7	1,928,465	610.0	6,004,453	1,899.4	699,594	221.3

[a]Populations are U.S. Census Bureau provisional estimates as of July 1 for each year except 2000 and 2010, which are decennial census counts.
[b]The figures shown in this column for the offense of rape were estimated using the legacy Uniform Crime Reporting definition of rape.
[c]The murder and nonnegligent homicides that occurred as a result of the events of September 11, 2001, are not included in this table.
[d]The crime figures have been adjusted.
Note: Although arson data are included in the trend and clearance tables, sufficient data are not available to estimate totals for this offense. Therefore, no arson data are published in this table.

SOURCE: "Table 1. Crime in the United States by Volume and Rate per 100,000 Inhabitants, 1994–2013," in *Crime in the United States 2013*, U.S. Department of Justice, Federal Bureau of Investigation, November 10, 2014, http://www.fbi.gov/about-us/cjis/ucr/crime-in-the-u.s/2013/crime-in-the-u.s.-2013/tables/1tabledatadecoverviewpdf/table_1_crime_in_the_united_states_by_volume_and_rate_per_100000_inhabitants_1994-2013 .xls (accessed November 12, 2014)

at 9 murders per 100,000 inhabitants. The rate began a sustained decline and dipped below 5 murders per 100,000 inhabitants for the first time in 2010. It should be noted that Table 2.1 does not include the thousands of people who were killed as a result of the September 11, 2001, terrorist attacks against the United States.

The FBI collects detailed homicide data in the UCR Program's Supplementary Homicide Report (SHR). SHR data include the age, sex, and race of the offenders and victims, the relationship between the offenders and victims, the circumstances surrounding the murders, and the types of weapons used in the murders. Note that not all these statistics are reported by all agencies for every reported murder, offender, and victim.

MURDER OFFENDERS AND VICTIMS. Table 2.2 includes SHR data for 14,132 murder offenders. Because offender data are based on reported crimes rather than on actual arrests, SHR tables classify the age, sex, or race of some offenders as "unknown." SHR categorizations for 2013 murder offenders by sex are:

- Male offenders—9,085 (64.3% of the total)
- Female offenders—1,085 (7.7%)
- Unknown—3,962 (28%)

SHR categorizations for 2013 murder offenders by race are:

- White offenders—4,396 (31.1% of the total)
- African American offenders—5,375 (38%)
- Other offenders—249 (1.8%)
- Unknown—4,112 (29.1%)

The ages of 4,674 murder offenders (33.1% of the total) are listed as unknown. (See Table 2.2.) Offenders for which ages are known fall mostly within the range of 17 to 34 years old.

SHR data for 12,253 murder victims in 2013 are shown in Table 2.3. The vast majority (9,523, or 77.7% of the total) were male, whereas 2,707 (22.1%) were female. Another 23 victims (0.2%) were of unknown sex. Whites accounted for 5,537 (45.2%) of the victims, and African Americans accounted for 6,261 (51.1%) of the victims. Another 308 victims (2.5%) were of other races, and 147 victims (1.2%) were of unknown race.

The vast majority of murder victims (11,101, or 90.6% of the total) were aged 18 years and older. (See Table 2.3.) Only 1,027 victims (8.4% of the total) were under the age of 18 years. Ages were reported as

TABLE 2.2

Murder offenders where age, sex, race, and ethnicity are known, 2013

| Age | Total | Sex | | | Race | | | | Ethnicity[a] | | |
		Male	Female	Unknown	White	Black or African American	Other[b]	Unknown	Hispanic or Latino	Not Hispanic or Latino	Unknown
Total	**14,132**	**9,085**	**1,085**	**3,962**	**4,396**	**5,375**	**249**	**4,112**	**1,096**	**2,861**	**2,909**
Percent distribution[c]	100.0	64.3	7.7	28.0	31.1	38.0	1.8	29.1	16.0	41.7	42.4
Under 18[d]	595	558	35	2	209	370	8	8	111	137	51
Under 22[d]	2,669	2,437	221	11	885	1,724	32	28	364	679	181
18 and over[d]	8,863	7,797	1,035	31	4,087	4,435	234	107	932	2,549	702
Infant (under 1)	0	0	0	0	0	0	0	0	0	0	0
1 to 4	0	0	0	0	0	0	0	0	0	0	0
5 to 8	3	3	0	0	0	3	0	0	0	2	0
9 to 12	11	11	0	0	6	5	0	0	0	5	0
13 to 16	288	265	21	2	104	173	5	6	45	64	30
17 to 19	1,227	1,123	102	2	399	808	13	7	183	314	78
20 to 24	2,496	2,237	249	10	899	1,524	46	27	276	667	195
25 to 29	1,541	1,369	168	4	671	799	53	18	178	437	129
30 to 34	1,131	977	151	3	550	535	34	12	139	328	90
35 to 39	701	605	95	1	365	304	21	11	81	205	52
40 to 44	564	473	90	1	317	222	23	2	59	156	45
45 to 49	477	403	73	1	298	155	17	7	30	145	44
50 to 54	415	347	64	4	266	130	13	6	25	136	38
55 to 59	230	201	29	0	146	73	6	5	11	76	21
60 to 64	140	128	12	0	88	43	6	3	10	57	10
65 to 69	104	96	8	0	83	15	3	3	6	37	7
70 to 74	43	40	3	0	36	7	0	0	0	16	4
75 and over	87	77	5	5	68	9	2	8	0	41	10
Unknown	4,674	730	15	3,929	100	570	7	3,997	53	175	2,156

[a]The ethnicity totals are representative of those agencies that provided ethnicity breakdowns. Not all agencies provide ethnicity data, therefore the race and ethnicity totals will not equal.
[b]Includes American Indian or Alaska Native; Asian; Native Hawaiian or other Pacific Islander.
[c]Because of rounding, the percentages may not add to 100.0.
[d]Does not include unknown ages.

SOURCE: "Expanded Homicide Data Table 3. Murder Offenders by Age, Sex, Race, and Ethnicity, 2013," in *Crime in the United States 2013*, U.S. Department of Justice, Federal Bureau of Investigation, November 10, 2014, http://www.fbi.gov/about-us/cjis/ucr/crime-in-the-u.s/2013/crime-in-the-u.s.-2013/offenses-known-to-law-enforcement/expanded-homicide/expanded_homicide_data_table_3_murder_offenders_by_age_sex_and_race_2013.xls (accessed November 12, 2014)

TABLE 2.3

Murder victims where age, sex, race, and ethnicity are known, 2013

Age	Total	Sex			Race				Ethnicity[a]		
		Male	Female	Unknown	White	Black or African American	Other[b]	Unknown	Hispanic or Latino	Not Hispanic or Latino	Unknown
Total	12,253	9,523	2,707	23	5,537	6,261	308	147	1,729	6,147	1,670
Percent distribution[c]	100.0	77.7	22.1	0.2	45.2	51.1	2.5	1.2	18.1	64.4	17.5
Under 18[d]	1,027	715	308	4	492	482	31	22	140	519	124
Under 22[d]	2,603	2,086	511	6	1,005	1,507	54	37	416	1,243	315
18 and over[d]	11,101	8,728	2,368	5	4,986	5,738	277	100	1,577	5,588	1,485
Infant (under 1)	162	96	64	2	110	44	4	4	19	105	22
1 to 4	251	148	102	1	118	113	11	9	26	131	33
5 to 8	78	39	39	0	46	26	4	2	8	40	10
9 to 12	68	42	26	0	35	25	5	3	5	32	11
13 to 16	247	194	52	1	105	134	5	3	41	113	22
17 to 19	911	803	107	1	287	602	13	9	163	400	121
20 to 24	2,249	1,923	324	2	756	1,438	39	16	371	1,056	261
25 to 29	1,746	1,468	278	0	617	1,065	51	13	230	746	237
30 to 34	1,497	1,213	283	1	618	840	32	7	193	757	206
35 to 39	1,101	850	251	0	489	564	36	12	170	554	162
40 to 44	826	618	208	0	413	377	25	11	216	421	116
45 to 49	803	570	233	0	436	340	17	10	94	433	114
50 to 54	689	506	183	0	409	258	20	2	74	398	82
55 to 59	543	384	159	0	335	186	17	5	53	322	79
60 to 64	340	233	107	0	233	89	14	4	25	207	48
65 to 69	214	144	70	0	163	42	5	4	12	136	31
70 to 74	140	86	54	0	102	30	6	2	7	83	21
75 and over	263	126	136	1	206	47	4	6	10	173	33
Unknown	125	80	31	14	59	41	0	25	12	40	61

[a]The ethnicity totals are representative of those agencies that provided ethnicity breakdowns. Not all agencies provide ethnicity data, therefore the race and ethnicity totals will not equal.
[b]Includes American Indian or Alaska Native; Asian; Native Hawaiian or Other Pacific Islander.
[c]Because of rounding, the percentages may not add to 100.0.
[d]Does not include unknown ages.

SOURCE: "Expanded Homicide Data Table 2. Murder Victims by Age, Sex, Race, and Ethnicity, 2013," in *Crime in the United States 2013*, U.S. Department of Justice, Federal Bureau of Investigation, November 10, 2014, http://www.fbi.gov/about-us/cjis/ucr/crime-in-the-u.s/2013/crime-in-the-u.s.-2013/offenses-known-to-law-enforcement/expanded-homicide/expanded_homicide_data_table_2_murder_victims_by_age_sex_and_race_2013.xls (accessed November 12, 2014)

unknown for 125 victims (1%). Overall, people between the ages of 17 and 34 years accounted for the largest numbers of murder victims in 2013.

MURDER CIRCUMSTANCES. Table 2.4 describes the circumstances for 12,253 of the total murders reported in 2013. The circumstances of 4,440 murders, or 36.2% of the total covered by the SHR, were unknown. Of the reported murders, 1,909 (15.8%) were known to be associated with felonies, mostly robberies and narcotic drug law violations. Nearly half (5,782, or 47.2%) of the reported murders occurred due to other circumstances, mainly arguments and brawls between people.

As shown in Table 2.4, the relationship between the murder offender and victim was unknown in 5,572 (45.5%) of the murders. Of the 6,681 murders in which the relationship could be ascertained, 1,281 murders (or 10.5%) were committed by strangers (people unknown to the victims). The three most common relationships were those in which the victim was the offender's:

- Acquaintance—2,660
- Wife—534
- Girlfriend—458

Overall, 1,664 of the victims were murdered by family members.

MURDER WEAPONS. Table 2.5 shows the weapons used in 12,253 of the murders committed during 2013, as reported in the SHR. About two-thirds (8,454, or 69%) of the murders involved firearms. Knives or other cutting instruments were used in 1,490 (12.2%) of the murders, and personal weapons (hands, fists, feet, etc.) were used in 686 (5.6%).

Rape

Rape is a crime of violence in which the victim may suffer serious physical injury and long-term psychological pain. According to the FBI in *Crime in the United States, 2013*, until 2013 the UCR Program categorized rape using what it called its "legacy" definition: "the carnal knowledge of a female forcibly and against her will." In 2013 the FBI revised its definition of rape for the UCR Program. Under the new definition, rape includes "penetration, no matter how slight, of the vagina or anus with any body part or object, or oral penetration by a sex organ of another person, without the consent of the victim. Attempts or assaults to commit rape are also

TABLE 2.4

Murder victims where relationship to offender and circumstances are known, 2013

Circumstances	Total murder victims	Husband	Wife	Mother	Father	Son	Daughter	Brother	Sister	Other family	Acquaintance	Friend	Boyfriend	Girlfriend	Neighbor	Employee	Employer	Stranger	Unknown
Total	12,253	108	534	128	142	230	148	99	30	245	2,660	346	137	458	127	6	2	1,281	5,572
Felony type total:	1,909	3	28	10	13	20	15	10	4	31	477	53	9	20	26	2	0	390	798
Rape*	20	0	1	0	0	0	0	0	0	2	6	1	0	1	1	0	0	4	4
Robbery	686	1	0	0	4	0	0	0	0	6	151	15	1	1	8	2	0	240	257
Burglary	94	0	0	0	0	0	0	0	0	1	22	2	1	2	3	0	0	23	41
Larceny-theft	16	0	0	0	0	0	0	0	0	2	2	1	0	0	2	0	0	2	7
Motor vehicle theft	27	0	2	1	0	0	0	0	0	4	5	1	0	1	1	0	0	4	6
Arson	37	0	0	1	2	0	0	4	2	2	11	0	1	0	4	0	0	6	5
Prostitution and commercialized vice	13	0	0	0	0	0	0	0	0	0	5	2	0	0	0	0	0	2	4
Other sex offenses	9	0	0	0	0	0	0	0	0	1	4	0	0	0	0	0	0	2	2
Narcotic drug laws	386	0	0	0	0	0	1	2	0	0	146	11	1	2	0	0	0	28	195
Gambling	7	0	0	0	0	0	0	0	0	0	4	0	0	0	0	0	0	0	3
Other-not specified	614	2	25	8	6	20	14	4	2	13	121	21	5	13	7	0	0	79	274
Suspected felony type	122	1	5	4	2	2	2	0	1	2	16	2	0	6	1	0	2	6	72
Other than felony type total:	5,782	89	410	72	102	173	94	72	19	163	1,644	210	109	348	83	4	2	617	1,571
Romantic triangle	69	0	2	0	1	0	0	0	0	0	36	8	3	9	0	0	0	3	0
Child killed by babysitter	30	0	0	0	0	2	0	0	0	2	25	0	0	0	1	0	0	0	0
Brawl due to influence of alcohol	93	0	4	1	2	1	1	1	0	6	27	14	0	3	1	0	0	21	11
Brawl due to influence of narcotics	59	0	1	0	1	0	0	0	0	1	28	5	1	2	1	0	0	6	13
Argument over money or property	133	0	4	3	0	1	0	3	1	6	59	14	1	6	4	0	0	11	20
Other arguments	2,889	65	298	46	74	39	14	56	10	98	891	117	90	273	56	2	2	250	508
Gangland killings	138	0	1	0	0	0	0	0	0	0	40	0	0	0	0	0	0	24	73
Juvenile gang killings	584	0	0	0	0	0	0	0	0	0	106	1	0	0	1	0	0	80	396
Institutional killings	15	0	0	0	0	0	0	0	0	0	10	0	0	0	0	0	0	3	2
Sniper attack	6	0	0	0	0	0	0	0	0	0	2	0	0	0	0	0	0	2	2
Other-not specified	1,766	24	100	22	24	130	79	12	8	50	420	51	14	55	19	2	0	217	539
Unknown	4,440	15	91	42	25	35	37	17	6	49	523	81	19	84	17	0	0	268	3,131

*The rape figures in this table are an aggregate total of the data submitted using both the revised and legacy Uniform Crime Reporting definitions.

Note: The relationship categories of husband and wife include both common-law and ex-spouses. The categories of mother, father, sister, brother, son, and daughter include stepparents, stepchildren, and stepsiblings. The category of acquaintance includes homosexual relationships and the composite category of other known to victim. Relationship is that of victim to offender.

SOURCE: "Expanded Homicide Data Table 10. Murder Circumstances by Relationship, 2013," in *Crime in the United States 2013*, U.S. Department of Justice, Federal Bureau of Investigation, November 10, 2014, http://www.fbi.gov/about-us/cjis/ucr/crime-in-the-u.s/2013/crime-in-the-u.s.-2013/offenses-known-to-law-enforcement/expanded-homicide/expanded_homicide_data_table_10_murder_circumstances_by_relationship_2013.xls (accessed November 12, 2014)

TABLE 2.5

Murder victims where murder weapon and circumstances are known, 2013

Circumstances	Total murder victims	Total firearms	Handguns	Rifles	Shotguns	Other guns or type not stated	Knives or cutting instruments	Blunt objects (clubs, hammers, etc.)	Personal weapons (hands, fists, feet, etc.)	Poison	Pushed or thrown out window	Explosives	Fire	Narcotics	Drowning	Strangulation	Asphyxiation	Other
Total	12,253	8,454	5,782	285	308	2,079	1,490	428	686	11	1	2	94	53	4	85	95	850
Felony type total:	1,909	1,381	1,026	32	36	287	174	79	64	1	1	0	42	21	0	17	11	118
Rape*	20	2	2	0	0	0	3	4	6	0	0	0	0	0	0	1	1	3
Robbery	686	536	435	8	10	83	52	39	20	0	0	0	1	0	0	6	5	27
Burglary	94	52	29	2	2	19	24	5	5	0	0	0	2	0	0	0	1	5
Larceny-theft	16	6	4	0	0	2	3	2	2	0	0	0	0	1	0	0	0	0
Motor vehicle theft	27	12	8	0	2	2	4	2	0	0	0	0	2	0	0	2	0	7
Arson	37	1	0	0	0	1	6	1	1	0	0	0	22	0	0	0	0	6
Prostitution and commercialized vice	13	7	4	0	0	3	3	0	1	0	0	0	0	0	0	1	0	1
Other sex offenses	9	0	0	0	0	0	3	0	3	0	0	0	0	0	0	2	0	1
Narcotic drug laws	386	327	244	5	8	70	25	4	4	0	0	0	1	18	0	0	1	6
Gambling	7	6	5	0	0	1	1	0	0	0	0	0	0	0	0	0	0	0
Other-not specified	614	432	295	17	14	106	50	22	22	1	1	0	14	2	0	5	3	62
Suspected felony type	122	87	59	2	7	19	15	5	2	0	0	0	1	2	0	4	1	7
Other than felony type total:	5,782	3,673	2,653	164	186	670	922	208	482	8	0	2	25	24	4	39	52	343
Romantic triangle	69	49	36	3	2	8	13	0	1	1	0	0	0	0	0	0	2	3
Child killed by babysitter	30	0	0	0	0	0	0	3	19	0	0	0	0	0	0	0	1	7
Brawl due to influence of alcohol	93	48	33	5	5	5	21	3	13	0	0	0	1	0	0	0	2	5
Brawl due to influence of narcotics	59	35	26	2	1	6	3	2	4	0	0	0	0	6	0	0	1	8
Argument over money or property	133	83	62	4	6	11	25	9	11	0	0	0	0	0	0	1	1	3
Other arguments	2,889	1,747	1,270	80	108	289	616	124	216	3	0	1	11	2	2	22	22	123
Gangland killings	138	117	87	3	1	26	15	0	2	0	0	0	0	0	0	0	0	4
Juvenile gang killings	584	547	428	9	9	101	28	2	2	0	0	0	0	0	0	0	0	5
Institutional killings	15	0	0	0	0	0	0	3	7	0	0	0	0	0	0	2	1	2
Sniper attack	6	6	2	1	0	3	0	0	0	0	0	1	0	0	0	0	0	0
Other-not specified	1,766	1,041	709	57	54	221	201	62	207	4	0	1	13	16	2	14	22	183
Unknown	4,440	3,313	2,044	87	79	1,103	379	136	138	2	0	0	26	8	2	25	31	382

*The rape figures in this table are an aggregate total of the data submitted using both the revised and legacy Uniform Crime Reporting definitions.

SOURCE: "Expanded Homicide Data Table 11. Murder Circumstances by Weapon, 2013," in *Crime in the United States 2013*, U.S. Department of Justice, Federal Bureau of Investigation, November 10, 2014, http://www.fbi.gov/about-us/cjis/ucr/crime-in-the-u.s/2013/crime-in-the-u.s.-2013/offenses-known-to-law-enforcement/expanded-homicide/expanded_homicide_data_table_11_murder_circumstances_by_weapon_2013.xls (accessed November 12, 2014)

included; however, statutory rape and incest are excluded." Statutory rape is an offense in which the victim cannot legally consent to sexual intercourse because the victim is either too young or is mentally or physically incapacitated in some way.

Rape is a very intimate crime, and rape victims may be unwilling, afraid, or ashamed to discuss it. As a result, many rapes are likely not reported to law enforcement authorities. In 2013, 79,770 rapes (legacy definition) were reported to law enforcement agencies for a rate of 25.2 rapes per 100,000 female inhabitants. (See Table 2.1.) The legacy rape rate has declined dramatically since 1994 when it was 39.3 rapes per 100,000 female inhabitants.

Table 2.6 provides additional information about selected offenses as reported by 14,540 agencies in 2013. The data show 54,785 completed rapes (legacy definition) and 3,778 attempted rapes (legacy definition) for 2013.

Robbery

According to the FBI in *Crime in the United States, 2013*, robbery is defined as "the taking or attempting to take anything of value from the care, custody, or control of a person or persons by force or threat of force or violence and/or by putting the victim in fear." The robbery count in 2013 was 345,031 for a rate of 109.1 per 100,000 inhabitants. (See Table 2.1.) This is down significantly from 1994, when the rate was 237.8 per 100,000 inhabitants.

Figure 2.3 shows the locations of robberies that were reported in 2013. Nearly 43% of these robberies occurred on the street or highway, 18.4% occurred at miscellaneous locations, 16.6% occurred at residences, and 13.3% occurred at commercial houses (i.e., nonresidential structures that are used for businesses other than gas stations, banks, or convenience stores). Robberies at convenience stores accounted for 5% of the total, whereas gas or service stations accounted for 2.4% and banks for 1.9% of the total. (Note that due to rounding the percentages sum to more than 100%.)

WEAPONS INVOLVED IN ROBBERIES. Table 2.6 provides additional information about 297,608 robberies reported by 14,540 law enforcement agencies in 2013. More than half (171,267, or 57.5%) involved a weapon, such as firearm (122,266), knife or other cutting instrument (22,553), or some other type of weapon (26,448). The other 42.5% (126,341) of the robberies were strong-arm robberies in which the offenders used bodily force to rob their victims.

Aggravated Assault

Aggravated assault is defined by the FBI in *Crime in the United States, 2013* as "an unlawful attack by one person upon another for the purpose of inflicting severe or aggravated bodily injury." The agency further notes that aggravated assault typically involves "the use of

a weapon or by other means likely to produce death or great bodily harm." Attempted aggravated assaults that involve weapons or the threat to use weapons are included in this category. However, an aggravated assault that occurs during a robbery is categorized as a robbery.

In 2013, 724,149 aggravated assaults were reported to law enforcement agencies nationwide for a rate of 229.1 aggravated assaults per 100,000 inhabitants. (See Table 2.1.) The rate has declined substantially since 1994 when it stood at 427.6 aggravated assaults per 100,000 inhabitants.

WEAPONS INVOLVED IN AGGRAVATED ASSAULTS. Table 2.6 provides additional information about 634,750 of the aggravated assaults that occurred in 2013 as reported by 14,540 law enforcement agencies. Nearly three-quarters of the assaults (465,106, or 73.3%) involved weapons. Perpetrators used their hands, fists, feet, and so on in the remaining 169,644 assaults for 26.7% of the total. Overall, firearms were involved in 139,931 (22%) of the aggravated assaults in 2013.

Violent Crime and Property Crime

As noted earlier, the FBI includes four crimes in the category of violent crime: forcible rape, murder and non-negligent manslaughter, aggravated assault, and robbery. A crime that includes more than one of these violent acts is counted only once, under the most serious offense committed. According to the FBI in *Crime in the United States, 2013*, the hierarchy is murder and nonnegligent homicide, forcible rape, robbery, and aggravated assault. Thus, a forcible rape in which the victim is also robbed would be counted as a forcible rape, not as a forcible rape and a robbery. In 2013 nearly 1.2 million violent crimes were reported by law enforcement agencies. (See Table 2.1.) As shown in Figure 2.4, the breakdown of reported violent crimes by percentage was:

- Murder and nonnegligent homicide—1% of reported violent crimes

- Forcible rape (legacy definition)—7% of reported violent crimes

- Robbery—30% of reported violent crimes

- Aggravated assault—62% of reported violent crimes

The FBI includes four crimes in the category of property crime: larceny-theft, burglary, arson, and motor vehicle theft. In 2013, 8.6 million of these property crimes were reported for a rate of 2,730.7 per 100,000 inhabitants. (See Table 2.1.) According to the FBI, the hierarchy for property crimes is burglary, larceny-theft, and motor vehicle theft. The property crime hierarchy lies below the violent crime hierarchy, meaning that a violent crime that includes one or more property crimes is counted only under the appropriate violent crime. Arson is not included in the hierarchy. It is always counted separately, even

TABLE 2.6

Details about selected offenses, 2012–13

Population group	Forcible rape*		Robbery				Aggravated assault				Burglary			Motor vehicle theft			Arson			Number of agencies	2013 estimated population
	Rape by force	Assault to rape-attempts	Firearm	Knife or cutting instru-ment	Other weapon	Strong-arm	Firearm	Knife or cutting instru-ment	Other weapon	Hands, fists, feet, etc.	Forcible entry	Unlawful entry	Attempted forcible entry	Autos	Trucks and buses	Other vehicles	Structure	Mobile	Other		
Total all agencies:																					
2012	57,904	4,034	125,366	23,532	26,784	129,662	146,045	125,595	218,469	180,637	1,133,013	642,852	121,877	489,915	100,562	72,193	22,052	10,970	14,985		
2013	54,785	3,778	122,266	22,553	26,448	126,341	139,931	120,063	205,112	169,644	1,032,491	595,997	110,688	474,529	98,265	70,768	18,896	9,834	12,904	14,540	277,860,576
Percent change	−5.4	−6.3	−2.5	−4.2	−1.3	−2.6	−4.2	−4.4	−6.1	−6.1	−8.9	−7.3	−9.2	−3.1	−2.3	−2.0	−14.3	−10.4	−13.9		

*The rape figures in this table are based on the legacy Uniform Crime Reporting (UCR) definition of rape. The rape figures shown for 2012 and 2013 include converted National Incident-Based Reporting System rape data and those states/agencies that reported the legacy UCR definition of rape for both years.

SOURCE: Adapted from "Table 15. Crime Trends: Additional Information About Selected Offenses by Population Group, 2012–2013," in *Crime in the United States 2013,* U.S. Department of Justice, Federal Bureau of Investigation, November 10, 2014, http://www.fbi.gov/about-us/cjis/ucr/crime-in-the-u.s/2013/crime-in-the-u.s.-2013/tables/table-15/table_15_crime_trends_by_additional_information_about_selected_offenses_2012-2013.xls (accessed November 12, 2014)

FIGURE 2.3

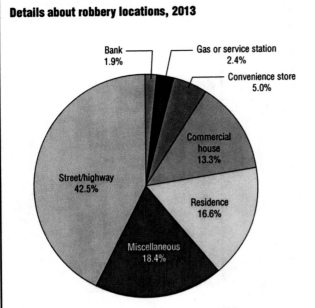

Details about robbery locations, 2013

- Bank 1.9%
- Gas or service station 2.4%
- Convenience store 5.0%
- Commercial house 13.3%
- Street/highway 42.5%
- Residence 16.6%
- Miscellaneous 18.4%

Note: Due to rounding, the percentages may not add to 100.0.

SOURCE: "Percent Distribution, 2013," in *Crime in the United States 2013*, U.S. Department of Justice, Federal Bureau of Investigation, November 10, 2014, http://www.fbi.gov/about-us/cjis/ucr/crime-in-the-u.s/2013/crime-in-the-u.s.-2013/violent-crime/robbery-topic-page (accessed November 12, 2014)

FIGURE 2.4

Breakdown of violent crimes reported to law enforcement, 2013

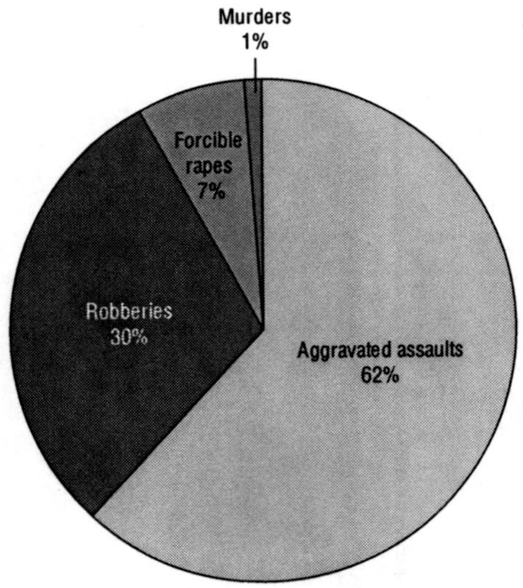

- Murders 1%
- Forcible rapes 7%
- Robberies 30%
- Aggravated assaults 62%

SOURCE: Adapted from "Violent Crime," in *Crime in the United States 2013*, U.S. Department of Justice, Federal Bureau of Investigation, November 10, 2014, http://www.fbi.gov/about-us/cjis/ucr/crime-in-the-u.s/2013/crime-in-the-u.s.-2013/violent-crime/violent-crime-topic-page/violentcrimemain_final (accessed November 12, 2014)

when it occurs in conjunction with another violent or property crime. The following four sections describe the statistics for individual property crimes.

Burglary

According to the FBI in *Crime in the United States, 2013*, burglary is defined as "the unlawful entry of a structure to commit a felony or theft." Unlawful entry includes both forcible and nonforcible entry (e.g., entering a home through an unlocked door without the owner's permission). The FBI's definition of structure includes houses, apartments, offices, barns, stables, and so on, but does not include automobiles. Attempted forcible entries are included in the burglary category.

Just over 1.9 million burglaries were reported in 2013 for a rate of 610 per 100,000 inhabitants. (See Table 2.1.) This rate is down from 1994, when it was 1,042.1 burglaries per 100,000 inhabitants. Table 2.6 provides additional information about 1.7 million of the robberies reported to 14,540 law enforcement agencies. More than one million of them (or 59.4%) involved forcible entry, while 595,997 (or 34.3%) involved nonforcible but unlawful entries. The remaining 110,688 offenses were attempted burglaries.

A separate data set by the FBI covering 1.7 million burglaries in 2013 (http://www.fbi.gov/about-us/cjis/ucr/crime-in-the-u.s/2013/crime-in-the-u.s.-2013/tables/table-23/table_23_offense_analysis_number_and_percent_change_2012-2013.xls) indicates that the vast majority of these burglaries (1.3 million) occurred at residences. The rest were at nonresidences, such as stores or offices.

Larceny-Theft

Larceny-theft is defined by the FBI in *Crime in the United States, 2013* as "the unlawful taking, carrying, leading, or riding away of property from the possession or constructive possession of another." Larceny-theft does not involve the use of force, violence, or fraud. Examples of fraud-based crimes are embezzlement, forgery, and passing bad checks. Larceny-theft does include offenses such as shoplifting, pocket picking, purse snatching, stealing items from motor vehicles, and stealing bicycles. Attempted larceny-thefts are also included.

In 2013 law enforcement agencies reported 6 million larceny-thefts for a rate of 1,899.4 per 100,000 inhabitants. (See Table 2.1.) This rate is down substantially from 1994, when it exceeded 3,000 per 100,000 inhabitants. According to the FBI, the total value of property lost by victims to larceny-theft during 2013 was $7.6 billion.

Table 2.7 provides details about nearly 5.4 million of the larceny-thefts that occurred in 2013 based on information from 14,230 law enforcement agencies. Thefts from motor vehicles (excluding accessories) accounted for nearly 1.3 million of the offenses. This was the largest category among the specifically identified larceny-theft crimes. It accounted for 23.3% of the total. Shoplifting crimes (1.1 million) and thefts from buildings (662,964) made up 20% and 12.3%, respectively, of the total.

TABLE 2.7

Details about larceny-theft crimes, 2012–13

[14,230 agencies. 2013 estimated population 289,935,142.]

Classification	Number of offenses 2013	Percent change from 2012	Percent distribution*	Average value
Larceny-theft (except motor vehicle theft):				
Total	5,392,153	−2.4	100.0	1,259
Larceny-theft by type:				
Pocket-picking	29,047	+1.1	0.5	514
Purse-snatching	23,171	−1.6	0.4	467
Shoplifting	1,074,188	+4.3	19.9	207
From motor vehicles (except accessories)	1,259,348	−5.0	23.4	937
Motor vehicle accessories	393,385	−6.4	7.3	556
Bicycles	190,703	−4.5	3.5	420
From buildings	662,964	−2.5	12.3	1,384
From coin-operated machines	14,248	−6.4	0.3	448
All others	1,745,099	−3.2	32.4	2,372
Larceny-theft by value:				
Over $200	2,525,685	−2.3	46.8	2,625
$50 to $200	1,202,569	−3.6	22.3	104
Under $50	1,663,899	−1.7	30.9	21

*Because of rounding, the percentages may not add to 100.0.

SOURCE: Adapted from "Table 23. Offense Analysis: Number and Percent Change, 2012–2013," in *Crime in the United States 2013*, U.S. Department of Justice, Federal Bureau of Investigation, November 10, 2014, http://www.fbi.gov/about-us/cjis/ucr/crime-in-the-u.s/2013/crime-in-the-u.s.-2013/tables/table-23/table_23_offense_analysis_number_and_percent_change_2012-2013.xls (accessed November 12, 2014)

According to the FBI, the average loss to victims due to larceny-thefts in 2013 was $1,259 per offense. A breakdown by average value is shown in Table 2.7:

- Value over $200—2.5 million offenses or 46.8% of the total

- Value of $50 to $200—1.2 million offenses or 22.3% of the total

- Value less than $50—1.7 million offenses or 30.9% of the total

Motor Vehicle Theft

In *Crime in the United States, 2013*, the FBI defines motor vehicle theft as "the theft or attempted theft of a motor vehicle." Included in the definition of motor vehicles are cars, trucks, sport-utility vehicles, buses, motorcycles and motor scooters, snowmobiles, and all-terrain vehicles. Other types of motorized vehicles (e.g., boats, tractors, and construction equipment) are not included.

In 2013, 669,594 cases of motor vehicle theft were reported in the United States for a rate of 221.3 motor vehicle thefts per 100,000 inhabitants. (See Table 2.1.) This rate is down considerably from 1994, when the rate was nearly 600 motor vehicle thefts per 100,000 inhabitants. Table 2.6 provides additional details about 643,562 of the motor vehicle thefts based on information from 14,540 law enforcement agencies. The vast majority (474,529, or 73.7%) of the thefts were of automobiles. Another 98,265 (15.3%) of the thefts were of trucks and

buses, and 70,768 (11%) were of other types of vehicles. According to the FBI, the total value of stolen motor vehicles in 2013 was more than $4.1 billion.

Arson

Arson, as defined by the FBI in *Crime in the United States, 2013*, is "any willful or malicious burning or attempting to burn, with or without intent to defraud, a dwelling house, public building, motor vehicle or aircraft, personal property of another, etc." Arson statistics only include fires determined to have been set on purpose; those that have been classified as suspicious or of unknown origin are excluded.

The FBI notes that statistics for arson crimes are incomplete due to limited reporting by law enforcement agencies. As reported in *Crime in the United States, 2013*, those agencies that did supply full- or partial-year arson statistics to the FBI reported 44,840 arsons in 2013. Table 2.6 provides detailed information about 41,634 of the arsons. Nearly half (18,896, or 45.4%) involved buildings, such as residences or other structures. Another 9,834 (23.6%) involved mobile property, such as cars, and 12,904 (31%) of the arsons involved other types of property, such as crops or fences.

GUNS AND CRIME

As noted earlier and shown in Table 2.5, the FBI reports that firearms were used in 8,454 (69%) of 12,253 murders reported in 2013. Likewise, Table 2.6 shows that firearms were used in 122,266 robberies (or 41.1% of the total) and in 139,931 aggravated assaults (or 22% of the total). The number of these crimes declined dramatically between 1994 and 2013. Thus, crime-related firearm use likewise decreased sharply. Nevertheless, highly publicized mass murders committed with firearms (particularly in schools) since the late 1990s have raised concerns about gun availability.

Gun Control

Laws that regulate gun ownership by certain groups of people date back to the country's founding. Worries about firearms in the hands of criminals have spurred legislative prohibitions targeting known felons (i.e., people who have been convicted of felony crimes). In addition, the state and federal governments have historically enacted restrictions on certain types of firearms, for example, the "tommy" submachine guns favored by gangsters during the 1930s. In 1968 President Lyndon Johnson (1908–1973) signed into law the Gun Control Act of 1968 noting, "Today we begin to disarm the criminal and the careless and the insane." Despite these strong words, violent crime escalated greatly over the following decades. As shown in Figure 2.5, the violent crime rate increased from about 150 reported offenses per 100,000 population in 1960 to nearly 760 reported offenses per 100,000 population in the early 1990s.

In 1993 Congress passed the Brady Handgun Violence Prevention Act (Brady Act). In *National Instant Criminal Background Check System (NICS) Operations 2013* (July 2014, http://www.fbi.gov/about-us/cjis/nics/reports/2013-operations-report), the FBI's Criminal Justice Information Services Division (CJISD) notes that the Brady Act strengthened federal firearms regulations and established the National Instant Criminal Background Check System (NICS). Licensed federal firearms dealers in some states use the NICS to confirm that potential purchasers can legally buy firearms. Provisions of federal law prohibit certain people from possessing or receiving a firearm. For example, the CJISD indicates that prohibited people include those convicted of a crime punishable by imprisonment for a year or more. Note that state laws can include additional prohibitive measures.

The NICS began operating in 1998. According to the CJISD in *National Instant Criminal Background Check System (NICS) Operations 2013*, as of December 31, 2013, nearly 182 million transactions had been processed through the system. The agency notes that nearly 1.1 million transactions were denied by the NICS during that period. Figure 2.6 provides a breakdown of the denial causes. The vast majority of the denials were based on the criminal histories of the potential purchasers.

FIGURE 2.5

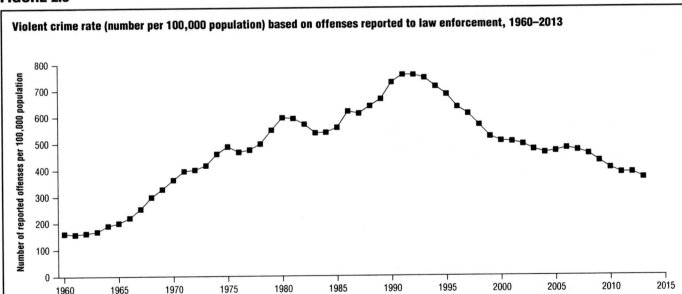

Violent crime rate (number per 100,000 population) based on offenses reported to law enforcement, 1960–2013

Notes: Offense totals are based on data from all reporting agencies and estimates for unreported areas. The 168 murder and nonnegligent homicides that occurred as a result of the bombing of the Alfred P. Murrah Federal Building in Oklahoma City in 1995 are included in the national estimate. The 2,823 murder and nonnegligent homicides that occurred as a result of the events of September 11, 2001, are not included in the national estimates. Arson data are not included.

SOURCE: Adapted from "Estimated Crime in United States-Total," in *Uniform Crime Reporting Statistics*, U.S. Department of Justice, Federal Bureau of Investigation, November 2, 2014, http://www.ucrdatatool.gov/Search/Crime/State/RunCrimeStatebyState.cfm (accessed November 2, 2014) and "Table 1. Crime in the United States by Volume and Rate per 100,000 Inhabitants, 1994–2013," in *Crime in the United States 2013*, U.S. Department of Justice, Federal Bureau of Investigation, November 10, 2014, http://www.fbi.gov/about-us/cjis/ucr/crime-in-the-u.s/2013/crime-in-the-u.s.-2013/tables/1tabledatadecoverviewpdf/table_1_crime_in_the_united_states_by_volume_and_rate_per_100000_inhabitants_1994-2013.xls (accessed November 12, 2014)

FIGURE 2.6

Reasons for denial of firearms transfers by federally licensed firearm dealers, 1998–2013

[Reasons why the NICS section denies (program to date). Population = 1,075,781.]

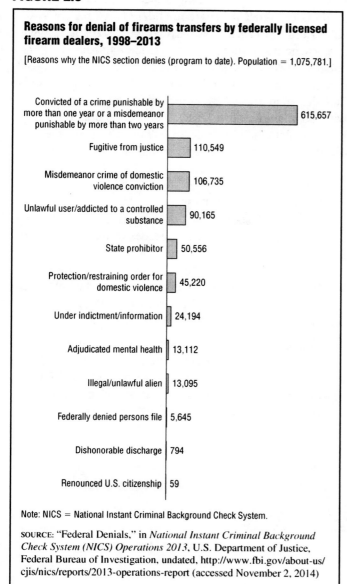

Convicted of a crime punishable by more than one year or a misdemeanor punishable by more than two years — 615,657

Fugitive from justice — 110,549

Misdemeanor crime of domestic violence conviction — 106,735

Unlawful user/addicted to a controlled substance — 90,165

State prohibitor — 50,556

Protection/restraining order for domestic violence — 45,220

Under indictment/information — 24,194

Adjudicated mental health — 13,112

Illegal/unlawful alien — 13,095

Federally denied persons file — 5,645

Dishonorable discharge — 794

Renounced U.S. citizenship — 59

Note: NICS = National Instant Criminal Background Check System.

SOURCE: "Federal Denials," in *National Instant Criminal Background Check System (NICS) Operations 2013*, U.S. Department of Justice, Federal Bureau of Investigation, undated, http://www.fbi.gov/about-us/cjis/nics/reports/2013-operations-report (accessed November 2, 2014)

HATE CRIMES

As noted in Chapter 1, hate crimes are crimes that are motivated by the offender's personal prejudice or bias against the victim. There is no single, comprehensive legal definition for the term *hate crime*; however, the FBI defines it in *Hate Crime Statistics, 2013: Methodology* (December 2014, http://www.fbi.gov/about-us/cjis/ucr/hate-crime/2013/resource-pages/methodology/methodology_final) as "criminal offenses that were motivated, in whole or in part, by the offender's bias against a race, gender, gender identity, religion, disability, sexual orientation, or ethnicity, and were committed against persons, property, or society."

In 1990 Congress passed the Hate Crime Statistics Act, which required the U.S. attorney general to "acquire data...about crimes that manifest evidence of prejudice based on race, religion, disability, sexual orientation, or ethnicity" and to publish a summary of the data. The Hate Crime Statistics Act was amended by the Violent Crime and Law Enforcement Act of 1994 to include bias-motivated acts against disabled people. Further amendments in the Church Arson Prevention Act of 1996 directed the FBI to track bias-related church arsons as a permanent part of its duties. According to the agency in "FBI Releases 2013 Hate Crime Statistics" (December 8, 2014, http://www.fbi.gov/news/pressrel/press-releases/fbi-releases-2013-hate-crime-statistics), the Matthew Shepard and James Byrd, Jr. Hate Crimes Prevention Act of 2009 requires the FBI to add the bias categories of gender and gender identity (transgender and gender nonconforming) to its hate crime monitoring program. The gender identity category covers people who self-identify and/or behave as being of a different gender than their birth gender.

The Constitutionality of Hate Crime Legislation

The constitutionality of hate crime legislation has been challenged on the grounds that these laws punish free thought. In 1992 the U.S. Supreme Court, in *R.A.V. v. City of St. Paul* (505 U.S. 377), found a Minnesota law outlawing certain "fighting words" to be unconstitutional. In this case, the defendant had burned a cross "inside the fenced yard of a black family." A law limiting pure speech or symbolic speech can only be upheld if it meets the "clear and present danger" standard of *Brandenburg v. Ohio* (395 U.S. 444 [1969]). This standard means that speech may only be outlawed if it incites or produces "imminent lawless action."

However, in *Wisconsin v. Mitchell* (508 U.S. 476 [1993]), the Supreme Court upheld laws that impose harsher prison sentences and greater fines for criminals who are motivated by bigotry. The court found that statutes such as the Wisconsin law in question to be constitutional because, unlike the Minnesota law, they do not criminalize protected speech. Instead, they allow for stiffer penalties to be imposed on people convicted of crimes when they are found to be motivated by hateful biases.

Hate Crime Statistics

Data on hate crimes are likely incomplete because many incidents may not be reported or cannot be verified as hate crimes. Some victims may not report hate crimes due to fear that the criminal justice system is biased against the group to which the victim belongs and that law enforcement authorities will not be responsive. Attacks against gays and lesbians may not be reported because the victims do not want to reveal their sexual orientation to others. In addition, proving that an offender acted from bias can be a long, tedious process, requiring much investigation. Until a law enforcement investigator can find enough evidence in a particular case to be sure the offender's actions came, at least in part, from bias, the crime is not counted as a hate crime.

In *Hate Crime Statistics, 2013* (December 2014, http://www.fbi.gov/about-us/cjis/ucr/hate-crime/2013), the FBI notes that in 2013, law enforcement agencies reported 5,928 hate crime incidents involving 6,933 specific offenses. Most of the incidents (5,922) were due to a single bias on behalf of the offender (note that the percentages sum to more than 100% due to rounding):

- Racial bias—49.3%
- Sexual-orientation bias—20.2%
- Religious bias—16.9%
- Ethnicity/national origin bias—11.4%
- Disability bias—1.4%
- Gender identity—0.5%
- Gender—0.4%

In total, 4,430 of the hate crime offenses in 2013 were considered crimes against people, while 2,424 were deemed crimes against property. The FBI notes that 43.5% of the hate crimes against people involved intimidation, whereas 38.8% involved simple assault, and 16.6% involved aggravated assault. Five murders and 21 rapes (legacy and revised definitions) were also reported as hate crimes.

THE DECLINE OF CRIME

As shown in Table 2.1, between 1994 and 2013 both the number of crimes reported each year and the crime rate decreased for all the crimes that are monitored by the DOJ under the UCR Program. Older UCR data are available from the agency's UCR Data Tool (http://www.bjs.gov/ucrdata/index.cfm), an online database. In "Frequently Asked Questions" (2014, http://www.bjs.gov/ucrdata/faq.cfm), the BJS notes that the database only includes data from law enforcement agencies of cities with populations of at least 10,000 people and counties with populations of at least 25,000 people. Thus, the data differ slightly from those presented in the FBI's annual *Crime in the United States* reports.

A Decline in Violent Crime

Figure 2.5 shows the violent crime rate climbed dramatically during the latter decades of the 20th century from about 150 reported offenses per 100,000 population in the early 1960s to nearly 760 reported offenses per 100,000 population in the early 1990s. The rate then tumbled to 367.9 reported offenses per 100,000 population in 2013.

Figure 2.7 shows the murder and nonnegligent manslaughter rate per 100,000 population between 1960 and 2013. The rate peaked at 10.2 offenses per 100,000 population in 1980 and remained at or above 7.9 offenses per 100,000 population into the 1990s. Starting in 1994, the rate began to decline. It dropped to 4.5 offenses per 100,000 population in 2013.

Figure 2.8 shows the forcible rape rate per 100,000 population between 1960 and 2013. The rate peaked at

FIGURE 2.7

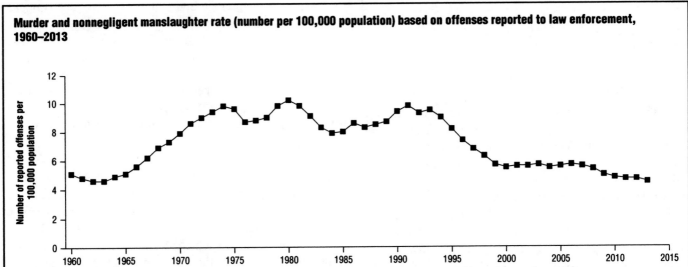

Murder and nonnegligent manslaughter rate (number per 100,000 population) based on offenses reported to law enforcement, 1960–2013

Notes: Offense totals are based on data from all reporting agencies and estimates for unreported areas. The 168 murder and nonnegligent homicides that occurred as a result of the bombing of the Alfred P. Murrah Federal Building in Oklahoma City in 1995 are included in the national estimate. The 2,823 murder and nonnegligent homicides that occurred as a result of the events of September 11, 2001, are not included in the national estimates.

SOURCE: Adapted from "Estimated Crime in United States-Total," in *Uniform Crime Reporting Statistics*, U.S. Department of Justice, Federal Bureau of Investigation, November 2, 2014, http://www.ucrdatatool.gov/Search/Crime/State/RunCrimeStatebyState.cfm (accessed November 2, 2014) and "Table 1. Crime in the United States by Volume and Rate per 100,000 Inhabitants, 1994–2013," in *Crime in the United States 2013*, U.S. Department of Justice, Federal Bureau of Investigation, November 10, 2014, http://www.fbi.gov/about-us/cjis/ucr/crime-in-the-u.s/2013/crime-in-the-u.s.-2013/tables/1tabledatadecoverviewpdf/table_1_crime_in_the_united_states_by_volume_and_rate_per_100000_inhabitants_1994-2013.xls (accessed November 12, 2014)

FIGURE 2.8

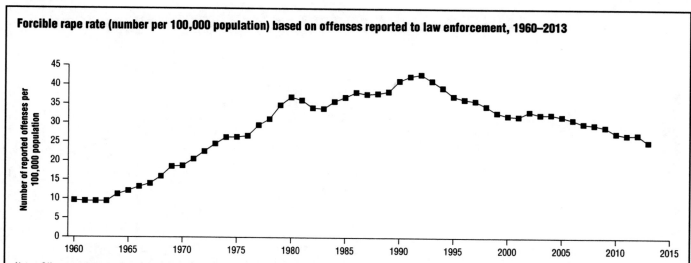

Forcible rape rate (number per 100,000 population) based on offenses reported to law enforcement, 1960–2013

Notes: Offense totals are based on data from all reporting agencies and estimates for unreported areas. Rape data were estimated using the legacy Uniform Crime Reporting definition of rape.

SOURCE: Adapted from "Estimated Crime in United States-Total," in *Uniform Crime Reporting Statistics*, U.S. Department of Justice, Federal Bureau of Investigation, November 2, 2014, http://www.ucrdatatool.gov/Search/Crime/State/RunCrimeStatebyState.cfm (accessed November 2, 2014) and "Table 1. Crime in the United States by Volume and Rate per 100,000 Inhabitants, 1994–2013," in *Crime in the United States 2013*, U.S. Department of Justice, Federal Bureau of Investigation, November 10, 2014, http://www.fbi.gov/about-us/cjis/ucr/crime-in-the-u.s/2013/crime-in-the-u.s.-2013/tables/1tabledatadecoverviewpdf/table_1_crime_in_the_united_states_by_volume_and_rate_per_100000_inhabitants_1994-2013.xls (accessed November 12, 2014)

FIGURE 2.9

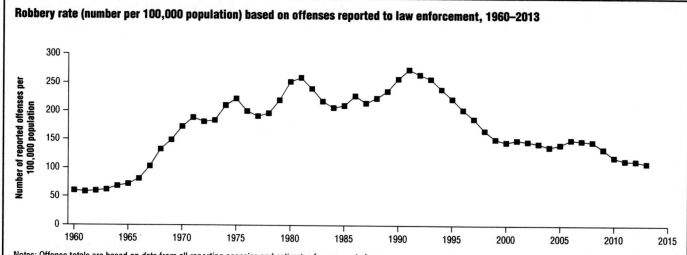

Robbery rate (number per 100,000 population) based on offenses reported to law enforcement, 1960–2013

Notes: Offense totals are based on data from all reporting agencies and estimates for unreported areas.

SOURCE: Adapted from "Estimated Crime in United States-Total," in *Uniform Crime Reporting Statistics*, U.S. Department of Justice, Federal Bureau of Investigation, November 2, 2014, http://www.ucrdatatool.gov/Search/Crime/State/RunCrimeStatebyState.cfm (accessed November 2, 2014) and "Table 1. Crime in the United States by Volume and Rate per 100,000 Inhabitants, 1994–2013," in *Crime in the United States 2013*, U.S. Department of Justice, Federal Bureau of Investigation, November 10, 2014, http://www.fbi.gov/about-us/cjis/ucr/crime-in-the-u.s/2013/crime-in-the-u.s.-2013/tables/1tabledatadecoverviewpdf/table_1_crime_in_the_united_states_by_volume_and_rate_per_100000_inhabitants_1994-2013.xls (accessed November 12, 2014)

42.8 forcible rapes per 100,000 population in 1992 and then began a general decline. In 2013 it was 25.2 forcible rapes per 100,000 population.

Figure 2.9 shows the robbery rate per 100,000 population between 1960 and 2013. The rate was above 200 robberies per 100,000 population much of the time from the mid-1970s onward, peaking at 272.7 offenses

per 100,000 population in 1991. A sharp decline followed. In 2013 the rate was 109.1 robberies per 100,000 population.

Figure 2.10 shows the aggravated assault rate per 100,000 population between 1960 and 2013. During the early 1960s the rate was less than 100 aggravated assaults per 100,000 population. The rate skyrocketed over the

FIGURE 2.10

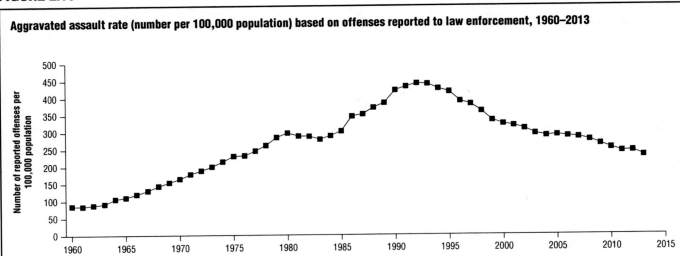

Aggravated assault rate (number per 100,000 population) based on offenses reported to law enforcement, 1960–2013

Notes: Offense totals are based on data from all reporting agencies and estimates for unreported areas.

SOURCE: Adapted from "Estimated Crime in United States-Total," in *Uniform Crime Reporting Statistics*, U.S. Department of Justice, Federal Bureau of Investigation, November 2, 2014, http://www.ucrdatatool.gov/Search/Crime/State/RunCrimeStatebyState.cfm (accessed November 2, 2014) and "Table 1. Crime in the United States by Volume and Rate per 100,000 Inhabitants, 1994–2013," in *Crime in the United States 2013*, U.S. Department of Justice, Federal Bureau of Investigation, November 10, 2014, http://www.fbi.gov/about-us/cjis/ucr/crime-in-the-u.s/2013/crime-in-the-u.s.-2013/tables/1tabledatadecoverviewpdf/table_1_crime_in_the_united_states_by_volume_and_rate_per_100000_inhabitants_1994-2013.xls (accessed November 12, 2014)

FIGURE 2.11

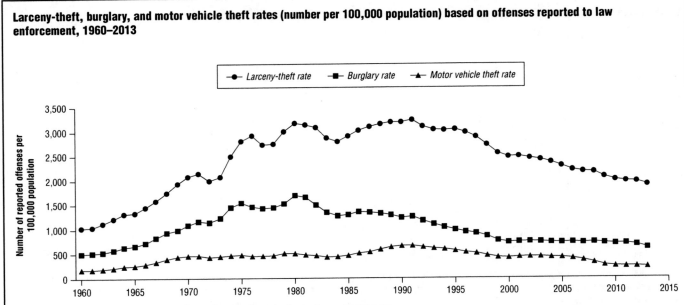

Larceny-theft, burglary, and motor vehicle theft rates (number per 100,000 population) based on offenses reported to law enforcement, 1960–2013

Notes: Offense totals are based on data from all reporting agencies and estimates for unreported areas.

SOURCE: Adapted from "Estimated Crime in United States-Total," in *Uniform Crime Reporting Statistics*, U.S. Department of Justice, Federal Bureau of Investigation, November 2, 2014, http://www.ucrdatatool.gov/Search/Crime/State/RunCrimeStatebyState.cfm (accessed November 2, 2014) and "Table 1. Crime in the United States by Volume and Rate per 100,000 Inhabitants, 1994–2013," in *Crime in the United States 2013*, U.S. Department of Justice, Federal Bureau of Investigation, November 10, 2014, http://www.fbi.gov/about-us/cjis/ucr/crime-in-the-u.s/2013/crime-in-the-u.s.-2013/tables/1tabledatadecoverviewpdf/table_1_crime_in_the_united_states_by_volume_and_rate_per_100000_inhabitants_1994-2013.xls (accessed November 12, 2014)

following decades, reaching 441.9 offenses per 100,000 population in 1992. The rate then began a dramatic decrease, dropping to 229.1 aggravated assaults per 100,000 population in 2013.

Property Crime Decreases

Figure 2.11 shows the rate per 100,000 population for property crimes (burglary, larceny-theft, and motor vehicle theft) between 1960 and 2013. The larceny-theft rate in particular soared from the 1960s through the early 1990s peaking at 3,229.1 offenses in 1991. It then declined over the following years reaching 1,899.4 larceny-thefts per 100,000 population in 2013. The burglary rate reached its climax in 1980, at 1,684.1 offenses per 100,000 population. It fell to 610 offenses per 100,000 population in 2013. The motor vehicle theft rate peaked in 1991 at 659 thefts per 100,000 population. It has dropped substantially since that time, and was 221.3 motor vehicle thefts per 100,000 population in 2013.

WHY DID CRIME RISE AND FALL?

According to Arthur J. Lurigio of Loyola University of Chicago in "Crime and Communities: Prevalence, Impact, and Programs" (Lawrence B. Joseph, ed., *Crime, Communities, and Public Policy*, 1995), the national crime rate fell from 1900 until the Prohibition era (1920–1933). Crime spiked during Prohibition and then fell and leveled off until World War II (1939–1945). Crime dropped dramatically during the war because many young men were away. Following the war, a baby boom occurred, meaning that there was a dramatic increase in births. The baby boom lasted from the late 1940s into the 1960s, resulting in a huge surge of teenagers and young adults in the population from the 1960s through the 1980s.

Figure 2.5 and Figure 2.11 show historical crime rates for violent crimes and property crimes, respectively, between 1960 and 2010. In both categories a huge increase occurred from 1960 through the 1980s and 1990s. A variety of social, economic, and even environmental reasons have been proposed to explain this increase:

- Huge influx in youth due to the baby boom
- Decrease in high-paying blue-collar manufacturing jobs for low-skilled workers
- Growth of ghettos and low-income housing projects in the inner cities
- Breakdown of the traditional family structure
- New drug culture, particularly heroin and cocaine during the 1970s and crack cocaine during the 1980s
- Growth of youth gangs
- Easy availability of firearms
- Better crime-tracking methods
- Exposure of infants and children to lead in paint and gasoline before the late 1970s (Lead exposure has been linked to a range of developmental and behavioral issues, including inattention, irritability, aggressiveness, and violent behavior.)

During the early 1990s the crime rate began a dramatic and sustained decline. (See Figure 2.5 and Figure 2.11.) Many of the conditions that had been blamed for the crime surge continued into the 1990s and the first decade of the 21st century, even as the crime rate decreased. The breakdown of the traditional family, the growth of youth gangs, and the loss of high-paying blue-collar jobs continued to occur even as the crime rate plummeted. Likewise, crime-tracking methods continued to improve over time. Sociologists and criminologists have struggled to explain why the crime rate increased and then decreased. During the 1990s and early years of the first decade of the 21st century, the strong economy was credited for the crime decline. In 2007, however, the United States entered into an economic downturn dubbed the Great Recession that saw huge spikes in unemployment and financial hardships for millions of people. Although the recession officially ended in 2009, the subsequent economic recovery was weak and slow to develop. Nevertheless, crime rates did not surge during and following the Great Recession. As a result, analysts have posited noneconomic causes as the possible reasons for the overall decrease in crime:

- Tougher sentencing rules took hard-core criminals off the streets and kept them behind bars for longer periods
- Tougher gun control laws made firearms less accessible to criminals
- The U.S. population aged and baby boomers became older and less prone to criminal behavior
- Some ghettos and low-income housing projects that had been hotbeds for crime in the inner cities were dismantled
- There were more police officers per capita
- Policing methods improved
- People increased their crime prevention efforts, such as the use of security systems and neighborhood watch programs
- The crack cocaine epidemic subsided
- The national legalization of abortion in 1973 prevented unwanted babies from being born and potentially growing up to become criminals
- Lead exposure in infants and children decreased dramatically after the 1970s

It remains to be seen whether these explanations for the crime decline will hold up to future scrutiny.

CHAPTER 3
CRIME VICTIMS

Millions of U.S. residents are victimized by crime each year. Some public and private organizations conduct surveys in order to estimate the national extent of victimization and the types of crimes that victims have experienced. For example, since 2000 the Gallup Organization has surveyed Americans annually (excluding 2012) about whether or not they or someone in their household was victimized during the previous 12 months by seven specific crimes. In 2014 the largest fraction (15%) said that they or someone in their household had experienced having money or property stolen from them. (See Table 3.1.) A smaller percentage (11%) said they had been personally victimized by such a crime during the previous year. Property vandalism was the second-most common crime with 14% of respondents saying they or someone in their household had experienced it. A smaller percentage (8%) said they had personally been victimized by vandalism during the previous 12 months. The prevalence rates for the other five crimes were all 6% or below.

Overall, in 2014 just over a quarter (26%) of the survey participants told Gallup that they or someone in their household had been a victim of at least one of the crimes during the previous year. (See Figure 3.1.) A smaller percentage (19%) said they had been personally victimized. For both measures the percentages have been fairly consistent since 2000. Gallup found that in 2014 approximately two-thirds (67%) of the victims reported the crime to the police, whereas 33% did not report it. (See Figure 3.2.) This breakdown is similar to that obtained in previous surveys dating back to 2000.

THE NATIONAL CRIME VICTIMIZATION SURVEY

As described in Chapter 2, the Federal Bureau of Investigation (FBI) operates the Uniform Crime Reporting (UCR) Program, which compiles national crime data that are submitted by thousands of law enforcement agencies from throughout the country. The UCR Program provides data on the types of crimes that are reported to law enforcement agencies. It also includes some data on the victims of these crimes. Another, more detailed examination of crime victims is spearheaded by the Bureau of Justice Statistics (BJS), an agency within the U.S. Department of Justice (DOJ). This program is called the National Crime Victimization Survey (NCVS).

Every year since 1972 the BJS has overseen the annual survey conducted by the U.S. Census Bureau in which data are collected from thousands of individuals and households on the frequency, characteristics, and consequences of criminal victimizations. The data are used to calculate national crime estimates. The data are available online from the BJS's NCVS Victimization Analysis Tool (NVAT; http://www.bjs.gov/index.cfm?ty =nvat). In addition, selected data are presented and discussed in annual publications. As of January 2015, the most recently published annual report was *Criminal Victimization, 2013* (September 2014, http://www.bjs.gov/ content/pub/pdf/cv13.pdf) by Jennifer L. Truman and Lynn Langton of the BJS. They indicate that a nationally representative sample of 160,040 individuals aged 12 years and older from 90,630 households was interviewed during 2013.

The BJS divides criminal victimizations into three categories: violent crimes, personal larceny crimes, and property crimes. Violent crimes include rape and sexual assault, robbery, aggravated assault, and simple assault. Personal larceny crimes include pocket picking and purse snatching. Both categories are known collectively as personal crimes because the victims are individuals. Victimization rates for personal crimes are expressed as the number of victims per 1,000 U.S. residents aged 12 years and older. By contrast, the victimization rates for property crimes (household burglary, motor vehicle theft, and other thefts) are expressed as the number of incidents per 1,000 U.S. households. (Note that murder and other killing crimes are not counted in the NCVS because the data are gathered only through interviews with victims.)

According to the BJS in *Survey Methodology for Criminal Victimization in the United States* (April 16, 2010, http://bjs.ojp.usdoj.gov/content/pub/pdf/ncvs_methodo logy.pdf), neither the interviewers nor the victims classify events as specific crimes during the interviews. A computer program later performs crime classification based on victim answers to specific detailed questions about the nature of each event. The NVAT website provides the following definitions for the crimes considered in the NCVS:

- Aggravated assault—an attack or attempted attack with a weapon, regardless of whether the victim is injured, or an attack without a weapon when serious injury results.

- Burglary—unlawful or forcible entry or attempted entry into a residence (i.e., house, garage, storage shed or any other structure on the premises) or hotel room. This crime usually, but not always, involves theft. Note that forcible entry is not required, as burglary occurs when the person entering has no legal right to be present in the structure.

- Motor vehicle theft—unlawful taking, or attempted taking, of a self-propelled road vehicle owned by another, with the intent of permanently or temporarily depriving the owner of possession. Excludes vehicle parts.

- Purse snatching or pocket picking—theft or attempted theft of property or cash directly from the victim by stealth, without force or the threat of force.

- Rape—unlawful penetration or attempted penetration of a person against the will of the victim, with use or threatened use of force, including psychological coercion and physical force. Also includes incidents where penetration is from a foreign object, such as a bottle. Attempted rape includes verbal threats of rape.

- Robbery—unlawful taking or attempted taking of property that is in the immediate possession of another, by force or threat of force, with or without a weapon, and with or without injury.

- Sexual assault—this includes a wide range of sexual victimizations (excluding rape or attempted rape) that

TABLE 3.1

Percentage of Americans saying they or their households were victimized by specific crimes during previous year, October 2014

	U.S households victimized %	U.S adults victimized %
Money or property stolen from you or another member of your household	15	11
A home, car, or property owned by you or another household member vandalized	14	8
Your house or apartment broken into	6	6
A car owned by you or another household member stolen	3	2
You or another household member mugged or physically assaulted	3	2
Money or property taken by force, with gun, knife, weapon or physical attack	1	1
You or another household member sexually assaulted	*	*

*= Less than 0.5%.

FIGURE 3.1

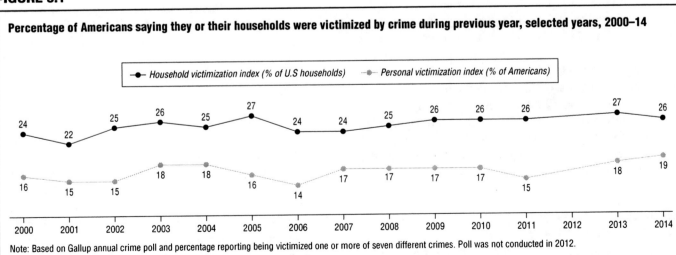

Percentage of Americans saying they or their households were victimized by crime during previous year, selected years, 2000–14

Note: Based on Gallup annual crime poll and percentage reporting being victimized one or more of seven different crimes. Poll was not conducted in 2012.

FIGURE 3.2

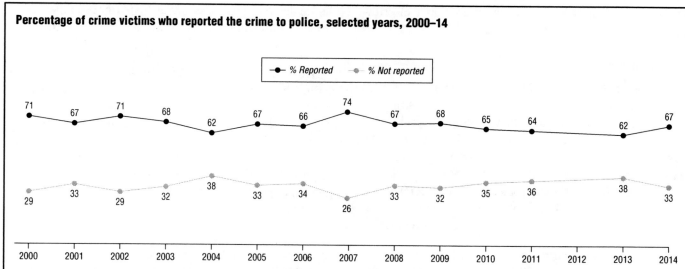

Percentage of crime victims who reported the crime to police, selected years, 2000–14

Note: Figures are based on the percentages of those who said they were a victim of burglaries, property thefts, car thefts, vandalism, robberies, physical assaults or sexual assaults. Survey not conducted in 2012.

SOURCE: Jeffrey M. Jones, "Crime Reporting to Police, 2000–2014 Gallup Polls," in *About One in Four U.S. Households Victimized by Crime*, The Gallup Organization, November 5, 2014, http://www.gallup.com/poll/179174/one-four-households-victimized-crime.aspx (accessed November 6, 2014). Copyright © 2014 Gallup, Inc. All rights reserved. The content is used with permission; however, Gallup retains all rights of republication.

may or may not involve force. The assaults, or attempted assaults, generally involve unwanted sexual contact between victim and offender, such as grabbing or fondling. Verbal threats are also included.

- Simple assault—an attack or attempted attack without a weapon that results in either no injury, minor injury (e.g., bruises, black eyes, cuts, scratches, or swelling) or an undetermined injury requiring less than two days of hospitalization.

- Theft—the unlawful taking or attempted unlawful taking of property or cash without personal contact with the victim, by an offender with a legal right to be in the house (e.g., a maid, delivery person, or guest).

For events that include more than one crime (e.g., rape and burglary), only the most serious crime is counted for NCVS purposes using the following hierarchy: rape, sexual assault, robbery, assault, burglary, motor vehicle theft, and theft.

It should be noted that the BJS used a different overall methodology during the 2006 NCVS data collection effort. As a result, Truman and Langton warn that victimization estimates for 2006 may not be comparable to estimates from other years.

Comparing NCVS and UCR Data

The NCVS was created because of a concern that the FBI's UCR Program did not fully portray the true volume of crime in the United States. The UCR provides data on crimes that are reported to law enforcement authorities, but not all crimes are reported by victims.

Some observers believe the NCVS is a better indicator than the UCR of the volume of crime in the United States. Nonetheless, like all surveys, the NCVS is subject to error. The accuracy of the survey data depends on people's truthful and complete reporting of incidents and events that have happened to them. Also, the NCVS and the UCR define and track some crimes differently. For example, Truman and Langton indicate that the NCVS covers simple assaults and sexual assaults, two crime categories excluded from the UCR. In addition, the UCR Program counts crimes committed against people less than 12 years old, whereas the NCVS only counts crimes against people aged 12 years and older. Thus, direct comparisons between UCR and NCVS data are difficult.

The NCVS and the UCR are generally considered the primary sources of statistical information on crime in the United States. Like all reporting systems, both have their shortcomings, but each provides valuable insights into crime in the United States.

CRIME VICTIMS AND VICTIMIZATIONS IN 2013

In *Criminal Victimization, 2013*, Truman and Langton report the number of victims who experienced certain crimes during 2013 and the number of victimizations that occurred. Note that these are different measures. For example, a person who was robbed twice in 2013 is counted twice in the victimization count but only once in the victim count. The number of victimizations reflects the number of victims that were present during a criminal incident. Because there can be multiple victims from a single criminal incident (e.g., a home invasion robbery in which several victims are present), the number of victimizations in 2013 may be larger than the number of criminal incidents that occurred that year.

Violent Crimes

As stated earlier, the NCVS considers rape/sexual assault, robbery, and aggravated and simple assault as violent crimes. With the exception of simple assault these crimes are also considered "serious violent crimes." As shown in Table 3.2, just over 3 million people aged 12 years and older experienced at least one violent victimization during 2013. This value was down from 2004, when it totaled nearly 3.5 million people. More than 1.1 million people in 2013 were victims of serious violent crimes.

Note that the victim counts provided for specific violent crime categories in Table 3.2 do not sum to the total victim count for each year. This is because victims of multiple crimes are counted each time for the crime type, but only once for the violent crime total. For example, a person who was robbed and assaulted during 2013 is counted once in the robbery total and once in the assault total, but only once in the violent crime total.

Truman and Langton estimate that 1.2% of the population aged 12 years and older "experienced at least one violent victimization" during 2013. The prevalence rate was down from 1.4% in 2004. (See Table 3.2.)

Domestic violence is a crime in which the offender and victim have a close personal relationship; that is, they are family members or current or former spouses, boyfriends, or girlfriends. As noted in Table 3.2, in 2013 there were 589,140 victims of domestic violence aged 12 years and older. Nearly two-thirds of them (369,310, or 63%) were victimized by their intimate partners—current or former spouses, boyfriends, or girlfriends. By contrast, 1.2 million people in 2013 were violently victimized by strangers.

Table 3.3 provides a breakdown by crime type for the 6.1 million violent victimizations estimated to have occurred in 2013 to U.S. residents aged 12 years and older. More than 1.9 million of the victimizations were associated with "serious violent crimes." Overall, the largest number of victimizations (5.2 million) were assaults, including 4.2 million simple assaults and nearly 1 million aggravated assaults. In addition, there were 645,650 robbery victimizations and 300,170 rapes or sexual assaults.

TABLE 3.2

Number of victims and prevalence rate, by type of crime, 2004, 2012, and 2013

Type of crime	Number of victims[a]			Prevalence rate[b]		
	2004	2012	2013	2004	2012	2013
Violent crime[c]	3,478,620	3,575,900	3,041,170	1.4%	1.4%	1.2%
Rape/sexual assault	134,860	170,400	173,610	0.1	0.1	0.1
Robbery	358,780	498,780	369,070	0.1	0.2	0.1
Assault	3,028,230	3,011,130	2,600,920	1.3	1.1	1.0
Aggravated assault	794,400	633,590	633,090	0.3	0.2	0.2
Simple assault	2,349,840	2,469,270	2,046,600	1.0	0.9	0.8
Domestic violence[d]	649,950	643,680	589,140	0.3	0.2	0.2
Intimate partner violence[e]	401,880	385,500	369,310	0.2	0.1	0.1
Stranger violence	1,592,450	1,610,520	1,244,560	0.7	0.6	0.5
Violent crime involving injury	1,064,350	940,010	849,240	0.4	0.4	0.3
Serious violent crime[f]	1,276,560	1,271,770	1,145,350	0.5%	0.5%	0.4%
Serious domestic violence[d]	208,190	244,230	231,170	0.1	0.1	0.1
Serious intimate partner violence[e]	135,380	160,790	163,480	0.1	0.1	0.1
Serious stranger violence	619,190	665,850	497,920	0.3	0.3	0.2
Serious violent crime involving weapons	930,350	824,320	738,540	0.4	0.3	0.3
Serious violent crime involving injury	446,260	469,120	420,890	0.2	0.2	0.2
Property crime[g]	12,085,300	13,111,940	11,531,420	10.4%	10.4%	9.0%
Burglary	2,450,560	2,694,260	2,458,360	2.1	2.1	1.9
Motor vehicle theft	785,460	519,540	555,660	0.7	0.4	0.4
Theft	9,589,480	10,595,290	9,070,680	8.3	8.4	7.1

[a]Number of persons age 12 or older who experienced at least one victimization during the year for violent crime, and number of households that experienced at least one victimization during the year for property crime.

[b]Percentage of persons age 12 or older who experienced at least one victimization during the year for violent crime, and percentage of households that experienced at least one victimization during the year for property crime.

[c]Excludes homicide because the National Crime Victimization Survey (NCVS) is based on interviews with victims and therefore cannot measure murder.

[d]Includes victimization committed by intimate partners and family members.

[e]Includes victimization committed by current or former spouses, boyfriends, or girlfriends.

[f]Includes rape or sexual assault, robbery, and aggravated assault.

[g]Includes household burglary, motor vehicle theft, and theft.

Note: Detail may not sum to total because a person or household may experience multiple types of crime.

SOURCE: Jennifer L. Truman and Lynn Langton, "Table 4. Number of Victims and Prevalence Rate, by Type of Crime, 2004, 2012, and 2013," in *Criminal Victimization, 2013*, U.S. Department of Justice, Office of Justice Programs, Bureau of Justice Statistics, September 19, 2014, http://www.bjs.gov/content/pub/pdf/cv13.pdf (accessed November 2, 2014)

TABLE 3.3

Violent victimizations, number and rate, by type of crime, 2004, 2012, and 2013

Type of violent crime	Number			Rate[a]		
	2004	2012	2013	2004	2012	2013
Violent crime[b]	6,726,060	6,842,590	6,126,420	27.8	26.1	23.2
Rape/sexual assault	255,770	346,830	300,170	1.1	1.3	1.1
Robbery	616,420	741,760	645,650	2.6	2.8	2.4
Assault	5,853,870	5,754,010	5,180,610	24.2	22.0	19.6
Aggravated assault	1,418,660	996,110	994,220	5.9	3.8	3.8
Simple assault	4,435,220	4,757,900	4,186,390	18.3	18.2	15.8
Domestic violence[c]	1,434,190	1,259,390	1,116,090	5.9	4.8	4.2
Intimate partner violence[d]	1,031,720	810,790	748,800	4.3	3.1	2.8
Stranger violence	2,672,240	2,710,110	2,098,170	11.1	10.3	7.9
Violent crime involving injury	1,984,920	1,573,460	1,603,960	8.2	6.0	6.1
Serious violent crime[e]	2,290,850	2,084,690	1,940,030	9.5	8.0	7.3
Serious domestic violence[c]	467,240	411,080	464,730	1.9	1.6	1.8
Serious intimate partner violence[d]	334,620	270,240	360,820	1.4	1.0	1.4
Serious stranger violence	966,390	1,020,400	737,940	4.0	3.9	2.8
Serious violent crime involving weapons	1,650,430	1,415,120	1,174,370	6.8	5.4	4.4
Serious violent crime involving injury	828,620	762,170	739,210	3.4	2.9	2.8

[a]Per 1,000 persons age 12 or older.
[b]Excludes homicide because the National Crime Victimization Survey (NCVS) is based on interviews with victims and therefore cannot measure murder.
[c]Includes victimization committed by intimate partners and family members.
[d]Includes victimization committed by current or former spouses, boyfriends, or girlfriends.
[e]Includes rape or sexual assault, robbery, and aggravated
Note: Detail may not sum to total due to rounding. Total population age 12 or older was 241,703,710 in 2004; 261,996,320 in 2012; and 264,411,700 in 2013.

SOURCE: Jennifer L. Truman and Lynn Langton, "Table 1. Violent Victimization, by Type of Violent Crime, 2004, 2012, and 2013," in *Criminal Victimization, 2013*, U.S. Department of Justice, Office of Justice Programs, Bureau of Justice Statistics, September 19, 2014, http://www.bjs.gov/content/pub/pdf/cv13.pdf (accessed November 2, 2014)

Table 3.4 provides information about weapon use during certain types of violent victimizations during 2013. Overall weapons were used by offenders in 60.5% of serious violent victimizations. The percentages by crime type were aggravated assaults (92.5%), robberies (37.6%), and rapes and sexual assaults (4.1%).

The violent crime victimization rate in 2013 was 23.2 victimizations per 1,000 population aged 12 years and older. (See Table 3.3.) Simple assault had the highest rate (15.8) followed by aggravated assault (3.8), robbery (2.4), and rape/sexual assault (1.1). As shown in Figure 3.3 the violent crime victimization rate has declined dramatically since 1993, when it was around 80 victimizations per 1,000 population aged 12 years and older.

Victim-Offender Relationships

As shown in Table 3.3, about 1.1 million of the violent victimizations in 2013 were classified as domestic violence. Approximately 67% (748,800) of them were committed by intimate partners.

Figure 3.4 categorizes the 6.1 million violent victimizations in 2013 by victim-offender relationship. Overall, well-known or casual acquaintances were the offenders in the largest share (40%) of the victimizations. They were followed by strangers (34%) and intimate partners (12%). Additional details about victim-offender relationships are provided in Table 3.5. More females than males were victimized by intimate partners, other relatives, and well-known or casual acquaintances. For example, 619,357

females were victimized by intimate partners compared with 129,438 males. By contrast, strangers were the offenders in more victimizations of men (1.3 million) than of women (824,969).

VICTIM DEMOGRAPHICS FOR VIOLENT CRIMES. Table 3.6 categorizes violent crime and serious violent crime victimization rates by victim demographics for 2004, 2012, and 2013. In 2013 the highest rate (90.3 victimizations per 1,000 population) was experienced by people of two or more races who were not of Hispanic or Latino origin. Native Americans and Alaskan Natives also had a high rate at 56.3 victimizations per 1,000 population aged 12 years and older. Children aged 12 to 17 years had a much higher rate (52.1 per 1,000 population aged 12 years and older) than other age groups. Likewise, the victimization rate for separated people (73.2 per 1,000 population aged 12 years and older) was much higher than the rates for people with other marital statuses.

Table 3.7 provides a breakdown by annual household income for people that were victimized by violent crimes in 2013. The NCVS data indicate that individuals from lower income households experienced much higher victimization rates than did individuals from higher income households. The victimization rate for people from households making less than $7,500 per year was 84 per 1,000 people aged 12 years and older. The next-highest victimization rate (62.3 per 1,000 people aged 12 years and older) was for those with a household

TABLE 3.4

Serious violent victimizations, by weapon use and weapon category, 2013

Crime type	Number	Percent
Serious violent victimization	**1,940,030**	
Yes, offender had weapon	1,174,370	60.5%
Firearm	332,951	17.2%
Knife	321,139	16.6%
Other type weapon	336,470	17.3%
Type weapon unknown	183,810	9.5%
No, offender did not have weapon	687,021	35.4%
Do not know if offender had weapon	78,638	4.1%
Rape/sexual assault	**300,165**	
Yes, offender had weapon	12,182	4.1%
Firearm	2,866	1.0%
Knife	9,316	3.1%
No, offender did not have weapon	265,366	88.4%
Do not know if offender had weapon	22,617	7.5%
Robbery	**645,645**	
Yes, offender had weapon	242,529	37.6%
Firearm	108,754	16.8%
Knife	91,535	14.2%
Other type weapon	24,511	3.8%
Type weapon unknown	17,730	2.7%
No, offender did not have weapon	350,775	54.3%
Do not know if offender had weapon	52,341	8.1%
Aggravated Assault	**994,220**	
Yes, offender had weapon	919,659	92.5%
Firearm	221,331	22.3%
Knife	220,288	22.2%
Other type weapon	311,959	31.4%
Type weapon unknown	166,081	16.7%
No, offender did not have weapon	70,880	7.1%
Do not know if offender had weapon	3,680	0.4%

Notes: Special tabulations from the NCVS Victimization Analysis Tool (NVAT). Detail may not sum to total due to rounding and/or missing data.

SOURCE: Adapted from "Number of Serious Violent Victimizations, Rape/Sexual Assaults, Robberies, and Aggravated Assaults by Weapon Use and Weapon Category, 2013," in *NCVS Victimization Analysis Tool (NVAT)*, U.S. Department of Justice, Office of Justice Programs, Bureau of Justice Statistics, 2014, http://www.bjs.gov/index.cfm?ty=nvat (accessed November 2, 2014)

income of $7,500 to $14,999 per year. These two rates were more than twice the overall rate of 23.2 violent victimizations per 1,000 people aged 12 years and older.

As shown in Table 3.8, in 2013 people living in the Northeast (27.5 per 1,000 population aged 12 years and older) and West (27.3 per 1,000 population aged 12 years and older) experienced higher victimization rates for violent crimes than did people in other regions. Those living in urban areas had a rate of 25.9 violent victimizations per 1,000 population aged 12 years and older. This compared with rates of 23.3 per 1,000 population aged 12 years and older for suburban dwellers and 16.9 per 1,000 population aged 12 years and older for rural dwellers.

Property Crimes

As noted earlier, the NCVS includes household burglaries (forced and unforced), motor vehicle thefts, and other thefts (excluding purse snatching and pocket picking) in the category of property crimes. As shown in Table 3.2, 11.5 million households experienced at least one property victimization during 2013. Truman and Langton calculate that 9% of all U.S. households suffered property crimes in 2013. Most of the victimized households (9.1 million) experienced thefts. The 9% prevalence rate for 2013 was down from the rate of 10.4% calculated for 2004.

According to NCVS data, nearly 16.8 million property victimizations occurred at households in 2013. (See Table 3.9.) Thefts made up 12.8 million of the total victimizations, followed by 3.3 million household burglaries, and 661,250 motor vehicle thefts.

As shown in Table 3.9, in 2013 the victimization rate for all property crimes was 131.4 per 1,000 households. The victimization rates for individual property crimes were:

• Motor vehicle theft—5.2 per 1,000 households

• Burglary—25.7 per 1,000 households

• Theft—100.5 per 1,000 households

Overall, the property victimization rate has declined significantly since 1993, when it was above 350 victimizations per 1,000 households. (See Figure 3.3.)

NCVS data indicate that households in the West had the highest property victimization rate in 2013 at 182.1 per 1,000 households. (See Table 3.8.) People living in urban areas had a rate of 165.3 victimizations per 1,000 households compared with rates of 115.3 for suburban households and 109.4 for rural households.

Personal Larceny Crimes

Truman and Langton do not provide victimization estimates for personal larceny crimes, such as pocket picking and purse snatching. However, the data are available online through the NVAT (http://www.bjs.gov/index.cfm?ty=nvat). In 2013 there were an estimated 140,603 victimizations of U.S. residents aged 12 years and older. This value is far lower than the 481,384 victimizations reported for 1993. The personal larceny victimization rate in 2013 was 0.5 per 1,000 population aged 12 years and older. The rate was down from 1993, when it was 2.3 per 1,000 population aged 12 years and older.

REPORTING VICTIMIZATIONS TO THE POLICE

Almost half (45.6%) of all violent crime victimizations covered in the 2013 NCVS were reported by the victims to the police. (See Table 3.10.) This percentage was down from 2004 when it was 50.3%. The reporting rate in 2013 was highest for victims of robbery (68%), followed by aggravated assault (64.3%), simple assault (38.5%), and rape/sexual assault (34.8%). A majority of domestic violence crimes (56.9%), intimate partner violence crimes

FIGURE 3.3

Rates of violent crimes and property crimes per 1,000 persons aged 12 or older, 1993–2013

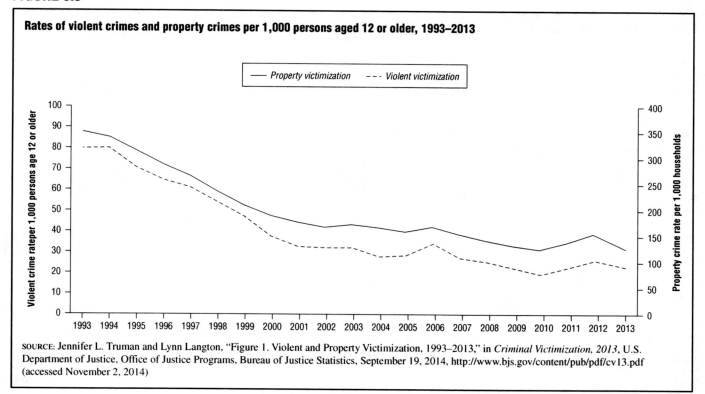

SOURCE: Jennifer L. Truman and Lynn Langton, "Figure 1. Violent and Property Victimization, 1993–2013," in *Criminal Victimization, 2013*, U.S. Department of Justice, Office of Justice Programs, Bureau of Justice Statistics, September 19, 2014, http://www.bjs.gov/content/pub/pdf/cv13.pdf (accessed November 2, 2014)

FIGURE 3.4

Breakdown of violent victimizations by victim–offender relationship, 2013

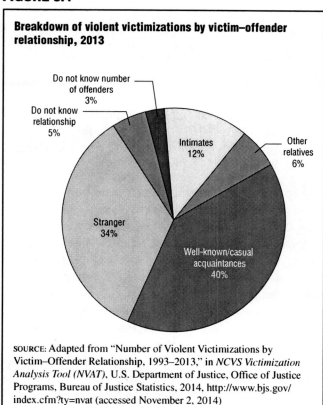

SOURCE: Adapted from "Number of Violent Victimizations by Victim–Offender Relationship, 1993–2013," in *NCVS Victimization Analysis Tool (NVAT)*, U.S. Department of Justice, Office of Justice Programs, Bureau of Justice Statistics, 2014, http://www.bjs.gov/index.cfm?ty=nvat (accessed November 2, 2014)

TABLE 3.5

Number of violent victimizations by victim–offender relationship and sex, 2013

Violent victimization	6,126,423
Intimates	748,795
Male	129,438
Female	619,357
Other relatives	367,291
Male	124,079
Female	243,212
Well-known/casual acquaintances	2,445,099
Male	1,166,903
Female	1,278,196
Stranger	2,098,170
Male	1,273,201
Female	824,969
Do not know relationship	288,795
Male	198,671
Female	90,124
Do not know number of offenders	178,273
Male	153,676
Female	24,597

Notes: Special tabulations from the NCVS Victimization Analysis Tool (NVAT). Detail may not sum to total due to rounding and/or missing data.

SOURCE: Adapted from "Number of Violent Victimizations by Victim–Offender Relationship and Sex, 1993–2013," in *NCVS Victimization Analysis Tool (NVAT)*, U.S. Department of Justice, Office of Justice Programs, Bureau of Justice Statistics, 2014, http://www.bjs.gov/index.cfm?ty=nvat (accessed November 2, 2014)

(57%), and violent crimes involving injury (55.5%) were reported by the victims to the police.

Only 36.1% of all property crime victimizations tallied in the 2013 NCVS were reported to the police. (See

Table 3.10.) Victims of motor vehicle theft were, by far, the most likely to have reported the crime, with 75.5% of the thefts reported to the police. This compares with 57.3% of household burglaries and 28.6% of other thefts. Overall, the reporting rate for property crime victimizations declined by 3.1 percentage points between 2004 and 2013.

TABLE 3.6

Violent victimizations, by victim demographic characteristics, 2004, 2012, and 2013

Victim demographic characteristic	Violent crime[a]			Serious violent crime[b]		
	2004	2012	2013	2004	2012	2013
Total	27.8	26.1	23.2	9.5	8.0	7.3
Sex						
Male	30.2	29.1	23.7	10.6	9.4	7.7
Female	25.5	23.3	22.7	8.4	6.6	7.0
Race/Hispanic origin						
White[c]	28.5	25.2	22.2	9.0	6.8	6.8
Black/African American[c]	30.2	34.2	25.1	16.3	11.3	9.5
Hispanic/Latino	20.1	24.5	24.8	6.5	9.3	7.5
American Indian/Alaska Native[c]	165.6	46.9	56.3	46.1!	26.2!	39.0!
Asian/Native Hawaiian/other Pacific Islander[c]	11.3	16.4	7.0	3.9	9.1	1.6!
Two or more races[c]	77.6	42.8	90.3	11.6!	9.5!	26.8
Age						
12–17	49.7	48.4	52.1	13.7	9.9	10.8
18–24	55.4	41.0	33.8	19.9	14.7	10.7
25–34	31.2	34.2	29.6	10.9	10.9	10.2
35–49	28.0	29.1	20.3	9.9	9.5	7.1
50–64	15.4	15.0	18.7	5.7	4.6	6.9
65 or older	2.5	5.7	5.4	0.8	1.6	1.1
Marital status						
Never married	46.2	40.7	36.3	16.5	11.9	9.6
Married	13.8	13.5	10.7	4.5	3.9	3.2
Widowed	9.3	8.3	8.6	1.8!	2.6	5.2
Divorced	36.7	37.0	34.4	11.8	10.9	16.0
Separated	110.7	83.1	73.2	38.9	39.5	33.3

!Interpret with caution. Estimate based on 10 or fewer sample cases, or the coefficient of variation is greater than 50%.
[a]Includes rape or sexual assault, robbery, aggravated assault, and simple assault.
[b]Includes rape or sexual assault, robbery, and aggravated assault.
[c]Excludes persons of Hispanic or Latino origin.
Note: Victimization rates are per 1,000 persons age 12 or older.

SOURCE: Jennifer L. Truman and Lynn Langton, "Table 9. Violent Victimization, by Victim Demographic Characteristics, 2004, 2012, and 2013," in *Criminal Victimization, 2013*, U.S. Department of Justice, Office of Justice Programs, Bureau of Justice Statistics, September 19, 2014, http://www.bjs.gov/content/pub/pdf/cv13.pdf (accessed November 2, 2014)

TABLE 3.7

Rates of violent victimizations by household income, 2013

Violent victimization	23.2
Less than $7,500	84.0
$7,500 to $14,999	62.3
$15,000 to $24,999	31.8
$25,000 to $34,999	21.6
$35,000 to $49,999	22.8
$50,000 to $74,999	17.8
$75,000 or more	14.4
Unknown	18.2

Note: Special tabulations from the NCVS Victimization Analysis Tool (NVAT). Detail may not sum to total due to rounding and/or missing data. Victimization rates are per 1,000 persons age 12 or older.

SOURCE: "Rates of Violent Victimizations by Household Income, 2013," in *NCVS Victimization Analysis Tool (NVAT)*, U.S. Department of Justice, Office of Justice Programs, Bureau of Justice Statistics, 2014, http://www.bjs.gov/index.cfm?ty=nvat (accessed November 2, 2014)

Reasons Victims Do Not Report Victimizations

In *Criminal Victimization, 2013*, Truman and Langton do not provide the reasons given by victims for reporting or not reporting victimizations to the police. However, historical data on this subject are presented by Lynn Langton et al. in *Victimizations Not Reported to the Police, 2006–2010* (August 2012, http://bjs.ojp.us doj.gov/content/pub/pdf/vnrp0610.pdf), the most recent report of its kind as of January 2015.

According to Langton et al., over half (58%) of victimizations occurring between 2006 and 2010 were not reported by victims to the police. Interviewers asked the crime victims who had not reported their victimizations to the police why they chose not to do so. The largest single reason given for not reporting a violent crime (attempted or completed rape/sexual assault, robbery, or aggravated or simple assault) was that the victim considered the incident to be a private or personal matter. About one-third (34%) of those asked gave this reason. Other oft-cited reasons were that the victimization was "not important enough" to report to the police (18%), the police would not or could not help (16%), or the victim feared reprisal from the offender or feared getting the offender in trouble (13%).

Langton et al. indicate that 60% of property crimes between 2006 and 2010 were not reported to the police by their victims. The primary reasons cited by victims were that they believed the police would or could not

TABLE 3.8

Violent and property victimization, by household location, 2004, 2012, and 2013

Household location	Violent crime[a]			Serious violent crime[b]			Property crime[c]		
	2004	2012	2013	2004	2012	2013	2004	2012	2013
Total	27.8	26.1	23.2	9.5	8.0	7.3	167.5	155.8	131.4
Region									
Northeast	19.6	24.7	27.5	8.0	4.6	7.8	113.8	116.9	92.1
Midwest	33.1	23.9	23.7	11.8	8.6	7.5	177.4	153.1	122.3
South	25.1	22.1	18.0	8.5	6.2	5.5	163.3	143.4	125.8
West	33.6	35.5	27.3	9.9	12.5	9.6	210.3	210.5	182.1
Location of residence									
Urban	37.3	32.4	25.9	14.6	11.4	8.8	220.1	187.0	165.3
Suburban	23.0	23.8	23.3	7.7	6.6	6.8	147.7	138.9	115.3
Rural	27.1	20.9	16.9	6.8	5.1	6.1	140.4	142.9	109.4

[a]Includes rape or sexual assault, robbery, aggravated assault, and simple assault.
[b]Includes rape or sexual assault, robbery, and aggravated assault.
[c]Includes household burglary, motor vehicle theft, and theft.
Note: Victimization rates are per 1,000 persons age 12 or older for violent crime and per 1,000 households for property crime.

SOURCE: Jennifer L.Truman and Lynn Langton, "Table 10. Violent and Property Victimization, by Household Location, 2004, 2012, and 2013," in *Criminal Victimization, 2013*, U.S. Department of Justice, Office of Justice Programs, Bureau of Justice Statistics, September 19, 2014, http://www.bjs.gov/content/pub/pdf/cv13.pdf (accessed November 2, 2014)

TABLE 3.9

Property victimizations, number and rate, by type of crime, 2004, 2012, and 2013

Type of crime	Number			Rate*		
	2004	2012	2013	2004	2012	2013
Total	19,394,780	19,622,980	16,774,090	167.5	155.8	131.4
Burglary	3,598,570	3,764,540	3,286,210	31.1	29.9	25.7
Motor vehicle theft	1,068,480	633,740	661,250	9.2	5.0	5.2
Theft	14,727,730	15,224,700	12,826,620	127.2	120.9	100.5

*Per 1,000 households.
Note: Detail may not sum to total due to rounding. Total number of households was 115,775,570 in 2004; 125,920,480 in 2012; and 127,622,320 in 2013.

SOURCE: Jennifer L. Truman and Lynn Langton, "Table 3. Property Victimization, by Type of Property Crime, 2004, 2012, and 2013," in *Criminal Victimization, 2013*, U.S. Department of Justice, Office of Justice Programs, Bureau of Justice Statistics, September 19, 2014, http://www.bjs.gov/content/pub/pdf/cv13.pdf (accessed November 2, 2014)

help them (36%) or that the crime was "not important enough" to report (30%). Smaller percentages of property crime victims said they chose not to report because the incident was a private or personal matter (15%) or because they feared reprisal from the offender or getting the offender in trouble (3%).

CONSEQUENCES OF VICTIMIZATION

Crime victims suffer a number of consequences from being victimized, including physical injuries, mental distress, and economic losses. The economic costs borne by crime victims include direct costs, such as the value of items that have been stolen, and indirect costs, such as the expenses of the criminal justice system, which must be shared by the entire society.

Physical Injuries

As shown in Table 3.3, NCVS data indicate that in 2013, more than 1.6 million violent victimizations (or 26% of the total of 6.1 million) involved injury to the victims. (Note that only people aged 12 years and older are included.) The percentage was down from 2004, when nearly 2 million out of 6.7 million victimizations (or 30%) involved physical injury to the victims. In 2013 an estimated 739,210 victimizations due to serious violent crimes (i.e., rape/sexual assault, robbery, or aggravated assault) left victims physically injured. This number accounted for more than a third (38%) of the 1.9 million serious violent victimizations that occurred that year.

Socio-emotional Impacts

Crime victims may also suffer social and emotional impacts due to victimizations. In *Socio-emotional Impact of Violent Crime* (September 2014, http://www.bjs.gov/content/pub/pdf/sivc.pdf), Lynn Langton and Jennifer Truman of the BJS discuss NCVS data collected from 2009 to 2012 regarding the socio-emotional impacts of violent criminal victimizations. Victims were quizzed about the level of distress they experienced due to the crimes. The results are shown in Figure 3.5 by crime

TABLE 3.10

Percentage of victimizations reported to police, by type of crime, 2004, 2012, and 2013

Type of crime	2004	2012	2013
Violent crime[a]	50.3%	44.2%	45.6%
Rape/sexual assault	29.3	28.2	34.8
Robbery	60.6	55.9	68.0
Assault	50.1	43.7	43.4
Aggravated assault	69.8	62.4	64.3
Simple assault	43.9	39.7	38.5
Domestic violence[b]	56.6	54.9	56.9
Intimate partner violence[c]	56.4	53.3	57.0
Stranger violence	54.4	48.9	49.6
Violent crime involving injury	60.8	58.6	55.5
Serious violent crime[d]	62.8%	54.4%	61.0%
Serious domestic violence[b]	69.7	60.9	65.3
Serious intimate partner violence[c]	69.1	55.4	60.4
Serious stranger violence	67.9	54.8	61.9
Serious violent crime involving weapons	68.5	56.3	65.7
Serious violent crime involving injury	69.0	56.1	66.2
Property crime[e]	39.2%	33.5%	36.1%
Household burglary	53.3	54.8	57.3
Motor vehicle theft	85.6	78.6	75.5
Theft	32.4	26.4	28.6

[a]Excludes homicide because the National Crime Victimization Survey (NCVS) is based on interviews with victims and therefore cannot measure murder.
[b]Includes victimization committed by intimate partners and family members.
[c]Includes victimization committed by current or former spouses, boyfriends, or girlfriends.
[d]Includes rape or sexual assault, robbery, and aggravated assault.
[e]Includes household burglary, motor vehicle theft, and theft.

SOURCE: Jennifer L. Truman and Lynn Langton, "Table 6. Percent of Victimizations Reported to Police, by Type of Crime, 2004, 2012, and 2013," in *Criminal Victimization, 2013*, U.S. Department of Justice, Office of Justice Programs, Bureau of Justice Statistics, September 19, 2014, http://www.bjs.gov/content/pub/pdf/cv13.pdf (accessed November 2, 2014)

FIGURE 3.5

Level of distress experienced by violent crime victims, by type of crime, 2009–12

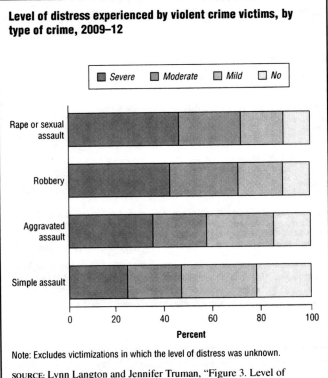

Note: Excludes victimizations in which the level of distress was unknown.

SOURCE: Lynn Langton and Jennifer Truman, "Figure 3. Level of Distress Experienced by Violent Crime Victims, by Type of Crime, 2009–2012," in *Socio-emotional Impact of Violent Crime*, U.S. Department of Justice, Office of Justice Programs, Bureau of Justice Statistics, September 2014, http://www.bjs.gov/content/pub/pdf/sivc.pdf (accessed November 2, 2014)

type. Overall, the highest levels of severe or moderate distress were seen for people who had experienced rape, sexual assault, or robbery. As illustrated in Figure 3.6, distress levels reported by the victims of serious violent crimes (i.e., rape or sexual assault, robbery, and aggravated assault) varied significantly depending on the victim-offender relationship. People victimized by relatives or intimate partners had much higher levels of distress than did people victimized by close friends, other acquaintances, or strangers.

As shown in Figure 3.7, victims who experienced moderate or severe distress were more likely to report the crime to police and/or to receive victim services than victims who experienced no distress or mild distress.

Langton and Truman present comprehensive data on violent crime victims that experienced one or more of the following socio-emotional problems:

- Moderate or severe distress

- Significant problems at work or school (e.g., trouble with bosses, coworkers, or peers)

- Significant problems with family members or friends (e.g., more arguments, inability to trust, or feelings of emotional distance)

Overall, 57% of the violent crime victims suffered socio-emotional problems. (See Table 3.11.) The percentage was highest for victims of rape or sexual assault (75%) and lowest for victims of simple assault (51%). Socio-emotional problems were most prevalent in victims who had endured firearm violence (74%) and those who had to receive medical treatment due to their injuries (77%). More people who were victimized by their intimate partners (85%) experienced socio-emotional problems than did people victimized by other types of offenders.

Table 3.12 lists specific physical and emotional symptoms suffered by the violent crime victims who experienced socio-emotional problems. The highest percentages of victims reported experiencing worry or anxiety (72%), anger (70%), or feeling unsafe (65%). Trouble sleeping was the most common physical symptom reported by the victims. Nearly half (47%) said they experienced this problem. The prevalence rates of the specific symptoms were highest for victims of serious violence and for people victimized by their intimate partners.

Economic Losses

During NCVS interviews crime victims are asked about economic losses they suffered as a result of being

FIGURE 3.6

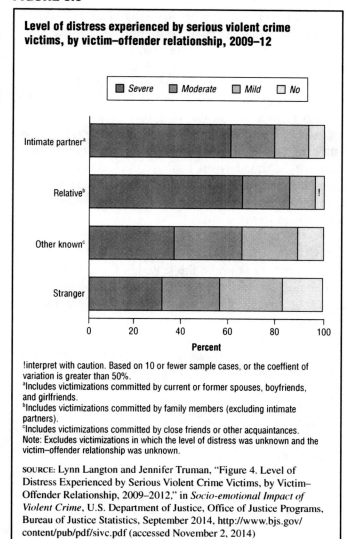

Level of distress experienced by serious violent crime victims, by victim–offender relationship, 2009–12

!interpret with caution. Based on 10 or fewer sample cases, or the coeffient of variation is greater than 50%.
[a]Includes victimizations committed by current or former spouses, boyfriends, and girlfriends.
[b]Includes victimizations committed by family members (excluding intimate partners).
[c]Includes victimizations committed by close friends or other acquaintances.
Note: Excludes victimizations in which the level of distress was unknown and the victim–offender relationship was unknown.

SOURCE: Lynn Langton and Jennifer Truman, "Figure 4. Level of Distress Experienced by Serious Violent Crime Victims, by Victim–Offender Relationship, 2009–2012," in *Socio-emotional Impact of Violent Crime*, U.S. Department of Justice, Office of Justice Programs, Bureau of Justice Statistics, September 2014, http://www.bjs.gov/content/pub/pdf/sivc.pdf (accessed November 2, 2014)

FIGURE 3.7

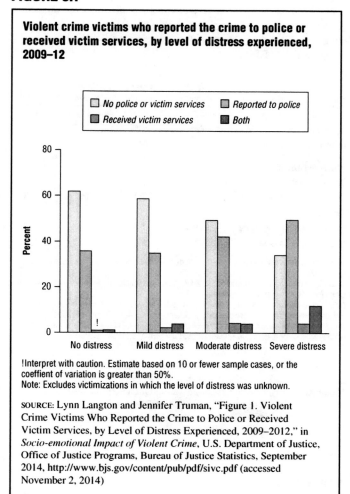

Violent crime victims who reported the crime to police or received victim services, by level of distress experienced, 2009–12

!Interpret with caution. Estimate based on 10 or fewer sample cases, or the coeffient of variation is greater than 50%.
Note: Excludes victimizations in which the level of distress was unknown.

SOURCE: Lynn Langton and Jennifer Truman, "Figure 1. Violent Crime Victims Who Reported the Crime to Police or Received Victim Services, by Level of Distress Experienced, 2009–2012," in *Socio-emotional Impact of Violent Crime*, U.S. Department of Justice, Office of Justice Programs, Bureau of Justice Statistics, September 2014, http://www.bjs.gov/content/pub/pdf/sivc.pdf (accessed November 2, 2014)

victimized, but such data were not published in *Criminal Victimization, 2013* and, as of January 2015, were not available through the NVAT.

The most recent publication containing economic loss data was *Criminal Victimization in the United States, 2008—Statistical Tables* (May 2011, http://www.bjs.gov/content/pub/pdf/cvus08.pdf), which was compiled by the BJS. There were 21.3 million personal and property victimizations in 2008. The majority (14.1 million or 66%) involved an economic loss of at least $1 to the victim. Another 2.4 million victimizations, or 11% of the total, included an economic loss of an unknown monetary value. The gross loss for all 21.3 million victimizations was $17.4 billion, including $16.2 billion from property crimes and $1.2 billion from personal crimes. The mean (average) dollar loss per victim was $816. The mean dollar loss was highest for victims of motor vehicle theft ($6,077), household burglary ($1,539), and robbery ($1,167).

Detailed economic loss data related to household burglaries are presented by Jennifer Hardison Walters et al. in *Household Burglary, 1994–2011* (June 2013, http://www.bjs.gov/content/pub/pdf/hb9411.pdf). NCVS data for 2011 indicate that nearly 3.4 million burglary victimizations occurred that year. According to Walters et al. the mean (average) loss of items and cash stolen from households that lost at least $1 during completed burglaries was $2,116. The median dollar value (i.e., half of the losses were greater than the median and the other half were lower) was $600.

VICTIMS' RIGHTS

For many years victims received little consideration in justice proceedings; to some it seemed that victims were victimized again by the very system to which they had turned for help. In *Final Report of the President's Task Force on Victims of Crime* (December 1982, http://www.ojp.gov/ovc/publications/presdntstskforcrprt/87299.pdf), Lois Haight Herrington observes that "somewhere along the way, the system began to serve lawyers and judges and defendants, treating the victim with institutionalized disinterest."

The report describes a number of problems that were commonly cited by crime victims. For example, police

TABLE 3.11

Victims who experienced socio-emotional problems as a result of violent victimization, by type of crime and victim–offender relationship, 2000–12

Type of violent crime	Total violence	Intimate partner[a]	Other known[b]	Stranger
Total	**57%**	**85%**	**60%**	**43%**
Serious violence	**68%**	**84%**	**75%**	**59%**
Rape or sexual assault	75	84	79	67
Robbery	74	82	88	66
Aggravated assault	62	84	66	53
Simple assault	**51%**	**85%**	**54%**	**34%**
Violence involving a weapon	**64%**	**84%**	**68%**	**59%**
Firearm	74	88	76	71
Violence involving an injury	**71%**	**88%**	**72%**	**59%**
Medical treatment received	77	95	77	73

[a]Includes victimizations committed by current or former spouses, boyfriends, or girlfriends.
[b]Includes victimizations committed by family members (excluding intimate partners), close friends, or other acquaintances.
Note: Socio-emotional problems are defined as the experience of one or more of the following: moderate to severe distress, problems with family or friend relationships, or problems at work or school as a result of the victimization. Excludes victimizations in which the level of distress was unknown and the victim–offender relationship was unknown.

SOURCE: Lynn Langton and Jennifer Truman, "Table 2. Victims Who Experienced Socio-emotional Problems as a Result of the Violent Victimization, by Type of Crime and Victim-Offender Relationship, 2009–2012," in *Socio-emotional Impact of Violent Crime*, U.S. Department of Justice, Office of Justice Programs, Bureau of Justice Statistics, September 2014, http://www.bjs.gov/content/pub/pdf/sivc.pdf (accessed November 2, 2014)

questioning seemed to accuse rape victims of enticing their attacker or participating willingly in the act. Assault victims found that hospitals were more concerned about whether they could pay for treatment than about helping them recover from the incident. In their efforts to make sure that each defendant received a fair trial, judges and lawyers appeared to be more concerned about the accused offenders than the victims. Crime victims were not informed of court dates, sentencing hearings, or probation or parole hearings concerning their cases. They were not informed when their attacker escaped or was released from prison. Also, victims participating in a trial were sometimes kept outside the courtroom without ever being called to the witness stand.

The Crime Victims' Rights Movement

Attempts to improve the situation for crime victims had begun during the 1960s. In 1965 California established the first crime victim compensation program. A growing victims' rights movement spurred the creation of victim assistance and compensation programs throughout the country. In 1975 the National Organization for Victim Assistance (http://www.trynova.org) was formed in Virginia. That same year the attorney Frank Carrington (1936–1992) published *The Victims*, a book that highlighted the problematic treatment of crime victims by the criminal justice system. He founded the Crime Victims' Legal Advocacy Institute, later renamed

TABLE 3.12

Physical and emotional symptoms suffered by violent crime victims who experienced socio-emotional problems as a result of the victimization, by type of crime and victim–offender relationship, 2009–12

Symptom	Type of crime			Victim–offender relationship		
	Total violence	Serious violence	Simple assault	Intimate partner[a]	Other known[b]	Stranger
Emotional	**91%**	**96%**	**87%**	**92%**	**91%**	**89%**
Worried or anxious	72	78	67	79	73	65
Angry	70	76	67	72	72	68
Unsafe	65	73	60	69	63	66
Violated	61	69	56	72	57	57
Vulnerable	60	64	58	69	58	57
Distrustful	56	66	50	60	57	52
Sad or depressed	53	58	50	72	54	37
Other	12	13	12	13	11	14
Physical	**61%**	**67%**	**57%**	**74%**	**61%**	**53%**
Trouble sleeping	47	51	44	61	45	38
Fatigue	34	36	33	52	33	24
Upset stomach	31	32	30	46	29	22
Muscle tension	31	34	28	39	31	25
Headaches	30	37	25	40	31	22
Problems with eating/drinking	27	33	23	43	26	16
High blood pressure	15	16	15	18	17	11
Other	9	12	7	12	8	8

[a]Includes victimizations committed by current or former spouses, boyfriends, or girlfriends.
[b]Includes victimizations committed by family members (excluding intimate partners), close friends, or other acquaintances.
Note: Includes victims who experienced symptoms for a month or more. Victims who did not report experiencing socio-emotional problems (one or more of the following: moderate to severe distress, problems with family or friend relationships, or problems at work or school) were not asked about physical and emotional symptoms and were excluded from the analysis. Excludes victimizations in which the level of distress was unknown.

SOURCE: Lynn Langton and Jennifer Truman, "Table 1. Physical and Emotional Symptoms Suffered by Violent Crime Victims Who Experienced Socio-Emotional Problems as a Result of the Victimization, by Type of Crime And Victim–Offender Relationship, 2009–2012," in *Socio-emotional Impact of Violent Crime*, U.S. Department of Justice, Office of Justice Programs, Bureau of Justice Statistics, September 2014, http://www.bjs.gov/content/pub/pdf/sivc.pdf (accessed November 2, 2014)

the Victims' Assistance Legal Organization (http://www.valor-national.org), and is widely considered to be the father of the victims' rights movement in the United States.

In 1976 a California probation officer named James Rowland introduced the first victim impact statements. These written statements provided the judiciary with information about the specific and often devastating impact of crimes on victims—a viewpoint that had not previously been considered by the criminal justice system.

By the early 1980s a number of programs had been developed at the state and local levels on behalf of crime victims. In 1981 President Ronald Reagan (1911–2004) proclaimed the first-ever National Victims' Rights Week. In 1982 he spearheaded passage of the federal Victim and Witness Protection Act, which was designed to protect and assist victims and witnesses of federal crimes. The law permits victim impact statements in sentencing hearings to provide judges with information concerning financial, psychological, and/or physical harm that is suffered by victims. The law also provides for restitution (monetary compensation) to victims and prevents victims and/or witnesses from being intimidated by threatening verbal harassment. The law establishes penalties for acts of retaliation by defendants against those who testify against them.

Also in 1982 Reagan appointed the Task Force on Victims of Crime, which included Herrington, Carrington, and a number of other well-known victims' advocates. The group's report, *Final Report of the President's Task Force on Victims of Crime*, presented dozens of recommendations to reform state and federal criminal justice systems to better protect victims' rights. The report was also generally critical of state crime victim compensation funds by noting that many of them were underfunded and poorly administrated.

In 1983 the DOJ created the Office for Victims of Crime (OVC; http://www.ojp.usdoj.gov/ovc) to implement the task force's recommendations. The following year Congress passed the Victims of Crime Act. The act established the Crime Victims Fund to be funded by money from federal criminal fines, penalties, and forfeited bonds. The fund, which is administered by the OVC, supports federal and state programs for victim services and compensation. The fund supports victim compensation and victim assistance grant programs that are overseen by the states. Victim compensation grant programs cover medical treatment and physical therapy costs, counseling fees, lost wages, funeral and burial expenses, and loss of support to dependents of homicide victims. Victim assistance grant programs cover the costs of crisis intervention, counseling, emergency shelter, and criminal justice advocacy. Deposits to the Crime Victims Fund come from fines, penalty assessments, and bond

forfeitures that are collected from convicted federal criminal offenders. In 2001 legislation was passed allowing the fund to receive gifts, donations, and bequests from private entities.

In *OVC Report to the Nation: Fiscal Years 2011–2012: Transforming Today's Vision into Tomorrow's Reality* (March 2014, http://www.ovc.gov/pubs/reporttonation2013/index.html), the OVC notes that it "supports some 4 million crime victims annually as they struggle to reclaim their lives." Figure 3.8 shows the receipts to the Crime Victims Fund for fiscal years (FYs) 1986 through 2012 and the funds that were available for distribution. A federal fiscal year extends from October 1 through September 30; thus, FY 2012 lasted from October 1, 2011, through September 30, 2012. In FY 2012 the Crime Victims Fund received nearly $2.8 billion and had about $700 million available for allocation.

Since the 1980s the federal and state governments, the judicial system, and private groups have all reflected an increased awareness of victims' concerns. Numerous crime laws passed at the federal and state levels have included provisions that pertain specifically to victims and their rights during criminal proceedings. For example, the Crime Victims' Rights Act was enacted in 2004. According to the OVC (2014, http://ojp.gov/ovc/rights/legislation.html), the act grants victims specific rights in federal criminal cases. Some states have passed constitutional amendments to ensure that victims' rights are preserved and protected in their criminal justice systems. Diverse organizations have begun offering services to victims of crime. These organizations include domestic violence shelters, rape crisis centers, and child abuse programs. Law enforcement agencies, hospitals, and social services agencies also provide victims' services. The types of services provided include crisis intervention, counseling, emergency shelter and transportation, and legal services.

Victims' Participation at Sentencing

According to the National Center for Victims of Crime, every state allows courts to consider or ask for information from victims concerning the effects of the offense on their lives. Most states permit victim input at sentencing and most allow written victim impact statements. Although impact statements are typically used at sentencing and parole hearings, they can also be used at bail hearings, pretrial release hearings, and plea-bargaining hearings.

VICTIM IMPACT STATEMENTS IN CAPITAL CASES. As noted earlier, the first use of victim impact statements was in California in 1976. Over the following decade this practice became widespread across the nation. In 1987 the U.S. Supreme Court ruled 5–4 in *Booth v. Maryland*

FIGURE 3.8

Crime Victims Fund receipts and funds available for distribution, fiscal years 1985–2012

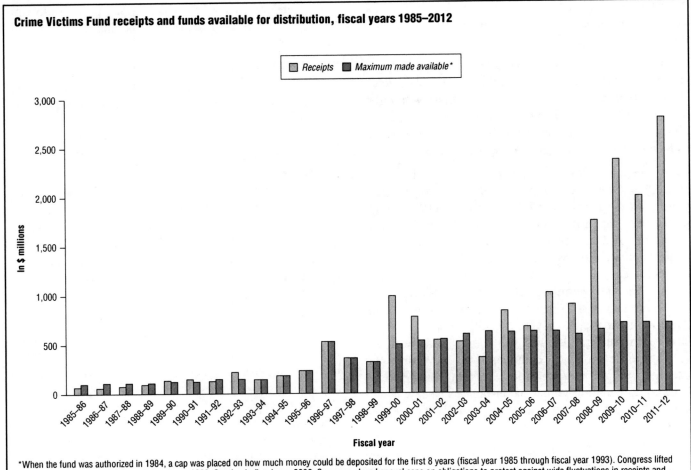

*When the fund was authorized in 1984, a cap was placed on how much money could be deposited for the first 8 years (fiscal year 1985 through fiscal year 1993). Congress lifted the cap for fiscal year 1994 through fiscal year 1999. Starting in fiscal year 2000, Congress placed annual caps on obligations to protect against wide fluctuations in receipts and ensure a stable level of funding in the future.

SOURCE: "Exhibit 2. Crime Victims Fund Receipts and Funds Available for Distribution," in *2013 OVC Report to the Nation: Fiscal Years 2011–2012: Transforming Today's Vision into Tomorrow's Reality*, U.S. Department of Justice, Office of Justice Programs, Office for Victims of Crime, undated, http://www.ovc.gov/pubs/reporttonation2013/pfv.html (accessed November 2, 2014)

(482 U.S. 496) that victim impact statements were unconstitutional when used in the sentencing phase of capital trials (i.e., those involving the death penalty). The court noted that "the admission of the family members' emotionally charged opinions and characterizations of the crimes could serve no other purpose than to inflame the jury and divert it from deciding the case on the relevant evidence concerning the crime and the defendant." Two years later the court narrowly reaffirmed this decision with a 5–4 ruling in *South Carolina v. Gathers* (490 U.S. 805).

The Supreme Court changed course in 1991, when it ruled 7–2 in *Payne v. Tennessee* (501 U.S. 808) that victim impact statements in capital cases are constitutional. The court concluded, "We are now of the view that a State may properly conclude that for the jury to assess meaningfully the defendant's moral culpability and blameworthiness, it should have before it at the sentencing phase evidence of the specific harm caused by the defendant."

Organizations Supporting Victims of Crime

The OVC (http://www.ovc.gov/help/index.html) provides a list of crime victim organizations, helplines, and other resources for crime victims. Table 3.13 lists several national organizations that offer assistance to victims of crime. One of the listed organizations is the National Center for Victims of Crime (2014, http://www.victimsofcrime.org), which describes itself as "the nation's leading resource and advocacy organization for victims of all types of crime and for the people who serve them." Besides the organizations listed in Table 3.13, the online database VictimLaw (https://www.victimlaw.org), which is funded by the OVC, serves as a clearinghouse of information regarding victims' rights at the federal, state, and tribal levels.

THE USE OF VICTIM SERVICE AGENCIES. During NCVS interviews, crime victims are quizzed about whether or not they used victim service agencies after being victimized. These agencies include public and

TABLE 3.13

National organizations for crime victims

Childhelp USA National Child Abuse Hotline	1–800–422–4453	www.childhelp.org
Child Welfare Information Gateway	1–800–394–3366	www.childwelfare.gov
Mothers Against Drunk Driving (MADD)	1–877–623–3435	www.madd.org
National Center for Missing & Exploited Children (NCMEC)	1–800–843–5678	www.missingkids.com
National Center for Victims of Crime (NCVC)	1–800–394–2255	www.victimsofcrime.org
National Clearinghouse for Alcohol and Drug Information	1–800–729–6686	http://ncadi.samhsa.gov
National Criminal Justice Reference Service (NCJRS)	1–800–851–3420	www.ncjrs.gov
National Domestic Violence Hotline	1–800–799–7233	www.ndvh.org
National Fraud Information Hotline	202–835–3323	www.fraud.org
National Human Trafficking Resource Center (NHTRC)	1–888–3737–888	http://nhtrc.polarisproject.org
National Organization for Victim Assistance (NOVA)	1–800–879–6682	www.trynova.org
National Resource Center on Domestic Violence	1–800–537–2238	www.nrcdv.org
National White Collar Crime Center (NW3C)	1–800–221–4424	www.nw3c.org
Parents of Murdered Children (POMC)	1–888–818–7662	www.pomc.org
Rape, Abuse & Incest National Network (RAINN)	1–800–656–4673	www.rainn.org

SOURCE: Adapted from "National Victim Organizations Stand Ready to Assist You," in *What You Can Do If You Are a Victim of Crime*, U.S. Department of Justice, Office of Justice Programs, Office for Victims of Crime, April 2010, http://www.ojp.usdoj.gov/ovc/publications/infores/whatyoucando_2010/WhatUCanDo_508.pdf (accessed November 9, 2014)

TABLE 3.14

Percentage of violent crime victims who received assistance from a victim service agency, by type of crime, 2004, 2012, and 2013

Type of crime	2004	2012	2013
Violent crime[a]	10.7%	8.2%	9.5%
Serious violent crime[b]	13.1	9.6	13.7
Simple assault	9.5	7.6	7.6
Violent crime resulting in injury	17.1%	14.9%	17.2%
Violent crime involving weapons	11.5%	8.8%	7.4%

[a]Includes rape or sexual assault, robbery, aggravated assault, and simple assault.
[b]Includes rape or sexual assault, robbery, and aggravated assault.

SOURCE: Jennifer L. Truman and Lynn Langton, "Table 8. Violent Crime Victims Who Received Assistance from a Victim Service Agency, by Type of Crime, 2004, 2012, and 2013," in *Criminal Victimization, 2013*, U.S. Department of Justice, Office of Justice Programs, Bureau of Justice Statistics, September 19, 2014, http://www.bjs.gov/content/pub/pdf/cv13.pdf (accessed November 2, 2014)

private groups that provide victims with a variety of services and other support. As shown in Table 3.14, Truman and Langton estimate that 9.5% of the victims of violent crimes (rape/sexual assault, robbery, aggravated assault, and simple assault) received assistance from such agencies in 2013. The percentage has declined since 2004, when it stood at 10.7%. In 2013 the highest percentage of crime victims who received assistance (17.2%) were those who suffered a physical injury during the victimization.

NATIONAL CRIME VICTIMS' RIGHTS WEEK. The OVC encourages local communities to observe a National Crime Victims' Rights Week. The event is held annually in April and includes rallies, candlelight vigils, and other activities that are designed to honor or memorialize crime victims and highlight their rights in the criminal justice system.

Offender Restitution Programs

Restitution programs require those who have harmed an individual to repay the victim. In the past, the criminal justice system focused primarily on punishing the criminal and leaving the victims to rely on civil court cases for damage repayment. By the 21st century most states permitted criminal courts to allow restitution payments as a condition of probation and/or parole. In addition, courts had the statutory authority to order restitution, and several states had passed constitutional amendments that specifically enumerated a victim's right to restitution.

Most restitution laws provide for restitution to the direct victim(s) of a crime, including the surviving family members of homicide victims. Restitution is usually only provided to victims of crimes for which a defendant was convicted. Many states allow victims to claim medical expenses and property damage or loss, and several permit families of homicide victims to claim costs for loss of support. In assessing damages, the courts must consider the offender's ability to pay.

Civil Suits

A victim can sue in civil court for damages even if the offender has not been found guilty of a criminal offense. In addition, any restitution amounts that remain unpaid at the end of an offender's parole or probation period may be converted into civil judgments. Victims often pursue civil suits because it is easier to win civil cases than criminal cases. In a criminal case, a jury or judge can find an alleged offender guilty only if the proof is "beyond a reasonable doubt." In a civil case, the burden of proof requires merely a "preponderance of the evidence" against the accused. Proof is still needed that a crime was committed, that there were damages, and that the accused is liable to pay for those damages. Nonetheless, even when victims secure a civil judgment, they often have trouble collecting their damage payments. Such has been the case with O. J. Simpson (1947–), a former professional football player, who was acquitted in 1995 of killing his former wife and her friend. In 1997 the victims' families won a multimillion-dollar civil judgment against Simpson. However, quirks of state laws shielded his pension and primary residence from seizure to pay the debts, and as of 2015 only a fraction of the awarded judgment had been recovered.

CHAPTER 4

DRUG CRIMES

Drug crime has grown to be an enormous national problem. In *Southwest Border Violence: Issues in Identifying and Measuring Spillover Violence* (February 28, 2013, http://fas.org/sgp/crs/homesec/R41075.pdf), Kristin M. Finklea of the Congressional Research Service (CRS) states, "The United States is the largest consumer of illegal drugs and sustains a multi-billion dollar market in illegal drugs."

U.S. history regarding the criminalization of drug use has been checkered. During the 1700s a number of potions containing opium and promising cures for a variety of ailments were available as so-called patent medicines, and physicians routinely prescribed opium medications to their patients. In 1805 the discovery of morphine by the German pharmacist Friedrich Sertürner (1783–1841) introduced another powerful drug to the medicines of the day. By the end of the 19th century, cocaine, codeine, and dozens of similar drugs were in common use. However, doctors were increasingly concerned about the side effects and addictiveness of these drugs and began issuing stern warnings about them to the public.

The Progressive movement and religious revival that swept the United States during the late 1800s and early 1900s made drug abuse socially unacceptable. Legislators at the state and federal levels responded by passing laws prohibiting the use of specific drugs, including opium and marijuana. By the 1950s many Americans considered drug abuse to be a problem only among marginalized populations, such as the African American inhabitants of inner-city ghettos and beatniks (nonconformist youths who defied societal conventions).

The 1960s ushered in a completely new drug culture to the United States: recreational drug use among middle- and upper-class white youths in suburban and rural areas. Marijuana and a relatively new hallucinogenic drug called D-lysergic acid diethylamide (LSD) surged in popularity. Other drugs of choice during this era were amphetamines (also called speed or uppers). Amphetamines stimulate the central nervous system. The drugs were widely dispensed by U.S. military authorities during World War II (1939–1945) to keep soldiers alert during battle. After the war amphetamines remained popular among students and workers who wanted to stay awake for long periods. They also used them to lose weight because amphetamines suppress the appetite. According to Celinda Franco of the CRS, in *Methamphetamine: Background, Prevalence, and Federal Drug Control Policies* (January 24, 2007, http://assets.opencrs.com/rpts/RL33857_20070124.pdf), amphetamines could be easily purchased over the counter (i.e., without a prescription) until 1951. By the end of the 1960s, new laws had been passed to combat the growing problems with LSD and amphetamine abuse.

In 1969 President Richard M. Nixon (1913–1994) asked Congress to pass extensive legislation giving the federal government more control over the problem of drug abuse. The result was the Comprehensive Drug Abuse Prevention and Control Act (CDAPCA) of 1970. The act gave the U.S. attorney general greater jurisdiction over drug crimes and provided for the rehabilitation of drug addicts. It placed new restrictions on the pharmaceutical industry and the medical professionals to better control and monitor the supply and dispensing of prescription drugs. The following year Nixon (http://www.presidency.ucsb.edu/ws/index.php?pid=3048&st=&st1=) made a statement to the public in which he called drug abuse "public enemy number one" and called for an "all-out offensive" against it. Over time, Nixon's statement became known as the declaration of the War on Drugs. In 1973 the U.S. Drug Enforcement Administration (DEA) was created to coordinate drug control efforts for the federal government. Over subsequent decades the national War on Drugs led to the arrests of millions of Americans for drug offenses.

DRUG OFFENSES AND ARRESTS

Titles II and III of the CDAPCA are called the Controlled Substances Act (CSA). The CSA places all illicit drugs into one of five schedules or categories based on the characteristics of the drugs and their potential for abuse. According to the DEA in *Drugs of Abuse, 2011 Edition: A DEA Resource Guide* (June 2011, http://www.justice.gov/dea/docs/drugs_of_abuse_2011.pdf), the five schedules are:

- Schedule I—these drugs have a high potential for abuse, have no accepted use in medical treatment in the United States, and lack acceptable safety for use even under medical supervision.

- Schedule II—these drugs have a high potential for abuse that could cause severe physical or psychological dependence. They have accepted uses in medical treatment in the United States (perhaps with many restrictions).

- Schedule III—these drugs have a lower abuse potential than Schedule I or II drugs, and such abuse "may lead to moderate or low physical dependence or high psychological dependence." They have accepted uses in medical treatment in the United States.

- Schedule IV—these drugs have a lower abuse potential than Schedule III drugs, and such abuse could cause limited physical or psychological dependence. They have accepted uses in medical treatment in the United States.

- Schedule V—these drugs have a lower abuse potential than Schedule IV drugs, and such abuse could cause limited physical or psychological dependence. They have accepted uses in medical treatment in the United States.

Table 4.1 lists common illicit drugs, their CSA schedule numbers, and how they are commonly administered. Heroin, morphine, cocaine, and the cannabinoids are derived primarily from organic sources. Heroin, morphine, and cocaine originate from opium poppies. The cannabinoids are from *Cannabis*, a genus of flowering plants. Some illicit drugs are considered synthetic or manufactured drugs because their origins are not primarily organic. Examples include amphetamines, methamphetamines, MDMA drugs (e.g., ecstasy), and LSD.

Many drug offenses are felonies and are punishable by at least one year in prison. Some drug offenses (particularly the possession of small amounts of marijuana) are misdemeanors. People convicted of misdemeanor drug crimes may receive a fine and/or a sentence of less than one year in a local jail. Some jurisdictions treat the possession of very small amounts of marijuana (e.g., less than 1 ounce [28 g]) as an infraction, rather than as a misdemeanor. Infractions are minor offenses, such as traffic violations, that are punishable only with fines, not with incarceration.

Drug laws are complex and can differ between jurisdictions. In general, the seriousness of an offense and the harshness of its penalty are based on the type and amount of drug involved and whether the offender possesses the drug for his or her own use or is a seller, manufacturer, or distributor. First-time offenders may receive less harsh charges and sentences than repeat offenders.

There is substantial overlap between federal law and state laws regarding drug offenses. In many cases perpetrators could be prosecuted by either federal or state authorities. People arrested for drug offenses on federal property (e.g., national parks), trafficking or distributing drugs across state lines, and those arrested by federal officers (e.g., DEA officers) fall under federal jurisdiction. In other cases federal and state prosecutors may negotiate which jurisdiction should have precedence. Federal authorities tend to handle cases involving the trafficking of large amounts of drugs and those in which conspiracies, organized crime groups, and/or firearms are a factor.

As shown in Figure 2.2 in Chapter 2, more than 30,000 people had drug cases filed against them in federal court during fiscal year (FY) 2012 (October 1, 2011, through September 30, 2012). Excluding immigration cases, drug cases far outnumbered other types of federal prosecutions from the late 1990s through FY 2012. In *Federal Justice Statistics 2011–2012* (January 22, 2015, http://www.bjs.gov/content/pub/pdf/fjs1112.pdf), Mark Motivans of the Bureau of Justice Statistics (BJS) within the U.S. Department of Justice (DOJ) reports that 30,292 felony drug cases were filed in federal court in FY 2012.

Many more drug cases are handled at the state and local level. Statistics about them are collected by the Federal Bureau of Investigation (FBI) as part of its Uniform Crime Reporting (UCR) Program. In "Drugs and Crime Facts" (undated, http://www.bjs.gov/content/dcf/tables/arrtot.cfm), the BJS presents UCR data indicating there were 580,900 arrests for drug crimes in 1980. By 1988 the number had soared to over a million a year and continued to grow. Drug arrests peaked in 2006 at nearly 1.9 million and slowly began to decline. According to the FBI in *Crime in the United States, 2013* (November 2014, http://www.fbi.gov/about-us/cjis/ucr/crime-in-the-u.s/2013/crime-in-the-u.s.-2013/tables/table-29/table_29_estimated_number_of_arrests_united_states_2013.xls), arrests for drug abuse violations in 2013 totaled 1.5 million. It was the largest number of arrests for any specific crime type followed by larceny-theft and driving under the influence, which each had 1.2 million arrests.

Table 4.2 breaks down state and local drug arrests in 2013 by drug law violation and drug type. The majority

TABLE 4.1

Characteristics of commonly abused drugs

Category & name	Examples of commercial & street names	DEA schedule (see note)	How administered
Cannabinoids			
Marijuana	Blunt, dope, ganja, grass, herb, joint, bud, Mary Jane, pot, reefer, green, trees, smoke, sinsemilla, skunk, weed	I	Smoked, swallowed
Hashish	Boom, gangster, hash, hash oil, hemp	I	Smoked, swallowed
Opioids			
Heroin	Diacetylmorphine: smack, horse, brown sugar, dope, H, junk, skag, skunk, white horse, China white; cheese (with OTC cold medicine and antihistamine)	I	Injected, smoked, snorted
Opium	Laudanum, paregoric: big O, black stuff, block, gum, hop	II, III, V	Swallowed, smoked
Stimulants			
Cocaine	Cocaine hydrochloride: blow, bump, C, candy, Charlie, coke, crack, flake, rock, snow, toot	II	Snorted, smoked, injected
Amphetamine	Biphetamine, Dexedrine: bennies, black beauties, crosses, hearts, LA turnaround, speed, truck drivers, uppers	II	Swallowed, snorted, smoked, injected
Methamphetamine	Desoxyn: meth, ice, crank, chalk, crystal, fire, glass, go fast, speed	II	Swallowed, snorted, smoked, injected
Club drugs			
Methylene-dioxy-methamph-etamine (MDMA)	Ecstasy, Adam, clarity, Eve, lover's speed, peace, uppers	I	Swallowed, snorted, injected
Flunitrazepam*	Rohypnol: forget-me pill, Mexican Valium, R2, roach, Roche, roofies, roofinol, rope, rophies	IV	Swallowed, snorted
Gamma-hydroxybutyrate (GHB)*	G, Georgia home boy, grievous bodily harm, liquid ecstasy, soap, scoop, goop, liquid X	I	Swallowed
Dissociative drugs			
Ketamine	Ketalar SV: cat Valium, K, Special K, vitamin K	III	Injected, snorted, smoked
Phencyclidine (PCP) and analogs	Angel dust, boat, hog, love boat, peace pill	I, II	Swallowed, smoked, injected
Salvia divinorum	Salvia, Shepherdess's Herb, Maria Pastora, magic mint, Sally-D	Not scheduled	Chewed, swallowed, smoked
Dextrometh-orphan (DXM)	Found in some cough and cold medications: Robotripping, Robo, Triple C	Not scheduled	Swallowed
Hallucinogens			
Lysergic acid diethylamide (LSD)	Acid, blotter, cubes, microdot yellow sunshine, blue heaven	I	Swallowed, absorbed through mouth tissues
Mescaline	Buttons, cactus, mesc, peyote	I	Swallowed, smoked
Psilocybin	Magic mushrooms, purple passion, shrooms, little smoke	I	Swallowed
Other compounds			
Anabolic steroids	Anadrol, Oxandrin, Durabolin, Depo-Testosterone, Equipoise: roids, juice, gym candy, pumpers	III	Injected, swallowed, applied to skin
Inhalants	Solvents (paint thinners, gasoline, glues); gases (butane, propane, aerosol propellants, nitrous oxide); nitrites (isoamyl, isobutyl, cyclohexyl): laughing gas, poppers, snappers, whippets	Not scheduled	Inhaled through nose or mouth

*Associated with sexual assaults.
Notes: Schedule I drugs have a high potential for abuse. They require greater storage security and have a quota on manufacturing, among other restrictions. Schedule I drugs are available for research only and have no approved medical use.
Schedule II drugs have a high potential for abuse. They require greater storage security and have a quota on manufacturing, among other restrictions. Schedule II drugs are available only by prescription (unrefillable) and require a form for ordering.
Schedule III drugs are available by prescription, may have five refills in 6 months, and may be ordered orally.
Schedule IV drugs are available by prescription, may have five refills in 6 months, and may be ordered orally.
Some Schedule V drugs are available over the counter.
DEA = Drug Enforcement Administration.

SOURCE: Adapted from "Commonly Abused Drugs Chart," in *Commonly Abused Drugs Chart*, U.S. Department of Health and Human Services, National Institutes of Health, National Institute on Drug Abuse, March 2011, http://www.drugabuse.gov/drugs-abuse/commonly-abused-drugs/commonly-abused-drugs-chart (accessed November 9, 2014)

(82.3%) of the arrests were for possession, whereas only 17.7% were for sale/manufacturing. Overall, marijuana was involved in nearly half (46.2%) of all arrests—40.6% of possession arrests and 5.6% of sale/manufacturing arrests. Heroin, cocaine, and its derivatives were involved in 22.4% of all arrests—6% of sales/manufacturing

TABLE 4.2

Arrests for drug abuse violations, by type and region, 2013

Drug abuse violations	United States total	Northeast	Midwest	South	West
Total*	100.0	100.0	100.0	100.0	100.0
Sale/manufacturing:					
Total	17.7	21.8	18.4	17.5	15.2
Heroin or cocaine and their derivatives	6.0	11.9	3.5	5.6	4.2
Marijuana	5.6	6.0	8.6	4.9	4.7
Synthetic or manufactured drugs	1.9	1.6	1.3	3.3	0.5
Other dangerous nonnarcotic drugs	4.2	2.3	5.0	3.7	5.8
Possession:					
Total	82.3	78.2	81.6	82.5	84.8
Heroin or cocaine and their derivatives	16.4	17.4	9.6	13.8	23.4
Marijuana	40.6	46.0	51.7	49.8	18.0
Synthetic or manufactured drugs	4.6	3.1	5.1	6.4	2.7
Other dangerous nonnarcotic drugs	20.7	11.6	15.1	12.5	40.8

*Because of rounding, the percentages may not add to 100.0.

SOURCE: "Arrest Table: Arrest for Dug Abuse Violations, Percent Distribution by Region, 2013," in *Crime in the United States 2013*, U.S. Department of Justice, Federal Bureau of Investigation, November 10, 2014, http://www.fbi.gov/about-us/cjis/ucr/crime-in-the-u.s/2013/crime-in-the-u.s.-2013/persons-arrested/arrest_table_arrests_for_drug_abuse_violations_percent_distribution_by_regions_2013.xls (accessed November 12, 2014)

arrests and 16.4% of possession arrests. Only 6.5% of the total arrests (1.9% of sales/manufacturing arrests and 4.6% of possession arrests) were related to synthetic or manufactured drugs, such as methamphetamine. Arrests for other types of drugs comprised 24.9% of the total arrests by making up 4.2% of sale/manufacturing arrests and 20.7% of possession arrests.

DRUG FACTORS IN OTHER CRIMINAL OFFENSES

Crimes such as assault, murder, and robbery clearly have victims. Drug abuse is different in that people other than the users are not specifically victimized by the offenses. However, illicit drug users may commit other crimes, such as stealing (to support their habits) or engaging in violent behavior.

Drug Trafficking and Violence

Drug trafficking is strongly associated with other criminal acts, particularly violent ones. In "Mexico Drug War Fast Facts" (CNN.com, November 18, 2014), CNN notes that more than 60,000 people were killed in Mexico between 2006 and 2012 due to drug crime related violence. Mexico is a major source and transit country for many of the illegal drugs smuggled into the United States, including cocaine, marijuana, and methamphetamine. Much of this illicit business is conducted by drug cartels or drug trafficking organizations (DTOs) that engage in extremely violent behaviors. In *Southwest Border Violence: Issues in Identifying and Measuring Spillover Violence*, Finklea states, "Mexican DTOs have formed relationships with U.S. street gangs, prison gangs, and outlaw motorcycle gangs. Although these gangs have historically been involved with retail-level drug distribution,

their ties to the Mexican DTOs have allowed them to become increasingly involved at the wholesale level as well. These gangs facilitate the movement of illicit drugs to urban, suburban, and rural areas of the United States."

Finklea notes that it is extremely difficult to quantify how many U.S. criminal acts are associated with drug trafficking because law enforcement authorities do not compile such data on a widespread basis. For example, the FBI's UCR Program contains very limited information about the role of drugs in other criminal offenses. As shown in Table 2.4 in Chapter 2, the FBI indicates that 386 murders during 2013 were related to "narcotic drug laws," and 59 murders were associated with "brawl due to influence of narcotics." However, no statistics are provided about the role of drugs in other criminal offenses.

Drug Use Reported by Prison Inmates and Arrestees

Some clues about the link between drug use and criminal behavior can be gleaned from studies of prison inmates. Between 1974 and 2004 the BJS conducted a periodic "Survey of Inmates in State and Federal Correctional Facilities" that included questions about drug use. In *Drug Use and Dependence, State and Federal Prisoners, 2004* (January 2007, http://bjs.ojp.usdoj.gov/content/pub/pdf/dudsfp04.pdf), Christopher J. Mumola and Jennifer C. Karberg of the BJS reported on drug-related findings from the 2004 survey. As reported by Mumola and Karberg, in 2004, 56% of all state prisoners reported using drugs in the month before committing their offense(s). This percentage had changed little from 1997, when 57% of state prisoners reported previous drug use. A slightly lower percentage of federal prison inmates, 50%, reported drug use in the month before their offense in 2004, compared with 45% in 1997. Nearly one-third (32.1%) of state prison inmates and 26.4% of federal prison inmates in 2004 said they had committed their current offense while under the influence of drugs. A follow-up survey of inmates had not been conducted as of January 2015.

Since 2007 the Office of National Drug Control Policy (ONDCP) within the Executive Office of the President has operated the Arrestee Drug Abuse Monitoring (ADAM) program. The ONDCP's ADAM II program replaces an earlier ADAM I program that was operated by the National Institute of Justice. In *ADAM II 2013 Annual Report* (January 2014, http://www.whitehouse .gov/sites/default/files/ondcp/policy-and-research/adam_ii_ 2013_annual_report.pdf), the ONDCP notes that the ADAM II program monitors drug use trends among newly arrested males. From 2007 through 2011 the program included 10 jail systems throughout the country; in 2012 and 2013 only five jail systems were included. Participation by arrestees is voluntary, and they are not limited to people arrested for drug crimes. As shown in Figure 4.1, the majority of arrestees subjected to urine drug testing at each location in 2013 tested positive for at least one drug. The drugs tested included amphetamine, barbiturates, benzodiazepines, cocaine, marijuana, methadone, methamphetamine, opiates, oxycodone, phencyclidine, and propoxyphene.

Marijuana was the most commonly used drug in all locations, with a range of 33.5% to 59.4% of arrestees testing positive for it. It was followed by cocaine, from 6.6% to 33.3%; opiates, from 6% to 17.9%; and methamphetamine, from 0.3% to 50.6%. Usage of the latter three drugs varied substantially from one city to another. Overall, the ONDCP reports that ADAM II results consistently show that marijuana has been the most commonly used illegal substance among booked arrestees since the original program began in 2000.

Drug-Facilitated Sexual Abuse

Two commonly abused drugs shown in Table 4.1— flunitrazepam and gamma-hydroxybutyrate (GHB)—are associated with sexual assaults. In "Drug Facilitated Sexual Assault" (2009, https://www.rainn.org/get-infor mation/types-of-sexual-assault/drug-facilitated-assault), the Rape, Abuse, and Incest National Network notes that alcohol and some drugs are used by perpetrators to facilitate sexual assaults. The substances lower victims' inhibitions, minimize their resistance to assault, and impair their memories. Since the 1990s there have been some well-publicized cases in which so-called "date rape drugs" were secretly slipped into the drinks of people who were then sexually assaulted. For example, in "Brown Student Tests Positive for Date-Rape Drug after Drinking Punch at Frat Party" (Boston.com, November 9, 2014), Justine Hofherr reports that authorities in Providence, Rhode Island, were investigating claims by two young women that they were secretly given drugs while drinking at a fraternity party at Brown University. One of the women reported being sexually assaulted following the incident. According to Hofherr, GHB was found in the blood of one of the women. As of January 2015

FIGURE 4.1

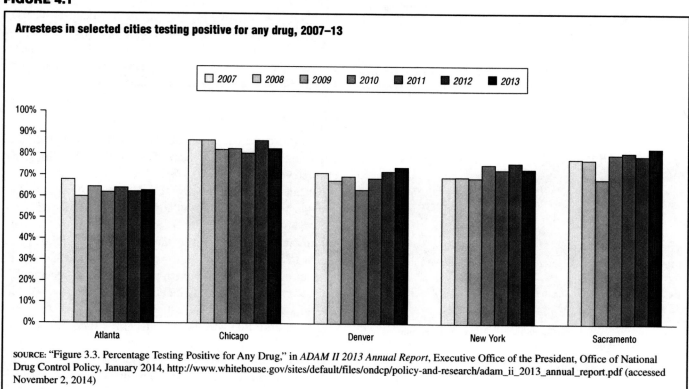

Arrestees in selected cities testing positive for any drug, 2007–13

SOURCE: "Figure 3.3. Percentage Testing Positive for Any Drug," in *ADAM II 2013 Annual Report*, Executive Office of the President, Office of National Drug Control Policy, January 2014, http://www.whitehouse.gov/sites/default/files/ondcp/policy-and-research/adam_ii_2013_annual_report.pdf (accessed November 2, 2014)

the fraternity that hosted the party had been suspended from the Brown campus for four years, but no arrests had been made in the case.

SELF-REPORTED ILLICIT DRUG USE

Substance Abuse and Mental Health Services Administration

The Substance Abuse and Mental Health Services Administration (SAMHSA), which is part of the U.S. Department of Health and Human Services, conducts an annual survey on the use of illegal drugs by the U.S. population. In *Results from the 2013 National Survey on Drug Use and Health: Summary of National Findings* (September 2014, http://www.samhsa.gov/data/sites/default/files/NSDUHresultsPDFWHTML2013/Web/NSDUHresults2013.pdf), SAMHSA notes that it surveys approximately 67,500 people each year in the civilian noninstitutionalized population (people who are not in the U.S. military, hospitals, jail, or similar facilities) of the United States.

SAMHSA finds that in 2013, 24.6 million Americans aged 12 years and older had used illicit drugs within the previous month. (See Figure 4.2.) The vast majority (19.8 million) had used marijuana. Much smaller numbers had used psychotherapeutics (6.5 million), cocaine (1.5 million),

hallucinogens (1.3 million), inhalants (500,000), and heroin (300,000). Psychotherapeutics are defined by SAMHSA as prescription drugs, such as pain relievers, tranquilizers, stimulants, and sedatives, that are used for nonmedical purposes.

Figure 4.3 shows past-month use of various illicit drugs by people aged 12 years and older between 2002 and 2013. In 2013, 9.4% of the U.S. population aged 12 years and older admitted using illicit drugs during the previous month. The most widely consumed illicit drug was marijuana (7.5%), followed by psychotherapeutics (2.5%), cocaine (0.6%), and hallucinogens (0.5%). As shown Figure 4.4, SAMHSA finds that self-reported illicit drug use in 2002 through 2013 was most common among teens and young adults aged 18 to 25 years (21.5%), followed by younger teens aged 12 to 17 years (8.8%); adults aged 26 years and older were the least likely to report having used illicit drugs (7.3%). Figure 4.5 shows the number of people aged 12 years and older who reported daily or almost daily use of marijuana in 2002 through 2013. In 2013, 8.1% said they used marijuana on 20 or more days during the past month, and 5.7% said they had used it on 300 or more days during the previous year.

Gallup Polling on Marijuana Use

The Gallup Organization has occasionally polled Americans about their use of marijuana. As shown in Figure 4.6, in 1969 only 4% of survey respondents admitted to ever trying marijuana; by 2013 that value had risen to 38%. According to Lydia Saad of the Gallup Organization, in *In U.S., 38% Have Tried Marijuana, Little Changed since '80s* (August 2, 2013, http://www.gallup.com/poll/163835/tried-marijuana-little-changed-80s.aspx), in 2013 nearly half (49%) of respondents aged 39 to 49 years had ever tried marijuana compared with 44% of those aged 50 to 64 years, 36% of those aged 18 to 29 years, and 17% of those aged 65 years and older.

COCAINE AND CRACK

Nonmedical use of cocaine has been illegal since the passage of the Harrison Narcotics Act of 1914. In 1970 cocaine was classified as a CSA Schedule II drug because it is considered highly addictive. During the 1970s and 1980s cocaine use soared in the United States with the rise of large well-funded drug cartels in South America, particularly in Colombia. The cartels used their extensive criminal networks to import the drug into the United States and sell it for premium prices. Cocaine in powdered form became the drug of choice for wealthy celebrities and professionals. It developed a reputation as a trendy, glamorous, and non-addictive drug that was too expensive for street users.

The Crack Epidemic

During the early 1980s a cheaper form of cocaine called crack cocaine was introduced to street users. Unlike

FIGURE 4.2

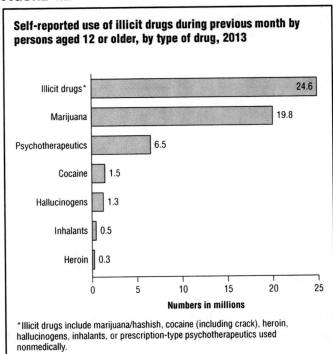

Self-reported use of illicit drugs during previous month by persons aged 12 or older, by type of drug, 2013

*Illicit drugs include marijuana/hashish, cocaine (including crack), heroin, hallucinogens, inhalants, or prescription-type psychotherapeutics used nonmedically.

SOURCE: "Figure 2.1. Past Month Illicit Drug Use among Persons Aged 12 or Older: 2013," in *Results from the 2013 National Survey on Drug Use and Health: Summary of National Findings*, U.S. Department of Health and Human Services, Substance Abuse and Mental Health Services Administration, Center for Behavioral Health Statistics and Quality, September 2014, http://www.samhsa.gov/data/sites/default/files/NSDUHresultsPDFWHTML2013/Web/NSDUHresults2013.pdf (accessed November 2, 2014)

FIGURE 4.3

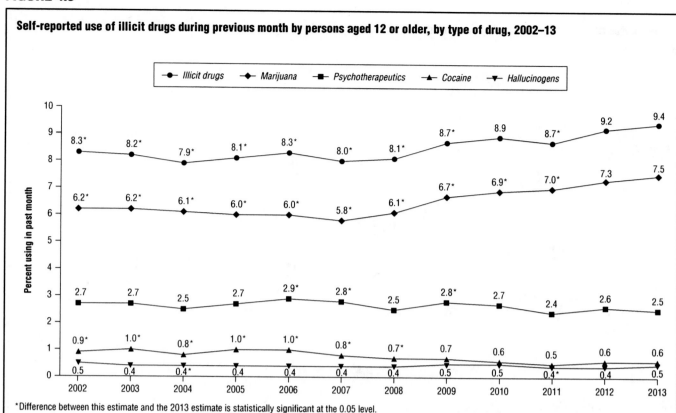

Self-reported use of illicit drugs during previous month by persons aged 12 or older, by type of drug, 2002–13

*Difference between this estimate and the 2013 estimate is statistically significant at the 0.05 level.

SOURCE: "Figure 2.2. Past Month Use of Selected Illicit Drugs among Persons Aged 12 or Older: 2002–2013," in *Results from the 2013 National Survey on Drug Use and Health: Summary of National Findings*, U.S. Department of Health and Human Services, Substance Abuse and Mental Health Services Administration, Center for Behavioral Health Statistics and Quality, September 2014, http://www.samhsa.gov/data/sites/default/files/NSDUHresultsPDFWHTML2013/Web/NSDUHresults2013.pdf (accessed November 2, 2014)

powdered cocaine, the crack version was a crystal that could be smoked. It was also more potent than the same amount of powdered cocaine and provided a much quicker high. Crack soon became the drug of choice among low-income users, particularly in inner cities with large minority populations, and the country experienced a so-called crack epidemic. Gang wars and other crack-related crimes skyrocketed. Americans were appalled by media reports about crack-induced street crime and crack-addicted babies born to mothers abusing the drug. The social effects of the crack epidemic are described by the DEA in *DEA History in Depth* (January 2009, http://www.justice.gov/dea/about/history/1985-1990.pdf): "The crack trade had created a violent sub-world, and crack-related murders in many large cities were skyrocketing. For example, a 1988 study by the Bureau of Justice Statistics found that in New York City, crack use was tied to 32% of all homicides and 60% of drug-related homicides. On a daily basis, the evening news reported the violence of drive-by shootings and crack users trying to obtain money for their next hit."

The Crackdown on Crack

In 1986 Congress passed the Anti-drug Abuse Act, a comprehensive law that imposed mandatory minimum prison sentences for people convicted of federal drug crimes. The new law made an important distinction between crack cocaine and powdered cocaine. A person convicted of possessing only 0.2 ounces (5 g) of crack cocaine faced the same mandatory prison sentence as a person convicted of possessing 17.6 ounces (500 g) of powdered cocaine. In other words, there was a 100 to 1 sentencing disparity between the two forms of the drug. At the time, politicians defended the disparity as a reasonable response to the harm that crack cocaine was doing to U.S. society. However, the law soon became controversial because relatively low-level crack users and suppliers (many of whom were low-income African Americans) received harsher sentences than users and suppliers of much larger amounts of powdered cocaine. Because most of the latter offenders were white, activists decried the law as racist.

After nearly two decades of controversy, the issue was addressed by the U.S. Supreme Court in *Kimbrough v. United States* (552 U.S. 85 [2007]). The case involved Derrick Kimbrough, an African American defendant who had pleaded guilty in federal court to offenses involving both powdered and crack cocaine. The original court sentenced Kimbrough in accordance with the federal guidelines for powdered cocaine, rather than with the harsher crack cocaine sentence structure. The Supreme

FIGURE 4.4

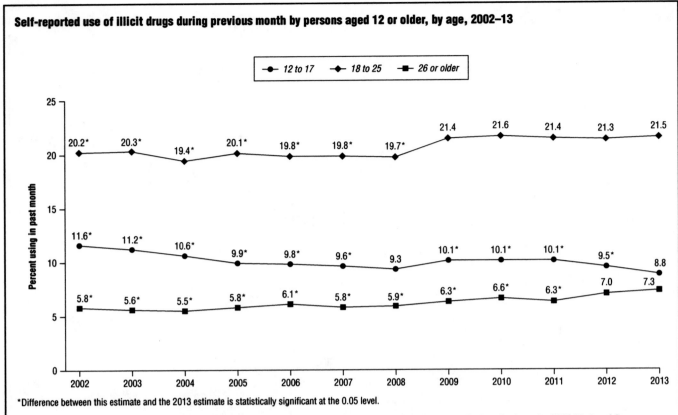

Self-reported use of illicit drugs during previous month by persons aged 12 or older, by age, 2002–13

Legend: ━●━ *12 to 17* ━◆━ *18 to 25* ━■━ *26 or older*

*Difference between this estimate and the 2013 estimate is statistically significant at the 0.05 level.

SOURCE: "Figure 2.6. Past Month Illicit Drug Use among Persons Aged 12 or Older, by Age: 2002–2013," in *Results from the 2013 National Survey on Drug Use and Health: Summary of National Findings*, U.S. Department of Health and Human Services, Substance Abuse and Mental Health Services Administration, Center for Behavioral Health Statistics and Quality, September 2014, http://www.samhsa.gov/data/sites/default/files/NSDUHresultsPDFWHTML2013/Web/NSDUHresults2013.pdf (accessed November 2, 2014)

Court ruled in December 2007 that federal judges can use discretion in such cases and impose shorter sentences for crack cocaine offenses than called for by federal guidelines, to reduce the powder-crack disparity. That same month the U.S. Sentencing Commission (USSC) ruled that crack cocaine sentences imposed by federal courts in the past could be shortened accordingly following petition by the convicted defendants. The USSC also recommended that Congress eliminate the 100 to 1 disparity in crack sentencing compared with sentencing for powdered cocaine offenses.

In August 2010 President Barack Obama (1961–) signed the Fair Sentencing Act. The act eliminated the five-year mandatory minimum prison sentence for first-time crack cocaine possession and increased to 1 ounce (28 g) the amount of crack cocaine that is required for the imposition of mandatory minimum prison terms for drug trafficking. In other words, the 100 to 1 sentencing disparity between crack cocaine and powdered cocaine was reduced to an 18 to 1 sentencing disparity.

The Crack Epidemic Ends

During the 1990s crack lost favor as the drug of choice among inner-city youths as they increasingly turned to marijuana. Denise Herd of the University of California, Berkeley, suggests in "Changes in Drug Use Prevalence in Rap Music Songs, 1979–1997" (*Addiction Research and Theory*, vol. 16, no. 2, April 2008) that rap music may have played a role in this social trend. Herd finds that popular rap songs decried the "destructiveness" of crack during the 1980s, but glorified marijuana during the 1990s by tying the drug to "creativity, wealth and status."

The end of the crack epidemic saw a brief downturn in the total number of drug arrests by state and local authorities. According to the BJS in "Drugs and Crime Facts," arrests dropped from 1.4 million in 1989 to 1 million in 1992. This decline coincided with a national drop in overall crime that is described in Chapter 2. The overall crime rate continued its downward trend, but arrests for drug crime resurged due in large part to the growing popularity of marijuana.

MARIJUANA

According to the BJS (http://www.bjs.gov/content/dcf/tables/drugtype.cfm), marijuana arrests at the state and local level fell throughout the 1980s, dropping to about 290,000 arrests in 1991. Over the following decade arrests more than doubled and continued to rise through

FIGURE 4.5

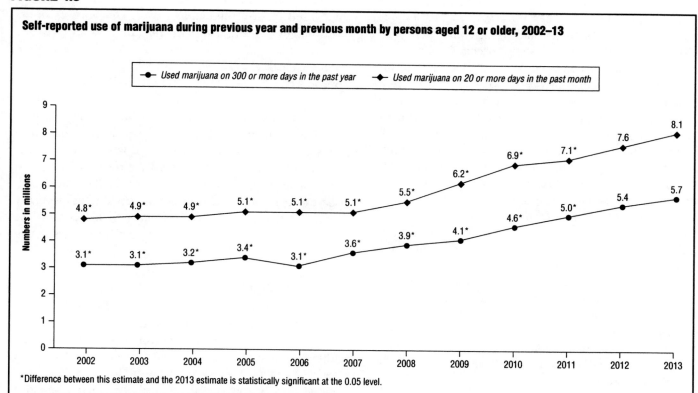

Self-reported use of marijuana during previous year and previous month by persons aged 12 or older, 2002–13

— Used marijuana on 300 or more days in the past year   — Used marijuana on 20 or more days in the past month

*Difference between this estimate and the 2013 estimate is statistically significant at the 0.05 level.

SOURCE: "Figure 2.15. Daily or Almost Daily Marijuana Use in the Past Year and Past Month among Persons Aged 12 or Older: 2002–2013," in *Results from the 2013 National Survey on Drug Use and Health: Summary of National Findings*, U.S. Department of Health and Human Services, Substance Abuse and Mental Health Services Administration, Center for Behavioral Health Statistics and Quality, September 2014, http://www.samhsa.gov/data/sites/default/files/NSDUHresultsPDFWHTML2013/Web/NSDUHresults2013.pdf (accessed November 2, 2014)

FIGURE 4.6

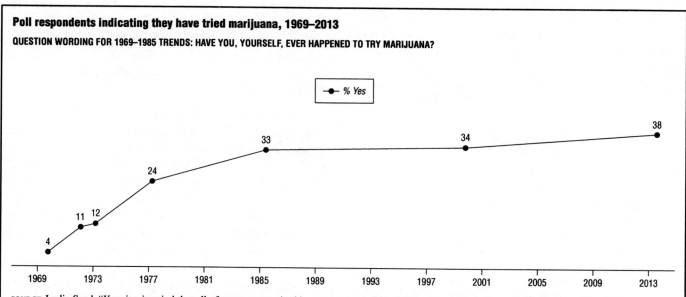

Poll respondents indicating they have tried marijuana, 1969–2013

QUESTION WORDING FOR 1969–1985 TRENDS: HAVE YOU, YOURSELF, EVER HAPPENED TO TRY MARIJUANA?

— % Yes

SOURCE: Lydia Saad, "Keeping in mind that all of your answers in this survey are confidential, have you, yourself, ever happened to try marijuana?," in *In U.S., 38% Have Tried Marijuana, Little Changed Since '80s*, The Gallup Organization, August 2, 2013, http://www.gallup.com/poll/163835/tried-marijuana-little-changed-80s.aspx (accessed November 2, 2014). Copyright © 2013 Gallup, Inc. All rights reserved. The content is used with permission; however, Gallup retains all rights of republication.

2007, before declining. As noted earlier there were 1.5 million total arrests in 2013 for drug crimes, and 46.2% of them involved marijuana. Thus, nearly 700,000 arrests in 2013 were associated with marijuana.

Marijuana Decriminalization

In *Beyond Our Control?: Confronting the Limits of Our Legal System in the Age of Cyberspace* (2003), Stuart Biegel of the University of California, Los Angeles, reports that marijuana arrests in the United States doubled from 7,000 to 15,000 between 1964 and 1966. By 1969 the national total for marijuana arrests had increased nearly 700% to 118,903. Court systems became overrun with cases involving marijuana possession, which at that time could elicit a prison sentence as long as five years for possession of only a single marijuana cigarette (or joint). In response, many jurisdictions began lowering the penalties for possession of small amounts of marijuana, for example, from a misdemeanor to an infraction payable only by a fine. This practice is called decriminalization and is not the same as legalization, which makes an action legal when it was previously illegal. In *State Marijuana Legalization Initiatives: Implications for Federal Law Enforcement* (December 4, 2014, http://www.fas.org/sgp/crs/misc/R43164.pdf), Lisa N. Sacco and Kristin Finklea of the CRS note, "A state decriminalizes conduct by removing the accompanying criminal penalties; however, civil penalties remain. If, for instance, a state decriminalizes the possession of marijuana in small amounts, possession of marijuana still violates state law; however, possession of marijuana within the specified small amount is considered a civil offense and subject to a civil penalty, not criminal prosecution."

Marijuana decriminalization began in Oregon in 1973 and then spread to other states and to dozens of cities and counties. Typically the laws specify threshold amounts of the drug and offender age limits. For example, in October 2014 Maryland decriminalized the possession of less than 10 grams (0.35 ounces) of marijuana. In "Having a Small Amount of Pot in Md. Is No Longer a Criminal Case" (WashingtonPost.com, October 1, 2014), Jenna Johnson reports that people aged 21 years and older caught with less than 10 grams of marijuana must pay a fine; younger offenders must also "attend a drug education program." Some decriminalization laws apply only in specific situations. According to Dan McQuade, in "Mayor Nutter Signs Marijuana Decriminalization Bill" (PhillyMag.com, October 1, 2014), a new decriminalization law that went into effect in October 2014 in Philadelphia, Pennsylvania, does not apply to offenders caught without identification; they can still be arrested on criminal charges of possession.

During the late 1990s some states began decriminalizing the use of small amounts of marijuana for medical reasons, such as to relieve pain or nausea. According to the National Conference of State Legislatures (January 2015, http://www.ncsl.org/research/health/state-medical-marijuana-laws.aspx), as of January 2015, 23 states, the District of Columbia, and Guam had passed laws allowing "comprehensive public medical marijuana and cannabis programs." Another 11 states allowed medical use of some low-dosage products under limited circumstances.

Despite these changes at the state level, marijuana remains illegal under federal law, and some of those who use or traffic in medical marijuana have been prosecuted by the federal government. However, Todd Garvey of the CRS notes in *Medical Marijuana: The Supremacy Clause, Federalism, and the Interplay between State and Federal Laws* (November 9, 2012, http://assets.opencrs.com/rpts/R42398_20121109.pdf) that in 2009 the U.S. attorney general issued a memorandum indicating that the federal government did not intend to prioritize the enforcement of federal laws against marijuana users acting in compliance with state laws. One reason is that the federal government lacks the resources to investigate and enforce federal drug laws at the state level. Garvey states that the Obama administration "has formally suggested that it will not prosecute individuals who use medicinal marijuana in a manner consistent with state laws."

Marijuana Legalization

In November 2012 voters in Colorado and Washington approved ballot initiatives legalizing the possession of small amounts of marijuana for recreational use and calling on their state governments to license and regulate marijuana sales. These actions posed direct challenges to federal laws against marijuana use. The DOJ responded on August 29, 2013, with a memorandum titled "Guidance Regarding Marijuana Enforcement" (http://www.justice.gov/iso/opa/resources/3052013829132756857467.pdf) indicating the federal government would not block the state legalization movement so long as the states "implement strong and effective regulatory and enforcement systems that will address the threat those state laws could pose to public safety, public health, and other law enforcement interests." In November 2014 voters in Alaska, Oregon, and the District of Columbia also passed legalization initiatives.

THE COLORADO EXPERIENCE. Colorado already allowed medicinal use of marijuana when it legalized the drug for recreational use by people aged 21 years and older. The new law (https://www.colorado.gov/pacific/sites/default/files/Section%2016%20-%20%20Retail.pdf) and the associated regulations are complex. The Marijuana Enforcement Division (https://www.colorado.gov/pacific/enforcement/marijuanaenforcement) within the Colorado Department of Revenue (CDOR) is responsible for licensing and regulating the state's medical and retail marijuana industries and provides lists of licensed commercial growers, testers, product manufacturers, and stores. In "Colorado Struggles to Adjust Marijuana Supply" (DenverPost.com, September 2, 2014), Kristen Wyatt notes that previously the state "limited pot-growers to the number of medical marijuana patients they served." With recreational use allowed, the state has begun implementing new production caps designed to prevent oversupply that could make its way out of the state. According to Wyatt, "commercial growers will need to prove they're selling 85 percent of their inventory before getting permission to add plants."

In January 2014 Colorado became the first jurisdiction in the country to allow retail stores to begin legally selling marijuana. It was joined later in the year by Washington State. According to Michael Martinez in "10 Things to Know about Nation's First Recreational Marijuana Shops in Colorado" (CNN.com, January 1, 2014), Colorado permits state residents to buy up to an ounce (28.4 grams) at a time. People visiting from out of state are limited to a quarter of an ounce (7.1 grams) per purchase. Retail sales have a 25% excise tax added on top of a state sales tax of 2.9%. Individual communities can impose additional taxes or refuse to allow retail sales. Colorado adults are allowed to grow up to six marijuana plants in an "enclosed and locked" area for their personal use. In "Marijuana Retailers in Colo. Woo Shoppers with Holiday Deals" (BostonGlobe.com, November 24, 2014), Wyatt points out that marijuana legally grown and sold in Colorado cannot leave the state per federal laws against interstate drug trafficking.

The CDOR (https://www.colorado.gov/pacific/sites/default/files/1014%20Marijuana%20Tax%2C%20License%2C%20and%20Fees%20Report.pdf) indicates that as of November 2014 its Marijuana Cash Fund had collected $30.6 million in taxes on sales made through the previous month. In addition, $5.9 million in license and application fees had been received for a total of $36.5 million. The opportunities for the state to raise funds and to reduce spending on marijuana law enforcement were two drivers behind the legalization effort. Critics, however, worry that other crimes, such as driving under the influence, will rise with increasing retail marijuana sales. As of January 2015, there were insufficient data on the issue to make a determination. There is also concern about marijuana edibles (food products containing marijuana or its active ingredient) being ingested accidentally by children. In "Colorado Wants Most Edible Marijuana Banned" (CBSNews.com, October 21, 2014), CBS News indicates that nine children had been seen at one Denver hospital during 2014 for ingesting such products. It was not known whether the edibles were commercially sold or homemade. According to CBS News, state regulators were considering banning retail sales of most marijuana edibles. No final decision had been made as of January 2015.

PUBLIC OPINION ON LEGALIZATION. Since 1969 the Gallup Organization has conducted polls gauging American public opinion about legalizing marijuana use. As shown in Table 4.3, only 12% of respondents in 1969 thought that marijuana should be legalized. By 2014 that percentage had risen to 51%. Support for legalization varies greatly by political ideology, with liberals most strongly in favor of it. (See Figure 4.7.) In 2014 nearly three-fourths (73%) of respondents identifying themselves

TABLE 4.3

Public opinion on legalizing marijuana, selected years, 1969–2014

	Yes, legal	No, illegal	No opinion
2014 Oct 12–15	51	47	2
2013 Oct 3–6	58	39	3
2012 Nov 26–29	48	50	1
2011 Oct 6–9	50	46	3
2010 Oct 7–10*	46	50	4
2009 Oct 1–4*	44	54	2
2005 Oct 13–16*	36	60	4
2003 Nov 10–12*	34	64	2
2001 Aug 3–5	34	62	4
2000 Aug 29–Sep 5*	31	64	5
1995 Aug 28–30	25	73	2
1985 May 17–20	23	73	4
1980 Jun 27–30	25	70	5
1979 May 18–21	25	70	5
1977 Apr 1–4	28	66	6
1973 Jan 26–29	16	78	6
1972 Mar 3–5	15	81	4
1969 Oct 2–7	12	84	4

*Asked of a half sample.

SOURCE: Jeff Jones and Lydia Saad, "Do you think the use of marijuana should be made legal, or not?" in *Gallup Poll Social Series: Crime*, The Gallup Organization, October 15, 2014, http://www.gallup.com/file/poll/179240/Marijuana_Legalization_141106.pdf (accessed November 12, 2014). Copyright © 2014 Gallup, Inc. All rights reserved. The content is used with permission; however, Gallup retains all rights of republication.

FIGURE 4.7

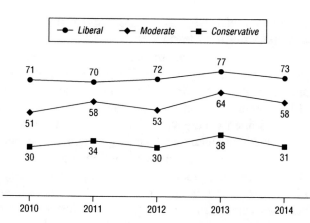

Percentage of Americans who support legalizing marijuana, by political ideology, 2010–14

[% Yes, should be legal]

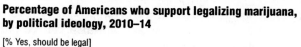

SOURCE: Lydia Saad, "Support for Legalizing the Use of Marijuana—Recent Trend by Party Ideology," in *Majority Continues to Support Pot Legalization in U.S.*, The Gallup Organization, November 6, 2014, http://www.gallup.com/poll/179195/majority-continues-support-pot-legalization.aspx (accessed November 12, 2014). Copyright © 2014 Gallup, Inc. All rights reserved. The content is used with permission; however, Gallup retains all rights of republication.

as liberal favored legalizing marijuana compared with 58% of moderates and 31% of conservatives. There are also substantial differences of opinion based on age. As shown in Table 4.4, in 2013 two-thirds (67%) of respondents aged 18 to 29 years favored legalizing marijuana compared with 45% of those aged 65 and older.

TABLE 4.4

Public opinion on legalizing marijuana, by age, October 2013

	% Yes, legal	% No, illegal
18 to 29 years	67	31
30 to 49 years	62	35
50 to 64 years	56	40
65+ years	45	53

SOURCE: Art Swift, "Americans' Views on Legalizing Marijuana, by Age," in *For First Time, Americans Favor Legalizing Marijuana*, The Gallup Organization, October 22, 2013, http://www.gallup.com/poll/165539/first-time-americans-favor-legalizing-marijuana.aspx (accessed November 2, 2014). Copyright © 2013 Gallup, Inc. All rights reserved. The content is used with permission; however, Gallup retains all rights of republication.

METHAMPHETAMINE

Methamphetamine (or meth) is a stimulant in the amphetamine group. Beginning in the 1990s, methamphetamine abuse became a major problem in some parts of the United States. The rise of this previously obscure drug is described by Franco in *Methamphetamine: Background, Prevalence, and Federal Drug Control Policies.*

Methamphetamine can be synthesized from a naturally occurring chemical called ephedrine. This so-called precursor chemical is commonly synthesized, as are two other methamphetamine precursors: phenylpropanolamine and pseudoephedrine. Both of the latter are widely used in cold and sinus medications, many of which can be purchased without a prescription.

The Evolution of Illicit Methamphetamine Laboratories

Franco notes that methamphetamine is classified as a Schedule II drug under the CSA. The drug had been used medically in the United States for several decades. During the 1950s methamphetamine was widely prescribed for a variety of ailments; however, growing concern about the abuse of methamphetamine (and amphetamines, in general) led to severe government restrictions on dispensing the drug. In response, underworld methamphetamine laboratories began springing up during the 1960s. These illicit laboratories were primarily located in the western United States and mostly operated by outlaw motorcycle gangs. They produced a crude form of methamphetamine that was known as crank on the streets. Crank was less potent than pharmaceutical-grade methamphetamine, but it still became popular with certain users. During the 1980s more sophisticated amateur chemists developed a new method for synthesizing a much more potent form of crank using ephedrine-based reactions. This led to a variety of forms that could be ingested, snorted, injected, or smoked. A popular type of smokable methamphetamine is a crystalline powder known as ice.

During the 1990s illicit amateur methamphetamine laboratories became a cause of great concern. Many of the laboratories were operated in homes, putting the residents (particularly children) at great danger of fires and explosions due to the volatile nature of the chemicals involved.

As the so-called methamphetamine epidemic attracted national attention, legislators rushed to pass laws making it more difficult for amateur chemists to obtain the ephedrine-type precursors that are used to synthesize methamphetamine. The Comprehensive Methamphetamine Control Act of 1996 added the precursor chemicals to Schedule II of the CSA. That act and a subsequent law, the Methamphetamine Trafficking Penalty Enhancement Act of 1998, increased the penalties for manufacturing and selling methamphetamine. After 2000, legislators tackled the easy availability of precursor chemicals in over-the-counter cold and sinus medications. In 2006 federal law was changed to set limits on how much of these precursor-containing products an individual could purchase at one time, as well as within a 30-day period. Furthermore, businesses were required to track who was purchasing these products and to keep the products in an area where customers could not access them directly, such as in a locked case.

In *Drug Control: State Approaches Taken to Control Access to Key Methamphetamine Ingredient Show Varied Impact on Domestic Drug Labs* (January 2013, http://www.gao.gov/assets/660/651709.pdf), the U.S. Government Accountability Office (GAO) analyzes DEA data regarding seizures of methamphetamine laboratories, dumpsites, chemicals, and glassware around the country. The number of seizures peaked in 2004 at 24,155 and then declined sharply to 6,951 in 2007. According to the GAO, this was likely the result of state and federal restrictions on the sale of cold and allergy medications. The GAO notes, however, that drug synthesizers have adopted new methods to circumvent the restrictions. One option is a manufacturing method that requires less precursor material than did older methods. In addition, some drug producers have recruited groups of individuals to acquire precursor chemicals for them. The process, dubbed smurfing, relies on multiple individuals to visit multiple stores and obtain the legally allowed amount of ephedrine-containing medications from each store. The implementation of these methods likely accounts for an increase in the number of seizures of methamphetamine laboratories, dumpsites, chemicals, and glassware between 2008 and 2010. Although methamphetamine abuse is often described by the media as a national epidemic, analysts assert that it is actually a regional problem in that certain so-called hot spots exist around the country. Most seizures of methamphetamine laboratories, dumpsites, chemicals, and glassware have occurred in the Midwest and the South.

According to the DEA (http://www.dea.gov/resource-center/meth-lab-maps.shtml), there were 11,210 methamphetamine laboratory incidents during 2012, the latest year for which data were available as of January 2015.

FEDERAL SPENDING ON DRUG CONTROL

Like all commodities, illicit drugs operate under the economic principles of supply and demand. Federal, state, and local law enforcement officials attack the supply side by arresting and prosecuting sellers and manufacturers of illicit drugs. Because many illicit drugs are imported from foreign countries, the federal government plays an active role in trying to control and stop these international suppliers. This has proved to be extremely difficult. In addition, the War on Drugs is an expensive war. According to Raphael Perl of the CRS in *Drug Control: International Policy and Approaches* (February 2, 2006, http://fpc.state.gov/documents/organization/61518 .pdf), between 1981 and 2001 the United States spent $8.6 billion on international narcotics control, primarily in Latin America. Nevertheless, estimated cocaine production in that region nearly quadrupled during that same period, and the average price per gram of cocaine in the United States decreased by half. Table 4.5 shows the federal government budget for drug control for FY 2013, enacted for FY 2014, and requested for FY 2015. The federal government spent $23.8 billion in FY 2013 on drug control. Another $25.2 billion was authorized for FY 2014, and $25.4 billion was expected to be spent in FY 2015.

TABLE 4.5

Federal drug control funding, fiscal years 2013–15

[In billions of dollars]

Function	Fiscal year 2013 final	Fiscal year 2014 enacted	Fiscal year 2015 request[a]
Treatment	$7.889	$8.825	$9.597
Prevention	1.275	1.279	1.337
Domestic law enforcement	8.850	9.274	9.177
Interdiction	3.941	4.048	3.863
International	1.846	1.786	1.389
Total	**23.800**	**25.212**	**25.363**
Demand reduction[b]	9.157	10.097	10.927
Supply reduction[c]	14.643	15.115	14.436
Total	**23.800**	**25.212**	**25.363**

[a]In September 2014, the Continuing Appropriations Resolution, 2015 (P.L. 113-164) continued funding the federal government at fiscal year 2014 spending levels through December 11, 2014. Details of fiscal year 2015 federal drug control spending remain unclear.
[b]Demand reduction includes treatment and prevention.
[c]Supply reduction includes domestic law enforcement, interdiction, and international.
Notes: Amounts may not add to total due to rounding.

SOURCE: Lisa N. Sacco and Kristin Finklea, "Table 1. Federal Drug Control Budget by Function," in *Reauthorizing the Office of National Drug Control Policy: Issues for Consideration*, Congressional Research Service, September 30, 2014, http://fas.org/sgp/crs/misc/R41535.pdf (accessed November 3, 2014)

CHAPTER 5
WHITE-COLLAR CRIME

OFFENSES AND ARRESTS

The term *white-collar crime* was first used by the American criminologist Edwin Hardin Sutherland (1883–1950) in 1939 to define a violation of the criminal law committed by "a person of respectability and high social status in the course of his occupation" (Cornell University Law School, "White Collar Crime," August 19, 2010, http://www.law.cornell.edu/wex/White-collar_crime). Over time, the definition has become much broader. In *Financial Crimes Report to the Public, Fiscal Years 2010–2011 (October 1, 2009–September 30, 2011)* (February 2012, http://www.fbi.gov/stats-services/publications/financial-crimes-report-2010-2011/financial-crimes-report-2010-2011.pdf), the Federal Bureau of Investigation (FBI) notes that white-collar crimes are "characterized by deceit, concealment, or violation of trust and are not dependent upon the application or threat of physical force or violence." Examples include bribery, computer hacking, confidence games, copyright violations, counterfeiting, embezzlement, environmental crimes, fraud, identity theft, money laundering, and swindles. Table 5.1 briefly describes dozens of types of white-collar crimes based on information from the FBI.

White-collar crimes are prohibited by federal and/or state laws. Some offenses fall directly under federal authority, particularly currency counterfeiting, mail fraud, and wire fraud. Mail fraud involves offenses perpetrated by use of the U.S. Postal Service or other interstate delivery services, such as FedEx. Wire fraud covers offenses committed via telecommunication systems, such as the telephone or the Internet. Because fraudsters frequently use one of these two methods to communicate with victims, many white-collar offenses are federal crimes. Federal authorities also focus on offenses involving corporate financial misdeeds, income tax fraud, public official corruption, and frauds perpetrated against insurance companies, financial institutions, and federal government programs, such as Medicaid and Medicare. White-collar criminals who operate across state lines and/or have international connections are also subject to federal prosecution.

The FBI (http://www.fbi.gov/news/stories/story-index/white-collar-crime) maintains a website on which it posts articles about white-collar crime cases it has investigated. For example, in "Egregious Case of Health Care Fraud: Cancer Doctor Admits Prescribing Unnecessary Chemotherapy" (November 6, 2014, http://www.fbi.gov/news/stories/2014/november/egregious-case-of-health-care-fraud/egregious-case-of-health-care-fraud), the agency describes a case in which a Michigan doctor pleaded guilty to ordering unnecessary tests and administering unnecessary treatments to patients in order to "fraudulently bill the federal Medicare program and private insurance companies for hundreds of millions of dollars." As of January 2015, the doctor had not been sentenced but faced up to 175 years in prison. At another website (http://www.fbi.gov/wanted/wcc), the FBI regularly posts photos and information about suspected white-collar criminals it is seeking. As of January 2015, the list included 10 individuals, most of whom are believed to have fled the country. They are wanted for a variety of federal crimes including wire fraud, mail fraud, bank fraud, mortgage fraud, health care fraud, identity theft, and being fugitives from justice.

In *Federal Justice Statistics, 2012—Statistical Tables* (January 22, 2015, http://www.bjs.gov/content/pub/pdf/fjs12st.pdf), Mark Motivans of the Bureau of Justice Statistics (BJS) within the U.S. Department of Justice (DOJ) categorizes the most serious offenses of the 172,248 suspects arrested for federal law violations during fiscal year (FY) 2012 (October 1, 2011, through September 30, 2012). For white-collar crimes the most arrests occurred for defendants charged with fraud

TABLE 5.1

White collar crimes

Fraud	Description and/or examples
Adoption scams	Women promise their unborn children to more than one couple or aren't even pregnant; phony domestic adoption agencies or facilitators; unsanctioned international adoptions.
Advance fee schemes	The victim pays money to someone in anticipation of receiving something of greater value—such as a loan, contract, investment, or gift—and then receives little or nothing in return.
Anti-aging product fraud	Con artists market and sell bogus products advertised as having anti-aging benefits.
ATM skimming	Surreptitious surveillance equipment installed on ATMs allows criminals to record customers' account information and PINs, create their own bank cards, and steal from customer accounts.
Bankruptcy fraud	Lying under oath or providing false documentation during bankruptcy proceedings or concealing or transferring financial assets. Using false identities to file for bankruptcy multiple times in multiple locations; bribing a bankruptcy trustee; intentionally running up credit card bills with no intention of paying them off (also known as "credit card bust-outs").
Corporate fraud	Accounting schemes designed to deceive investors, auditors, and analysts about the true financial condition of a corporation or business entity; insider trading; utilizing companies to perpetrate large-scale, high-yield fraud schemes, such as Ponzi schemes.
Credit card fraud	Criminals use stolen credit cards or the credit card numbers of victims to make purchases, apply for credit cards using the identities of others, or create counterfeit credit cards.
Financial institution fraud	Insider fraud (embezzlement and misapplication), check fraud, counterfeit negotiable instruments, check kiting, and fraud contributing to the failure of financial institutions.
Foreclosure fraud	Con artists take money from homeowners in danger of foreclosure by offering bogus services such as mortgage loan modifications or other means touted as a way to avoid foreclosure.
Funeral fraud (prepaid funeral scams)	Victims pay in advance for funeral services that are never provided. Typically the victims are led to believe their money will be invested in a life insurance policy that will pay off in the event of their death.
Gameover malware	Spam e-mails—purportedly from the National Automated Clearing House Association (NACHA), the Federal Reserve Bank, or the Federal Deposit Insurance Corporation (FDIC)—that can infect recipients' computers with malware and allow access to their bank accounts.
Grandparent scam	Typically involves a phone call or an e-mail from someone who identifies himself or herself as the victim's grandchild or other relative and claims to need money wired as soon as possible for an emergency.
Health care fraud	Fraudulent billings to health care programs including medically unnecessary services billed to health care insurers.
Hedge fund fraud	Hedge funds are minimally regulated private investment partnerships that historically accept only high-wealth investors. Fraud is perpetrated when investors are given false information about the fund's performance or otherwise deceived.
House stealing	Criminals assume the identities of homeowners and then fill out transfer property forms and file deeds with the authorities to transfer ownership of the homes to themselves.
Identity theft	Someone wrongfully obtains another's personal information without their knowledge in order to commit theft or fraud.
Income tax refund fraud	Schemes in which criminals file false income tax forms with stolen identities in order to obtain tax refunds.
Insider trading	The trading of securities or stocks by "insiders" with material, non-public information pertaining to significant, often market-moving developments to benefit themselves or others financially.
Insurance fraud	Fraudsters obtain insurance under false circumstances or file bogus or inflated claims.
Internet fraud	Fraud perpetrated over the internet, for example, via phishing or malware.
Internet pharmacy fraud	Online businesses that fill orders without prescriptions and sell drugs that may be expired, counterfeit, mislabeled, adulterated, or contaminated.
Investment fraud	Schemes in which investors in securities, stocks, commodities, real estate, or businesses are deceived and defrauded.
Jury duty scam	People claiming to be court officials call victims and threaten them with arrest for not reporting for jury duty. The perpetrators ask for personal information including a credit card number which they claim is for the purpose of paying a fine and avoiding arrest.
Letter of credit fraud	Legitimate letters of credit are issued by banks to ensure payment for goods shipped in international trade. Payment on a letter of credit generally requires that the paying bank receive documentation certifying that the goods ordered have been shipped and are en route to their intended destination. Con artists present fake letters of credit to banks to lure them to pay for goods that were not shipped or were inferior.
Lottery scams	Scam artists sell victims fake lottery tickets or notify victims they have won large amounts in foreign lotteries and request money to pay for taxes or fees.
Mass marketing fraud	Scams that exploit mass communication techniques like bulk mail, e-mail, or telemarketing.
Mortgage fraud	Material misstatements, misrepresentations, or omissions relating to real estate transactions; includes foreclosure rescue schemes, loan modification schemes, illegal property flipping, builder bailout/condo conversion, equity skimming, silent second, home equity conversion mortgage, bogus commercial real estate loans, and air loans (i.e., loans obtained by brokers for properties and applicants that do not actually exist).
Natural disaster fraud	Frauds perpetrated in the aftermath of natural disasters involving fake insurance claims or theft of government-provided assistance.
Nigerian letter or "419" fraud	An advance fee scheme in which a letter or e-mail from Nigeria offers the recipient the "opportunity" to share in a percentage of millions of dollars that the author—a self-proclaimed government official—is trying to transfer illegally out of Nigeria. The victim is asked to transmit bank information and pay "expenses" with fake promises of reimbursement.
Online auction fraud	Schemes designed to defraud sellers or buyers participating in online auctions.
Online auto auction fraud	Con artists offer vehicles for sale—often at below-market prices—on legitimate websites, but convince victims to conclude the transactions at other websites controlled by the criminals. The victims are often convinced to purchase buyer protection plans and instructed to wire funds to the fake sellers.
Online dating scams	Con artists establish relationships through online dating sites and then ask for money from unsuspecting victims.
Online rental housing scheme	Online scheme in which victims prepay for rental or vacation housing not actually owned by the individuals pretending to be the owners.
Phishing	Victims receive faked e-mails that appear to be from their banks or other trusted institutions and are designed to con them into providing personal information (PINs, social security numbers, credit card information, etc.).
Ponzi schemes	"Ponzi" schemes promise high financial returns or dividends not available through traditional investments. Instead of investing the funds of victims, however, the con artist pays "dividends" to initial investors using the funds of subsequent investors. The scheme generally falls apart when the operator flees with all of the proceeds or when a sufficient number of new investors cannot be found to allow the continued payment of "dividends."
Prime bank note fraud	An investment scheme that supposedly offers extremely high yields in a relatively short period of time. The con artists claim to have access to "bank guarantees" that they can buy at a discount and sell at a premium.

(12,541), tax law violations (1,125), and counterfeiting (795). Figure 2.2 in Chapter 2 shows that 11,000 to 14,000 defendants per year were involved in fraud cases filed in federal courts between FYs 1994 and 2012, making fraud the most commonly prosecuted white-collar crime at the federal level.

TABLE 5.1

White collar crimes [CONTINUED]

Fraud	Description and/or examples
Pump-and-dump stock scheme	Con artists hype a small company with little actual worth. Unsuspecting investors purchase the stock in droves, pumping up the price. But when the fraudsters behind the scheme sell their shares at the peak price and stop hyping the stock, the price plummets, and innocent investors lose their money.
Pyramid schemes	Marketing and investment frauds in which an individual is offered a distributorship or franchise to market a particular product. The real profit is earned, not by the sale of the product, but by the sale of new distributorships. Emphasis on selling franchises rather than the product eventually leads to a point where the supply of potential investors is exhausted and the pyramid collapses.
Ransomware	Malware that causes the victim's computer to lock up, and the monitor to display a message claiming to be from the FBI or other authority stating there has been a violation of federal law, for example, viewing of child pornography. To unlock their computers, users are instructed to pay a fine using a prepaid money card service.
Redemption/strawman/bond fraud	Con artists claim that the U.S. government or the Treasury Department control bank accounts—often referred to as "U.S. Treasury Direct Accounts"—for all U.S. citizens that can be accessed by submitting the appropriate paperwork to state and federal authorities. Individuals promoting this scam often charge large fees for "kits" that teach individuals how to perpetrate this scheme.
Reverse mortgage scams	Scams engineered by unscrupulous professionals in real estate, financial services, and related companies to steal the equity from the property of unsuspecting senior citizens or to use these seniors to unwittingly aid the fraudsters in stealing equity from a flipped property.
Scareware	Faked pop-up messages appear on computers telling users they have a computer virus and must buy antivirus software to solve the problem.
Securities and commodities fraud	Schemes involving the purchase and selling of securities, such as stock, and commodities.
Senior citizen fraud	Scams that target senior citizens.
Smishing	Criminals set up an automated dialing system to text or call people in a particular region or area code (or sometimes they use stolen customer phone numbers from banks or credit unions). The victims receive messages like: "There's a problem with your account," or "Your ATM card needs to be reactivated," and are directed to a phone number or website asking for personal information.
Social Security card fraud	These crimes typically involve falsified social security cards that can be used by illegal aliens or for other criminal purposes.
Spear phishing	A type of "phishing" in which con artists target a group of people with something in common, such as membership in a particular organization. The phishing e-mails appear to come from a legitimate organization with which the targeted individuals are familiar.
Sports memorabilia fraud	Fraud committed by forgers and counterfeiters who prey on sports fans and try to sell them faked memorabilia, such as baseballs with forged signatures of famous players.
Staged auto accident fraud	Frauds in which con artists purposely cause unsuspecting drivers to crash into cars driven by the con artists so they can file bogus and inflated insurance claims against the innocent drivers' insurance companies.
Stock options backdating	Company executives look back over their company's stock performance and pick a low point on the stock chart to set the options price, thereby boosting the value of the options—and the executive's portfolio. When the practice isn't documented in financial statements, it amounts to fraud.
Surrogacy scam	Con artists take advantage of couples who desperately want children by offering them seemingly legitimate surrogacy situations in exchange for money.
Telemarketing fraud	Frauds in which con artists use telecommunications systems to contact victims.
Telephone denial of service fraud	Using automated dialing programs, crooks flood victims' phone lines with multiple calls. While the lines are tied up, the criminals—masquerading as the victims themselves—raid the victims' bank accounts and online trading or other money management accounts.
Timeshare schemes	Victims—mostly owners trying to sell—are scammed by criminals posing as representatives of timeshare resale companies or by actual employees of companies that are committing fraud.
Vishing	A type of "phishing" in which con artists target victims with Voice Over Internet Protocol, or VoIP, which enables telephone calls to be made over the internet.
Work-at-home scams	Con artists recruit victims for supposed work-at-home jobs that require payment of a fee up front. In another scam "mystery shoppers" are sent a check and told to shop for certain items and send them to the con artists. The ruse continues until the check bounces.

ATM = automated teller machine.
PIN = personal identification number.

SOURCE: Adapted from "Frauds from A to Z," in *Scams and Safety*, U.S. Department of Justice, Federal Bureau of Investigation, 2014, http://www.fbi.gov/scams-safety/frauds-from-a-to-z (accessed November 6, 2014) and "Major Threats & Programs," in *White-Collar Crime*, U.S. Department of Justice, Federal Bureau of Investigation, 2014, http://www.fbi.gov/about-us/investigate/white_collar/whitecollarcrime (accessed November 6, 2014)

The FBI's Uniform Crime Reporting (UCR) Program gathers crime data from local law enforcement agencies throughout the country and publishes selected data in an annual report. Arrest data for 2013 are provided in *Crime in the United States, 2013* (November 2014, http://www.fbi.gov/about-us/cjis/ucr/crime-in-the-u.s/2013/crime-in-the-u.s.-2013/tables/table-29/table_29_estimated_number_of_arrests_united_states_2013.xls). The UCR Program provides 2013 arrest data for only three crime types widely considered white-collar crimes:

• Fraud—143,528 arrests

• Forgery and counterfeiting—60,969 arrests

• Embezzlement—15,730 arrests

The FBI (http://www.fbi.gov/about-us/cjis/ucr/crime-in-the-u.s/2013/crime-in-the-u.s.-2013/resource-pages/ offense-definitions/13-offensedefinitions_final) defines these crimes as:

• Fraud—"The intentional perversion of the truth for the purpose of inducing another person or other entity in reliance upon it to part with something of value or to surrender a legal right. Fraudulent conversion and obtaining of money or property by false pretenses. Confidence games and bad checks, except forgeries and counterfeiting, are included."

• Forgery and counterfeiting—"The altering, copying, or imitating of something, without authority or right, with the intent to deceive or defraud by passing the copy or thing altered or imitated as that which is original or genuine; or the selling, buying, or possession of an altered, copied, or imitated thing with the intent to deceive or defraud. Attempts are included."

- Embezzlement—"The unlawful misappropriation or misapplication by an offender to his/her own use or purpose of money, property, or some other thing of value entrusted to his/her care, custody, or control."

According to the UCR Program, there were 11.3 million total arrests in 2013; thus, arrests for these three white-collar crimes made up only a very small portion (about 2%) of the total arrests.

IDENTITY THEFT

One of the most pervasive white-collar crimes is identity theft, which is defined in various terms in federal and state law. In general, identity thieves steal personal information from victims, such as their Social Security, driver's license, credit card, or other identification numbers, and then set up new bank or credit card accounts or otherwise misrepresent themselves as their victims to obtain money, goods, or services fraudulently.

Identity thievery is accomplished in various ways. In some cases the thieves steal or find (for example, in the garbage) paper records containing the information they seek. Since the late 20th century more and more financial transactions are handled remotely using cellular phones, computers, and the Internet. Perpetrators may steal phones, tablets, or computers to obtain stored identity information or hack (digitally access without permission) these devices or the computer networks used to transfer or store sensitive data. In addition, identity thieves may use trickery and deception to get people to voluntarily provide identifying information to them, for example, through phone calls, e-mail, or over the Internet.

Data Breaches

Since the 1990s well-organized rings of identity thieves have emerged that engage in large-scale thefts known as data breaches. These are crimes in which the computer records of businesses, government agencies, universities, or other organizations are breached for the purpose of obtaining the personal and/or financial data of large numbers of people. Large-scale data breaches first gained public attention in 2005, when thieves stole the financial records of approximately 163,000 consumers from the computer systems of Choicepoint, Inc. The company notified California consumers about the breach in accordance with a 2003 law requiring companies to alert individuals whose data records have been stolen. Since that time other large data breaches have prompted many states to pass similar legislation.

The Privacy Rights Clearinghouse (PRC; https://www.privacyrights.org) is a California-based organization that educates consumers about personal privacy issues. One of its projects is an onsite listing (http://www.privacyrights.org/data-breach/new) of data breaches arranged chronologically by year. The organization learns about the

breaches through publicly released information, for example, media stories. The PRC notes that identity thieves gain large-scale access to personal information through five means:

- Unintended data releases, for example, information mistakenly posted on a company website

- Data accessed by computer hackers or perpetrators using malware or other computer applications

- Direct card access. One method used by thieves is called skimming. They secretly install devices that look like authentic card readers at banks or other businesses. Users unknowingly swipe their credit or debit cards in these devices, which provide the thieves with personal information taken from the cards.

- Insider access. This involves company employees or other insiders accessing data for illicit purposes.

- Access via lost, stolen, or improperly disposed of paper records, computers, or data storage devices containing sensitive information

As of January 2015, the PRC website listed 4,478 known data breaches that had occurred since 2005 that involved the possible release of personal information, and in some cases financial data, for hundreds of millions of individuals.

Identity Theft in Tax Refund Fraud

During the 21st century the Internal Revenue Service (IRS) has seen a huge increase in income tax fraud facilitated by identity theft. In "With Personal Data in Hand, Thieves File Early and Often" (NYTimes.com, May 26, 2012), Lizette Alvarez notes that fraudsters use stolen identities to file false tax returns with the IRS showing that refunds are due to the filers. The scam costs taxpayers hundreds of millions of dollars each year. According to Alvarez, in May 2012 an IRS official told Congress that the agency detected 940,000 fake 2010 income tax returns whose filers would have received refunds totaling $6.5 billion. Regardless, the IRS failed to catch another 1.5 million possibly fraudulent returns that reaped refunds totaling more than $5.2 billion. As shown in Figure 5.1, identity thieves carrying out the scheme typically file tax returns early in the filing season and obtain refunds before returns are filed by the legitimate owners of the stolen names and Social Security numbers. The legitimate returns are subsequently rejected by the IRS system as duplicate returns. This is the point at which many legitimate tax filers first learn that their identities have been stolen.

David Adams indicates in "Florida Hit by 'Tsunami' of Tax Identity Fraud" (Reuters, February 17, 2013), that the number of tax identity theft cases identified by the Treasury Department soared from 48,000 in 2008 to more

FIGURE 5.1

Methods by which the Internal Revenue Service (IRS) detects identity theft refund fraud

Example: Identity theft (IDT) refund fraud IRS detects after a duplicate return is filed

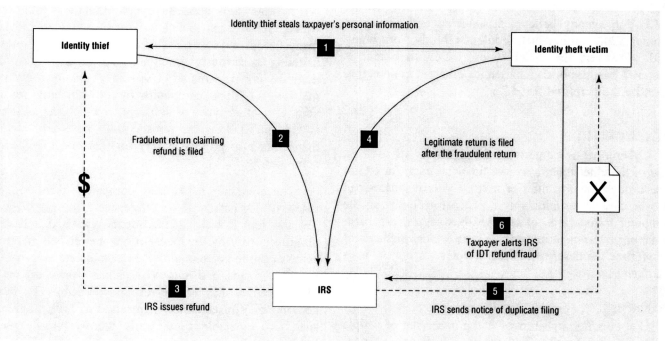

Example: IDT refund fraud IRS detects during information return matching

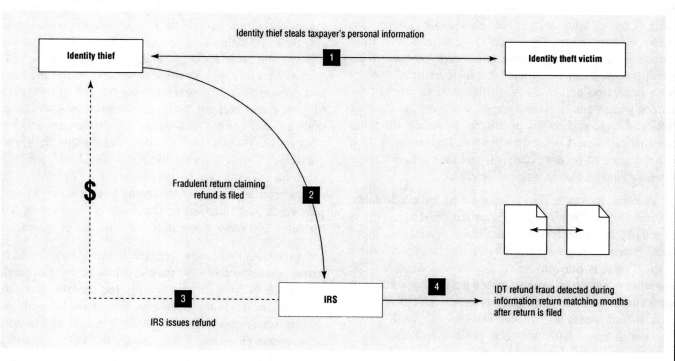

Notes: Numbers represent the order in which these actions occur in the examples.

SOURCE: "Figure 2. Examples of Identity Theft Refund Fraud that IRS Detects," in *Identity Theft: Additional Actions Could Help IRS Combat the Large, Evolving Threat of Refund Fraud*, U.S. Government Accountability Office, August 2014, http://www.gao.gov/assets/670/665368.pdf (accessed November 3, 2014)

than 1.2 million in 2012. In *Identity Theft: Additional Actions Could Help IRS Combat the Large, Evolving Threat of Refund Fraud* (August 2014, http://www.gao .gov/assets/670/665368.pdf), the U.S. Government Accountability Office (GAO) notes that the IRS estimates it paid $5.2 billion in fraudulent identity theft refunds during 2013. The agency believes it detected and prevented another $24.2 billion in fraudulent refunds from being paid. However, the GAO states, "the full extent is unknown because of the challenges inherent in detecting [identity theft] refund fraud."

CYBERCRIME

Cybercrime is perpetrated for a variety of reasons. One of the chief motivations is financial gain, for example, through identity theft or fraud. Cyber resources can also be used by criminals as a means for disrupting the computer transactions of targeted businesses, organizations, or government agencies. Three typical methods of cybercrime are described in this chapter: deception, malware, and hacking.

Deception

One common cybercrime is the deceiving of people online into voluntarily divulging their personal or financial information or turning over their money. One type of traditional white-collar crime is called a confidence game. People who engage in confidence games are known as con artists. They gain the confidence of their victims by establishing a personal and/or business relationship with them and then take their victims' money using deception and trickery. In the modern world confidence games can be easily perpetrated over the Internet thanks in large part to the popularity of online shopping and auction sites. Con artists pose as legitimate sellers, gain the trust of potential buyers, and then take payment for merchandise that is never delivered.

Another means of deception used by cybercriminals, particularly for identity theft, is called phishing. This is an activity in which Internet fraudsters impersonate legitimate businesses, government agencies, or organizations to trick victims into providing desired information. The anonymous nature of Internet-based transactions makes it particularly easy for criminals to create deceptive websites, e-mail messages, or text messages through which they can interact with potential victims and trick them into turning over information and/or money.

Criminals engaged in Internet fraud may also use spam as a means to find potential victims. Spam refers to unsolicited bulk e-mail. The e-mails are unsolicited because the recipients have not chosen to receive the messages. Generally, spam involves simultaneously sending identical e-mail messages to large numbers of e-mail accounts. Spam e-mails containing a phishing ploy, for example, could be sent to many thousands of individuals in the hope that at least a few of the recipients will fall for the scam.

Malware

Another tool used by cybercriminals is malware, which is short for malicious software. Malware takes many forms, and its effects can range from being mildly irritating to seriously damaging, depending on how the malware is programmed. Users may unknowingly put malware on their computers by downloading music, games, or other types of software in which the malware is hidden. Clicking on website links or e-mail attachments can also provide a way for malware to access a computer.

The computer networking company Cisco Systems notes in "What Is the Difference: Viruses, Worms, Trojans, and Bots?" (2014, http://www.cisco.com/web/ about/security/intelligence/virus-worm-diffs.html) that some of the most common types of malware are viruses, worms, Trojans, and bots. Viruses and worms are capable of replicating themselves and spreading to other computers. Viruses attach themselves to host programs, such as executable files, while worms operate more independently. By contrast, Trojans cannot replicate themselves. In addition, they are malware programs that appear to be legitimate. They get their name from a legendary story in which Greek soldiers constructed and then hid within a huge wooden horse. Their enemies mistook the horse for a gift and pulled it inside the walls of the city of Troy. The soldiers secretly exited the horse and opened the city gates, allowing the rest of their army to invade and conquer Troy. In a similar manner Trojan malware can open "back doors" to computers and networks that allow criminals to use them for their own purposes. Cisco Systems indicates that bots (which is short for robots) can be programmed to conduct automated processes, such as recording keystrokes, gathering passwords and financial information, or interacting with websites and other computers for criminal purposes.

Individual malware programs often have colorful names given to them by their creators or by the people who work to discover and destroy the harmful software. In addition, malware programs are often lumped into descriptive categories based on their means of operation or intended purposes. For example, the term *spyware* is broadly used to refer to malware that secretly collects information about a computer user. Likewise, *hijackers* are computer programs that allow criminals to seize control of others' computers for their own purposes. Malware classifications are not always mutually exclusive. For example, a Trojan or other piece of malware could conduct both spying and hijacking. The Daprosy worm, first reported in 2009, is an example of a keylogger. It monitors whatever is typed on the keyboard of an infected computer, and sends reports of this information to its originator. In this manner the malware's creator can gain access to Internet usernames, passwords, and other sensitive information.

In the press release "Three Alleged International Cyber Criminals Responsible for Creating and Distributing Virus That Infected over One Million Computers and Caused Tens of Millions of Dollars in Losses Charged in Manhattan Federal Court" (January 23, 2013, http://www.justice.gov/usao/nys/pressreleases/January13/GoziVirusPR.php?print=1), the DOJ notes that in January 2013 it secured indictments against three individuals accused of creating and distributing the Gozi virus, which infected more than 1 million computers and caused financial losses in the tens of millions of dollars. The agency calls the virus "one of the most financially destructive computer viruses in history." The virus was discovered and named in 2007 by security experts in the United States. Approximately 40,000 computers in the United States were infected, including computers used by individuals, businesses, and government agencies, such as the National Aeronautics and Space Administration. The virus collected personal bank account information from infected computers. It also created false bank websites that tricked users into voluntarily providing personal and financial information. The perpetrators allegedly used the information to steal money from bank accounts throughout the world. The DOJ notes that the virus was "virtually undetectable" by virus prevention software.

Hacking

Criminals that are particularly savvy in computer programming may engage in hacking (i.e., gaining unauthorized access to computers by identifying and exploiting system vulnerabilities). Criminal hackers use their expertise to crack passwords and security codes in order to access stored information or hijack computers (i.e., take control of computers and instruct them to perform certain tasks).

In "The Great Cyberheist" (NYTimes.com, November 10, 2010), James Verini details the life and crimes of Albert Gonzalez (1981–), who is considered to be the most financially successful hacker in U.S. history. Gonzalez was first arrested in 2003 and became an informant for the federal government to help the U.S. Secret Service capture top members of the Shadowcrew, a semiorganized group of sophisticated cybercriminals. However, Gonzalez secretly continued his own hacking career. He masterminded schemes for breaching corporate computer systems and gained access to millions of credit and debit card account numbers. In 2008 the FBI arrested Gonzalez on multiple charges. He pleaded guilty and in March 2010 was sentenced to 20 years in prison. Verini notes

that Gonzalez's crimes allegedly cost the victimized corporations more than $400 million in losses.

Some cybercriminals use hacking not for direct financial gain but to damage or disrupt the operations of computers used by others, particularly businesses or government agencies. These attacks may be designed to impose economic losses on the targets or to punish them for perceived wrongs. The hackers may claim responsibility online or through media outlets for their actions using assumed names to hide their actual identities. In late November 2014 the Sony Pictures Entertainment corporation suffered a large-scale hack attack. In "Sony Hack: Signs Point to North Korea" (CNN.com, December 5, 2014), Jose Pagliery indicates that security analysts suspect the hackers might be North Korean because of similarities to 2013 attacks on South Korean companies. In addition, the Sony hack occurred only weeks before the company was set to release *The Interview*, a comedy film with a plot involving the assassination of North Korean leader Kim Jong-Un (1983–). As a result, revenge is strongly suspected as the motive in the attack. Pagliery states, "The Sony Pictures hack was purely about destroying information and embarrassing the company. Hackers stole movie scripts, entire films, internal memos and personal information on movie stars and Sony employees. Then they wiped computers."

FEDERAL COMPUTER CRIME LEGISLATION. In 1986 Congress passed the Computer Fraud and Abuse Act (CFAA), which makes it illegal to perpetrate fraud on a computer. This law was followed in 1994 by the Computer Abuse Amendments Act, which makes it a federal crime "through means of a computer used in interstate commerce or communications... [to] damage, or cause damage to, a computer, computer system, network, information, data, or program... with reckless disregard" for the consequences of these actions to the computer owner. Robert Tappan Morris (1965–) was the first person ever to be charged under the CFAA. In 1988 Morris allegedly released the first-known computer worm on the Internet. He did not serve prison time but was put on probation for his crime and had to perform community service and pay a fine. As of January 2015, Morris was a computer science professor at the Massachusetts Institute of Technology.

The 2001 Uniting and Strengthening America by Providing Appropriate Tools Required to Intercept and Obstruct Terrorism (USA PATRIOT) Act, which gave increased powers to U.S. law enforcement and intelligence agencies to help prevent terrorist attacks, amended the CFAA. The act was expanded to include the types of electronic records that law enforcement authorities may obtain without a subpoena, including records of Internet session times and durations, as well as temporarily assigned network addresses. The PATRIOT Act was reauthorized in 2006 and again in 2010.

The Controlling the Assault of Non-Solicited Pornography and Marketing (CAN-SPAM) Act of 2003 established requirements for those who send commercial e-mail. CAN-SPAM requires that all spam contain a legitimate return address as well as instructions on how to opt out of receiving additional spam from the sender. Spam must also state in the subject line if the e-mail is pornographic in nature. Violators of these rules are subject to heavy fines.

The law's main provisions include:

- Banning false or misleading header information—the "from," "to," and routing information (including the originating name and e-mail address) must be accurate and identify the person who initiated the e-mail.

- Prohibiting deceptive subject lines—the subject line must not mislead the recipient about the e-mail's content or subject matter.

- Requiring an opt-out method—senders must provide a return e-mail address or another Internet-based way that allows the recipient to ask the sender not to send any more e-mail messages to him or her.

The first person convicted by a jury in a CAN-SPAM case was Jeffrey Brett Goodin (1961–) of California. He was found guilty in January 2007 of operating an Internet-based scheme to obtain personal and credit card information. Goodin sent e-mails to AOL users that appeared to be from AOL's billing department. The messages, which instructed recipients to update their AOL billing information or lose service, referred users to web pages that were actually scam pages set up by Goodin to collect the users' personal and credit card information. Goodin was sentenced to 70 months in federal prison and released in November 2011.

Some states have also enacted cybercrime legislation. For example, California's Consumer Protection against Computer Spyware Act makes it illegal for anyone to install software on someone else's computer deceptively and use it to modify settings, including the user's home page, default search page, or bookmarks. The act also outlaws collecting, through intentionally deceptive means, personally identifiable information by logging keystrokes, tracking website visits, or extracting personal information from a user's hard drive.

INTELLECTUAL PROPERTY CRIMES

According to the World Intellectual Property Organization (2014, http://www.wipo.int/about-ip/en), intellectual property consists of "creations of the mind, such as inventions; literary and artistic works; designs; and symbols, names and images used in commerce." These include industrial property such as trademarks, chemical formulas, patents, and designs, and copyrighted material such as literary works, films, musical compositions and recordings, graphic and architectural designs, works of art in any medium, and domain names.

In the United States intellectual property is protected by the joint efforts of the U.S. Patent and Trademark Office, the U.S. Copyright Office, the DOJ's Computer Crime and Intellectual Property Section (CCIPS), the U.S. Department of Commerce, and two agencies that focus on international aspects of intellectual property: U.S. Customs and Border Protection, which monitors incoming goods arriving from other nations, and the Office of the U.S. Trade Representative, which negotiates on behalf of U.S. interests and develops and implements trade agreements and policies.

Intellectual property fraud takes many forms. A scan of 2015 CCIPS press releases (2015, http://www.justice.gov/criminal/cybercrime/press-releases/2015.html) reveals many releases concerning counterfeiting of copyright-protected merchandise. The U.S. Patent and Trademark Office in "Scam Prevention" (November 7, 2014, http://www.uspto.gov/inventors/scam_prevention/index.jsp#heading-1) warns inventors to be wary of scams perpetrated by individuals or firms pretending to be invention promoters. The fraudsters may charge inventors large up-front fees and promise to research, develop, and promote their inventions, but do not actually provide these services. The agency notes that the American Inventors Protection Act of 1999 requires invention promoters to disclose to potential customers certain information about their operations and past clients, such as the total number of customers that the promoter knows received a "net financial profit as a direct result of the invention promotion services" provided by the promoter. In "Be Aware of Trademark and Patent Scams" (NatLawReview.com, October 15, 2011), Monica Riva Talley of the Washington, D.C., law firm Sterne, Kessler, Goldstein & Fox P.L.L.C. warns holders of patents and trademarks not to fall prey to e-mails and letters that appear to be from government agencies and illegally solicit fees for various services related to intellectual property.

COUNTERFEITING MONEY

Making counterfeit U.S. currency or altering genuine currency to increase its value is punishable by a fine, imprisonment, or both. Possession of counterfeit U.S. currency is also a crime, as is manufacturing counterfeit U.S. coins.

In response to the growing use of computer-generated counterfeit paper money, the Treasury Department began redesigning currency notes; for example, a watermark was added to notes of higher denominations to make them harder to copy accurately. According to the Bureau of Engraving and Printing in "Currency Redesign" (2014, http://www.newmoney.gov/currency/default.htm), another change in currency design was made in 2014 to add additional security features to the $100 bill. One of these features is a blue ribbon across the center of the bill including symbols that appear to change shape as the bill is tilted back and forth.

In "Know Your Money: Advanced Technologies in Counterfeiting" (2014, http://www.secretservice.gov/money_technologies.shtml), the Secret Service explains that many counterfeiters have abandoned the traditional method of offset printing, which requires specialized skills and machinery. Instead, counterfeiters produce fake currency with basic computer training and typical office equipment. The number of counterfeit notes in circulation is likely to increase because more people have access to the machines and methods that are required to produce them; however, the security features added to the design and manufacture of U.S. currency have also made it easier to detect bogus notes.

CORPORATE FRAUD AND SECURITIES FRAUD

Corporate fraud and securities (or investment) fraud are particularly troublesome because they can involve large numbers of victims and inflict high monetary losses. Two notable cases from the early 21st century demonstrate these principles.

Enron Corporation

The collapse of Enron Corporation is one of the most glaring examples of corporate crime and falsification of corporate data in recent history. Based in Houston, Texas, Enron was an energy broker that traded in electricity and other energy commodities. During the late 1990s, however, instead of simply brokering energy deals, Enron devised increasingly complex contracts with buyers and sellers that allowed Enron to profit from the difference in the selling price and the buying price of commodities such as electricity. Enron executives created a number of partnerships—in effect, companies that existed only on paper whose sole function was to hide debt and make Enron appear to be much more profitable than it actually was.

In December 2001 Enron filed for bankruptcy protection, listing some $13.1 billion in liabilities and $24.7 billion in assets—$38 billion less than the assets it claimed only two months earlier. As a result, thousands of Enron employees lost their jobs. In addition, many Enron staff—who had been encouraged by company executives to invest monies from their 401(k) retirement plans in Enron stock—had their retirement savings reduced to almost nothing as a result of the precipitous decline in value of Enron stock.

In the wake of Enron's collapse, several committees in the U.S. Senate and U.S. House of Representatives began to investigate whether Enron defrauded investors by deliberately concealing financial information. Many lawsuits were filed against Enron, its accounting firm

Arthur Andersen, and former Enron executives including the former chairman Kenneth L. Lay (1942–2006) and the former chief executive officer Jeffrey Skilling (1953–).

Enron treasurer Ben Glisan Jr. (1966–) was convicted of conspiracy charges to commit wire and securities fraud. He was sentenced to five years in prison and was released in January 2007. Lay and Skilling went on trial in January 2006. Kristen Hays reports in "Prosecutor: Lay, Skilling Committed Crimes" (Associated Press, May 16, 2006) that the federal prosecutor Kathryn H. Ruemmler (1971–) accused the men of using "accounting tricks, fiction, hocus-pocus, trickery, misleading statements, half-truths, omissions and outright lies" in committing their crimes. In May 2006 a jury found Lay guilty of all six counts against him in the corporate trial; he was also convicted of four counts of fraud in a separate trial relating to his personal finances. He faced 20 to 30 years in prison but died of a heart attack in July 2006, before the judge set his sentence. The jury found Skilling guilty of 19 of the 28 counts against him, and he was sentenced to 24 years and four months in federal prison. In "Ex-Enron CEO Skilling Has 10 Years Lopped off Sentence" (CNN.com, June 21, 2013), Aaron Smith reports that in 2013 Skilling's sentence was reduced by 10 years in exchange for his agreement "to stop challenging his conviction and forfeit roughly $42 million that will be distributed among the victims of the Enron fraud." As of January 2015, Skilling was serving his sentence at a federal minimum security prison in Alabama with an expected release date in February 2019.

Dozens of other people were also charged in the Enron scandal. In June 2002 the accounting firm Arthur Andersen was convicted of destroying Enron documents during an ongoing federal investigation of Enron's accounting practices. As a result of the verdict, Arthur Andersen faced a fine of $500,000 and a probation term of up to five years. In 2005 the U.S. Supreme Court overturned this conviction due to flaws in the instructions that had been given to the jury. However, the firm was effectively out of the accounting business, with its few remaining U.S. employees responsible for administrating the many legal cases generated by the scandal.

The Enron scandal helped lead to the passage of the Sarbanes-Oxley Act (SOX), which was signed into law in July 2002. The law was designed to rebuild public trust in the U.S. corporate sector by imposing new criminal and civil penalties for security violations and establishing a new certification system for internal audits. SOX also grants independent auditors more access to company data and requires increased disclosure of compensation methods and systems, especially for upper management.

Bernard Madoff's Ponzi Scheme

One of the most famous white-collar crimes in history was the enormous Ponzi scheme managed by Bernard

Madoff (1938–), an influential Wall Street executive who had served as the chairman of NASDAQ during the 1990s. At the time of Madoff's arrest, the U.S. Securities and Exchange Commission (SEC) reported in the press release "SEC Charges Bernard L. Madoff for Multi-billion Dollar Ponzi Scheme" (December 11, 2008, http://www.sec.gov/news/press/2008/2008-293.htm) that Madoff estimated the fraud losses to his victims to total "at least $50 billion."

Ponzi schemes are named after Charles Ponzi (1883–1949), an Italian immigrant who defrauded investors in Boston, Massachusetts, in the early 20th century. The victims of a Ponzi scheme are lured with promises of large, quick returns on their investments. Rather than generating legitimate profits, however, the swindler makes payments to his or her clients out of the funds that they and others have invested. If the swindler can convince enough people to continue investing large enough sums in the scheme, he or she can maintain the illusion of a legitimately profitable enterprise for years, all while diverting funds from his or her clients for personal use. However, this arrangement is inherently unstable. Eventually, circumstances will develop where the swindler is unable to give his or her clients the money that they expect and the scheme will be exposed (provided the swindler does not run off with all of the money first).

Madoff was the founder and chairman of Bernard L. Madoff Investment Securities LLC, a leading Wall Street firm established in 1960. Ruthie Ackerman indicates in "Market Maker Arrested in Ponzi Scheme He Estimated at $50B" (Forbes.com, December 11, 2008) that at the time of Madoff's arrest the firm claimed $700 million in capital and prided itself, according to its website, on the "unblemished record of value, fair-dealing, and high ethical standards that has always been the firm's hallmark." However, besides the investment firm, Madoff also conducted a side business as an investment adviser, kept multiple sets of books, maintained secrecy about his investments, and provided false reports of his activities to federal regulators and to his clients. In the press release "Statement Regarding Madoff Investigation" (December 16, 2008, http://www.sec.gov/news/press/2008/2008-297.htm), Christopher Cox (1952–), the chairman of the SEC, explains that Madoff's influence included an advisory role to the SEC, a relationship Madoff used to his advantage and one that led SEC staff to dismiss accusations against him that first came to their attention during the late 1990s.

When Madoff's list of clients was made public in early February 2009, it included thousands of institutions and individuals, including investment funds, pension funds, charitable organizations, financiers, Hollywood celebrities, and many private investors who expressed alarm at the sudden, unsought media exposure of their personal finances. In March 2009 Madoff pleaded guilty to 11 felony counts against him in federal court, including securities fraud, investment adviser fraud, mail fraud, wire fraud, money laundering, making false statements, perjury, filing false information with the SEC, and theft from an employee benefit plan. In June 2009 Madoff was sentenced to 150 years in prison. As of 2015 he was serving his sentence in a medium security federal prison in North Carolina.

PUBLIC CORRUPTION

The abuse of public trust may be found wherever the interest of individuals or businesses overlaps with government interest. It ranges from the health inspector who accepts a bribe from a restaurant owner or the police officer who "shakes down" a drug dealer, to the council member or legislator who accepts money to vote a certain way. These crimes are often difficult to uncover because typically few willing witnesses are available.

According to the DOJ in *Report to Congress on the Activities and Operations of the Public Integrity Section for 2013* (September 2014, http://www.justice.gov/criminal/pin/docs/2013-Annual-Report.pdf), the number of people convicted federally for offenses involving the abuse of public office has remained relatively stable since 2002, when it stood at 1,011. In 2013, 1,134 federal, state, and local officials and private citizens were indicted, and 1,037 were convicted, in public corruption cases.

Because public officials have sworn to uphold the law and to act in the interest of the communities they represent, their failure to do so is considered particularly reprehensible, and cases of public corruption often receive much media attention. Common public corruption charges include perjury (lying when one is legally required to tell the truth), obstruction of justice, and bribery. "Pay-to-play" is a form of bribery in which a public official demands benefits (often in the form of campaign contributions) in exchange for government appointments or contracts. Some notable public corruption cases in the 21st century have included:

- Kwame Kilpatrick (1970–): The former mayor of Detroit, Michigan, pleaded guilty to two felony counts of obstruction of justice and resigned from office as part of a September 2008 plea agreement. Two years later, while in prison, he was indicted by a federal grand jury and charged with committing racketeering (operating a criminal organization), bribery, extortion, and fraud while in office. He was convicted on 24 counts and sentenced to 28 years in prison.

- Rod R. Blagojevich (1956–): The former Illinois governor was impeached and removed from office in January 2009 following his arrest the previous month on federal charges of solicitation of bribery, mail fraud, and abuse of power. Later that year the federal charges were expanded in a 19-count indictment that included wire fraud, attempted extortion, and racketeering conspiracy, among other charges. In August 2010 Blagojevich was convicted of only one of the charges against him: making false statements to investigators. A mistrial was declared for the other charges against him. In 2011 he was retried and convicted of multiple charges, including wire fraud, attempted extortion, and bribery. Blagojevich was sentenced to 14 years in prison and fined more than $20,000.

- Jesse Jackson Jr. (1965–; D-IL): In February 2013 former Representative Jesse Jackson Jr., the son of the civil rights leader and politician Jesse Jackson (1941–), was charged with misusing hundreds of thousands of dollars in campaign funds. Later that month he pleaded guilty to the charges and was sentenced to two and a half years in prison.

VICTIMIZATION SURVEYS AND COMPLAINT CENTERS

Information about the prevalence of white-collar crime can be gleaned from victim surveys and complaint centers operated by various government and private organizations. The results reflect the observations of participants about events that happened to them or their households. It should be noted that not all of these events necessarily rise to the level of criminality. In addition, organizations use different terms to refer to events that might legally be deemed white-collar crimes; for example, they might define identity theft in different ways.

National White Collar Crime Center

The National White Collar Crime Center (NW3C) is a congressionally funded nonprofit corporation whose members are involved in the investigation and enforcement of laws dealing with white-collar crime. Every five years the NW3C conducts a national survey in which the participants are asked if they or their households have experienced specific events during the previous 12 months. As of December 2014 the most recent survey results were published in 2010 and presented by Rodney Huff, Christian Desilets, and John Kane in *The 2010 National Public Survey on White Collar Crime* (December 2010, http://www.nw3c.org/docs/publications/2010-national-public-survey-on-white-collar-crime.pdf?sfvrsn=8).

During the survey the participants were asked questions intended to discern if any of eight specific victimizations had occurred:

- Credit card fraud
- False stockbroker information
- Fraudulent business venture
- Identity theft

- Monetary loss (Internet)
- Mortgage fraud
- Price misrepresentation
- Unnecessary repairs

For example, the question involving identity theft read as follows: "In the last 12 months, has someone in your household discovered that their personal information had been used by someone else to obtain new credit cards or accounts without permission?"

Overall, 24% of households and 17% of individuals reported they had been victimized during the previous year. The most common household victimizations were credit card fraud (39.6%), being misled about the price of a product or service (28.1%), paying for unnecessary repairs (22.3%), monetary losses due to Internet fraud (15.8%), and identity theft (12.2%). Of the households that experienced a victimization, 54.7% reported the incident to at least one organization (such as a credit card company, business, or personal attorney), including 18.8% that reported it to the police. The types of incidents most commonly reported to law enforcement by individuals were false stockbroker information (56.3%), identity theft (46.6%), and mortgage fraud (42.9%).

National Crime Victimization Survey

As noted in Chapter 3, the BJS performs a detailed examination of U.S. crime victims through its National Crime Victimization Survey (NCVS). This annual survey measures the levels of victimization resulting from specific criminal acts. The data collected are extrapolated to the entire U.S. population to provide estimates of criminal victimization at the national level.

TRENDS FROM 2005 THROUGH 2010. In *Identity Theft Reported by Households, 2005–2010* (November 2011, http://www.bjs.gov/content/pub/pdf/itrh0510.pdf), Lynn Langton of the BJS notes that the agency first added questions about identity theft to the NCVS survey in 2004. However, data are only available for several months for 2004 and 2008; thus, Langton presents and discusses data only for 2005 through 2007 and for 2009 through 2010.

According to Langton, the NCVS defines identity theft as "the unauthorized use or attempted misuse of an existing credit card or other existing account, the misuse of personal information to open a new account or for another fraudulent purpose, or a combination of these types of misuse."

Based on the survey results, an estimated 8.6 million U.S. households experienced identity theft in 2010, representing 7% of all U.S. households. The latter value is up from 5.5% in 2005. More than half (54%) of the victimized households in 2010 experienced unauthorized

TABLE 5.2

Victims age 16 or older who experienced at least one identity theft incident during the previous year, by type of theft, 2012

Type of identity theft	Anytime during the past 12 months[a]		Most recent incident[b]		
	Number of victims	Percent of all persons	Number of victims	Percent of all persons	Percent of all victims
Total	16,580,500	6.7%	16,580,500	6.7%	100%
Existing account	15,323,500	6.2%	14,022,100	5.7%	84.6%
Credit card	7,698,500	3.1	6,676,300	2.7	40.3
Bank	7,470,700	3.0	6,191,500	2.5	37.3
Other	1,696,400	0.7	1,154,300	0.5	7.0
New account	1,125,100	0.5%	683,400	0.3%	4.1%
Personal information	833,600	0.3%	622,900	0.3%	3.8%
Multiple types	—	—	1,252,000	0.5%	7.6%
Existing account[b]	—	—	824,700	0.3	5.0
Other[c]	—	—	427,400	0.2	2.6

—Not applicable.
[a]Identity theft classified as a single type.
[b]Includes victims who experienced two or more of the following: unauthorized use of a credit card, bank account, or other existing account.
[c]Includes victims who experienced two or more of the following: unauthorized use of an existing account, misuse of personal information to open a new account, or misuse of personal information for other fraudulent purposes.
Note: Detail may not sum to total due to victims who reported multiple incidents of identity theft and rounding.

SOURCE: Erika Harrell and Lynn Langton, "Table 1. Persons Age 16 of Older Who Experienced at Least One Identity Theft Incident in the Past 12 Months, by Type of Theft, 2012," in *Victims of Identity Theft, 2012*, U.S. Department of Justice, Office of Justice Programs, Bureau of Justice Statistics, December 2013, http://www.bjs.gov/content/pub/pdf/vit12.pdf (accessed November 3, 2014)

use or attempted misuse of an existing credit card. Just over a quarter (25.6%) of the victimized households reported unauthorized use or attempted misuse of some other existing account, and 9% reported misuse of their personal information for fraudulent purposes. In addition, 11.4% reported being victimized through multiple types of identity theft. The overall financial losses were estimated at $13.3 billion.

In both 2005 and 2010 high-income households (i.e., those with annual incomes of $75,000 or more) were more likely to be victimized than lower-income households. Urban and suburban dwellers were victimized by identity theft more than rural dwellers. Lastly, households containing six or more people were more likely than smaller households to be victimized.

RESULTS FROM THE 2012 SURVEY. In *Victims of Identity Theft, 2012* (December 2013, http://www.bjs.gov/content/pub/pdf/vit12.pdf), Erika Harrell and Langton summarize identity theft data collected during the 2012 NCVS. As shown in Table 5.2 nearly 16.6 million people aged 16 years and older were believed victimized during the previous year. This represents 6.7% of the total population within that age group. Most of the victims (15.3 million) had experienced unauthorized use or attempted use of an existing account, such as a credit card or bank account.

The financial impact of the identity theft incidents in 2012 was enormous, with the total loss estimated at $24.7 billion. (See Table 5.3.) This includes both direct and indirect losses. Harrell and Langton define a direct loss as "the monetary amount the offender obtained from misusing the victim's account or personal information, including the estimated value of goods, services, or cash

TABLE 5.3

Mean, median, and total losses attributed to identity theft and property crime, 2012

	Mean	Median	Total (in thousands)
Identity theft[a]	$2,183	$300	$24,696,300
Property crime[b]	$915	$150	$13,991,700
Burglary	2,378	600	5,234,800
Motor vehicle theft	7,963	4,000	3,079,900
Theft	447	100	5,677,000

[a]Based on 11.3 million persons 16 or older who experienced one or more incidents of identity theft with known losses of $1 or more.
[b]Based on 15.3 million household property crimes, 2.2 million burglaries, 400,000 motor vehicle thefts, and 12.7 million household thefts with known losses of $1 or more. In 2012, 19% of completed burglaries had unknown loss amounts.

SOURCE: Erika Harrell and Lynn Langton, "Table 4. Mean, Median, and Total Losses Attributed to Identity Theft and Property Crime, 2012," in *Victims of Identity Theft, 2012*, U.S. Department of Justice, Office of Justice Programs, Bureau of Justice Statistics, December 2013, http://www.bjs.gov/content/pub/pdf/vit12.pdf (accessed November 3, 2014)

obtained." Indirect losses include victim expenses such as fees, e.g., bank fees for bounced checks. (Note that victims may have been reimbursed for some or all of the direct and indirect financial losses resulting from the identity theft incidents.) Table 5.3 includes estimates for the mean (average) and median total loss amounts for the 11.3 million people who experienced one or more incidents with known losses of at least $1. The mean loss was $2,183, and the median loss was $300, meaning that half of the losses were greater than $300 and half were less than $300. As shown in Table 5.3, the total identity theft loss in 2012 was much higher than the losses associated with property crimes, such as burglary, motor vehicle thefts, and other thefts.

FIGURE 5.2

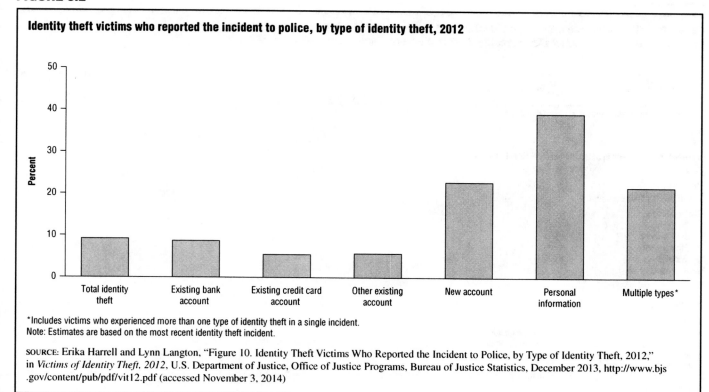

Identity theft victims who reported the incident to police, by type of identity theft, 2012

*Includes victims who experienced more than one type of identity theft in a single incident.
Note: Estimates are based on the most recent identity theft incident.

SOURCE: Erika Harrell and Lynn Langton, "Figure 10. Identity Theft Victims Who Reported the Incident to Police, by Type of Identity Theft, 2012," in *Victims of Identity Theft, 2012*, U.S. Department of Justice, Office of Justice Programs, Bureau of Justice Statistics, December 2013, http://www.bjs.gov/content/pub/pdf/vit12.pdf (accessed November 3, 2014)

The survey indicates that less than 10% of identity theft victims in 2012 reported the incidents to police. (See Figure 5.2.) Those who suffered personal information fraud were far more likely to file a report than victims of other types of identity theft.

During the 2012 NCVS, participants were asked if they had ever experienced identity theft "at any point in their lives." Overall, the results indicate that an estimated 34.2 million people aged 16 years and older had been victimized. (See Table 5.4.) This number represents 13.9% of the total population in that age group. As of 2012, 7.8% of the victims still had "unresolved problems" relating to their victimizations.

Consumer Sentinel Network

The Federal Trade Commission (FTC) operates a complaint database known as the Consumer Sentinel Network (CSN) that compiles consumer complaints about identity theft, consumer fraud, and related offenses. The data are made available to law enforcement agencies, such as the FBI, to assist in their investigations of white-collar crimes. The FTC publishes an annual report that summarizes CSN data collected within the previous year. According to the FTC in *Consumer Sentinel Network Data Book for January–December 2013* (February 2014, http://www.ftc.gov/system/files/documents/reports/consumer-sentinel-network-data-book-january-december-2013/sentinel-cy2013.pdf), the CSN compiles complaints that are filed with the FTC and other federal and state

agencies and private organizations (such as the Council of Better Business Bureaus) in North America.

Table 5.5 shows the number of complaints that were registered each year between 2001 and 2013. In 2012 and 2013 the CSN received 2.1 million complaints per year, the highest numbers ever recorded. More than half of the complaints in each year involved fraud. Table 5.6 lists the top-20 complaint categories processed by the CSN during 2013. Identity theft (14%) was the most prevalent complaint. It was followed by complaints about debt collection (10%), and complaints about banks and lenders (7%).

FRAUD VICTIMS. The CSN notes that 61% of the fraud complaints it received in 2013 identified the monetary amount paid by the victims to the fraudsters. The total involved was more than $1.6 billion. In addition, 48% of the complainants identified the method by which they were contacted by fraudsters. The breakdown by method was telephone (40%), e-mail (33%), the Internet, for example, websites (15%), and mail (5%). The remaining 7% of contacts were by other means.

IDENTITY THEFT VICTIMS. As reported in the *Consumer Sentinel Network Data Book for January–December 2013*, misuse of government documents or benefits was reported by 33.9% of identity theft complainants during 2013. (See Table 5.7.) Thieves used stolen identities to file fraudulent tax returns or to apply for or obtain government benefits or documents, such as driver's licenses or Social Security cards. Another significant type of identity theft

TABLE 5.4

Victims age 16 or older who experienced identity theft at any point in their lives, type of identity theft they experienced outside of the past year, and ongoing problems from identity theft that occurred outside of the past year, 2012

	Number of persons	Percent of all persons	Percent with unresolved problems resulting from identity theft[a]
Experienced at least one incident of identity theft during lifetime			
No	211,327,500	86.0%	—
Yes	34,237,400	13.9	7.8%
Experienced at least one incident of identity theft outside of past 12 months			
No	225,127,300	91.6%	—
Yes	20,334,600	8.3	7.3%
Type of identity theft experienced			
Existing account	15,311,100	6.2%	4.0%
Credit card	8,860,400	2.3	2.8
Bank account	5,721,700	3.6	5.9
Other account	729,000	0.3	7.7
New account	1,585,100	0.6	16.1
Personal information	1,947,700	0.8	14.9
Multiple types	1,450,300	0.6%	20.6%
Existing accounts[b]	572,800	0.2	11.1
Other[c]	877,500	0.4	26.7

—Not applicable.
[a]Based on number of persons who experienced the identity theft.
[b]Includes victims who experienced two or more of the following: unauthorized use of a credit card, bank account, or other existing account.
[c]Includes victims who experienced two or more of the following: unauthorized use of an existing account, misuse of personal information to open a new account, or misuse of personal information for other fraudulent purposes.
Note: Detail may not sum to same population total due to a small number of victims who did not know whether they experienced identity theft during the lifetime or outside of the past 12 months.

SOURCE: Erika Harrell and Lynn Langton, "Table 5. Persons Age 16 Or Older Who Experienced Identity Theft at Any Point in their Lives, Type of Identity Theft They Experienced Outside of the Past Year, and Ongoing Problems from Identity Theft That Occurred Outside of the Past Year, 2012," in *Victims of Identity Theft, 2012*, U.S. Department of Justice, Office of Justice Programs, Bureau of Justice Statistics, December 2013, http://www.bjs.gov/content/pub/pdf/vit12.pdf (accessed November 3, 2014)

TABLE 5.5

Consumer Sentinel Network complaints, by type of complaint, 2001–13

Calendar year	Fraud	Identity theft	Other	Total complaints
2001	137,306	86,250	101,963	325,519
2002	242,783	161,977	146,862	551,622
2003	331,366	215,240	167,051	713,657
2004	410,298	246,909	203,176	860,383
2005	437,585	255,687	216,042	909,314
2006	423,672	246,214	236,243	906,129
2007	505,563	259,314	305,570	1,070,447
2008	620,832	314,587	325,705	1,261,124
2009	708,781	278,360	441,836	1,428,977
2010	819,399	251,080	398,963	1,469,442
2011	1,040,439	279,216	577,597	1,897,252
2012	1,111,119	369,145	630,652	2,110,916
2013	1,165,090	290,056	646,634	2,101,780

Note: Complaint counts from calendar year 2001 to calendar year 2008 represent historic figures as per the Consumer Sentinel Network's five-year data retention policy. These complaint figures exclude National Do Not Call Registry complaints.

SOURCE: "Consumer Sentinel Network Complaint Type Count: Calendar Years 2001 through 2013," in *Consumer Sentinel Network Data Book for January through December 2013*, U.S. Federal Trade Commission, February 2014, http://www.ftc.gov/system/files/documents/reports/consumer-sentinel-network-data-book-january-december-2013/sentinel-cy2013.pdf (accessed November 3, 2014)

was credit card fraud, which accounted for 16.9% of the complaints. This entails thieves using stolen identities to open new credit card accounts or tap into victims' existing credit card accounts. In 13.5% of the total complaints, stolen identities were used by thieves to open new telephone, wireless, or utilities accounts or to fraudulently make charges to victims' existing accounts.

CSN data indicate that 61% of identity theft victims filed reports about the incidents with the police in 2013. Another 13% said they notified the police about the incidents, but either the reports were not filed or the victims did not indicate if a report was taken. The remaining 26% of self-reported identity theft victims in 2013 said they did not notify the police about the incidents.

Internet Crime Complaint Center

The Internet Crime Complaint Center (IC3) is a joint effort of the FBI, the DOJ's Bureau of Justice Assistance, and the National White Collar Crime Center. The IC3 collects complaints about Internet (and other types of) fraud from consumers and refers them, as appropriate, to law enforcement agencies. In *2013 Internet Crime Report* (May 2014, http://www.ic3.gov/media/annualreport/2013_IC3Report.pdf), the IC3 notes that it received 262,813 complaints in 2013. This value was down from the peak number of 336,655 complaints in 2009. The total dollar loss in 2013 was an estimated $782 million.

The IC3 provides victim numbers for a handful of specific scams for which it received complaints in 2013.

TABLE 5.6

Top-20 Consumer Sentinel Network complaint categories, 2013

Rank	Category	No. of Complaints	Percentages
1	Identity theft	290,056	14%
2	Debt collection	204,644	10%
3	Banks and lenders	152,707	7%
4	Impostor scams	121,720	6%
5	Telephone and mobile services	116,261	6%
6	Prizes, sweepstakes and lotteries	89,944	4%
7	Auto-related complaints	82,701	4%
8	Shop-at-home and catalog sales	66,024	3%
9	Television and electronic media	53,087	3%
10	Advance payments for credit services	50,422	2%
11	Internet services	50,311	2%
12	Health care	39,452	2%
13	Credit cards	35,086	2%
14	Business and job opportunities	32,939	2%
15	Credit bureaus, information furnishers and report users	31,810	2%
16	Travel, vacations and timeshare plans	30,094	1%
17	Foreign money offers and counterfeit check scams	24,752	1%
18	Internet auction	21,026	1%
19	Mortgage foreclosure relief and debt management	20,540	1%
20	Office supplies and services	19,584	1%

Note: Percentages are based on the total number of Consumer Sentinel Network (CSN) complaints (2,101,780) received by the Federal Trade Commission (FTC) between January 1 and December 31, 2013. Fourteen percent (293,668) of the total CSN complaints received by the FTC were coded "Other (note in comments)."

SOURCE: Adapted from "Consumer Sentinel Network Complaint Categories: January 1–December 31, 2013," in *Consumer Sentinel Network Data Book for January through December 2013*, U.S. Federal Trade Commission, February 2014, http://www.ftc.gov/system/files/documents/reports/ consumer-sentinel-network-data-book-january-december-2013/sentinel-cy2013.pdf (accessed November 3, 2014)

For example, 14,169 complaints were received about online auto-auction frauds. The IC3 indicates that "in most cases the criminal attempts to sell vehicles they do not own." The fraudsters advertise the cars for sale on the Internet at low prices and pressure potential buyers to buy quickly and to pay by wire transfer. The IC3 notes "once payment is made, the criminal pockets the money and the victim never receives the vehicle." Another 10,384 complaints were lodged over real estate rental scams perpetrated online. The fraudsters typically copy information and photos of actual properties from other websites and advertise them at low rental rates. Prospective renters are told to wire deposit money and may be asked to fill out credit applications in which they divulge sensitive financial information that can be used for identity theft purposes. The ICS states that it received 9,169 complaints in 2013 regarding FBI imposter frauds. These scams feature threatening letters or e-mails in which victims are accused of Internet crimes (such as downloading child pornography) and ordered to pay fines. The fraudsters typically pretend to be high-ranking officials with the FBI or other law enforcement agencies.

TABLE 5.7

Consumer Sentinel Network identity theft complaints, by how victim information was misused, 2013

	Percentages
	Calendar year 2013
Government documents or benefits fraud:	
Theft subtype	
Tax- or wage-related fraud	30.0%
Government benefits applied for/recieved	2.3%
Other government documents issued/forged	1.0%
Driver's license issued/forged	0.6%
Total	**33.9%**
Credit card fraud:	
Theft subtype	
New accounts	11.2%
Existing account	5.7%
Total	**16.9%**
Phone or utilities fraud:	
Theft subtype	
Utilities – new accounts	8.8%
Wireless – new accounts	3.5%
Telephone – new accounts	0.6%
Unauthorized charges to existing accounts	0.6%
Total	**13.5%**
Bank fraud:	
Theft subtype	
Electronic fund transfer	3.7%
New accounts	2.2%
Existing accounts	1.8%
Total	**7.7%**
Employment-related fraud:	
Theft subtype	
Employment-related fraud	5.6%
Loan fraud:	
Theft subtype	
Business/personal/student loan	2.0%
Auto loan/lease	1.1%
Real estate loan	0.8%
Total	**3.9%**
Other identity theft:	
Theft subtype	
Miscellaneous	8.7%
Uncertain	8.5%
Internet/email	1.7%
Data breach	1.3%
Evading the law	1.0%
Medical	0.9%
Apartment or house rented	0.5%
Insurance	0.3%
Securities/other investments	0.2%
Bankruptcy	0.1%
Property rental fraud	0.1%
Child support	0.1%
Magazines	0.1%
Total	**23.5%**
Attempted identity theft:	
Theft subtype	
Attempted identity theft	7.2%

TABLE 5.7

Consumer Sentinel Network identity theft complaints, by how victim information was misused, 2013 [CONTINUED]

Note: Percentages are based on the total number of Consumer Sentinel Network (CSN) identity theft complaints for calendar year 2013 (290,056). Note that 16% of identity theft complaints include more than one type of identity theft in calendar year 2013.

SOURCE: Adapted from "Consumer Sentinel Network Identity Theft Complains, How Victims' Information Is Misused: Calendar Years 2011 through 2013," in *Consumer Sentinel Network Data Book for January through December 2013*, U.S. Federal Trade Commission, February 2014, http://www.ftc.gov/system/files/documents/reports/consumer-sentinel-network-data-book-january-december-2013/sentinel-cy2013.pdf (accessed November 3, 2014)

CHAPTER 6
CONTROLLING CRIME

Criminologists state that every criminal act involves three elements: motivation, resources, and opportunity. A person who is motivated to commit a crime and has the resources to do so (e.g., a weapon or the physical or mental prowess needed to carry out a crime) seeks criminal opportunities, such as victims or targets. Societies try to control crime by controlling these three primary elements of criminality.

Controlling crime in the United States is a multipronged effort that includes interrelated acts of prevention, deterrence, and punishment. Private citizens may take actions that are designed to prevent and deter crimes on their person and property. Examples include installing an alarm system in their home, taking self-defense classes, and participating in neighborhood watch programs. Taxpayer funds are used by governments to establish crime-controlling entities at the local, state, and federal levels for the overall good of society. There are four major governmental components that work together to control crime:

- Law enforcement agencies

- The legal system

- The judiciary system

- The corrections system

The corrections system is described in detail in Chapters 7, 8, and 9. The remainder of this chapter addresses the three other arms of crime control.

LAW ENFORCEMENT AGENCIES

The primary role of law enforcement agencies is to investigate crimes, gather evidence, and arrest suspected perpetrators. Agencies differ by geographic jurisdictions (e.g., federal, state, or local) and by enforcement responsibilities (e.g., the types of laws they enforce or the types of crimes they investigate).

Agencies and Employees

The vast majority of law enforcement in the United States is carried out by local agencies. The Federal Bureau of Investigation (FBI) tracks local law enforcement employment as part of its Uniform Crime Reporting (UCR) Program. For 2013 the UCR Program reported that 13,051 city and county police agencies around the country had 902,410 full-time employees. (See Table 6.1.) Of these employees, 626,942 were law enforcement officers, such as police officers or sheriff deputies, and the remainder were civilian employees (e.g., receptionists or clerks). More than half of all local law enforcement employees worked for city governments, most for cities with populations of 250,000 or more.

In addition, all states operate some type of state police agency, state patrol, or highway patrol force. These officers patrol state highways and often provide law enforcement assistance to local agencies within their state, particularly those in rural areas or small towns.

The federal government has several law enforcement agencies with specific responsibilities. The largest agencies are:

- FBI

- U.S. Drug Enforcement Administration

- Bureau of Alcohol, Tobacco, Firearms, and Explosives

- U.S. Customs and Border Protection

- U.S. Immigration and Customs Enforcement

- U.S. Secret Service

The first three of these agencies are part of the U.S. Department of Justice. The latter three agencies operate under the U.S. Department of Homeland Security.

OFFICERS KILLED AND ASSAULTED IN THE LINE OF DUTY. The UCR Program tracks the number of law

TABLE 6.1

Number of full-time law enforcement employees (officers and civilians) and number of law enforcement agencies, total and by jurisdiction size, 2013

Population group	Total law enforcement employees	Percent law enforcement employees		Total officers	Percent officers		Total civilians	Percent civilians		Number of agencies	2013 estimated population
		Male	Female		Male	Female		Male	Female		
Total agencies:	**902,410**	**73.4**	**26.6**	**626,942**	**88.4**	**11.6**	**275,468**	**39.3**	**60.7**	**13,051**	**268,684,780**
Total cities	**503,227**	**75.6**	**24.4**	**389,934**	**88.3**	**11.7**	**113,293**	**32.1**	**67.9**	**9,894**	**179,802,240**
Group I (250,000 and over)	175,797	72.0	28.0	133,309	84.0	16.0	42,488	34.3	65.7	73	51,744,651
1,000,000 and over (Group I subset)	87,468	70.1	29.9	64,168	83.0	17.0	23,300	34.5	65.5	8	20,834,644
500,000 to 999,999 (Group I subset)	49,447	75.5	24.5	39,168	85.1	14.9	10,279	38.7	61.3	23	16,417,960
250,000 to 499,999 (Group I subset)	38,882	72.0	28.0	29,973	84.8	15.2	8,909	28.8	71.2	42	14,492,047
Group II (100,000 to 249,999)	63,410	73.3	26.7	48,284	88.1	11.9	15,126	26.0	74.0	193	28,587,514
Group III (50,000 to 99,999)	57,806	76.8	23.2	44,972	90.4	9.6	12,834	29.2	70.8	405	27,923,876
Group IV (25,000 to 49,999)	53,525	78.1	21.9	42,624	90.8	9.2	10,901	28.1	71.9	719	24,881,626
Group V (10,000 to 24,999)	58,127	79.7	20.3	47,120	92.1	7.9	11,007	26.8	73.2	1,597	25,483,611
Group VI (under 10,000)	94,562	79.4	20.6	73,625	90.8	9.2	20,937	39.0	61.0	6,907	21,180,962
Metropolitan counties	287,561	70.2	29.8	172,044	87.1	12.9	115,517	44.9	55.1	1,256	66,747,452
Nonmetropolitan counties	111,622	71.6	28.4	64,964	92.6	7.4	46,658	42.5	57.5	1,901	22,135,088
Suburban areas*	434,810	73.2	26.8	287,855	88.6	11.4	146,955	42.9	57.1	6,969	117,915,697

*Suburban areas include law enforcement agencies in cities with less than 50,000 inhabitants and county law enforcement agencies that are within a metropolitan statistical area. Suburban areas exclude all metropolitan agencies associated with a principal city. The agencies associated with suburban areas also appear in other groups within this table.

SOURCE: "Table 74. Full-time Law Enforcement Employees by Population Group, Percent Male and Female, 2013," in *Crime in the United States 2013*, U.S. Department of Justice, Federal Bureau of Investigation, November 10, 2014, http://www.fbi.gov/about-us/cjis/ucr/crime-in-the-u.s-2013/tables/table-74/table_74_full_time_law_enforcement_employees_by_population_group_percent_male_and_female_2013.xls (accessed November 12, 2014)

enforcement officers that are killed and assaulted in the line of duty each year. As of January 2015, the most recent results were reported by the FBI in *Law Enforcement Officers Killed and Assaulted 2013* (November 24, 2014, http://www.fbi.gov/about-us/cjis/ucr/leoka/2013). Between 2004 and 2013, 511 federal, state, and local law enforcement officers were feloniously killed (i.e., their deaths were caused by another person and were not accidental) in the line of duty. (See Figure 6.1.) Another 573,456 officers were assaulted between 2004 and 2013. Figure 6.1 provides a percentage breakdown of the circumstances under which these law enforcement officers were killed or assaulted. The largest percentage (23.5%) of felonious killings occurred during arrest situations. This was followed by ambushes (21.7%) and traffic pursuits or stops (16.4%). By contrast, the largest percentage (31.9%) of assaults occurred during disturbance calls, followed by arrest situations (18%) and other circumstances (14.5%).

Key Law Enforcement Agency Components

Law enforcement agencies differ in their geographic and criminal jurisdictions, but there are some components that are considered key to modern crime control, particularly at the local level. These components are proactive policing, detectives, high-technology tools, and forensic science.

PROACTIVE POLICING. Local law enforcement agencies may assign uniformed officers to regularly patrol specific neighborhoods for the purpose of developing relationships with the residents and business owners in the area. These officers are known informally as "beat cops" because each officer patrols a particular "beat" within the community. The use of beat cops is an example of community policing, whereby law enforcement agencies seek to forge a cooperative bond with people in the community to better fight crime.

Community policing was commonly practiced in the United States in the early part of the 20th century. However, beginning in the 1950s and 1960s police departments shifted beat cops from their foot patrols to patrol cars so that larger areas could be covered. Eventually, law enforcement agencies became almost completely reactive—that is, they reacted after a crime was committed with officers dispatched in response to 911 calls. During the high-crime decades of the 1970s and 1980s, some criminologists began advocating a return to community policing. Joseph F. Ryan describes this evolution in "Community Policing and the Impact of the COPS Federal Grants: A Potential Tool in the Local War on Terrorism" (Albert R. Roberts, ed., *Critical Issues in Crime and Justice*, 2003). Ryan notes that community policing was a key component of the Violent Crime

FIGURE 6.1

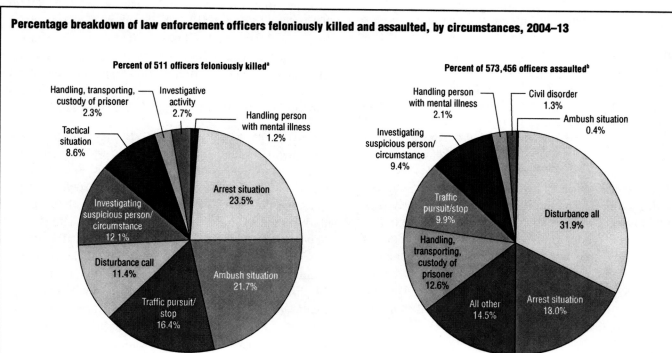

Percentage breakdown of law enforcement officers feloniously killed and assaulted, by circumstances, 2004–13

ᵃThe circumstance category of "All other" does not apply to the data collected for law enforcement officers feloniously killed.
ᵇThe circumstance categories of "Investigative activity" and "Tactical situation" are included in the "All other" data collected for law enforcement officers assaulted.
Note: Because of rounding, the percentages may not add to 100.0.

SOURCE: "Figure 4. Law Enforcement Officers Feloniously Killed and Assaulted: Percent Distribution by Circumstances at Scene of Incident, 2004–2013," in *Law Enforcement Officers Killed and Assaulted 2012*, U.S. Department of Justice, Federal Bureau of Investigation, November 24, 2014, http://www.fbi.gov/about-us/cjis/ucr/leoka/2013/figures/pdfs-figures-1-10/figure_4_2013.pdf (accessed December 16, 2014)

Control and Law Enforcement Act of 1994, which allocated billions of federal dollars for the hiring of more police officers and the development of community policing programs.

Community policing is an example of proactive policing. Proactive means taking action before a situation or event becomes a problem. Proactive policing is intended to prevent crimes from occurring in the first place. Activities that are designed to deter criminals include visible police patrols, such as beat cops regularly walking or driving around neighborhoods. Some jurisdictions install video cameras in public places, such as parks or street corners, to deter criminal activity. Local law enforcement agencies also work with private citizens and business owners to encourage the reporting of suspicious-acting people or situations that present opportunities to criminals.

DETECTIVES. Many law enforcement agencies also employ detectives. These are plainclothes officers who are specially trained to investigate particular crimes (such as homicides). Detectives interview witnesses and suspects, gather facts, examine records, and collect evidence. They may also participate in the apprehension of perpetrators.

HIGH-TECHNOLOGY TOOLS. As noted earlier, some jurisdictions deter criminal activity by employing video cameras in public areas. Video cameras are also useful for solving crimes that have already occurred, as video images can help detectives identify perpetrators and provide evidence for the prosecution. During the late 20th century law enforcement agencies began employing a variety of high-technology resources devoted to crime control. For example, agencies equipped their patrol cars with personal computers and global positioning systems to better provide officers with the data they need to perform their job. Another option that has become popular in some jurisdictions, particularly large cities, is the employment of gunfire locators. These devices recognize and record the sound of gunfire and determine the location of its source. The information can be instantly transmitted to patrol officers so that they can quickly go to the scene. Facial recognition software is another high-tech tool used by some law enforcement agencies. The software can scan crowds of people and notify officers if any viewed faces match photos of suspects. Advanced biometric technology is also increasingly being employed for crime fighting, for example, to digitally take fingerprints or scan the irises of arrestees.

FORENSIC SCIENCE. Forensic science is the application of scientific knowledge and methods to solve crime. Forensic investigators (or criminalists) are employed by some law enforcement agencies. These specialists commonly investigate crime scenes where they collect and analyze physical evidence. They may perform deoxyribonucleic acid or firearms analyses or conduct laboratory tests on blood, semen, hair, tissue, fibers, and other evidentiary materials that are associated with criminal acts.

Police Controversies

In the 21st century some law enforcement departments have come under intense criticism for the killing of unarmed civilians during encounters by their officers. Incidents involving white officers and African American civilians have severely stoked racial tensions in the United States. There is also growing concern about the increased militarization of the nation's police departments.

RACIALLY CHARGED KILLINGS. In 2014 two incidents in which white police officers killed unarmed African Americans inflamed public anger and spurred complaints about racial bias. On July 17, 2014, an African American man was subjected to a chokehold by a New York City police officer during an arrest for a minor offense. The incident was captured on video and shows the victim, Eric Garner (1970–2014), gasping "I can't breathe." Garner died as a result of the chokehold. Despite the fact that the use of chokeholds for restraining suspects has been banned by the New York City Police Department since 1993, a grand jury chose not to indict the officer who had employed this technique on Garner. This decision prompted public demonstrations and criticism of the New York City Police Department. On August 9, 2014, the African American teenager Michael Brown Jr. (1996–2014) was shot and killed by a white police officer in Ferguson, Missouri, a suburb of St. Louis. The shooting sparked prolonged public protests in Ferguson and other parts of the country. After a grand jury decided not to indict the officer, the protests increased in intensity and sometimes resulted in rioting and property destruction.

MILITARY EQUIPMENT AND TACTICS. Some police departments around the country have acquired military-type weapons and equipment, such as armored vehicles, and deploy officers trained in military tactics. These measures have grown increasingly controversial, particularly as the nation's violent crime rate has decreased. In "The Rise of the SWAT Team in American Policing" (NYTimes.com, September 7, 2014), Clyde Haberman traces this militarization trend back to the 1960s, when the first special weapons and tactics (SWAT) units were created in Los Angeles in the wake of deadly rioting in the Watts neighborhood. As the nation's war on drugs intensified over subsequent decades, SWAT-like units became routinely used in drug raids. Haberman notes that critics decry the tactics employed by these units, claiming that the "show of force . . . often far exceeds the threat to them." However, others argue these tactics are necessary because drug gangs are often heavily armed with powerful weapons.

In 1990 the National Defense Authorization Act included provisions for transferring U.S. military equipment to local police departments. These transfers attracted little public attention until the summer of 2014, when rioting broke out in Ferguson over the police killing of Michael Brown Jr. Local police responded to the rioting equipped with military-type body armor, weapons, and vehicles. Media images of this response against mostly unarmed protestors caused a public outcry. Haberman states, "What the world saw were lawmen looking more like combat troops in the Mideast than peacekeepers in the Midwest."

The furor prompted calls by community activists and some legislators to demilitarize local police departments. President Barack Obama (1961–) ordered federal agencies to reexamine their policies regarding transfers of military weapons and gear to local police departments. Evan Perez explains in "Police Militarization: The Ferguson Issue That Wasn't" (CNN.com, December 8, 2014) that the Obama administration decided to continue the transfer program, but instituted stricter tracking methods for the equipment and called for more training for officers using the equipment.

Another incident that stirred concern about police militarization was the accidental wounding of a toddler during a May 2014 drug raid in Georgia by a SWAT unit. According to the article "Toddler Critically Burned during SWAT Raid" (WSBTV.com, May 30, 2014), the raid was conducted using a "no-knock warrant," which allows police officers to enter a building without warning the people inside. The raid was conducted around 2 a.m. while the residents of the home were sleeping. The toddler was wounded by a flash-bang grenade that landed in his crib. The article notes that the child suffered severe burns and a collapsed lung. The target of the raid was not home at the time, but was arrested later at another location. The article "Family of Toddler Injured in SWAT Raid Faces $1M in Medical Bills" (WSBTV.com, December 19, 2014) notes that the injured child spent five weeks in the hospital, which resulted in medical bills that totaled nearly $1 million. Local authorities refused to pay the expenses, and a grand jury decided not to indict the officers involved in the raid. Nevertheless, the SWAT unit that conducted the raid was subsequently disbanded.

Arrests

One of the most important aspects of crime control that law enforcement agencies practice is the apprehension and arrest of suspected perpetrators. According to the FBI, in 2013 law enforcement agencies made over 11.3 million arrests for all criminal infractions, excluding traffic violations. (See Table 6.2.)

The FBI notes that there were 480,360 arrests for violent crimes (murder and nonnegligent manslaughter,

TABLE 6.2

Estimated number of arrests, by offense, 2013

Total[a]	11,302,102
Murder and nonnegligent manslaughter	10,231
Rape[b]	16,863
Robbery	94,406
Aggravated assault	358,860
Burglary	252,629
Larceny-theft	1,231,580
Motor vehicle theft	64,566
Arson	10,509
Violent crime[c]	480,360
Property crime[c]	1,559,284
Other assaults	1,097,741
Forgery and counterfeiting	60,969
Fraud	143,528
Embezzlement	15,730
Stolen property; buying, receiving, possessing	92,691
Vandalism	201,168
Weapons; carrying, possessing, etc.	137,779
Prostitution and commercialized vice	48,620
Sex offenses (except rape and prostitution)	57,925
Drug abuse violations	1,501,043
Gambling	6,024
Offenses against the family and children	101,247
Driving under the influence	1,166,824
Liquor laws	354,872
Drunkenness	443,527
Disorderly conduct	467,993
Vagrancy	25,755
All other offenses	3,282,651
Suspicion	1,096
Curfew and loitering law violations	56,371

[a]Does not include suspicion.
[b]The rape figures in this table are an aggregate total of the data submitted using both the revised and legacy Uniform Crime Reporting definitions.
[c]Violent crimes in this table are offenses of murder and nonnegligent manslaughter, rape (revised and legacy definitions), robbery, and aggravated assault. Property crimes are offenses of burglary, larceny-theft, motor vehicle theft, and arson.

SOURCE: "Table 29. Estimated Number of Arrests, United States, 2013," in *Crime in the United States 2013*, U.S. Department of Justice, Federal Bureau of Investigation, November 10, 2014, http://www.fbi.gov/about-us/cjis/ucr/crime-in-the-u.s/2013/crime-in-the-u.s.-2013/tables/table-29/table_29_estimated_number_of_arrests_united_states_2013.xls (accessed November 12, 2014)

rape, robbery, and aggravated assault) and 1.6 million arrests for property crimes (burglary, larceny-theft, motor vehicle theft, and arson) in 2013. (See Table 6.2.) Of the arrests for specific offenses on which the FBI collects statistics, the five crimes with the most arrests were:

- Drug abuse violations—1.5 million arrests

- Larceny-theft—1.2 million arrests

- Driving under the influence—1.2 million arrests

- Assaults, other than aggravated assaults—1.1 million arrests

- Disorderly conduct—468,000 arrests

Based on data from 7,858 law enforcement agencies, Table 6.3 provides the percentage changes in the number of people arrested between 2004 and 2013. Overall, arrests were down 15.3% over this period. The largest decreases were reported for suspicion (down 90.6%), curfew and loitering law violations (down 61.9%), fraud

TABLE 6.3

Arrests and percentage change in arrests, by offense, 2004–13

[7,858 agencies. 2013 estimated population 192,473,854; 2004 estimated population 178,805,123.]

	Number of persons arrested					
	Total all ages			18 years of age and over		
Offense charged	2004	2013	Percent change	2004	2013	Percent change
Total[a]	8,402,488	7,120,525	−15.3	7,175,623	6,454,262	−10.1
Murder and nonnegligent manslaughter	7,872	6,695	−15.0	7,229	6,203	−14.2
Rape[b]	15,019	10,471	−30.3	12,605	8,987	−28.7
Robbery	64,349	61,019	−5.2	49,413	48,679	−1.5
Aggravated assault	270,826	234,554	−13.4	234,914	215,203	−8.4
Burglary	180,617	163,261	−9.6	130,896	135,301	+3.4
Larceny-theft	721,769	771,869	+6.9	523,698	654,728	+25.0
Motor vehicle theft	87,337	41,385	−52.6	64,553	34,018	−47.3
Arson	9,093	6,792	−25.3	4,500	4,422	−1.7
Violent crime[c]	358,066	312,739	−12.7	304,161	279,072	−8.2
Property crime[c]	998,816	983,307	−1.6	723,647	828,469	+14.5
Other assaults	769,970	696,659	−9.5	621,227	605,223	−2.6
Forgery and counterfeiting	71,993	37,884	−47.4	69,005	37,235	−46.0
Fraud	196,788	88,245	−55.2	192,166	85,490	−55.5
Embezzlement	11,995	10,202	−14.9	11,297	9,969	−11.8
Stolen property; buying, receiving, possessing	78,027	58,443	−25.1	64,148	52,089	−18.8
Vandalism	160,941	128,589	−20.1	99,679	98,913	−0.8
Weapons; carrying, possessing, etc.	110,697	91,150	−17.7	85,219	78,379	−8.0
Prostitution and commercialized vice	55,369	35,562	−35.8	54,212	35,012	−35.4
Sex offenses (except rape and prostitution)	54,292	35,604	−34.4	43,369	29,355	−32.3
Drug abuse violations	1,080,301	976,882	−9.6	961,909	901,115	−6.3
Gambling	6,365	4,400	−30.9	5,266	3,831	−27.3
Offenses against the family and children	73,249	60,479	−17.4	69,641	58,811	−15.6
Driving under the influence	840,325	710,351	−15.5	829,113	706,036	−14.8
Liquor laws	343,782	206,285	−40.0	271,806	172,002	−36.7
Drunkenness	363,978	300,708	−17.4	352,861	295,601	−16.2
Disorderly conduct	364,859	258,950	−29.0	254,485	205,479	−19.3
Vagrancy	23,137	18,154	−21.5	19,999	17,609	−12.0
All other offenses (except traffic)	2,372,952	2,080,548	−12.3	2,142,413	1,954,572	−8.8
Suspicion	4,249	399	−90.6	3,714	361	−90.3
Curfew and loitering law violations	66,586	25,384	−61.9	—	—	—

[a]Does not include suspicion.
[b]The rape figures in this table are based on the legacy definition of rape only. The rape figures shown include converted National Incident-Based Reporting System rape data and those states/agencies that reported the legacy definition of rape for both years.
[c]Violent crimes in this table are offenses of murder and nonnegligent manslaughter, rape (legacy definition), robbery, and aggravated assault. Property crimes are offenses of burglary, larceny-theft, motor vehicle theft, and arson.

SOURCE: Adapted from "Table 32. Ten-Year Arrest Trends: Totals, 2004–2013," in *Crime in the United States 2013*, U.S. Department of Justice, Federal Bureau of Investigation, November 10, 2014, http://www.fbi.gov/about-us/cjis/ucr/crime-in-the-u.s/2013/crime-in-the-u.s.-2013/tables/table-32/table_32_ten_year_ arrest_trends_totals_2013.xls (accessed November 12, 2014)

(down 55.2%), motor vehicle theft (down 52.6%), and forgery and counterfeiting (down 47.4%). Arrests increased between 2004 and 2013 only for larceny-theft (up 6.9%).

Overall, arrests were down 12.7% for violent crimes and down 1.6% for property crimes between 2004 and 2013. (See Table 6.3.)

AGE OF ARRESTEES. Age data were reported to the FBI in 2013 for nearly 9.1 million arrestees. (See Table 6.4.) Of this number, 875,000 were under the age of 18 years and 8.2 million were aged 18 years and older. As explained in Chapter 10, people under the age of 18 years are considered juveniles in most states and are typically handled by the juvenile court system.

Over 4.8 million (or 53.3% of the total) people arrested nationwide in 2013 were under the age of 30 years. (See Table 6.4.) People in this age group made up

the majority of people arrested for violent crimes (54.8%) and property crimes (59.8%). In general, for all crimes, the number of arrests per age group decreased with increasing age for arrestees aged 30 years and older.

GENDER OF ARRESTEES. In Table 6.5 the FBI provides a gender breakdown for nearly 9.1 million arrestees in 2013. Male arrestees outnumbered female arrestees by a margin of almost three to one (73.5% male to 26.5% female). Overall, males accounted for 79.9% of people arrested for violent crimes, while females made up 20.1%. For property crimes the gender ratio was 62.2% male and 37.8% female. Males accounted for huge majorities of arrestees for most crimes, particularly rape (98.1%), sex offenses excluding rape and prostitution (92.2%), weapons charges (91.3%), murder and non-negligent manslaughter (88.3%), and robbery (86.6%). Female arrestees outnumbered male arrestees for only one crime: prostitution and commercialized vice. Nearly

TABLE 6.4

Arrests, by age, 2013

[11,951 agencies. 2013 estimated population 245,741,701.]

Offense charged	Total all ages	Ages under 18	Ages 18 and over	18	19	20	21	22	23	24	25–29	30–34	35–39	40–44	45–49	50–54	55–59	60–64	65 and over
Total	9,069,992	875,262	8,194,730	334,841	371,156	376,711	377,447	371,177	358,242	337,984	1,430,952	1,156,177	810,769	699,790	603,569	486,501	272,335	122,664	84,415
Total percent distribution[a]	100.0	9.7	90.3	3.7	4.1	4.2	4.2	4.1	3.9	3.7	15.8	12.7	8.9	7.7	6.7	5.4	3.0	1.4	0.9
Murder and nonnegligent manslaughter	8,401	614	7,787	440	480	565	539	477	439	360	1,422	952	572	464	377	317	158	97	128
Rape[b]	13,617	2,089	11,528	580	607	596	574	486	442	403	1,661	1,657	1,231	1,075	795	615	378	212	216
Robbery	78,753	15,932	62,821	5,920	5,443	4,959	4,383	3,897	3,471	2,965	10,976	7,283	4,372	3,537	2,720	1,787	766	229	113
Aggravated assault	292,007	25,016	266,991	7,542	9,082	9,776	11,150	11,144	11,189	10,823	48,607	40,695	28,742	24,231	20,916	16,451	9,008	4,227	3,408
Burglary	203,709	34,760	168,949	11,827	11,094	10,065	9,300	8,823	8,131	7,520	30,938	23,328	14,749	11,980	9,593	6,797	3,186	1,082	536
Larceny-theft	996,495	151,427	845,068	50,282	46,851	43,092	40,151	38,385	36,006	33,759	143,866	114,257	78,899	69,734	59,567	45,908	25,055	11,066	8,190
Motor vehicle theft	52,507	9,469	43,038	2,810	2,488	2,228	2,221	2,081	1,984	1,860	8,154	6,768	4,376	3,262	2,422	1,461	631	197	95
Arson	8,413	2,943	5,470	270	266	269	235	199	212	196	893	755	493	459	433	368	223	112	87
Violent crime[c]	392,778	43,651	349,127	14,482	15,612	15,896	16,646	16,004	15,541	14,551	62,666	50,587	34,917	29,307	24,808	19,170	10,310	4,765	3,865
Violent crime percent distribution[a]	100.0	11.1	88.9	3.7	4.0	4.0	4.2	4.1	4.0	3.7	16.0	12.9	8.9	7.5	6.3	4.9	2.6	1.2	1.0
Property crime[c]	1,261,124	198,599	1,062,525	65,189	60,699	55,654	51,907	49,488	46,333	43,335	183,851	145,108	98,517	85,435	72,015	54,534	29,095	12,457	8,908
Property crime percent distribution[a]	100.0	15.7	84.3	5.2	4.8	4.4	4.1	3.9	3.7	3.4	14.6	11.5	7.8	6.8	5.7	4.3	2.3	1.0	0.7
Other assaults	885,822	118,253	767,569	23,071	25,144	27,541	32,206	32,685	32,382	30,889	136,313	115,864	84,266	73,313	61,047	47,281	25,333	11,143	9,091
Forgery and counterfeiting	48,826	850	47,976	1,277	1,745	2,032	1,907	2,007	2,116	2,115	9,551	8,081	5,643	4,407	3,288	2,152	1,045	417	193
Fraud	113,510	3,542	109,968	2,368	3,262	3,845	3,887	4,053	4,240	4,192	19,250	17,616	13,438	11,741	9,056	6,430	3,620	1,643	1,327
Embezzlement	12,664	318	12,346	506	748	774	728	654	580	530	2,055	1,642	1,202	1,057	788	584	268	149	81
Stolen property; buying, receiving, possessing	74,792	8,388	66,404	3,623	3,582	3,487	3,307	3,192	3,165	2,978	12,596	10,440	6,779	5,223	3,693	2,580	1,075	433	251
Vandalism	162,068	37,678	124,390	8,128	7,612	7,090	7,402	6,917	6,258	5,705	22,411	16,386	10,646	8,708	6,969	5,300	2,661	1,220	977
Weapons; carrying, possessing, etc.	112,673	16,683	95,990	5,444	5,435	5,267	5,428	5,442	5,035	4,597	18,173	13,625	8,357	6,152	4,813	3,794	2,270	1,163	995
Prostitution and commercialized vice	42,110	655	41,455	1,202	1,722	1,843	1,990	2,027	1,913	1,874	7,410	5,785	4,161	4,042	3,290	2,256	1,055	489	396
Sex offenses (except rape and prostitution)	46,832	8,389	38,443	1,568	1,493	1,446	1,310	1,340	1,276	1,131	5,053	4,701	3,987	3,632	3,462	3,073	2,118	1,326	1,527
Drug abuse violations	1,209,661	94,187	1,115,474	61,494	66,235	64,345	61,524	58,989	55,457	51,148	205,771	157,451	100,040	79,587	65,380	49,239	25,159	9,592	4,063
Gambling	5,089	615	4,474	254	268	269	247	246	184	175	670	431	323	292	295	277	231	149	163
Offenses against the family and children	78,812	2,224	76,588	950	1,140	1,421	1,855	2,101	2,386	2,543	13,884	14,923	11,752	9,402	6,685	4,300	2,045	707	494
Driving under the influence	918,462	5,963	912,499	13,087	19,543	24,754	39,725	42,165	42,350	40,106	167,636	128,832	93,720	83,940	74,392	64,915	40,487	21,230	15,617
Liquor laws	280,860	48,126	232,734	43,972	48,601	41,435	7,043	5,107	4,215	3,528	13,392	11,113	9,039	10,039	11,395	11,526	7,253	3,280	1,796
Drunkenness	358,036	5,902	352,134	7,376	9,117	9,506	15,302	14,273	13,403	12,055	52,315	44,698	34,133	34,677	37,016	34,590	20,659	8,727	4,287
Disorderly conduct	375,142	76,318	298,824	13,371	13,079	12,988	17,125	15,269	13,841	12,623	48,627	37,777	27,060	24,154	22,893	20,038	11,293	4,999	3,687
Vagrancy	21,633	733	20,900	659	728	670	713	592	555	597	2,416	2,355	1,817	2,017	2,367	2,545	1,726	787	356
All other offenses (except traffic)	2,620,320	156,079	2,464,241	66,783	85,363	96,414	107,144	108,581	106,968	103,278	446,800	368,665	260,912	222,627	189,884	151,889	84,613	37,985	26,335
Suspicion	844	175	669	37	28	34	51	45	44	34	112	97	60	38	33	28	19	3	6
Curfew and loitering law violations	47,934	47,934	—	—	—	—	—	—	—	—	—	—	—	—	—	—	—	—	—

[a]Because of rounding, the percentages may not add to 100.0.

[b]The rape figures in this table are an aggregate total of the data submitted using both the revised and legacy Uniform Crime Reporting definitions.

[c]Violent crimes in this table are offenses of murder and nonnegligent manslaughter, rape (revised and legacy definitions), robbery, and aggravated assault. Property crimes are offenses of burglary, larceny-theft, motor vehicle theft, and arson.

SOURCE: Adapted from "Table 38. Arrests by Age, 2013," in *Crime in the United States 2013*, U.S. Department of Justice, Federal Bureau of Investigation, November 10, 2014, http://www.fbi.gov/about-us/cjis/ucr/crime-in-the-u.s/2013/crime-in-the-u.s.-2013/tables/table-38/table_38_arrests_by_age_2013.xls (accessed November 12, 2014)

TABLE 6.5

Arrests, by sex, 2013

[11,951 agencies. 2013 estimated population 245,741,701.]

Offense charged	Number of persons arrested			Percent male	Percent female
	Total	Male	Female		
Total	9,069,992	6,662,833	2,407,159	73.5	26.5
Murder and nonnegligent manslaughter	8,401	7,415	986	88.3	11.7
Rape[a]	13,617	13,362	255	98.1	1.9
Robbery	78,753	68,239	10,514	86.6	13.4
Aggravated assault	292,007	224,735	67,272	77.0	23.0
Burglary	203,709	169,018	34,691	83.0	17.0
Larceny-theft	996,495	567,174	429,321	56.9	43.1
Motor vehicle theft	52,507	42,078	10,429	80.1	19.9
Arson	8,413	6,752	1,661	80.3	19.7
Violent crime[b]	392,778	313,751	79,027	79.9	20.1
Property crime[b]	1,261,124	785,022	476,102	62.2	37.8
Other assaults	885,822	639,502	246,320	72.2	27.8
Forgery and counterfeiting	48,826	30,570	18,256	62.6	37.4
Fraud	113,510	68,270	45,240	60.1	39.9
Embezzlement	12,664	6,536	6,128	51.6	48.4
Stolen property; buying, receiving, possessing	74,792	58,734	16,058	78.5	21.5
Vandalism	162,068	129,202	32,866	79.7	20.3
Weapons; carrying, possessing, etc.	112,673	102,864	9,809	91.3	8.7
Prostitution and commercialized vice	42,110	13,818	28,292	32.8	67.2
Sex offenses (except rape and prostitution)	46,832	43,193	3,639	92.2	7.8
Drug abuse violations	1,209,661	953,984	255,677	78.9	21.1
Gambling	5,089	4,349	740	85.5	14.5
Offenses against the family and children	78,812	57,806	21,006	73.3	26.7
Driving under the influence	918,462	689,383	229,079	75.1	24.9
Liquor laws	280,860	199,751	81,109	71.1	28.9
Drunkenness	358,036	291,223	66,813	81.3	18.7
Disorderly conduct	375,142	270,299	104,843	72.1	27.9
Vagrancy	21,633	17,114	4,519	79.1	20.9
All other offenses (except traffic)	2,620,320	1,952,465	667,855	74.5	25.5
Suspicion	844	647	197	76.7	23.3
Curfew and loitering law violations	47,934	34,350	13,584	71.7	28.3

[a]The rape figures in this table are an aggregate total of the data submitted using both the revised and legacy Uniform Crime Reporting definitions.
[b]Violent crimes in this table are offenses of murder and nonnegligent manslaughter, rape (revised and legacy definitions), robbery, and aggravated assault. Property crimes are offenses of burglary, larceny-theft, motor vehicle theft, and arson.

SOURCE: Adapted from "Table 42. Arrests by Sex, 2013," in *Crime in the United States 2013*, U.S. Department of Justice, Federal Bureau of Investigation, November 10, 2014, http://www.fbi.gov/about-us/cjis/ucr/crime-in-the-u.s/2013/crime-in-the-u.s.-2013/tables/table-42/table_42_arrests_by_sex_2013.xls (accessed November 12, 2014)

two-thirds (67.2%) of the people arrested for this offense in 2013 were female. Other crimes in which female arrestees made up relatively large portions of those arrested were embezzlement (48.4%), larceny-theft (43.1%), fraud (39.9%), and forgery and counterfeiting (37.4%).

In *Crime in the United States, 2013* (November 10, 2014, http://www.fbi.gov/about-us/cjis/ucr/crime-in-the-u.s/2013/crime-in-the-u.s.-2013/cius-home), the FBI presents gender-based arrest data obtained from 7,858 law enforcement agencies between 2004 and 2013. The results indicate that over this period the number of males arrested declined by 18.3%, whereas female arrests decreased by 5.2%. Male arrests during this period declined for all crimes. Female arrests between 2004 and 2013 increased for several crimes, particularly larceny-theft (up 19.8%), gambling (up 16.9%), and robbery (up 15.8%).

Overall, male arrests were down 14.9% for violent crimes and down 9.6% for property crimes between 2004 and 2013. Female arrests decreased by 2.2% for violent crimes and increased by 15.5% for property crimes during this same period.

RACE AND ETHNICITY OF ARRESTEES. Of the 9 million arrests reported to the UCR Program that included race information in 2013, 68.9% of the arrestees were white and 28.3% were African American. (See Table 6.6.) The remaining arrestees were Native American or Alaskan Native (1.6%), Asian American (1.2%), or Native Hawaiian or other Pacific Islander (0.1%). Whites accounted for large percentages of those arrested for driving under the influence (84.2%), drunkenness (80.8%), and liquor law violations (80.1%). African American arrestees accounted for nearly two-thirds (66.5%) of all arrests for illegal gambling and around half of all arrests for robbery (56.4%) and murder and nonnegligent manslaughter (52.2%). Whites made up 58.4% of arrests for violent crimes, whereas African Americans accounted for 38.7%. Likewise, whites made up a larger percentage of those arrested for property crimes (68.2%) than did African Americans (29%).

TABLE 6.6

Arrests, by race, 2013

[11,951 agencies. 2013 estimated population 245,741,701.]

Offense charged	Total arrests						Percent distribution[a]					
		Race										
	Total	White	Black or African American	American Indian or Alaska Native	Asian	Native Hawaiian or other Pacific Islander	Total	White	Black or African American	American Indian or Alaska Native	Asian	Native Hawaiian or other Pacific Islander
Total	**9,014,635**	**6,214,197**	**2,549,655**	**140,290**	**105,109**	**5,384**	**100.0**	**68.9**	**28.3**	**1.6**	**1.2**	**0.1**
Murder and nonnegligent manslaughter	8,383	3,799	4,379	98	101	6	100.0	45.3	52.2	1.2	1.2	0.1
Rape[b]	13,515	8,946	4,229	160	173	7	100.0	66.2	31.3	1.2	1.3	0.1
Robbery	78,538	32,945	44,271	579	649	94	100.0	41.9	56.4	0.7	0.8	0.1
Aggravated assault	291,031	183,092	98,748	4,356	4,423	412	100.0	62.9	33.9	1.5	1.5	0.1
Burglary	203,089	136,990	61,709	1,966	2,196	228	100.0	67.5	30.4	1.0	1.1	0.1
Larceny-theft	990,936	677,173	284,358	16,402	12,605	398	100.0	68.3	28.7	1.7	1.3	*
Motor vehicle theft	52,307	34,864	15,960	685	725	73	100.0	66.7	30.5	1.3	1.4	0.1
Arson	8,364	6,198	1,925	130	107	4	100.0	74.1	23.0	1.6	1.3	*
Violent crime[c]	391,467	228,782	151,627	5,193	5,346	519	100.0	58.4	38.7	1.3	1.4	0.1
Property crime[c]	1,254,696	855,225	363,952	19,183	15,633	703	100.0	68.2	29.0	1.5	1.2	0.1
Other assaults	881,086	573,546	283,357	14,041	9,717	425	100.0	65.1	32.2	1.6	1.1	*
Forgery and counterfeiting	48,581	31,208	16,375	288	677	33	100.0	64.2	33.7	0.6	1.4	0.1
Fraud	112,920	74,682	35,958	1,145	1,094	41	100.0	66.1	31.8	1.0	1.0	0.1
Embezzlement	12,574	7,882	4,386	87	207	12	100.0	62.7	34.9	0.7	1.6	0.1
Stolen property; buying, receiving, possessing	74,541	50,237	22,687	684	862	71	100.0	67.4	30.4	0.9	1.2	0.1
Vandalism	161,078	113,842	42,566	2,951	1,638	81	100.0	70.7	26.4	1.8	1.0	0.1
Weapons; carrying, possessing, etc.	112,228	65,317	44,671	888	1,251	101	100.0	58.2	39.8	0.8	1.1	0.1
Prostitution and commercialized vice	41,946	22,666	17,378	386	1,492	24	100.0	54.0	41.4	0.9	3.6	0.1
Sex offenses (except rape and prostitution)	46,553	33,695	11,462	622	744	30	100.0	72.4	24.6	1.3	1.6	0.1
Drug abuse violations	1,204,162	815,181	365,785	9,408	12,930	858	100.0	67.7	30.4	0.8	1.1	0.1
Gambling	5,055	1,433	3,362	27	226	7	100.0	28.3	66.5	0.5	4.5	0.1
Offenses against the family and children	78,465	51,017	25,519	1,414	511	4	100.0	65.0	32.5	1.8	0.7	*
Driving under the influence	910,470	766,440	113,928	12,575	16,831	696	100.0	84.2	12.5	1.4	1.8	0.1
Liquor laws	277,444	222,201	40,665	10,861	3,672	45	100.0	80.1	14.7	3.9	1.3	*
Drunkenness	356,427	288,146	56,885	7,399	3,550	447	100.0	80.8	16.0	2.1	1.0	0.1
Disorderly conduct	372,202	231,604	129,782	7,982	2,775	59	100.0	62.2	34.9	2.1	0.7	*
Vagrancy	21,354	13,732	6,802	581	222	17	100.0	64.3	31.9	2.7	1.0	0.1
All other offenses (except traffic)	2,602,939	1,741,855	790,854	43,953	25,090	1,187	100.0	66.9	30.4	1.7	1.0	*
Suspicion	825	499	303	12	11	0	100.0	60.5	36.7	1.5	1.3	0.0
Curfew and loitering law violations	47,622	25,007	21,351	610	630	24	100.0	52.5	44.8	1.3	1.3	0.1

*Less than one-tenth of 1 percent.

[a]Because of rounding, the percentages may not add to 100.0.

[b]The rape figures in this table are an aggregate total of the data submitted using both the revised and legacy Uniform Crime Reporting definitions.

[c]Violent crimes in this table are offenses of murder and nonnegligent manslaughter, rape (revised and legacy definitions), robbery, and aggravated assault. Property crimes are offenses of burglary, larceny-theft, motor vehicle theft, and arson.

SOURCE: Adapted from "Table 43A. Arrests by Race, 2013," in *Crime in the United States 2013*, U.S. Department of Justice, Federal Bureau of Investigation, November 10, 2014, http://www.fbi.gov/about-us/cjis/ucr/crime-in-the-u.s/2013/crime-in-the-u.s.-2013/tables/table-43 (accessed November 12, 2014)

OFFENSES CLEARED BY ARREST OR EXCEPTIONAL MEANS. Figure 6.2 shows the percentage of known offenses that were cleared by arrest or exceptional means in 2013. Offenses cleared by exceptional means are those for which there can be no arrest, such as in a murder-suicide, when the perpetrator is known to be deceased.

Because murder is considered the most serious crime, it receives the most police attention and, therefore, has the highest arrest rate of all felonies. In 2013, 64.1% of murders and nonnegligent manslaughters were cleared by arrest or exceptional means. (See Figure 6.2.) The only other offense for which more than half of the crimes were cleared in 2013 was aggravated assault (57.7%). Clearance rates were much lower for the other crimes, particularly motor vehicle theft (14.2% clearance rate) and burglary (13.1% clearance rate).

Making an arrest does not mean the alleged offender is guilty or will be convicted of the crime. Law enforcement agencies do not determine the guilt or innocence of suspected perpetrators. That task is left up to the judicial system.

THE LEGAL SYSTEM

Although *mala in se* (morally wrong or inherently wrong) behaviors are universally condemned as wrong, punishments for these crimes can vary significantly between societies. Many of the legal decisions concerning *mala in se* crimes have evolved over time through what is known as common law. Common law refers to the legal precedents that are established by court decisions over time, as opposed to laws that are passed by legislative bodies. The U.S. legal system relies heavily on common-law decisions dating back to the legal system that was used in England before the establishment of the United States.

People enter the U.S. criminal justice system through a variety of means. They may be issued a citation for a traffic violation witnessed by a law enforcement officer. They may be arrested for a more serious crime by a law enforcement officer who has probable cause to believe they committed a crime. They may be arrested due to issuance of a warrant for their arrest by a court. An arrest warrant is a legal document signed by a judge or a magistrate who believes there is compelling evidence that the person named in the warrant has committed a particular crime.

A person charged with a crime falls under the legal and judicial system of the government body with appropriate jurisdiction, for example, the city, county, state, or federal government. These systems may differ in structure and mode of operation, but under U.S. law they all must provide certain legal rights to arrested people.

The Rights of the Arrested

People placed under arrest (with or without a warrant) must be told their Miranda rights before being questioned about their alleged crime by law enforcement officials. Miranda rights stem from the 1966 U.S. Supreme Court decision *Miranda v. Arizona* (384 U.S. 436). The court ruled that arrested individuals must be told about their constitutional rights to an attorney and against self-incrimination before they are subjected to any questioning about their alleged crime. Although the so-called Miranda warning takes several forms, it must cover the following basic concepts:

- The arrestee has the right to remain silent during police questioning.

- Anything the arrestee says to the police can be used against him or her at trial.

- The arrestee has the right to an attorney.

- If the arrestee cannot afford an attorney, one will be appointed for him or her at the government's expense.

In addition, arrested individuals have the right to know the charges against them and to see any arrest warrants that are used to make the arrest. According to the American Bar Association, in "Steps in a Trial: Arrest Procedures" (2015, http://www.americanbar.org/groups/public _education/resources/law_related_education_network/ how_courts_work/arrestprocedure.html), a person arrested

FIGURE 6.2

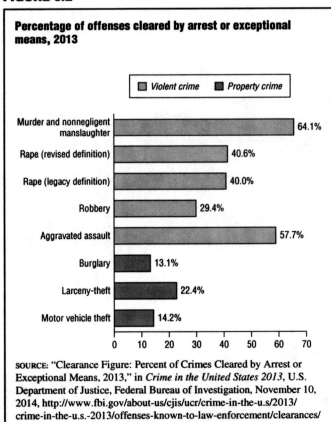

Percentage of offenses cleared by arrest or exceptional means, 2013

Legend: ▨ Violent crime ▨ Property crime

Offense	Percentage
Murder and nonnegligent manslaughter	64.1%
Rape (revised definition)	40.6%
Rape (legacy definition)	40.0%
Robbery	29.4%
Aggravated assault	57.7%
Burglary	13.1%
Larceny-theft	22.4%
Motor vehicle theft	14.2%

SOURCE: "Clearance Figure: Percent of Crimes Cleared by Arrest or Exceptional Means, 2013," in *Crime in the United States 2013*, U.S. Department of Justice, Federal Bureau of Investigation, November 10, 2014, http://www.fbi.gov/about-us/cjis/ucr/crime-in-the-u.s/2013/ crime-in-the-u.s.-2013/offenses-known-to-law-enforcement/clearances/ clearancetopic_final (accessed November 12, 2014)

without a warrant can be held by the police for only a limited period (typically 48 hours) before making his or her first court appearance, or arraignment, before a judge or magistrate. The granting of bail is not specifically a right, but most arrestees are given a bail hearing during which a court sets the monetary amount for bail. The U.S. Constitution prohibits excessive bail. It also guarantees the defendant the right to a speedy trial and prohibits the imposition of cruel and unusual punishment.

The Role of Prosecutors

Government jurisdictions have their own unique legal systems. Each system is typically headed by a public official. At the state level this official may be called the state attorney. At the lower levels of government, such as counties or cities, officials may be called district attorneys, county or city attorneys, or simply prosecutors. A prosecutor represents the legal authority of his or her geographical area and supervises the legal prosecution of suspected criminals. These cases are often referred to prosecutors' offices by law enforcement agencies. Some states also use grand juries to file criminal charges against suspected criminals. Grand juries consist of local citizens who are summoned by a court to serve for a specified period. They do not determine the guilt or innocence of the accused, but they do determine if there is enough evidence to bind over the accused to stand trial. If so, the grand jury issues a formal charge called an indictment.

Some district attorneys are elected into office, whereas others are appointed by higher public officials. A prosecutor acts on behalf of the people within a jurisdiction to ensure that its criminal laws are enforced and that criminals are prosecuted. Prosecution for criminal activity sometimes proceeds to court, where the guilt or innocence of the defendant is determined during a trial. The judicial system tries perpetrators in a court of law and, if they are found guilty, sentences them to a period of incarceration or some other form of punishment, restitution (an amount of money that is set by a court to be paid to the victim of a crime for property losses or injuries caused by the crime), and/or treatment.

Not all criminal cases proceed to trial. In fact, many are settled through alternative means, such as plea bargains.

PLEA BARGAINS. In a plea bargain the prosecutor and the defendant's attorney reach an agreement about how a case should be settled before it goes to trial. A typical example involves an offer from the prosecutor for the defendant to plead guilty to a lesser charge than the one originally filed against him or her. Another common plea bargain occurs when the defendant agrees to plead guilty to a charge in exchange for a recommendation by the prosecutor for a lighter sentence than would be expected to result from a guilty verdict if the case went to trial.

Prosecutors are motivated to negotiate plea bargains because criminal trials can be long and costly and their outcomes are not certain. Defendants may choose to plea bargain to avoid the publicity and legal expense of a trial and the likely harsher sentence that will result from a guilty verdict. The American Bar Association indicates in "Steps in a Trial: Plea Bargaining" (2015, http://www.americanbar.org/groups/public_education/resources/law_related_education_network/how_courts_work/pleabargaining.html) that plea bargains resolve most of the criminal cases in most jurisdictions in the United States.

THE JUDICIARY SYSTEM

The judiciary system includes all criminal courts and the judges and juries that operate within them. There are two main levels of the judiciary system in the United States: federal courts and state/local courts. In "District Courts" (2014, http://www.uscourts.gov/districtcourts.html), U.S. Courts notes that the federal judiciary system includes 94 U.S. judicial districts that are organized into 12 regional circuits. (See Figure 6.3; note that the 12th circuit is the District of Columbia.) The district courts serve as trial courts in the federal system. Each circuit has a U.S. court of appeals. The U.S. Supreme Court is the highest court in the United States. It hears a limited number of cases each year that primarily address issues related to federal law or the U.S. Constitution.

Every state has its own court system. These systems differ by state, but in general they include local or municipal courts, county-level courts, district courts, state appeals courts, and state supreme courts. Typically, local, municipal, and county courts have jurisdiction over misdemeanors, whereas district courts have jurisdiction over felony criminal cases.

Some defendants have their cases dismissed or are acquitted (found not guilty) at trial. Defendants who plead guilty or are found guilty at trial face measures including incarceration, fines, payment of restitution, and/or probation. According to Erinn J. Herberman and Thomas P. Bonczar of the Bureau of Justice Statistics (BJS), in *Probation and Parole in the United States, 2013* (January 21, 2015, http://www.bjs.gov/content/pub/pdf/ppus13.pdf), probation is defined as "a court-ordered period of correctional supervision in the community." Convicted defendants can be sentenced to prison or probation or receive split sentences including a period of incarceration followed by a period of probation. Another alternative is a suspended sentence. In an unconditional suspended sentence the convicted defendant faces no penalty, but the conviction stays on his or her record. In a conditional suspended sentence the convicted defendant is given an amount of time in which he or she must meet certain conditions (e.g., pay restitution and/or commit no further crimes). If the conditions are met, the person avoids any

FIGURE 6.3

Map of the geographical boundaries of the U.S. Courts of Appeal and U.S. District Courts

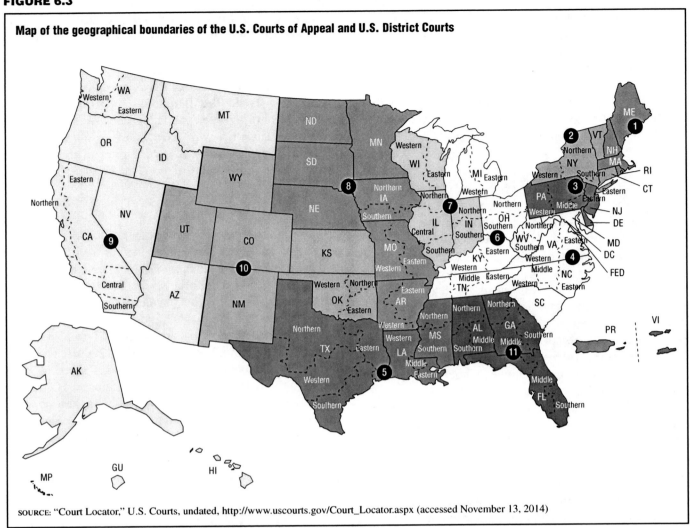

SOURCE: "Court Locator," U.S. Courts, undated, http://www.uscourts.gov/Court_Locator.aspx (accessed November 13, 2014)

prison time included in the sentence. If the conditions are not met, however, the person faces incarceration.

Adjudication and Sentencing Outcomes

The BJS compiles national conviction and sentencing data for the federal and state courts. Figure 2.1 in Chapter 2 shows the number of defendants processed between 1994 and 2012 in the federal justice system. According to Mark Motivans of the BJS, in *Federal Justice Statistics, 2011–2012* (January 2015, http://www.bjs.gov/content/pub/pdf/fjs10.pdf), 96,260 felons were adjudicated in 2012. The vast majority (91.3%) were convicted— 88.9% through guilty pleas, many presumably as a result of plea bargains, and 2.2% through trials before a judge or jury. Overall, 77.3% of the convicted felons received some prison time at sentencing. Another 10.4% were put on probation only, while 2.3% were fined only. The remainder (10.1%) received suspended sentences. (Note that these percentages do not sum to 100% due to rounding.)

As of January 2015, the most recent data available from a nationally representative survey for state courts

were for 2006. In *Felony Sentences in State Courts, 2006—Statistical Tables* (November 22, 2010, http://www.bjs.gov/content/pub/pdf/fssc06st.pdf), Sean Rosenmerkel, Matthew Durose, and Donald Farole of the BJS report that 1.1 million defendants were convicted of felonies in state courts in 2006. Nearly all of the felons (94%) pleaded guilty, many presumably as a result of plea bargains. Only 6% were convicted through a trial—4% by juries and 2% by the bench (i.e., by a judge). The percentage of felons convicted by a guilty plea exceeded 90% for all felonies except murder (61% convicted by a guilty plea), sexual assault (88% convicted by a guilty plea), and robbery (89% convicted by a guilty plea). In 2006 more than two-thirds (69%) of the convicted felons were sentenced to prison or jail time. Another 27% were given probation with no prison or jail time. The remaining 4% faced no prison or jail time or probation, but received other sentences including payment of fines or restitution; court-ordered testing (e.g., for drug use), treatment, or community service; or some other penalty.

Truth-in-Sentencing

During the 1970s and early 1980s the United States experienced a historically high crime rate. Politicians responded to public pressure with policies that aimed to "get tough on crime," including new sentencing guidelines that imposed mandatory minimum sentences and other reforms that established stiffer penalties for certain offenses. Some of the sentencing reforms enacted by states were known as "truth-in-sentencing" statutes. They required offenders to spend substantial portions of their sentence in prison. One effect of the laws was to reduce the practice of corrections officials releasing inmates early (i.e., before their court-imposed incarceration times were served). Nora V. Demleitner of the Hofstra University School of Law notes in "Good Conduct Time: How Much and for Whom? The Unprincipled Approach of the Model Penal Code: Sentencing" (*Florida Law Review*, 2009) that "back-end discretion" by the corrections system has long been a component of the U.S. justice system. For example, inmates can get "time off for good behavior." Many inmates who finish incarceration are then subject to community supervision under the parole system, which is explained in detail in Chapter 9. Decisions about transitioning inmates from prison to parole are typically made by panels called parole boards, which also decide when parolees can be released from supervision.

Truth-in-sentencing laws include provisions that set minimum or fixed terms of incarceration and take some decision-making power away from corrections officials and parole boards. In addition, the laws often include mandatory minimum sentences for specific offenses and circumstances. Guidelines define the range of sentences that may apply, and they depend on the offense and the prior history of the offender (e.g., first-time or repeat offender, severity of the offense, and so on).

Setting uniform sentences for offenses and requiring that fixed proportions of them be served by those convicted put pressure on prison and jail capacities. In response, Congress passed the Violent Crime Control and Law Enforcement Act of 1994. The act gave the federal government the authority to offer grants to states to expand their prison capacity if they imposed truth-in-sentencing requirements on violent offenders. To qualify for the grants, the states had to pass laws requiring that serious violent offenders serve at least 85% of their imposed sentences in prison.

JUDGES' SENTENCING POWER. Some states that adopted truth-in-sentencing laws during the 1970s and 1980s included provisions allowing judges great leeway in deciding sentencing factors. This was also true for some state hate crime laws that were first passed during the 1980s. Legal analysts, however, complained that these provisions violated the Sixth and 14th Amendments to the U.S. Constitution. The Sixth Amendment states in part "in all criminal prosecutions, the accused shall enjoy the right to a speedy and public trial, by an impartial jury." The 14th Amendment states in part "nor shall any state deprive any person of life, liberty, or property, without due process of law." Both provisions have historically been interpreted as a limit on the power of judges (as opposed to juries) in the criminal justice system.

In 2000 the U.S. Supreme Court found in *Apprendi v. New Jersey* (530 U.S. 466) that a state judge had violated the due process clause of the 14th Amendment by deciding on his own that a defendant who had pleaded guilty to a firearms charge had actually committed a hate crime and should receive an enhanced sentence allowed under New Jersey's hate crime law. In 2004 the court ruled in *Blakely v. Washington* (542 U.S. 296) that a state judge cannot impose a longer sentence when the basis for the enhanced sentence was not admitted by the defendant or found by the jury. In 2007 the Supreme Court similarly ruled in *Cunningham v. California* (No. 05-6551) that a state judge had violated a defendant's right to trial by jury by making findings on his own (i.e., findings not considered by the jury) that justified a longer sentence for a crime than the sentence called for under state law. In simple terms, these rulings mean that only facts proved to a jury (or admitted to by a defendant pleading guilty) can justify imposition by a state judge of a sentence longer than that called for under state law.

Federal Sentencing Guidelines

The Sentencing Reform Act of 1984 was the federal approach to truth-in-sentencing, or determinate sentencing. The act was designed to eliminate the unregulated power of federal judges to impose sentences of indeterminate length. Because of this unregulated power, some people were convicted of the same crime but sentenced by different judges to receive entirely different terms of incarceration. The U.S. Sentencing Commission (USSC) developed federal guidelines to give a range of sentencing options to federal judges while guaranteeing minimum and maximum sentencing lengths.

The USSC continues to update the guidelines as laws administered by the federal courts are changed or new laws are passed. The USSC also issues supplemental volumes. As of January 2015, the most recent edition of the guidelines was *U.S. Sentencing Commission Guidelines Manual* (November 1, 2014, http://www.ussc.gov/sites/default/files/pdf/guidelines-manual/2014/GLMFull.pdf).

At the core of the guidelines are offenses as defined by federal statutes. In its guidelines, the USSC assigns an offense level to each offense, known as the base offense level, which ranges from 1 to 43. Based on the circumstances that are associated with an offense, additional levels can be added or taken away until a particular offense has been assigned to the appropriate level. Judges and prosecutors use these levels to find the relevant sentence in the federal sentencing table, which determines the number of months of imprisonment.

DEPARTURES FROM THE GUIDELINES. As noted earlier, U.S. Supreme Court decisions in *Apprendi v. New Jersey*, *Blakely v. Washington*, and *Cunningham v. California* struck down state laws that allowed state judges to make findings on their own (i.e., not jury findings) that imposed longer sentences than those called for under state law.

In 2005 the Supreme Court made a related ruling in *United States v. Booker* (543 U.S. 220). In this case the subject, Freddie J. Booker, had been charged with possession with intent to distribute 1.8 ounces (50 grams) of crack cocaine, a crime for which the federal sentencing guidelines set a 262-month sentence. However, the judge later determined that Booker had possessed 3.2 ounces (92 grams) of crack cocaine and had also obstructed justice. Because of these additional offenses, the judge sentenced Booker to 360 months in prison. In language similar to the *Blakely* ruling, the court ruled that federal judges cannot determine facts that are used to increase a defendant's punishment beyond what is authorized by a jury verdict or the defendant's own admissions. In its ruling, the court struck down the mandatory application of sentencing guidelines and instructed courts to apply reasonableness in determining sentences. Guidelines should be considered, but judges are not required to follow them. The legal impact of these two decisions continues to be worked out in the courts.

"Three Strikes, You're Out"

Nine years after passing the first truth-in-sentencing law, the state of Washington passed the first of the so-called three-strikes laws in December 1993. The measure took effect in the wake of a voter initiative, which passed by a three-to-one margin. Three-strikes laws are the functional equivalent of sentencing guidelines in that they mandate a fixed sentence length for repeat offenders for specified crimes or a mix of crimes—but their formulation in public debate, using the baseball analogy, is much easier to understand than the complexities of thick books of codes and sentencing tables.

Three-strikes laws were originally intended to ensure that an offender receives a mandatory long sentence upon conviction for the third offense, for example, life imprisonment without parole (as in the state of Washington) or 25 years without parole (as in California). These sentences guaranteed that a repeat criminal would be removed from society for a long time or, in some instances, for life. Although three-strikes laws are best known for their imposition of long sentences on a third offense, they also feature longer-than-average sentences for second offenses.

The Washington law identifies specific offenses that are "strikable." California, which passed its own (and more famous) three-strikes law just months after Washington passed its measure, specifies the categories of offenses that must precede the third felony conviction.

OPPOSITION AND CHALLENGES TO THREE-STRIKES LAWS. Opponents of three-strikes laws charge that the laws unfairly target African Americans, who are disproportionately represented among felony convicts. They argue that three-strikes laws remove proportion and reasonableness from sentencing by making all third strikes punishable by the same prison sentence, whether it is for stealing a small item or killing someone. Opponents also note that incarcerating more people for longer periods requires more prisons and increases corrections costs for maintaining prisoners. Reducing the possibility of parole results in an increasing number of elderly prisoners, who are statistically much less likely to commit crimes than younger prisoners and who have increasing health care needs. Lastly, some critics suggest that the finality of three-strikes laws may make active criminals more desperate and, thus, more violent. According to this view, if criminals know they will be sentenced to life in prison, then they have nothing to lose and might be more likely to kill witnesses or to resist arrest through violent means.

As of January 2015, the constitutionality of California's three-strikes law had been considered twice by the U.S. Supreme Court. Both cases involved defendants with two strikes who triggered the third strike penalty by committing relatively minor third offenses. In *Lockyer v. Andrade* (538 U.S. 63 [2003]) and *Ewing v. California* (538 U.S. 11 [2003]) the Supreme Court upheld the California law.

AMENDING THREE-STRIKES LAWS. The three-strikes laws were a product of the early 1990s, a time of historically high crime rates and a booming national economy. By the end of the first decade of the 21st century, however, protests about the laws, decreasing crime rates, and increasing budget pressures led many states to water down their three-strikes laws. The National Conference of State Legislators is a bipartisan organization that provides research and technical assistance on legislative issues to state policy makers. In "Three Strikes and You're Out: Changes in California's Law" (February 2013, http://www.ncsl.org/Documents/CJ/BulletinFeb-2013.pdf), the National Conference of State Legislators indicates that at least 16 of the 24 states that enacted three-strikes laws during the early 1990s have amended their laws to make them less rigid. The most common change is the elimination of mandatory sentences in favor of "judicial discretion." In other words, judges do not have to automatically apply specific sentences, although they may be bound by sentencing guidelines. The Sentencing Project indicates in *Life Goes On: The Historic Rise in Life Sentences in*

America (2013, http://sentencingproject.org/doc/publications/inc_Life%20Goes%20On%202013.pdf) that as of 2013, only 13 states and the federal government maintained three-strikes laws providing for life without parole on the third strike.

In November 2012 California voters approved Proposition 36, which amended the state's three-strikes law. Aaron Sankin reports in "California Prop 36, Measure Reforming State's Three Strikes Law, Approved by Wide Majority of Voters" (HuffingtonPost.com, November 7, 2012) that the proposition revised the law so that only a serious or violent crime counts as a third strike. In addition, it gave judges the discretion to resentence offenders serving life sentences for third-strike convictions if their third crime was not serious or violent.

Other Penalty Reforms

Amended three-strikes laws are one example of reforms that are designed to soften the penalties imposed for certain criminal acts. Public concern about perceived unfairness in the criminal justice system has been one motivator, as explained in Chapter 4 regarding relaxed sentencing guidelines for crack cocaine possession. Other drivers have been problems in many jurisdictions with overcrowded prisons and the high costs to taxpayers of incarcerating large numbers of people. Both of these issues are examined in detail in Chapter 7. The nation's declining crime rate has also played a role, as political pressure has eased somewhat to be "tough on crime."

The U.S. attorney general Eric Holder Jr. (1951–) made headlines in August 2013 when he presented new federal penalty reforms during a speech before the American Bar Association. Holder (August 12, 2013, http://www.justice.gov/opa/speech/attorney-general-eric-holder-delivers-remarks-annual-meeting-american-bar-associations) explained "that too many Americans go to too many prisons for far too long, and for no truly good law enforcement reason." He indicated that the Department of Justice's policies would be changed "so that certain low-level, nonviolent drug offenders who have no ties to large-scale organizations, gangs, or cartels will no longer be charged with offenses that impose draconian mandatory minimum sentences. They now will be charged with offenses for which the accompanying sentences are better suited to their individual conduct, rather than excessive prison terms more appropriate for violent criminals or drug kingpins." In addition, he urged Congress to support legislation "giving federal judges more discretion in applying mandatory minimums to certain drug offenders." Holder noted that such changes could "save our country billions of dollars while keeping us safe."

In July 2014 the USSC (http://www.ussc.gov/sites/default/files/pdf/news/press-releases-and-news-advisories/press-releases/20140718_press_release.pdf) voted to reduce sentences for most federal offenders charged with drug trafficking. The change is retroactive, meaning that existing inmates who were convicted of the covered offenses can apply to have their sentence reduced. The USSC notes, "Under the guidelines, no offender would be released unless a judge reviews the case to determine whether a reduced sentence poses a risk to public safety and is otherwise appropriate." The change is scheduled to go into effect in November 2015.

In November 2014 California voters approved Proposition 47 to downgrade the classification of some nonviolent felonies to misdemeanors and hence reduce the penalties for them. In "Prop. 47 Floods Courts with Pleas for Resentencing and Records Purges" (LATimes.com, November 26, 2014), Maura Dolan reports that the retroactive measure prompted hundreds of inmates to apply immediately to have their convictions reduced. Tens of thousands more are eligible for the reduction. In addition, former inmates who have been released from prison can have their records amended to reflect the change. Dolan explains that "the incentive to take advantage of the new law is strong: a felony conviction can make it impossible to get a job, obtain government student loans, receive public housing or get a license for a wide range of positions, from hairstyling to nursing."

The Legislative Analyst's Office for the California legislature (November 4, 2014, http://www.lao.ca.gov/ballot/2014/prop-47-110414.aspx) provides a list of the covered offenses, which include drug possession and some property crimes, such as grand theft, shoplifting, receiving stolen property, writing bad checks, and check forgery. The reclassification to misdemeanor applies under specific circumstances. For example, previously the crime of receiving stolen property could be charged as a felony or a misdemeanor based on the prosecutor's discretion. Under the new measure the crime will be considered a misdemeanor in all cases in which the value of the stolen property is $950 or less.

Kristina Davis notes in "Calif Cuts Penalties for Small Drug Crimes" (UTSanDiego.com, November 4, 2014) that the ballot measure was called the Safe Neighborhoods and Schools Act. It is projected to save the state an estimated $200 million annually in prison spending. According to Davis, that money will be used "to fund programs that rehabilitate drug addicts, treat mental health needs, keep kids in school and support crime victims."

The transference of money spent on incarceration to funding for social programs has become a popular idea in the 21st century. The Urban Institute (UI), an organization that researches and makes public policy recommendations, describes in "The Justice Reinvestment Initiative: Experiences from the States" (July 2013, http://www.urban.org/UploadedPDF/412879-the-justice-reinvestment-initiative.pdf) the Justice Reinvestment Initiative (JRI), a program funded by the federal government that "convenes states' justice system stakeholders and policy leaders to devise data-driven approaches to criminal justice reform designed to generate cost savings that can be reinvested in high-performing public safety strategies." Many JRI reforms involve the probation and parole systems, which are described in Chapter 9. According to the Urban Institute, JRI penalty reforms have been implemented in 17 states. For example, the institute notes that in 2013 the Oregon legislature reduced sentence lengths for certain drug and property crimes.

Alternative Sentencing

Forms of sentencing other than incarceration, probation, or a combination of the two (split sentences) are widely used in the United States. These programs can vary, but options include work-release and weekender programs, community service programs, day fines, day reporting centers, intensive probation supervision, house arrest and electronic monitoring, residential community corrections, and diversionary treatment programs. Other types of alternative sentencing options, such as mediation and restitution, are sometimes available.

WORK RELEASE AND WEEKENDER PROGRAMS. Work-release programs permit selected prisoners nearing the end of their sentence to work in the community and return to prison facilities or community residential facilities during nonworking hours. Such programs are designed to prepare inmates to return to the community in a relatively controlled environment while they are learning how to work productively. Work release also allows inmates to earn an income, reimburse the state for part of their confinement costs, build up savings for their eventual full release, and acquire more positive living habits. Those on weekender programs spend certain days in prison, usually weekends, but are free the remainder of the time. Both of these types of sentences are known as intermittent incarceration. Violent offenders and those convicted of drug offenses are usually excluded from these programs by the courts.

COMMUNITY SERVICE PROGRAMS. Community service is most often a supplement to other penalties and mainly given to white-collar criminals, juvenile delinquents, and those who commit nonserious crimes. Offenders are usually required to work for government or private nonprofit agencies cleaning parks, collecting roadside trash, setting up chairs for community events, painting community projects, and helping out at nursing homes.

DAY FINES. Under the day-fines type of alternative sentence, the offender pays a monetary sum rather than spending time in jail or prison. Day fines are fines that are assessed for a specific number of days in which the fine amount is based on the seriousness of the crime, the criminal record of the offender, and the offender's income. The fines are paid into the jurisdiction's treasury.

DAY REPORTING CENTERS. Day reporting centers (DRCs) allow offenders to reside in the community. DRCs are often populated by people with drug and alcohol problems and require offenders to appear on a frequent and regular basis to participate in services or activities that are provided by the center or other community agencies. Random drug screening and breathalyzer tests may be administered. The centers may provide employment and educational training and conduct classes on topics such as anger management, substance abuse, life skills, and cognitive skills. Failure to adhere to program requirements or to report at stated intervals can lead to commitment to prison or jail. DRC participation can also be terminated if the offender is charged with a new crime.

INTENSIVE PROBATION SUPERVISION. Intensive probation supervision (IPS) is another method of closely supervising offenders while they reside in the community. Routine probation is not designed or structured to handle high-risk probationers. Therefore, IPS was developed as an alternative that is stricter than routine probation.

The caseloads of officers assigned to IPS offenders are kept low. In most IPS programs the offender must contact a supervising officer frequently, pay restitution to victims, participate in community service, have and keep a job, and, if appropriate, undergo random and unannounced drug testing. Offenders are often required to pay a probation fee.

HOUSE ARREST AND ELECTRONIC MONITORING. Some nonviolent offenders are sentenced to house arrest (or home confinement), which means that they are legally required to remain confined in their own home. They are allowed to leave only for medical purposes or to go to work, although some curfew programs permit offenders to work during the day and have a specified number of hours of free time before returning home. The idea began as a way to keep drunk drivers off the street, but it quickly expanded to include other nonviolent offenders.

The most severe type of house arrest is home incarceration, where the offender's home actually becomes a prison that he or she cannot leave except for very special reasons, such as medical emergencies. Home-detention programs require the offender to be at home when he or she is not working. Some offenders are required to perform a certain number of hours of community service and, if they are employed, to repay the cost of probation and/or restitution.

An electronic monitoring program (EMP) that is used in tandem with house arrest involves attaching a small radio transmitter to the offender in a nonremovable bracelet or anklet. Some systems send a signal to a small monitoring box, which is programmed to call a department of corrections computer if the signal is broken; other systems randomly call probationers and the computer verifies each prisoner's identity through voice recognition software. In some cases a special device in the electronic monitor sends a confirmation to the computer. Some systems have global positioning system technologies to help corrections officers ensure that offenders are not violating any territorial restrictions.

EMPs are often used to monitor the whereabouts of those who are under house arrest and permitted to work. Electronic monitoring is sometimes used to ensure that child molesters stay a specified distance from schools. EMPs cost much less than building new prison cells or housing more inmates. However, close supervision by officers is crucial to the success of EMPs. Officers must ensure that the participants are indeed working when they leave the house and that they are not using illegal drugs. Electronic monitoring equipment must also be checked periodically to make certain that the offenders have not attempted to disable the equipment.

RESIDENTIAL COMMUNITY CORRECTIONS. Residential community corrections facilities are known informally as halfway houses because they are designed as a halfway step from prison to help prisoners reintegrate into community life. Some offenders are sentenced to halfway houses directly in lieu of incarceration if their offenses and general profile indicate they will benefit from the structure and counseling available in such facilities. Many states frequently use halfway houses to relieve prison overcrowding.

Residential centers house offenders in a structured environment. Offenders work full time, maintain the residence center, perform community service, and sometimes attend educational or counseling programs. They may leave the centers only for work or approved programs such as substance-abuse treatment. One type of residential program, called a restitution center, allows offenders to work to pay restitution and child support. The centers regularly test the residents for drugs.

DIVERSIONARY TREATMENT PROGRAMS. Probation combined with mandatory treatment programs is used as an alternative sentence for nonviolent offenders convicted of drug offenses, alcohol abuse, or nonviolent sex offenses. Sentenced individuals are free on probation but typically are required to attend group therapy and supervised professional treatment sessions.

MEDIATION AND RESTITUTION. In mediation victims and offenders meet under the auspices of a community representative and work out a "reconciliation," usually involving some type of restitution and requiring the offenders to take responsibility for their actions. This technique is used mainly for minor crimes and often involves private organizations; therefore, the judiciary does not always accept its resolution. Most often, restitution is not considered the complete punishment but part of a broader punishment, such as probation or working off the restitution dollar amount while in prison.

Death Penalty

The ultimate penalty that can be imposed by the U.S. judiciary system is the death penalty, also known as capital punishment. The Eighth Amendment of the U.S. Constitution guarantees that "cruel and unusual punishments [not be] inflicted." In recent decades debates have raged about the morality and deterrent effect of the death penalty and whether capital punishment is cruel and unusual punishment under the Constitution. According to Tracy L. Snell of the BJS, in *Capital Punishment, 2013—Statistical Tables* (December 2014, http://www.bjs.gov/content/pub/pdf/cp13st.pdf), 2,979 state and federal prisoners were under a sentence of death at yearend 2013. Between 1977 and 2013 there were 1,359 executions, including 39 executions conducted in 2013.

KEY U.S. SUPREME COURT CASES. Three Supreme Court cases, all decided during the 1970s, have produced the current interpretation of the Eighth Amendment relative to the death penalty. In *Furman v. Georgia* (408 U.S. 238 [1972]), the court held that the death penalty in three cases under review was cruel and unusual because under the then-prevailing statutes juries had "untrammeled discretion...to pronounce life or death in capital cases." Due process required procedural fairness, including consideration of the severity and circumstances of the crime. In the three cases decided in *Furman*, three individuals were condemned to die, two for rape and one for murder.

In response to *Furman*, states modified their statutes. North Carolina imposed a mandatory death sentence for first-degree murder. This law was tested by the Supreme Court in *Woodson v. North Carolina* (428 U.S. 280 [1976]). The court held that although the death penalty was not a cruel and unusual punishment in every circumstance, a mandatory death sentence did not satisfy the requirements laid down in *Furman*. The court stated, "North Carolina's mandatory death penalty statute for first-degree murder departs markedly from contemporary standards respecting the imposition of the punishment of death and thus cannot be applied consistently with the Eighth and Fourteenth Amendments' requirement that the State's power to punish 'be exercised within the limits of civilized standards.'" The court overturned the North Carolina law.

Woodson was decided on July 2, 1976. On that same day the court rendered its judgment in *Gregg v. Georgia* (428 U.S. 153), the case of a man who was sentenced to death for murder and robbery under new legislation that passed in Georgia following *Furman*. In this case the court upheld the death penalty, saying, in part:

> The Georgia statutory system under which petitioner was sentenced to death is constitutional. The new procedures on their face satisfy the concerns of *Furman*, since before the death penalty can be imposed there must be specific jury findings as to the circumstances of the crime or the character of the defendant, and the State Supreme Court thereafter reviews the comparability of each death sentence with the sentences imposed on similarly situated defendants to ensure that the sentence of death in a particular case is not disproportionate. Petitioner's contentions that the changes in Georgia's sentencing procedures have not removed the elements of arbitrariness and capriciousness condemned by *Furman* are without merit.

As explained in Chapter 10, the death penalty for juveniles was deemed unconstitutional by the U.S. Supreme Court in 2005 in *Roper v. Simmons* (543 U.S. 551).

CHAPTER 7
CORRECTIONAL FACILITIES: PRISONS AND JAILS

Public views of crime and punishment have changed over the centuries. In general, most societies have moved away from the extraction of personal or family justice (vengeful acts such as blood feuds or the practice of taking "an eye for an eye") toward formal systems that are based on written codes and orderly processes. Prisons and jails have changed from being holding places where prisoners awaited deportation, maiming, whipping, or execution to places of extended—even lifelong—incarceration. Confinement itself has become the punishment.

THE HISTORY OF CORRECTIONS IN THE UNITED STATES

During the colonial period in U.S. history physical punishment was more common than incarceration. Stocks, pillories, branding, flogging, and maiming (such as cutting off an ear or slitting the nostrils) were typical punishments meted out to offenders. The death penalty was also used frequently. The Puritans of Massachusetts believed that humans were naturally depraved, which made it easier for some of the colonies and the first states to enforce harsh punishments. In addition, because Puritans maintained the view that individuals had no control over their fate (predestination), few early Americans supported the idea that criminals could be rehabilitated.

The Quakers, led by William Penn (1644–1718), made colonial Pennsylvania an exception to the harsh practices that were often found in the other colonies. The early criminal code of colonial Pennsylvania abolished executions for all crimes except homicide, replaced physical punishments with imprisonment and hard labor, and did not charge the prisoners for their food and housing.

The Reform Movement

The idea of individual freedom and the concept that people could change society for the better by using reason permeated American society during the 1800s. Reformers worked to abolish slavery, secure women's

rights, and prohibit liquor, as well as to change the corrections system. Rehabilitation of prisoners became the goal of criminal justice, and inmates were given work to keep them busy and to defray the cost of their confinement. Prison administrators began constructing factories within prison walls or hiring inmates out as laborers in chain gangs. In rural areas inmates worked on prison-owned farms. In the South prisoners were often leased out to local farmers. Prison superintendents justified the hard labor by arguing that it taught the offenders the value of work and self-discipline. With the rise of labor unions in the North, the 1930s saw an end to the large-scale prison industry. Unions complained about competing with the inmates' free labor, especially amid the rising unemployment of the Great Depression (1929–1939). As a result, states began limiting what inmates could produce.

As crime increased from the 1970s through the early 1990s, criminal justice practices such as probation, parole, and treatment programs came under attack. Support decreased for rehabilitative programs and increased for keeping offenders incarcerated; many people subscribed to the idea that keeping criminals off the streets was the surest way to keep them from committing more crimes. In response, the federal government and a growing number of states introduced mandatory sentencing and life terms for habitual criminals. They also limited the use of probation, parole, and time off for good behavior. As a result, the incarceration rate skyrocketed through the early 1990s. Crime rates began falling during the late 1990s and this trend continued through the first decade of the 21st century. The decrease in crime rates led to a much slower growth in the incarcerated population.

TYPES OF PRISONER COUNTS

The Bureau of Justice Statistics (BJS) within the U.S. Department of Justice (DOJ) compiles detailed data on federal, state, and local correctional facilities and inmates. It is important to note that some BJS reports distinguish between two different types of prisoner counts: a custody count and a count of the number of inmates under jurisdiction. A custody count is the number of inmates physically located within a particular facility, correctional system, or state. The number of inmates under jurisdiction is the number of inmates under the legal authority of a particular jurisdiction, for example, the state of California. These inmates may or may not be physically located in facilities in the same jurisdiction. Inmates under the legal authority of one type of jurisdiction, such as a state, may be physically located in a facility of another jurisdiction, such as a county jail.

PRISONS AND JAILS COMPARED

Corrections institutions are organized into tiers by level of government, and at each level (federal, state, and local) specific types of institutions provide corrections functions based on the relative severity of the offenses committed. The most restrictive form of corrections is incarceration in a prison. Both the federal and state governments operate their own prison systems; within the federal government, the military maintains its own prisons. Prison inmates serve time for serious offenses that carry a sentence of at least one year of incarceration.

State correctional facilities, including prisons, are commonly overseen by state corrections or public safety agencies. Table 7.1 lists the responsible agency for each state and the District of Columbia.

Most people sentenced to jail serve less than a year for misdemeanors and offenses against the public order.

TABLE 7.1

State correctional departments, 2014

Alabama	Alabama Department of Corrections	http://www.doc.state.al.us/
Alaska	Alaska Department of Corrections	http://www.correct.state.ak.us/corrections/index.jsf
Arizona	Arizona Department of Corrections	https://corrections.az.gov/
Arkansas	Arkansas Department of Correction	http://www.adc.arkansas.gov/
California	California Department of Corrections and Rehabilitation	http://www.cdcr.ca.gov/
Colorado	Colorado Department of Corrections	http://www.doc.state.co.us/
Connecticut	Connecticut Department of Correction	http://www.ct.gov/doc/site/default.asp
Delaware	Delaware Department of Correction	http://www.doc.delaware.gov/
District of Columbia	District of Columbia Department of Corrections	http://doc.dc.gov/
Florida	Florida Department of Corrections	http://www.dc.state.fl.us/
Georgia	Georgia Department of Corrections	http://www.dcor.state.ga.us/
Hawaii	Hawaii Department of Public Safety, Corrections Division	http://hawaii.gov/psd/corrections
Idaho	Idaho Department of Correction	http://www.corr.state.id.us/
Illinois	Illinois Department of Corrections	http://www2.illinois.gov/idoc/Pages/default.aspx
Indiana	Indiana Department of Correction	http://www.in.gov/idoc/
Iowa	Iowa Department of Corrections	http://www.doc.state.ia.us/
Kansas	Kansas Department of Corrections	http://www.dc.state.ks.us/
Kentucky	Kentucky Department of Corrections	http://www.corrections.ky.gov/
Louisiana	Louisiana Department of Public Safety and Corrections	http://www.corrections.state.la.us/
Maine	Maine Department of Corrections	http://www.maine.gov/corrections/
Maryland	Maryland Department of Public Safety and Correctional Services	http://www.dpscs.state.md.us/
Massachusetts	Massachusetts Department of Correction	http://www.mass.gov/eopss/agencies/doc/
Michigan	Michigan Department of Corrections	http://www.michigan.gov/corrections
Minnesota	Minnesota Department of Corrections	http://www.doc.state.mn.us/
Mississippi	Mississippi Department of Corrections	http://www.mdoc.state.ms.us/
Missouri	Missouri Department of Corrections	http://doc.mo.gov/
Montana	Montana Department of Corrections	http://www.cor.mt.gov/default.mcpx
Nebraska	Nebraska Department of Correctional Services	http://www.corrections.nebraska.gov/
Nevada	Nevada Department of Corrections	http://www.doc.nv.gov/
New Hampshire	New Hampshire Department of Corrections	http://www.nh.gov/nhdoc/
New Jersey	New Jersey Department of Corrections	http://www.state.nj.us/corrections/
New Mexico	New Mexico Corrections Department	http://www.corrections.state.nm.us/
New York	New York State Department of Corrections and Community Supervision	http://www.doccs.ny.gov/
North Carolina	North Carolina Department of Public Safety	https://www.ncdps.gov/
North Dakota	North Dakota Department of Corrections and Rehabilitation	http://www.nd.gov/docr/
Ohio	Ohio Department of Rehabilitation and Correction	http://www.drc.ohio.gov/
Oklahoma	Oklahoma Department of Corrections	http://www.ok.gov/doc/
Oregon	Oregon Department of Correction	http://www.oregon.gov/DOC/index.shtml
Pennsylvania	Pennsylvania Department of Corrections	http://www.cor.pa.gov/Pages/default.aspx
Rhode Island	Rhode Island Department of Corrections	http://www.doc.ri.gov/index.php
South Carolina	South Carolina Department of Corrections	http://www.doc.sc.gov/
South Dakota	South Dakota Department of Corrections	http://doc.sd.gov/
Tennessee	Tennessee Department of Correction	http://www.state.tn.us/correction/
Texas	Texas Department of Criminal Justice	http://tdcj.state.tx.us/
Utah	Utah Department of Corrections	http://corrections.utah.gov/
Vermont	Vermont Department of Corrections	http://www.doc.state.vt.us/
Virginia	Virginia Department of Corrections	http://www.vadoc.state.va.us/
Washington	Washington State Department of Corrections	http://www.doc.wa.gov/
West Virginia	West Virginia Division of Corrections	http://www.wvdoc.com/wvdoc/
Wisconsin	Wisconsin Department of Corrections	http://doc.wi.gov/Home
Wyoming	Wyoming Department of Corrections	http://doc.state.wy.us/

SOURCE: Created by Kim Masters Evans for Gale, © 2014

The vast majority of jails are operated at the local level by cities and counties. The federal government operates some jails as well, and within the federal government the U.S. Immigration and Customs Enforcement has its own detention facilities. Prisons and jails are operated under a single state authority in Alaska, Connecticut, Delaware, Hawaii, Rhode Island, and Vermont.

PUBLIC VERSUS PRIVATE CORRECTIONAL FACILITIES

During the 1980s the rapidly rising prison and jail populations led a few jurisdictions to privatize some of their correctional facilities. The basic assumption behind this idea is that the private sector is inherently more efficient, flexible, and cost effective than the government sector because it is less constrained by bureaucracy. It is also argued that private facilities save the public the initial costs of prison construction because those costs are assumed by private contractors. This saves the government from taking on long-term debt to build housing for more prisoners. In this view, a privatized or even a partially privatized corrections system would cost taxpayers less money. Corrections functions, however, are ultimately vested in governmental hands, and private prisons must operate under established rules and regulations.

According to E. Ann Carson of the BJS, in *Prisoners in 2013* (September 30, 2014, http://www.bjs.gov/content/pub/pdf/p13.pdf), at yearend 2013, 6.8% of the prisoners under state jurisdiction and 19.1% of the prisoners under federal jurisdiction were incarcerated in private correctional facilities.

FEDERAL CORRECTIONS

The Federal Bureau of Prisons (BOP; http://www.bop.gov) was established in 1930 as an agency of the DOJ to oversee the corrections system for federal inmates and to administer federal prisons. The BOP notes in "Statistics" (http://www.bop.gov/about/statistics/population_statistics.jsp) that as of January 29, 2014, it oversaw 210,436 federal inmates. Most of the inmates (169,465 or 80.5% of the total) were in BOP facilities. An additional 26,848 inmates (12.6% of the total) were in privately managed facilities, and 14,123 inmates (6.7% of the total) were held in other contract facilities, such as jails or community corrections centers, or were under home confinement. (Note that the individual percentages do not sum to 100% due to rounding.)

The BOP (http://www.bop.gov/locations/list.jsp) directly operated 111 prisons around the country at that time. In addition, federal inmates were incarcerated at 15 privately operated facilities (http://www.bop.gov/about/statistics/population_statistics.jsp). Overall, the 10 facilities housing the largest number of federal inmates were:

- Fort Dix Federal Correctional Institute, New Jersey—4,394 inmates
- Big Spring Correctional Institute (private), Texas—3,316 inmates
- Willacy Correctional Institute (private), Texas—2,886 inmates
- D. Ray James Correctional Facility (private), Georgia—2,332 inmates
- Reeves Correctional Institute (private), Texas—2,284 inmates
- Adams County Correctional Center (private), Mississippi—2,143 inmates
- Atlanta U.S. Penitentiary, Georgia—2,013 inmates
- Fort Worth Correctional Institute, Texas—1,990 inmates
- Brooklyn Metropolitan Detention Center, New York—1,887 inmates
- McRae Correctional Institute (private), Georgia—1,870 inmates

Security Levels of Federal Prisons

The BOP maintains institutions at four different security levels, and each prisoner is assigned to a particular level based on that individual's offenses and behavioral history:

- Minimum security—at the lowest security level are federal prison camps. These facilities have dormitory housing, a relatively low staff-to-inmate ratio, and limited or no perimeter fencing. They are located on or near larger institutions or military bases, where the inmates participate in work programs.

- Low-security federal correctional institutions (FCIs)—these FCIs have fenced perimeters and a dormitory that consists of cubicle housing. Inmates are typically involved in work programs.

- Medium-security FCIs—these facilities feature reinforced perimeter fencing, usually a double fence with an electronic detection system. In addition, inmates are housed in cells and have access to work and treatment programs.

- High-security U.S. penitentiaries—the most secure environment in the federal prison system includes highly secured perimeters with walls and reinforced fences. Inmates are held in multiple- or single-occupant cells, are closely watched, and do not have freedom to move around within the facility without supervision.

In addition, the BOP operates a number of administrative facilities. Many of them hold prisoners of several different security categories. Some are for offenders awaiting trial. Others treat inmates with serious medical needs. Special facilities may also be used to house the most dangerous, violent, or escape-prone inmates. Among the administrative facilities are metropolitan correctional centers; metropolitan detention centers; federal detention centers; federal medical centers; the Federal Transfer Center in Oklahoma City, Oklahoma; and the Administrative-Maximum U.S. Penitentiary in Florence, Colorado.

PRISON ADMISSIONS AND RELEASES

Figure 7.1 shows state and federal admissions and releases of sentenced inmates and yearend sentenced inmate populations between 1978 and 2012. Total admissions outpaced total releases into the first decade of the 21st century. As a result, the sentenced inmate population grew at a very fast rate from the late 1970s through around 2007 before leveling off and then declining slightly.

As shown in Table 7.2, admissions totaled 609,781 in 2012. The majority of these inmates (444,591 or 72.9%) were incarcerated due to new court commitments. Around a quarter (152,780 or 25.1%) were admitted to prison because of parole violations. As explained in Chapter 9, parolees face incarceration for violating certain terms and conditions of their parole agreements. These include technical infractions, such as failing to follow instructions, and committing crimes while on parole. Table 7.3 provides a breakdown of prison releases between 1978 and 2012.

Overall, 637,411 inmates were released from prison in 2012. Nearly two-thirds of them (408,186 or 64%) were given conditional releases, meaning that they were subject to some type of continuing supervision or conditions. Another 213,204 (or 33.4%) of the inmates received unconditional releases.

PRISON INMATES AT YEAREND 2013

Every year the DOJ collects data on the nation's state and federal inmate population. Survey results from yearend 2013 are reported by Carson in *Prisoners in 2013*. The report provides two different types of prisoner counts: sentenced inmates and inmates under the jurisdiction of correctional authorities. The latter group includes inmates that had been convicted but not sentenced at yearend 2013, as well as those awaiting trial.

According to Carson, nearly 1.6 million inmates were under state or federal jurisdiction at yearend 2013. The vast majority (1.4 million or 86.3%) of the inmates were in state prisons and 13.7% (215,900) were in federal prisons. According to Carson, sentenced prisoners numbered 1.5 million at yearend 2013, meaning that they made up 96.3% of all inmates under the jurisdiction of state and federal prison authorities.

As shown in Figure 7.2, the total prison population grew dramatically from 1978 through the first decade of the 21st century. Carson notes that the population peaked in 2009 at 1.6 million before beginning to decline.

FIGURE 7.1

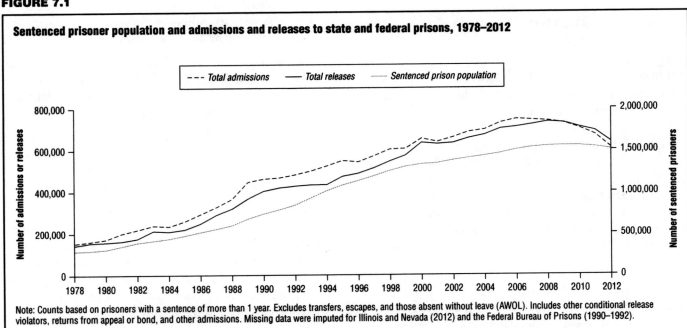

Sentenced prisoner population and admissions and releases to state and federal prisons, 1978–2012

Note: Counts based on prisoners with a sentence of more than 1 year. Excludes transfers, escapes, and those absent without leave (AWOL). Includes other conditional release violators, returns from appeal or bond, and other admissions. Missing data were imputed for Illinois and Nevada (2012) and the Federal Bureau of Prisons (1990–1992).

SOURCE: E. Ann Carson and Daniela Golinelli, "Figure 1. Sentenced State and Federal Prison Admissions and Releases and Yearend Sentenced Prison Population, 1978–2012," in *Prisoners in 2012: Trends in Admissions and Releases, 1991–2012*, U.S. Department of Justice, Office of Justice Programs, Bureau of Justice Statistics, September 2, 2014, http://www.bjs.gov/content/pub/pdf/p12tar9112.pdf (accessed November 7, 2014)

TABLE 7.2

Sentenced prisoners admitted to state and federal prisons, by type of admission, 1978–2012

Year	All admissions[a]			New court commitments			Parole violations[b]		
	Total	Federal	State	Total	Federal	State	Total	Federal	State
1978	152,039	14,724	137,315	126,121	13,247	112,874	23,844	1,429	22,415
1979	161,280	14,120	147,160	131,057	12,619	118,438	25,668	1,454	24,214
1980	171,884	12,598	159,286	142,122	10,907	131,215	28,817	1,640	27,177
1981	199,943	12,830	187,113	160,272	11,086	149,186	35,674	1,709	33,965
1982	218,087	14,818	203,269	177,109	12,461	164,648	39,003	2,317	36,686
1983	237,925	16,745	221,180	187,408	14,119	173,289	45,568	2,583	42,985
1984	234,293	16,013	218,280	180,418	13,491	166,927	52,007	2,475	49,532
1985	258,514	17,916	240,598	198,499	15,368	183,131	58,694	2,502	56,192
1986	291,903	18,501	273,402	219,382	16,067	203,315	71,184	2,401	68,783
1987	326,228	18,709	307,519	241,887	16,260	225,627	82,959	2,435	80,524
1988	365,724	18,696	347,028	261,242	15,932	245,310	101,354	2,744	98,610
1989	447,388	23,491	423,897	316,215	18,388	297,827	122,156	1,611	120,545
1990[c]	462,500	/	460,739	328,300	/	323,069	133,600	/	133,870
1991[c]	468,000	/	466,285	322,500	/	317,237	141,800	/	142,100
1992[c]	482,400	/	480,676	339,600	/	334,301	141,700	/	141,961
1993	500,335	25,235	475,100	341,722	23,653	318,069	147,712	1,346	146,366
1994	523,577	27,271	496,306	345,035	23,956	321,079	170,974	3,146	167,828
1995	549,313	27,337	521,976	361,464	23,972	337,492	178,641	2,915	175,726
1996	542,863	30,239	512,624	353,893	27,346	326,547	175,311	2,672	172,639
1997	572,281	33,906	538,375	365,085	30,560	334,525	189,765	3,106	186,659
1998	603,510	38,219	565,291	381,646	34,376	347,270	209,782	3,630	206,152
1999	606,728	41,972	564,756	375,796	37,455	338,341	202,163	4,292	197,871
2000	654,534	43,732	610,802	389,734	39,303	350,431	207,755	4,186	203,569
2001	638,978	45,140	593,838	405,422	40,193	365,229	220,064	4,720	215,344
2002	660,576	48,144	612,432	433,959	42,303	391,656	213,455	5,600	207,855
2003	686,471	52,288	634,183	445,556	45,713	399,843	205,062	6,357	198,705
2004	697,066	52,982	644,084	457,096	45,796	411,300	226,211	7,178	219,033
2005	730,141	56,057	674,084	470,149	48,723	421,426	239,560	7,331	232,229
2006	747,031	57,495	689,536	492,315	50,204	442,111	246,571	7,286	239,285
2007	742,875	53,618	689,257	479,710	48,691	431,019	252,775	4,924	247,851
2008	738,631	53,662	684,969	477,100	49,270	427,830	253,035	4,390	248,645
2009	728,686	56,153	672,533	474,997	51,524	423,473	242,347	4,628	237,719
2010	703,798	54,121	649,677	458,360	49,515	408,845	231,917	4,606	227,311
2011[d]	671,551	60,634	610,917	454,526	55,817	398,709	205,297	4,816	200,481
2012[d, e]	609,781	55,938	553,843	444,591	51,241	393,350	152,780	4,696	148,084

/Not reported.

BOP = Federal Bureau of Prisons.

[a]Counts based on prisoners with a sentence of more than 1 year. Excludes transfers, escapes, and those absent without leave (AWOL). Totals for all admissions include other conditional release violations, returns from appeal or bond, and other admissions.

[b]Includes all conditional release violators returned to prison for either violations of conditions of release or for new crimes.

[c]The Federal Bureau of Prisons did not report admission data. National totals include an imputed count for BOP admissions.

[d]Alaska did not report type of admission. State and national totals for all admissions include Alaska counts, but totals for admission types do not.

[e]Missing 2012 data were imputed for Illinois and Nevada.

SOURCE: E. Ann Carson and Daniela Golinelli, "Table 1. Sentenced State and Federal Prison Admissions, by Type of Admissions, 1978–2012," in *Prisoners in 2012: Trends in Admissions and Releases, 1991–2012*, U.S. Department of Justice, Office of Justice Programs, Bureau of Justice Statistics, September 2, 2014, http://www.bjs.gov/content/pub/pdf/p12tar9112.pdf (accessed November 7, 2014)

The 10 states with the highest number of inmates under their jurisdiction at yearend 2013 were:

- Texas—168,280

- California—135,981

- Florida—103,028

- Georgia—54,004

- New York—53,550

- Ohio—51,729

- Pennsylvania—50,312

- Illinois—48,653

- Michigan—43,759

- Arizona—41,104

Table 7.4 shows the imprisonment rates for sentenced prisoners under the jurisdiction of federal or state authorities at yearend 2013. The overall rate was 623 sentenced prisoners per 100,000 U.S. residents aged 18 years and older. The federal rate was only 80 sentenced prisoners per 100,000 U.S. residents aged 18 years and older. Louisiana had, by far, the highest rate (1,114) of any of the states, followed by Mississippi (918), Oklahoma (873), Alabama (840), and Texas (819).

Prison Capacities and Overcrowding

As shown in Figure 7.2, approximately 330,000 prisoners were under state and federal correctional jurisdiction in 1978. The incarcerated population has skyrocketed since that time, and federal and state governments have responded by building new prisons and expanding

TABLE 7.3

Sentenced prisoners released from state and federal prisons, by type of release, 1978–2012

Year	All releases[a]			Conditional releases[b]			Unconditional releases[c]		
	Total	Federal	State	Total	Federal	State	Total	Federal	State
1978	142,033	17,361	124,672	107,691	9,651	98,040	25,902	4,146	21,756
1979	154,277	18,518	135,759	117,135	10,442	106,693	26,754	4,493	22,261
1980	157,604	14,748	142,856	122,952	8,252	114,700	25,915	3,647	22,268
1981	162,294	11,715	150,579	124,415	6,431	117,984	27,901	3,396	24,505
1982	174,808	13,373	161,435	140,179	7,086	133,093	28,913	4,862	24,051
1983	212,302	14,415	197,887	166,345	8,151	158,194	38,307	5,264	33,043
1984	208,608	15,024	193,584	166,417	8,933	157,484	39,192	5,177	34,015
1985	219,310	13,410	205,900	174,916	8,748	166,168	41,915	4,188	37,727
1986	247,619	15,115	232,504	202,530	10,118	192,412	42,832	4,572	38,260
1987	288,781	16,012	272,769	232,871	11,358	221,513	53,253	4,260	48,993
1988	318,889	15,302	303,587	253,651	9,511	244,140	62,675	5,437	57,238
1989	367,388	18,104	349,284	302,327	13,136	289,191	62,107	4,864	57,243
1990[d]	404,000	/	403,777	337,000	/	339,439	57,900	/	55,243
1991[d]	420,000	/	419,831	351,300	/	353,774	58,200	/	55,579
1992[d]	428,300	/	428,110	355,300	/	357,731	61,100	/	58,425
1993	434,082	18,676	415,406	355,773	5,742	350,031	69,636	12,801	56,835
1994	434,766	21,062	413,704	353,020	4,790	348,230	72,836	15,986	56,850
1995	474,296	22,292	452,004	374,483	3,747	370,736	88,081	18,054	70,027
1996	488,748	24,647	464,101	369,808	3,176	366,632	103,435	19,699	83,736
1997	514,322	27,280	487,042	386,076	2,445	383,631	109,896	22,294	87,602
1998	546,616	29,239	517,377	406,050	2,148	403,902	126,086	23,939	102,147
1999	574,624	31,816	542,808	420,306	1,919	418,387	128,923	26,089	102,834
2000	635,094	35,259	599,835	426,617	1,991	424,626	148,336	29,180	119,156
2001	628,626	38,370	590,256	438,449	2,234	436,215	162,007	31,715	130,292
2002	633,947	42,339	591,608	443,996	3,154	440,842	161,293	33,904	127,389
2003	656,574	44,135	612,439	444,771	2,603	442,168	163,607	36,221	127,386
2004	672,202	46,624	625,578	483,215	2,488	480,727	166,862	43,715	123,147
2005	701,632	48,323	653,309	497,475	2,105	495,370	179,651	45,708	133,943
2006	709,874	47,920	661,954	499,950	1,746	498,204	193,720	45,749	147,971
2007	721,161	48,764	672,397	505,726	1,545	504,181	199,393	46,804	152,589
2008	734,144	52,348	681,796	505,350	1,225	504,125	216,036	50,708	165,328
2009	729,749	50,720	679,029	505,504	1,479	504,025	211,324	49,208	162,116
2,010	708,677	52,487	656,190	494,249	962	493,287	202,499	51,110	151,389
2011[e]	691,072	55,239	635,833	474,681	649	474,032	202,602	54,163	148,439
2012[e,f]	637,411	56,037	581,374	408,186	591	407,595	213,204	55,079	158,125

/Not reported.

BOP = Federal Bureau of Prisons.

[a]Counts based on prisoners with a sentence of more than 1 year. Excludes transfers, escapes, and those absent without leave (AWOL). Totals for all releases include deaths, releases to appeal or bond, and other releases.

[b]Includes releases to probation, supervised mandatory releases, and other unspecified conditional releases.

[c]Includes expirations of sentence, commutations, and other unconditional releases.

[d]The Federal Bureau of Prisons did not report release data. National totals include an imputed count for BOP releases.

[e]Alaska did not report type of release. State and national totals for all releases include Alaska counts, but totals for release types do not.

[f]Missing 2012 data were imputed for Illinois and Nevada.

SOURCE: E. Ann Carson and Daniela Golinelli, "Table 2. Sentenced State and Federal Prison Releases, by Type of Release, 1978–2012," in *Prisoners in 2012: Trends in Admissions and Releases, 1991–2012*, U.S. Department of Justice, Office of Justice Programs, Bureau of Justice Statistics, September 2, 2014, http://www.bjs.gov/content/pub/pdf/p12tar9112.pdf (accessed November 7, 2014)

older prisons. Nevertheless, at yearend 2013 prison capacities in some jurisdictions were far less than the numbers of inmates being housed in them. This overcrowding is a cause for serious concern. When overcrowding occurs, two inmates are often assigned to a cell that is designed for one person, or temporary housing units are set up to take prison overflow. Overcrowding makes it more likely that disagreements will arise between inmates, leading to violence and injuries. In addition, diseases are more likely to spread among the inmate population.

Table 7.5 shows three types of capacity measures (as available) for state and federal prisons. The measures are defined as follows:

• Design capacity—the number of inmates that planners or architects intended for a facility

• Operational capacity—the number of inmates that can be accommodated based on a facility's staff, existing programs, and services

• Rated capacity—the number of beds or inmates assigned by a rating official to institutions within a jurisdiction

Table 7.5 lists custody populations by jurisdiction at yearend 2013 and the custody populations as percentages of the lowest and highest capacity measures. Around half of the state prison systems had custody populations that exceeded 100% of their lowest capacity rating. Put another way, when judged by the least favorable of the available ratings of their capacities (i.e., lowest capacity), the prison systems of around half the states were overcrowded at yearend 2013. Alabama (197.3%), Illinois

FIGURE 7.2

Total state and federal prison populations, 1978–2013

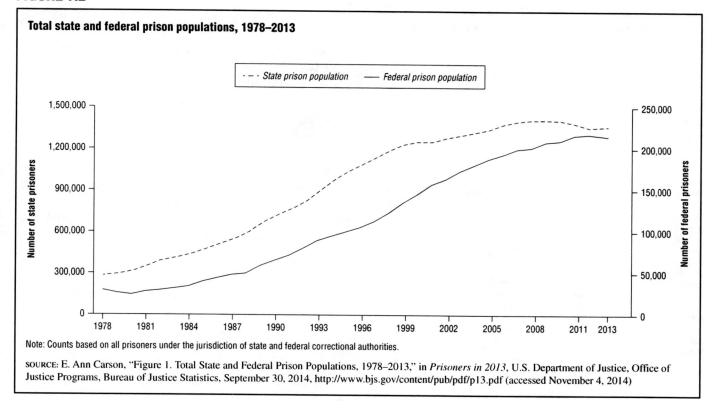

Note: Counts based on all prisoners under the jurisdiction of state and federal correctional authorities.

SOURCE: E. Ann Carson, "Figure 1. Total State and Federal Prison Populations, 1978–2013," in *Prisoners in 2013*, U.S. Department of Justice, Office of Justice Programs, Bureau of Justice Statistics, September 30, 2014, http://www.bjs.gov/content/pub/pdf/p13.pdf (accessed November 4, 2014)

(172.6%), Hawaii (163.8%), Delaware (163.4%), and North Dakota (158.5%) had the most severe overcrowding by this measurement. Even when using the most favorable ratings of prison capacities (highest capacity), 18 states had prisons at more than 100% capacity at yearend 2013. In addition, the federal prison system's population was at 133.1% of its rated capacity measure.

In September 2012 the U.S. Government Accountability Office (GAO) issued a report on the consequences of overcrowding in federal prisons. In *Bureau of Prisons: Growing Inmate Crowding Negatively Affects Inmates, Staff, and Infrastructure* (http://www.gao.gov/assets/650/648123.pdf), the GAO cites the following negative impacts:

- "More inmates are sharing cells and other living units, which brings together for longer periods of time inmates with a higher risk of violence and more potential victims."

- "Inmates may experience crowded bathroom facilities, reductions in shower times, shortened meal times coupled with longer waits for food service, and more limited recreational activities."

- "The growth in the inmate population affects the availability of program opportunities, resulting in waiting lists and inmate idleness. BOP provides programs including education, vocational training, drug treatment, and faith-based reentry programs that help to

rehabilitate inmates and support correctional management."

- "It is difficult to find meaningful work for all inmates, even though generally all inmates are required to have a job."

- "Crowded visiting rooms make it more difficult for inmates to visit with their families."

- "The number of staff positions generally has not increased as BOP's population has grown, affecting staff stress and overtime hours worked."

- "The increased population taxes the infrastructure that was designed for a smaller inmate population, affecting use of toilets, showers, water, and electricity, and wear and tear on food service equipment (e.g., freezer units)."

- "Increasing inmate population and staffing ratios negatively affect inmate conduct and the imposition of discipline, thereby affecting security and safety."

The negative consequences of overcrowding identified by the GAO are likely also found in state prisons that are over their design capacities.

As discussed in Chapter 6, there is a growing movement in the 21st century to reform the criminal justice system by reducing penalties for certain nonviolent crimes. These measures are designed to lower incarceration spending and to ease pressure on overcrowded prisons. Similar initiatives for the nation's probation

TABLE 7.4

Imprisonment rates of sentenced prisoners under state and federal jurisdiction, by jurisdiction, yearend 2013

Jurisdiction	Total adult[a]	Jurisdiction	Total adult[a]
U.S. total[b, c, d]	623	Mississippi	918
Federal[e]	80	Missouri	676
State[b, c, d]	542	Montana	458
		Nebraska	349
Alabama	840	Nevada[g, i]	—
Alaska[c, d, f]	489	New Hampshire	270
Arizona	775	New Jersey	325
Arkansas	760	New Mexico	423
California	464	New York	345
Colorado	502	North Carolina	463
Connecticut[f]	431	North Dakota	273
Delaware[f]	566	Ohio	578
Florida	659	Oklahoma[h]	873
Georgia	710	Oregon	492
Hawaii[f]	328	Pennsylvania	497
Idaho	634	Rhode Island[f]	243
Illinois[g]	492	South Carolina	577
Indiana[h]	597	South Dakota	568
Iowa	364	Tennessee	568
Kansas	437	Texas	819
Kentucky	600	Utah	350
Louisiana	1,114	Vermont[f]	312
Maine	185	Virginia[h]	575
Maryland	456	Washington[e]	332
Massachusetts	242	West Virginia	462
Michigan	570	Wisconsin[h]	478
Minnesota	247	Wyoming	517

NPS = National Prisoner Statistics.

[a]Imprisonment rate per 100,000 U.S. residents age 18 or older.
[b]Includes imputed counts for Nevada.
[c]Alaska did not submit sex-specific counts in 2013.
[d]Alaska did not submit sentence length data in 2013.
[e]Includes inmates held in nonsecure privately operated community corrections facilities and juveniles held in contract facilities.
[f]Prisons and jails form one integrated system. Data include total jail and prison populations.
[g]State did not submit 2012 NPS data.
[h]Counts for 2013 are not comparable to earlier years due to a change in reporting methodology.
[i]State did not submit 2013 NPS data.
Note: Jurisdiction refers to the legal authority of state or federal correctional officials over a prisoner, regardless of where the prisoner is held. Counts are based on prisoners with sentences of more than a year under the jurisdiction of state or federal correctional officials. As of December 31, 2001, sentenced felons from the District of Columbia are the responsibility of the Federal Bureau of Prisons.

SOURCE: E. Ann Carson, "Table 7. Imprisonment Rate of Sentenced Prisoners under the Jurisdiction of State or Federal Correctional Authorities per 100,000 U.S. Residents, by Sex, December 31, 2012 and 2013," in *Prisoners in 2013*, U.S. Department of Justice, Office of Justice Programs, Bureau of Justice Statistics, September 30, 2014, http://www.bjs.gov/content/pub/pdf/p13.pdf (accessed November 4, 2014)

and parole systems are described in Chapter 9. In most cases, overcrowded state prisons are a state problem. However, the federal government can become involved if the problem becomes so acute that it violates the U.S. Constitution. The Eighth Amendment forbids "cruel and unusual punishment." This prohibition has served as the basis for numerous lawsuits filed by inmates against the government regarding overcrowding.

CALIFORNIA'S LEGAL WOES. California's long-standing legal troubles in regards to prison overcrowding are described by the U.S. Supreme Court in *Brown v. Plata* (No. 09-1233), which was decided in May 2011. Justice Anthony M. Kennedy (1936–) notes that in 1990 a suit—

Coleman v. Brown—was brought against the state of California regarding lack of proper mental health care for prison inmates. A federal district court appointed a special master (overseer) to supervise the state's efforts to remedy the problem. According to Kennedy, in 2002 the special master reported that mental health care in California's prisons was "deteriorating due to increased overcrowding." Meanwhile, a separate lawsuit—*Plata v. Brown*—filed in 2001, resulted in the state conceding that its prison medical care violated the Eighth Amendment rights of the state's inmates. The state agreed to make improvements laid out in a remedial injunction (a court order specifying that certain actions be taken or not taken). However, the state's progress was stymied due to continuing problems with overcrowding in the prisons.

In 2008 the original plaintiffs in both cases succeeded in having a special three-judge panel convened to assess prison overcrowding in California. The panel was allowed under the Prison Litigation Reform Act of 1995, a federal law that lays out certain legal procedures for inmate lawsuits. The panel heard testimony on the issues involved and ordered California to decrease its prison population to 137.5% of design capacity within two years. Kennedy notes, "Because it appears all but certain that the State cannot complete sufficient construction to comply fully with the order, the prison population will have to be reduced to at least some extent." The state appealed the decision, but lost in the district courts and before the U.S. Supreme Court.

California formulated a Public Safety Realignment policy to reduce its prison population. According to Carson, the policy calls for "sentencing new nonviolent, nonserious, and nonsex offenders to local jail facilities starting on October 1, 2011." As shown in Table 7.6, between 2003 and 2012 California increased its prison design capacity on average by 0.4% annually while decreasing its custody population by 1.8% annually. However, the custody population was still at 142.7% of design capacity at yearend 2013. Carson notes that in February 2014 the state's deadline for reaching 137.5% of design capacity was extended to February 2016.

ALABAMA FEARS FEDERAL INTERVENTION. As noted earlier and shown in Table 7.5, Alabama's prisons were the most overcrowded at yearend 2013 as measured using the lowest capacity. According to Challen Stephens, in "Alabama Prisons: Why We Cannot Look Away from Alabama's Shame" (AL.com, October 2, 2014), in January 2014 the DOJ notified Alabama that it had found numerous problems involving inmate sexual abuse at the state's Julia Tutwiler Prison for women. Stephens notes, "The Justice Department, citing 'catastrophically low staffing and supervision levels,' threatened a lawsuit that could lead to the courts giving the federal government control over Tutwiler." In "Time, Money, Cooperation

TABLE 7.5

State and federal prison capacities and inmate populations, yearend 2013

Jurisdiction	Type of capacity measure			Custody population	Custody population as a percent of—	
	Rated	Operational	Design		Lowest capacity[a]	Highest capacity[a]
Federal[b]	130,907	—	—	174,242	133.1%	133.1%
Alabama[c]	—	26,145	13,318	26,271	197.3%	100.5%
Alaska[d]	*	*	*	5,054	*	*
Arizona	36,681	42,025	36,681	34,626	94.4	82.4
Arkansas	14,424	14,479	13,885	14,295	103.0	98.7
California[e]	—	—	86,054	122,798	142.7	142.7
Colorado	—	14,121	13,183	16,286	123.5	115.3
Connecticut	*	*	*	16,594	*	*
Delaware[c]	5,775	5,210	4,161	6,798	163.4	117.7
Florida[e]	—	114,995	—	100,940	87.8	87.8
Georgia[e]	60,638	54,583	—	53,701	98.4	88.6
Hawaii	—	3,327	2,291	3,752	163.8	112.8
Idaho[c, e]	—	6,924	7,010	7,219	104.3	103.0
Illinois	32,075	32,075	28,192	48,653	172.6	151.7
Indiana	—	30,917	—	28,495	92.2	92.2
Iowa[f]	—	—	7,109	8,106	114.0	114.0
Kansas	9,180	9,233	9,164	9,515	103.8	103.1
Kentucky	12,157	13,062	13,857	12,141	99.9	87.6
Louisiana[e]	18,121	15,531	16,764	18,794	121.0	103.7
Maine	2,339	2,033	2,339	2,073	102.0	88.6
Maryland	—	23,465	—	21,676	92.4	92.4
Massachusetts	—	—	8,029	10,622	132.3	132.3
Michigan[c, g]	44,846	43,985	—	43,704	99.4	97.5
Minnesota	—	9,099	—	9,391	103.2	103.2
Mississippi[e]	—	25,691	—	15,591	60.7	60.7
Missouri[c]	—	31,681	—	31,499	99.4	99.4
Montana	1,679	—	—	1,666	99.2	99.2
Nebraska[c]	—	3,969	3,175	5,012	157.9	126.3
Nevada[h]	*	*	*	*	*	*
New Hampshire[c]	—	2,848	2,190	2,848	130.0	100.0
New Jersey	19,461	20,959	22,902	19,528	100.3	85.3
New Mexico	6,485	7,428	7,428	3,783	58.3	50.9
New York	52,855	53,408	52,330	53,312	101.9	99.8
North Carolina	—	39,206	33,615	37,176	110.6	94.8
North Dakota[i]	1,044	991	1,044	1,571	158.5	150.5
Ohio	34,986	—	—	46,224	132.1	132.1
Oklahoma[c]	18,607	18,607	18,607	18,313	98.4	98.4
Oregon[i]	—	—	14,362	14,605	101.7	101.7
Pennsylvania[c]	47,780	47,780	47,780	49,735	104.1	104.1
Rhode Island	3,989	3,774	3,973	3,168	83.9	79.4
South Carolina	—	23,806	—	21,534	90.5	90.5
South Dakota[c]	—	3,633	—	3,596	99.0	99.0
Tennessee	22,264	21,528	—	15,655	72.7	70.3
Texas[c]	161,173	154,901	161,173	140,839	90.9	87.4
Utah	—	7,191	7,431	5,382	74.8	72.4
Vermont	1,681	1,681	1,322	1,579	119.4	93.9
Virginia[c]	31,658	—	—	28,431	89.8	89.8
Washington	16,799	16,488	—	17,760	107.7	105.7
West Virginia	4,948	5,778	4,948	5,708	115.4	98.8
Wisconsin[c]	—	22,923	17,181	22,443	130.6	97.9
Wyoming	2,288	2,288	2,407	2,036	89.0	84.6

—Not available. Specific type of capacity is not measured by State.

NPS = National Prisoner Statistics. BJS = Bureau of Justice Statistics.

*Not reported.

[a]Population counts are based on the number of inmates held in custody of facilities operated by the jurisdiction. Excludes inmates held in local jails, other states, or private facilities unless otherwise stated.

[b]Federal custody count reported for the calculation of capacity includes an additional 412 inmates compared to the yearend custody reported in National Prisoner Statistics (NPS).

[c]State defines capacity in a way that differs from BJS's definition.

[d]Alaska did not report 2013 capacity data to NPS, and new facility construction prevents BJS from using prior years' data.

[e]Private facilities included in capacity and custody counts.

[f]Both capacity and custody counts exclude inmates in community-based work release facilities.

[g]Capacity counts include institution and camp net operating capacities and the population of community programs on December 31 since these programs do not have a fixed capacity.

[h]Nevada did not report 2013 NPS data.

[i]State did not report 2013 capacity or custody data to NPS. Data are from 2012.

SOURCE: E. Ann Carson, "Appendix Table 1. Prison Facility Capacity, Custody Population, and Percent Capacity, December 31, 2013," in *Prisoners in 2013*, U.S. Department of Justice, Office of Justice Programs, Bureau of Justice Statistics, September 30, 2014, http://www.bjs.gov/content/pub/pdf/p13.pdf (accessed November 4, 2014)

Crucial for Lasting Criminal Justice Reform in Alabama, State Leaders Say" (AL.com, June 10, 2014), Kelsey Stein indicates that in June 2014 Alabama joined the Justice Reinvestment Initiative, a program that is described in Chapter 6. Justice Reinvestment Initiative reforms are intended to lower incarceration costs and use

TABLE 7.6

California state prison status and prisoner population, 2000–13

[California state prison custody population, facility operational and design capacities, and percent capacity, December 31, 2000–2013]

Year	Design capacity	Custody population	Custody population as a percent of design capacity
2000	80,467	152,859	190.0%
2001	79,957	149,654	187.2
2002	80,587	152,225	188.9
2003	80,487	155,657	193.4
2004	80,890	158,307	195.7
2005	87,250	162,545	186.3
2006	83,551	166,445	199.2
2007	82,936	162,841	196.3
2008	84,066	158,931	189.1
2009	84,056	160,866	191.4
2010	84,181	152,575	181.2
2011	84,130	138,274	164.4
2012	84,130	123,090	146.3
2013	86,054%	122,798	142.7

Percent change

Average annual,			
2003–2012	0.4%	−1.8%	
2012–2013	2.3	−0.2	

Note: Counts based on all inmates in physical custody of California state prisons and camps, regardless of sentence length. These may differ from previously published custody counts due to the exclusion of private prison beds from the custody population in this table.

SOURCE: E. Ann Carson, "Table 10. California State Prison Custody Population, Facility Operational and Design Capacities, and Percent Capacity, December 31, 2000–2013," in *Prisoners in 2013*, U.S. Department of Justice, Office of Justice Programs, Bureau of Justice Statistics, September 30, 2014, http://www.bjs.gov/content/pub/pdf/p13.pdf (accessed November 4, 2014)

the money saved to fund public safety programs. The changes, such as reduced sentences, also help relieve prison overcrowding over time.

JAILS

Besides confining offenders for short terms (usually a sentence of less than one year), jails administer community justice programs that offer alternatives to incarceration. Jails also hold suspects awaiting arraignment, trial, or sentencing, and detainees such as juveniles and mental patients who are being transferred to other facilities.

Jail Inmates at Midyear 2013

Data from the DOJ survey of the nation's jail population, conducted June 30, 2013, were reported by Todd D. Minton and Daniela Golinelli of the BJS in *Jail Inmates at Midyear 2013—Statistical Tables* (August 12, 2014, http://www.bjs.gov/content/pub/pdf/jim13st.pdf). At midyear 2013, 731,208 inmates were being held in local jails. (See Figure 7.3.) The jail inmate population grew at an average annual rate of around 2% to 5% between 2000 and 2007 before undergoing a substantial shift. By 2009 the annual change was −2.3%. After surging briefly in 2012 the jail population dropped again in 2013 by −1.8%. According to Minton and Golinelli, the majority (62%) of jail inmates at midyear 2013 were unconvicted. The other 38% had been convicted and were either awaiting sentencing or were serving their jail sentences.

FIGURE 7.3

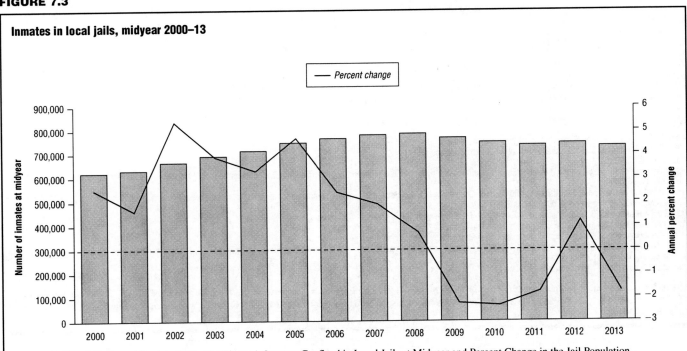

SOURCE: Todd D. Minton and Daniela Golinelli, "Figure 1. Inmates Confined in Local Jails at Midyear and Percent Change in the Jail Population, 2000–2013," in *Jail Inmates at Midyear 2013 – Statistical Tables*, U.S. Department of Justice, Office of Justice Programs, Bureau of Justice Statistics, August 12, 2014, http://www.bjs.gov/content/pub/pdf/jim13st.pdf (accessed November 4, 2014)

TABLE 7.7

Inmates in local jails at midyear, by size of jurisdiction, 2012 and 2013

Jurisdiction size[b]	Inmates confined at midyear[a]				Percent of all inmates	
	2012	2013	Difference	Percent change	2012	2013
Total	744,524	731,208	−13,316	−1.8%	100%	100%
Fewer than 50 inmates	25,091	23,545	−1,546	−6.2%	3.4%	3.2%
50 to 99	41,630	38,970	−2,660	−6.4	5.6	5.3
100 to 249	93,085	95,031	1,946	2.1	12.5	13.0
250 to 499	102,640	102,362	−278	−0.3	13.8	14.0
500 to 999	123,512	123,155	−357	−0.3	16.6	16.8
1,000 or more	358,567	348,145	−10,422	−2.9	48.2	47.6

[a]Number of inmates held on the last weekday in June.
[b]Based on the average daily population (ADP) during the 12-month period ending June 30, 2006, the first year in the current annual survey of jails series. ADP is the sum of all inmates in mail each day for a year, divided by the number of days in the year.
Note: Detail may not sum to total due to rounding.

SOURCE: Todd D. Minton and Daniela Golinelli, "Table 4. Inmates Confined in Local Jails at Midyear, by Size of Jurisdiction, 2012–2013," in *Jail Inmates at Midyear 2013 – Statistical Tables*, U.S. Department of Justice, Office of Justice Programs, Bureau of Justice Statistics, August 12, 2014, http://www.bjs.gov/content/pub/pdf/jim13st.pdf (accessed November 4, 2014)

TABLE 7.8

Rated capacities of local jails and percentage of capacity occupied, midyear 2000–13

Year	Rated capacity[b]	Percent of capacity occupied[a]	
		Midyear[c]	Average daily population[d]
2000	677,787	92.0%	91.2%
2001	699,309	90.0	89.5
2002	713,899	93.0	91.3
2003	736,471	94.0	92.4
2004	755,603	94.0	93.5
2005	786,954	95.0	93.2
2006	794,984	96.3	95.0
2007	810,543	96.3	95.4
2008	828,714	94.8	93.7
2009	849,895	90.3	90.4
2010	857,918	87.3	87.3
2011	870,422	84.5	84.5
2012	877,396	84.9	84.0
2013	872,943	83.8	83.8

Average annual change

2000–2012	2.2%
2012–2013	−0.5

[a]Based on the confined inmate population divided by the rated capacity and multiplied by 100.
[b]Maximum number of beds or inmates assigned by a rating official to a facility, excluding separate temporary holding areas.
[c]Number of inmates held on the last weekday in June.
[d]Sum of all inmates in jail each day for a year, divided by the number of days in the year.
Note: Based on revised data for 2010 to 2012.

SOURCE: Adapted from Todd D. Minton and Daniela Golinelli, "Table 5. Rated Capacity of Local Jails and Percent of Capacity Occupied, 2000–2013," in *Jail Inmates at Midyear 2013—Statistical Tables*, U.S. Department of Justice, Office of Justice Programs, Bureau of Justice Statistics, August 12, 2014, http://www.bjs.gov/content/pub/pdf/jim13st.pdf (accessed November 4, 2014)

TABLE 7.9

Percentage of jail capacity occupied, by jurisdiction size, midyear 2012 and 2013

Jurisdiction size[a]	2012[b]	2013
Total	84.9%	83.8%
Fewer than 50 inmates	66.2%	64.4%
50 to 99	72.1	69.4
100 to 249	79.5	77.9
250 to 499	87.5	87.3
500 to 999	85.9	84.9
1,000 or more	88.8	87.9

[a]Based on the average daily population (ADP) during the 12-month period ending June 30, 2006, the first year in the current annual survey of jails series.
[b]Number of inmates held on the last weekday in June divided by the rated capacity multiplied by 100. Based on revised data for 2012.

SOURCE: Todd D. Minton and Daniela Golinelli, "Table 6. Percent of Jail Capacity Occupied at Midyear, by Size of Jurisdiction, 2012–2013," in *Jail Inmates at Midyear 2013 – Statistical Tables*, U.S. Department of Justice, Office of Justice Programs, Bureau of Justice Statistics, August 12, 2014, http://www.bjs.gov/content/pub/pdf/jim13st.pdf (accessed November 4, 2014)

Overall, the nation's jails do not suffer as much overcrowding as the state and federal prisons. Table 7.8 shows the rated capacity of local jails and the percentage of capacity occupied between 2000 and 2013. (Note that data were compiled based on midyear surveys.) Local jails had a rated capacity of 677,787 beds or inmates at midyear 2000. By midyear 2013 the local jail capacity had reached 872,943 beds or inmates. At midyear 2000 local jails were at approximately 92% of rated capacity. By midyear 2013 they were at 83.8% of rated capacity.

The percentages of capacity occupied at local jails differ greatly by jurisdiction size. As shown in Table 7.9, jails with fewer than 50 inmates were at 64.4% of capacity at midyear 2013, whereas those holding 1,000 or more inmates were at 87.9% of capacity.

Local Jail Sizes and Capacities

Table 7.7 breaks down the nation's local jail inmates by size of facility as of midyear 2012 and 2013. In 2013 only 3.2% of the inmates were incarcerated in jail facilities that held fewer than 50 inmates each. The largest percentage (47.6%) of inmates were in facilities that held 1,000 or more inmates each.

Jail-Supervised People at Midyear 2013

As noted earlier, local jails perform services other than full-time confinement of inmates. Table 7.10 provides a breakdown of the numbers of people under jail supervision at midyear 2000 and from 2006 to 2013. Overall, jails supervised 790,649 people as of midyear 2013—731,208 inmates held in jail facilities full time and 59,441 people being supervised in other ways. The largest numbers of people being supervised were in community service programs (13,877), electronic monitoring programs (12,023), and weekend confinement programs (10,950).

COSTS OF INCARCERATION

As is explained in Chapter 6, the nation's criminal justice system includes police protection, judicial and legal functions, and corrections. As is shown in Table 1.1 in Chapter 1, the total amount spent on corrections at the federal, state, and local levels in fiscal year (FY) 2011 was $80.7 billion. Federal direct expenditures on corrections were $7.9 billion, state direct expenditures were $46.7 billion, and local direct expenditures were $26.1 billion. It is important to note that the correctional system includes both incarceration and community supervision (i.e., parole and probation programs). Determining the amount that the nation spends solely on incarceration each year is difficult because of the many jurisdictions involved. Each state and local government has its own budgeting system. In addition, there are significant funds transferred between different government levels. For example, the federal government spends money directly on the federal prison system and also provides grants and other funding to state and local governments to help with their incarceration costs. Likewise, state governments provide intergovernmental funds to local jurisdictions.

Incarceration costs are most easily ascertained for the federal government. The federal fiscal year runs from October 1 through September 30. Thus, FY 2015 covers October 1, 2014, through September 30, 2015. In *Federal Prison System Federal Bureau of Prisons* (February 2014, http://www.justice.gov/sites/default/files/jmd/legacy/2013/12/21/bop.pdf), the DOJ indicates that the BOP's requested budget for FY 2015 was $6.9 billion, virtually unchanged from the funding that was enacted for FY 2014.

Tracey Kyckelhahn of the BJS examines in *State Corrections Expenditures, FY 1982–2010* (April 30, 2014, http://bjs.ojp.usdoj.gov/content/pub/pdf/scefy8210.pdf) trends in state government corrections expenditures between FYs 1982 and 2010. Overall, corrections spending in FY 2010 totaled $48.5 billion. (See Figure 7.4.) The majority ($38.6 billion, or 79.6% of the total) was spent on correctional institutions, such as prisons. This amount included $37.3 billion to operate the institutions and $1.3 billion for institutional capital outlays (e.g., construction, renovations, major repairs, and major equipment costs). Noninstitutional expenditures in FY 2010 totaled $10 billion, or 20.6% of total state correctional spending. These noninstitutional expenses included training of employees, operation of probation and parole systems, and operation of other nonresidential correctional facilities and programs.

TABLE 7.10

Persons under jail supervision, by confinement status and program type, midyear 2000 and 2006–13

Confinement status and type of program	2000	2006	2007	2008	2009	2010	2011	2012	2013
Total	**687,033**	**826,041**	**848,419**	**858,385**	**837,647**	**809,360**	**798,417**	**808,622**	**790,649**
Held in jail[a]	621,149	765,819	780,174	785,533	767,434	748,728	735,601	744,524	731,208
Supervised outside of a jail facility[b]	65,884	60,222	68,245	72,852	70,213	60,632	62,816	64,098	59,441
Weekend programs[c]	14,523	11,421	10,473	12,325	11,212	9,871	11,369	10,351	10,950
Electronic monitoring	10,782	10,999	13,121	13,539	11,834	12,319	11,950	13,779	12,023
Home detention[d]	332	807	512	498	738	736	809	2,129	1,337
Day reporting	3,969	4,841	6,163	5,758	6,492	5,552	5,200	3,890	3,683
Community service	13,592	14,667	15,327	18,475	17,738	14,646	11,680	14,761	13,877
Other pretrial supervision	6,279	6,409	11,148	12,452	12,439	9,375	10,464	7,738	7,542
Other work programs[e]	8,011	8,319	7,369	5,808	5,912	4,351	7,165	7,137	5,341
Treatment programs[f]	5,714	1,486	2,276	2,259	2,082	1,799	2,449	2,164	2,002
Other	2,682	1,273	1,857	1,739	1,766	1,983	1,731	2,149	2,687

[a]Number of inmates held on the last weekday in June.
[b]Number of persons under jail supervision but not confined on the last weekday in June. Excludes persons supervised by a probation or parole agency.
[c]Offenders serve their sentences of confinement on weekends only (i.e., Friday to Sunday).
[d]Includes only persons without electronic monitoring.
[e]Includes persons in work release programs, work gangs, and other alternative work programs.
[f]Includes persons under drug, alcohol, mental health, and other medical treatment.

SOURCE: Todd D. Minton and Daniela Golinelli, "Table 9. Persons under Jail Supervision, by Confinement Status and Type of Program, Midyear 2000 and 2006–2013," in *Jail Inmates at Midyear 2013 – Statistical Tables*, U.S. Department of Justice, Office of Justice Programs, Bureau of Justice Statistics, August 12, 2014, http://www.bjs.gov/content/pub/pdf/jim13st.pdf (accessed November 4, 2014)

FIGURE 7.4

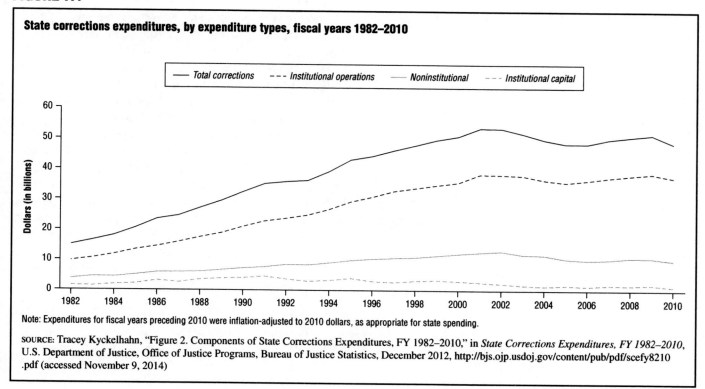

State corrections expenditures, by expenditure types, fiscal years 1982–2010

Legend: Total corrections — — — Institutional operations — Noninstitutional — — Institutional capital

Note: Expenditures for fiscal years preceding 2010 were inflation-adjusted to 2010 dollars, as appropriate for state spending.

SOURCE: Tracey Kyckelhahn, "Figure 2. Components of State Corrections Expenditures, FY 1982–2010," in *State Corrections Expenditures, FY 1982–2010*, U.S. Department of Justice, Office of Justice Programs, Bureau of Justice Statistics, December 2012, http://bjs.ojp.usdoj.gov/content/pub/pdf/scefy8210 .pdf (accessed November 9, 2014)

Closing Prisons to Save Costs

According to Kyckelhahn, correctional institutional costs skyrocketed from 1982 through the end of the 20th century before leveling off. Near the end of the first decade of the 21st century the United States underwent a severe economic downturn dubbed the Great Recession. As a result, many states suffered significant budget shortfalls and looked for ways to cut expenses. Some states began closing prisons to reduce their corrections expenditures. This was particularly true for states with declining inmate populations. The Sentencing Project notes in *On the Chopping Block 2013: State Prison Closures* (April 2014, http://sentencingproject.org/doc/publications/ inc_On%20the%20Chopping%20Block%202013.pdf) that in 2013 Georgia, Kentucky, New York, North Carolina, Pennsylvania, and Texas closed prisons. Between 2011 and 2013, 17 states had reduced their prison capacities.

The Illinois governor Pat Quinn (1948–) has pushed to close prisons to save costs, but this decision has proved to be quite controversial because of overcrowding in the state's overall prison system. In "Quinn Stands by Decision to Close 2 Prisons, Despite Inmate Crowding" (Chicago-Tribune.com, February 18, 2013), Monique Garcia and Rafael Guerrero indicate that as of February 2013 Quinn had closed two prisons in the state and was planning to close additional correctional facilities. The closures forced some remaining prisons to house minimum-security inmates in their gymnasiums instead of in regular cells. This practice spurred fierce criticism from the state's union for corrections officers, some of whom would lose their job

if prisons closed. They argued that already overcrowded prisons were being further strained, making their job more difficult and dangerous. In 2013 Illinois closed two more prison facilities: the Dwight Correctional Center and the Tamms Super Maximum Security Correctional Center.

WORK, EDUCATIONAL, AND COUNSELING PROGRAMS FOR INMATES

Many state and federal prisons offer inmate work, educational, and counseling programs. For example, the New York State Department of Corrections and Community Supervision (2014, http://www.doccs.ny.gov/Pro gramServices/program_list_alpha.html) lists dozens of programs and services that are available to inmates in certain state prisons.

Prisoner Work Programs

State and local governments prevent prisoners from working at some jobs because they would be in competition with private enterprise or workers. In 1936 Congress barred convicts from working on federal contracts worth more than $10,000. In 1940 Congress made it illegal to transport convict-made goods through interstate commerce. These rules were changed in 1979, when Congress established the Prison Industry Enhancement Certification Program (PIECP). The PIECP allows state correctional industries that meet certain requirements to sell inmate-produced goods to the federal government and in interstate commerce. The National Correctional Industries Association, the professional organization for prison industry employees, provides training and technical assistance to the PIECP.

Many prison administrators generally favor work programs. Some believe work keeps prisoners productive and occupied, thus leading to a safer prison environment. Another benefit is that work programs prepare prisoners for reentry into the noninstitutionalized world by helping them develop job skills and solid work habits that will be needed for post-incarceration employment. Some prisons report that inmates who work in industry are less likely to cause problems in prison or be rearrested after release than convicts who do not participate in work programs.

In addition, many inmates report they like the opportunity to work. They assert that it provides relief from boredom and gives them some extra money. Inmates find that the money they earn helps them to meet financial obligations for their families even while they are in prison.

Work Programs for Federal Inmates

The BOP explains in "Work Programs" (2014, http://www.bop.gov/inmates/custody_and_care/work_programs.jsp?) that federal prison inmates are required to work if they are medically able to do so. Their work assignments typically contribute to the facility operations and maintenance in areas such as food service, plumbing, painting, or landscaping. Inmates earn $0.12 to $0.40 per hour for these in-house work assignments. In "UNICOR" (2014, http://www.bop.gov/inmates/custody_and_care/unicor.jsp), the BOP also reports that 16% of federal prison inmates work in Federal Prison Industries factories. This program provides slightly higher wages to inmates, from $0.23 to $1.15 per hour. Work includes manufacturing jobs in areas such as furniture, electronics, textiles, and graphic arts. A high school diploma or its equivalent is required for all but entry-level positions.

CHAPTER 8
CHARACTERISTICS AND RIGHTS OF INMATES

CHARACTERISTICS OF INMATES

As of January 2015, recent national information about inmate characteristics was available from two primary sources: the Federal Bureau of Prisons (BOP) and the Bureau of Justice Statistics (BJS). Both are agencies of the U.S. Department of Justice (DOJ). Because these sources compile inmate data at different times for different inmate population subsets, they provide somewhat differing datasets of inmate counts and characteristics. In addition, some inmate counts include only adults, while others also include juveniles. (Detailed information about the juvenile justice system is provided in Chapter 10.) Lastly, it is important to distinguish between the different ways in which inmates are officially counted:

- Inmates under jurisdiction—the number of inmates under the jurisdiction of a governmental entity regardless of where the inmates are held and their incarceration status

- Inmates in custody—the number of inmates in the physical custody of a particular jurisdiction (i.e., the number of inmates held within the facilities of that jurisdiction)

- Sentenced inmates—the number of inmates that have been sentenced by the justice system and are serving sentences in prison or jail

Federal and State Inmates

As shown in Table 8.1, nearly 1.6 million adults were under the jurisdiction of federal or state prisons at year-end 2013. The vast majority (1.4 million or 86.3%) were under state jurisdiction, while 215,900 (13.7%) were under federal jurisdiction. Overall, the prison population was predominantly male (1.5 million or 92.9%) with only 111,300 female prisoners (7.1% of the total).

Table 8.2 provides a breakdown for 1.5 million federal and state inmates at yearend 2013 by age, sex, race,

and Hispanic origin. (Note that individual percentages may not sum to 100% due to rounding and other data adjustments.) The largest single age category was 30 to 34 years; 16.7% of the inmates fell into this age group. Over four out of 10 (44.4%) of all the inmates were under the age of 35 years. On a racial basis, 526,000 (37.2%) of the male prisoners were non-Hispanic African American, 454,100 (32.1%) were non-Hispanic white, and 118,100 (8.4%) were non-Hispanics of other races. The racial makeup of the female non-Hispanic inmate population was 51,500 (49.5%) white, 23,100 (22.2%) African American, and 11,900 (11.4%) another race. In addition, 17,600 (16.9%) of the female inmates were of Hispanic origin.

The overall adult incarceration rate at yearend 2013 was 478 prisoners per 100,000 U.S. residents. (See Table 8.3; note that the rates shown are for the 1.5 million inmates for which demographic data were available.) The age group with the highest incarceration rate was 30 to 34 years, which had a rate of 1,187 prisoners per 100,000 U.S. residents. The incarceration rate for men (904) was much higher than that for women (65). The highest rate for any specific group was 6,746 for non-Hispanic African American males aged 30 to 34 years. Overall, non-Hispanic African American males had a much higher incarceration (2,805) than did non-Hispanic white males (466).

OFFENSES OF FEDERAL INMATES. Table 8.4 provides a breakdown by offense for sentenced federal prisoners between September 30, 2001, and September 30, 2013. As of September 2013, 50.7% of the inmates had been incarcerated for violating federal drug laws. Weapons offenses were listed for 15.5% of the inmates, and other public order offenses were listed for 10.4% of the inmates. Dating back to September 2001 at least half of all federal inmates were in prison because of drug charges.

TABLE 8.1

Inmates under state and federal jurisdiction by gender, yearend 2013

Jurisdiction	2013 Total	2013 Male	2013 Female
U.S. total[a, b]	1,574,741	1,463,454	111,287
Federal[c]	215,866	201,697	14,169
State[a, b]	1,358,875	1,261,757	97,118
Alabama	32,381	29,660	2,721
Alaska[b, d]	5,081	4,450	631
Arizona	41,104	37,332	3,772
Arkansas[e]	17,235	15,904	1,331
California	135,981	129,684	6,297
Colorado	20,371	18,556	1,815
Connecticut[d]	17,563	16,328	1,235
Delaware[d]	7,004	6,405	599
Florida	103,028	95,757	7,271
Georgia	54,004	50,445	3,559
Hawaii[d]	5,632	4,972	660
Idaho	7,549	6,523	1,026
Illinois[f]	48,653	45,737	2,916
Indiana[g]	29,913	27,078	2,835
Iowa	8,697	7,983	714
Kansas	9,763	9,026	737
Kentucky	21,030	18,717	2,313
Louisiana	39,299	37,071	2,228
Maine	2,173	2,013	160
Maryland	21,335	20,410	925
Massachusetts	10,950	10,143	807
Michigan	43,759	41,700	2,059
Minnesota	10,289	9,566	723
Mississippi	21,969	20,352	1,617
Missouri	31,537	28,755	2,782
Montana	3,642	3,230	412
Nebraska	5,026	4,656	370
Nevada[h]	13,056	11,971	1,085
New Hampshire	3,018	2,781	237
New Jersey	22,452	21,427	1,025
New Mexico	6,849	6,195	654
New York	53,550	51,193	2,357
North Carolina	36,922	34,430	2,492
North Dakota	1,513	1,356	157
Ohio	51,729	47,579	4,150
Oklahoma[g]	27,547	24,769	2,778
Oregon	15,362	14,066	1,296
Pennsylvania	50,312	47,668	2,644
Rhode Island[d]	3,361	3,169	192
South Carolina	22,060	20,669	1,391
South Dakota	3,651	3,209	442
Tennessee	28,521	26,069	2,452
Texas	168,280	154,450	13,830
Utah	7,075	6,413	662
Vermont[d]	2,078	1,924	154
Virginia[g]	36,982	34,133	2,849
Washington	17,984	16,535	1,449
West Virginia	6,824	6,016	808
Wisconsin[g]	22,471	21,232	1,239
Wyoming	2,310	2,050	260

—Not calculated.
NPS = National Prisoner Statistics.
[a]Includes imputed counts for Nevada.
[b]Alaska did not submit sex-specific jurisdiction counts to NPS in 2013.
[c]Includes inmates held in nonsecure privately operated community corrections facilities and juveniles held in contract facilities.
[d]Prisons and jails form one integrated system. Data include total jail and prison populations.
[e]Changes to Arkansas' parole system in 2013 contributed to higher counts of inmates under jurisdiction.
[f]State did not submit 2012 NPS data.
[g]Counts for 2013 are not comparable to earlier years due to a change in reporting methodology.
[h]State did not submit 2013 NPS data.
Note: Jurisdiction refers to the legal authority of state or federal correctional officials over a prisoner, regardless of where the prisoner is held. As of December 31, 2001, sentenced felons from the District of Columbia were the responsibility of the Federal Bureau of Prisons.

SOURCE: Adapted from E. Ann Carson, "Table 2. Prisoners under the Jurisdiction of State or Federal Correctional Authorities, by Sex, December 31, 2012 and 2013," in *Prisoners in 2013*, U.S. Department of Justice, Office of Justice Programs, Bureau of Justice Statistics, September 30, 2014, http://www.bjs.gov/content/pub/pdf/p13.pdf (accessed November 4, 2014)

OFFENSES OF STATE INMATES. Table 8.7 provides a breakdown by offense for 1.3 million sentenced state prisoners as of yearend 2012. More than half (53.8%) had committed a violent offense as their most serious offense. Overall, the largest fractions of inmates had been incarcerated for robbery (13.7%), murder (12.7%), rape/sexual assault (12.2%), or drug offenses other than possession (12.2%). There were stark differences between males and females in regards to the most serious offense committed. Most of the male inmates had been incarcerated for robbery (14%), rape/sexual assault (13%), or drug crimes other than possession (11.8%). By contrast, most of the female inmates had been incarcerated for drug crimes other than possession (17.9%), murder (11.1%), or larceny-theft (9.1%). A violent offense was the most serious offense listed for 59.9% of Hispanic inmates, 58.8% of non-Hispanics of other races, 58.3% of non-Hispanic African American inmates, and 49.3% of non-Hispanic white inmates.

Some historical perspective on the offenses of state inmates is provided for selected years between 1991 and 2011 in Table 8.8. The percentage of inmates incarcerated for a violent crime was 44.6% in 1991 but climbed to 53.5% by 2011. This corresponded with reductions in the percentages of inmates held for property and drug offenses over that period. However, the percentages of inmates in prison for public order offenses (e.g., weapons crimes) and for other crimes increased between 1991 and 2011.

Death Row Inmates

In *Capital Punishment, 2013—Statistical Tables* (December 2014, http://www.bjs.gov/content/pub/pdf/cp13st.pdf), Tracy L. Snell of the BJS indicates that 2,979 state and federal prisoners were under a sentence

In "Statistics" (2014, http://www.bop.gov/about/statistics), the BOP provides a snapshot in time of the federal inmate population. Offense information available as of September 27, 2014, is provided in Table 8.5. The largest number of inmates (98,482) were incarcerated under federal drug charges. Weapons, explosives, and/or arson offenses were listed for 32,141 inmates, while another 20,447 inmates were incarcerated for violating federal immigration laws. As shown in Table 8.6, the largest fraction of federal inmates (25.5%) was serving a sentence of five to 10 years. The second-largest contingent (20.3%) had been sentenced to 10 to 15 years in prison.

TABLE 8.2

Percentage of sentenced prisoners under state and federal jurisdiction, by sex, race, Hispanic origin, and age, yearend 2013

| Age | Total[a] | Male | | | | | Female | | | | |
		Total male[a, b]	White[c]	Black[c]	Hispanic	Other[b, c]	Total female[a, b]	White[c]	Black[c]	Hispanic	Other[b, c]
Total[d]	100%	100%	100%	100%	100%	100%	100%	100%	100%	100%	100%
18–19	1.0%	1.1%	0.6%	1.3%	1.3%	1.1%	0.6%	0.4%	0.9%	1.1%	0.8%
20–24	11.4	11.4	8.6	13.0	12.7	12.4	10.2	8.7	11.3	12.5	10.9
25–29	15.3	15.2	13.2	15.5	17.2	17.2	17.3	16.6	16.5	20.5	20.2
30–34	16.7	16.6	15.1	16.8	18.6	17.9	18.3	18.4	16.9	19.9	21.0
35–39	13.9	13.9	12.7	14.1	15.5	14.2	14.4	14.5	13.9	14.8	14.3
40–44	12.5	12.5	13.0	12.2	12.3	12.4	13.2	13.7	13.4	11.4	11.8
45–49	10.8	10.8	12.2	10.5	9.1	9.5	11.3	11.7	12.1	9.1	9.2
50–54	8.4	8.5	10.4	8.2	6.3	7.0	7.7	8.2	7.8	5.7	6.7
55–59	4.9	5.0	6.4	4.6	3.6	4.0	3.8	3.9	4.3	2.8	3.4
60–64	2.5	2.6	3.7	2.1	1.8	2.1	1.7	2.0	1.7	1.1	1.7
65 or older	2.1	2.2	3.8	1.2	1.4	1.8	1.2	1.4	0.9	1.1	0.8
Total number of sentenced prisoners	1,516,879	1,412,745	454,100	526,000	314,600	118,100	104,134	51,500	23,100	17,600	11,900

NPS = National Prisoner Statistics.

[a]Detail may not sum to total due to rounding, inclusion of inmates age 17 or younger in the total count, and missing race or Hispanic origin data.

[b]Includes American Indians, Alaska Natives, Asians, Native Hawaiians, Pacific Islanders, persons of two or more races, or additional racial categories in reporting information systems.

[c]Excludes persons of Hispanic or Latino orgin.

[d]Includes persons age 17 or younger.

Note: Jurisdiction refers to the legal authority of state or federal correctional officials over a prisoner, regardless of where the prisoner is held. Counts are based on prisoners with sentences of more than a year under the jurisdiction of state or federal correctional officials. Nevada did not submit 2013 data to NPS and Alaska did not submit sex-specific counts or sentence length data in 2013.

SOURCE: E. Ann Carson, "Table 7. Sentenced Prisoners under the Jurisdiction of State or Federal Correctional Authorities, by Age, Sex, Race, and Hispanic Origin," in *Prisoners in 2013*, U.S. Department of Justice, Office of Justice Programs, Bureau of Justice Statistics, September 30, 2014, http://www.bjs.gov/content/pub/pdf/p13.pdf (accessed November 4, 2014)

TABLE 8.3

Imprisonment rates of sentenced prisoners under state and federal jurisdiction per 100,000 U.S. residents, by sex, race, Hispanic origin, and age, yearend 2013

| Age | Total[a] | Male | | | | | Female | | | | |
		Total male[a]	White[b]	Black[b]	Hispanic	Other[a, b]	Total female[a]	White[b]	Black[b]	Hispanic	Other[a, b]
Total[c]	478	904	466	2,805	1,134	963	65	51	113	66	90
18–19	181	340	115	1,092	412	344	14	7	33	17	24
20–24	755	1,382	601	3,956	1,617	1,472	95	73	154	100	131
25–29	1,067	1,937	954	5,730	2,289	2,082	168	140	260	173	232
30–34	1,187	2,183	1,104	6,746	2,529	2,257	180	156	277	169	235
35–39	1,071	1,994	1,009	6,278	2,321	1,951	151	133	240	133	178
40–44	917	1,713	938	5,244	2,007	1,730	131	113	224	107	144
45–49	782	1,464	827	4,486	1,700	1,495	112	90	202	99	135
50–54	567	1,082	615	3,382	1,382	1,171	70	54	128	72	94
55–59	348	679	389	2,132	1,016	750	36	26	72	44	52
60–64	208	415	252	1,269	714	497	19	14	34	25	27
65 or older	70	153	108	406	301	206	5	4	7	8	8
Total number of sentenced prisoners	1,516,879	1,412,745	454,100	526,000	314,600	118,100	104,134	51,500	23,100	17,600	11,900

NPS = National Prisoner Statistics.

[a]Includes American Indians, Alaska Natives, Asians, Native Hawaiians, Pacific Islanders, persons of two or more races, or additional racial categories in the reporting information systems.

[b]Excludes persons of Hispanic or Latino origin.

[c]Includes persons age 17 or younger.

Note: Counts based on prisoners with sentences of more than a year under the jurisdiction of state or federal correctional officials. Imprisonment rate is the number of prisoners under state or federal jurisdiction with a sentence of more than a year per 100,000 U.S. residents of corresponding sex, age, and race or Hispanic origin. Resident population estimates are from the U.S. Census Bureau for January 1 of the following year. Nevada did not submit 2013 data to NPS, and Alaska did not submit sex-specific counts or sentence length data in 2013.

SOURCE: E. Ann Carson, "Table 8. Imprisonment Rate of Sentenced State and Federal Prisoners per 100,000 U.S. Residents, by Sex, Race, Hispanic Origin, and Age, December 31, 2013," in *Prisoners in 2013*, U.S. Department of Justice, Office of Justice Programs, Bureau of Justice Statistics, September 30, 2014, http://www.bjs.gov/content/pub/pdf/p13.pdf (accessed November 4, 2014)

of death at yearend 2013. California had the largest number (735), followed by Florida (398), Texas (273), and Pennsylvania (190) and Alabama (190). Over half (56%) of all death row inmates were white, while 42% were African American. Snell notes that Hispanics accounted for 14% of the death row inmates for which

TABLE 8.4

Percentage of sentenced prisoners under federal jurisdiction, by offense, September 30, 2001–13

Most serious offense	2001	2002	2003	2004	2005	2006	2007	2008	2009	2010	2011	2012	2013
Total	100%	100%	100%	100%	100%	100%	100%	100%	100%	100%	100%	100%	100%
Violent	10.2%	10.1%	9.5%	9.8%	9.4%	9.0%	8.5%	8.3%	7.7%	7.5%	7.2%	7.1%	7.0%
Homicide[a]	1.4	1.5	1.4	1.6	1.5	1.5	1.5	1.5	1.4	1.3	1.2	1.2	1.2
Robbery	6.7	6.5	6.1	6.1	5.8	5.5	5.0	4.8	4.5	4.3	4.0	3.9	3.8
Other violent	2.1	2.1	2.0	2.1	2.1	2.1	2.0	2.0	1.9	1.9	1.9	2.0	2.0
Property	7.4%	7.2%	7.0%	5.4%	5.1%	5.1%	5.2%	5.4%	5.5%	5.5%	5.6%	5.8%	6.0%
Burglary	0.4	0.4	0.3	0.3	0.3	0.3	0.3	0.2	0.2	0.2	0.2	0.2	0.2
Fraud	4.5	4.4	4.4	3.4	3.2	3.3	3.5	3.8	4.0	4.0	4.1	4.3	4.5
Other property	2.5	2.3	2.3	1.7	1.5	1.5	1.4	1.4	1.3	1.3	1.3	1.2	1.2
Drug[b]	56.0%	56.1%	55.9%	55.5%	54.7%	54.8%	54.7%	53.6%	53.0%	52.4%	51.8%	51.0%	50.7%
Public-order	25.8%	26.0%	27.0%	28.7%	30.0%	30.3%	30.8%	32.0%	33.2%	34.0%	34.9%	35.5%	35.7%
Immigration	10.8	10.7	10.9	10.9	11.2	10.5	10.2	10.1	10.6	10.6	11.1	10.6	9.9
Weapons	8.8	9.5	10.3	12.2	13.2	14.0	14.4	15.0	15.1	15.2	15.1	15.3	15.5
Other	6.2	5.8	5.7	5.6	5.5	5.8	6.2	6.9	7.5	8.2	8.7	9.6	10.4
Other/unspecified[c]	0.6%	0.6%	0.6%	0.6%	0.8%	0.8%	0.7%	0.7%	0.7%	0.6%	0.6%	0.6%	0.6%
Total number of sentenced prisoners	137,574	143,690	152,693	153,776	160,524	167,051	173,979	176,081	184,553	186,545	193,043	193,861	193,775

BJS = Bureau of Justice Statistics. NPS = National Prisoner Statistics.
[a]Includes murder, negligent, and nonnegligent manslaughter.
[b]Includes trafficking, possession, and other drug offenses.
[c]Includes offenses not classified.

Note: Estimates are based on prisoners with sentences of more than 1 year under federal custody as of September 30 of each year, and include inmates sentenced on U.S. district court commitments, District of Columbia superior court commitments, and violators of probation, parole, supervised release, and mandatory release. Estimates may differ from federal offense statistics previously published by BJS due to differences in methodology. Data are from the Federal Justice Statistics Program (FJSP) and may differ from NPS and the online FJSP data tool.

SOURCE: E. Ann Carson, "Table 16. Estimated Percent of Sentenced Prisoners under the Custody of Federal Correctional Authorities, by Offense, September 30, 2001–2013," in Prisoners in 2013, U.S. Department of Justice, Office of Justice Programs, Bureau of Justice Statistics, September 30, 2014, http://www.bjs.gov/content/pub/pdf/p13.pdf (accessed November 4, 2014)

TABLE 8.5

Federal inmates, by type of offense, September 27, 2014

Offense	# of inmates	% of inmates
Banking and insurance, counterfeit, embezzlement	739	0.4%
Burglary, larceny, property offenses	7,937	3.9%
Continuing criminal enterprise	454	0.2%
Courts or corrections	832	0.4%
Drug offenses	98,482	48.8%
Extortion, fraud, bribery	12,455	6.2%
Homicide, aggravated assault, and kidnapping offenses	5,776	2.9%
Immigration	20,447	10.1%
Miscellaneous	1,544	0.8%
National security	79	0.0%
Robbery	7,500	3.7%
Sex offenses	13,369	6.6%
Weapons, explosives, arson	32,141	15.9%

Note: Data is limited due to the availability of offense-specific information.

SOURCE: Adapted from "Offenses," in *Statistics*, U.S. Department of Justice, Federal Bureau of Prisons, November 2014, http://www.bop.gov/about/statistics/statistics_inmate_sentences.jsp (accessed November 4, 2014)

TABLE 8.6

Federal inmates, by sentence imposed, September 27, 2014

Sentence	# of inmates	% of inmates
Less than 1 year	6,367	2.3%
1–3 years	23,669	11.7%
3–5 years	26,966	13.4%
5–10 years	51,356	25.5%
10–15 years	40,931	20.3%
15–20 years	22,280	11.1%
More than 20 years	24,447	12.1%
Life	5,488	2.7%
Death	57	0.0%

Note: Data is limited by availability of sentencing information.

SOURCE: "Sentences Imposed," in Statistics, U.S. Department of Justice, Federal Bureau of Prisons, November 2014, http://www.bop.gov/about/statistics/statistics_inmate_sentences.jsp (accessed November 4, 2014)

ethnicity was known. Nearly all (98%) of the inmates on death row at yearend 2013 were male; only 2% were female. The average inmate age was 47 years. On average, the prisoners under penalty of death had spent 14.6 years on death row as of yearend 2013.

Local Jail Inmates

Table 8.9 provides demographic and conviction status data for jail inmates as of midyear 2013. (Note that both adults and juveniles are included.) At that time nearly all (99.4%) of the inmates were adults and most (85.4%) of them were male. In regards to racial and ethnic origin, the largest contingent of the jail inmates was non-Hispanic white (47.2%), followed by non-Hispanic African American (35.8%) and Hispanic (14.8%). Another 0.2% of the inmates were identified as non-Hispanics of two or more races. Lastly, 2.1% of the inmates were non-Hispanic and were of other races. As of midyear 2013, 38% of the

inmates in the nation's jails had been convicted of crimes, while 62% had not been convicted.

WOMEN PRISONERS

Female prisoners make up a small part of the overall prison population, but their treatment is an issue for many human rights groups. The American Civil Liberties Union (ACLU) is particularly critical of the practice of shackling pregnant inmates. Shackling can consist of handcuffs and/or chains around the ankles or midsection. It is a common practice at many prisons for inmates to be shackled under certain circumstances, for example, during transport to and from court or other locations and while being treated in hospitals. Critics suggest that shackled women are in danger of seriously harming their unborn babies if they should fall. Human rights advocates also abhor the practice of shackling women inmates to their hospital beds while the women are in labor.

According to Audrey Quinn, in the op-ed "In Labor, in Chains: The Outrageous Shackling of Pregnant Inmates" (NYTimes.com, July 26, 2014), as of July 2014, 21 states had passed laws that prohibit or restrict the shackling of women during pregnancy, delivery, and/or postpartum (after delivery). However, Quinn notes that there have been complaints that the laws are not being followed. She states, "In many correctional systems, doctors, guards and prison officials simply are not told about anti-shackling laws, or are not trained to comply." In 2012 a group of dozens of inmates who had been shackled while pregnant at the Cook County jail in Illinois won a $4.1 million settlement against the state, which had outlawed such shackling practices in 1999.

MEDICAL PROBLEMS IN INMATES

The BJS also collects information about the medical conditions of state and federal prisoners. As of January 2015, the most recent comprehensive report available was published in 2008. In *Medical Problems of Prisoners* (April 22, 2008, http://bjs.ojp.usdoj.gov/content/pub/pdf/mpp.pdf), Laura M. Maruschak of the BJS presents findings from the 2004 Survey of Inmates in State and Federal Correctional Facilities. According to Maruschak, 43.8% of state inmates and 38.5% of federal inmates reported a current medical problem other than a cold or virus. The most common medical problems reported by inmates were arthritis (15.3% of state inmates and 12.4% of federal inmates), hypertension (13.8% of state inmates and 13.2% of federal inmates), and asthma (9.1% of state inmates and 7.2% of federal inmates). In addition, 9.4% of state inmates and 7.1% of federal inmates reported ever having tuberculosis. Female inmates were more likely to report a current medical problem than male inmates. In addition, inmates aged 45 years and older were more likely than younger age groups to report a medical problem.

TABLE 8.7

Percentage of sentenced prisoners under state jurisdiction, by offense, sex, race, and Hispanic origin, yearend 2012

Most serious offense	Total inmates[a]	Male	Female	White[b]	Black[b]	Hispanic	Other[a, b]
Total	100%	100%	100%	100%	100%	100%	100%
Violent	53.8%	55.0%	37.1%	49.3%	58.3%	59.9%	58.8%
Murder[c]	12.7	12.8	11.1	9.9	13.7	14.9	17.0
Manslaughter	1.3	1.3	2.5	1.6	1.0	1.2	1.9
Rape/sexual assault	12.2	13.0	2.3	17.0	8.0	13.2	12.6
Robbery	13.7	14.0	8.7	8.2	20.4	13.4	10.0
Aggravated or simple assault	10.7	10.8	8.9	9.3	11.5	13.6	13.2
Other violent	3.2	3.2	3.7	3.3	3.6	3.6	4.1
Property	18.8%	18.1%	28.2%	24.5%	16.0%	12.9%	17.3%
Burglary	9.9	10.2	6.9	12.0	9.4	8.0	8.6
Larceny-theft	3.7	3.3	9.1	5.2	3.2	1.9	3.3
Motor vehicle theft	0.9	0.9	0.8	1.2	0.5	1.0	1.6
Fraud	2.0	1.5	8.4	2.9	1.4	0.8	2.1
Other property	2.2	2.2	3.0	3.2	1.4	1.2	1.9
Drug	16.0%	15.4%	24.6%	14.0%	15.9%	15.1%	11.7%
Drug possession	3.7	3.5	6.7	4.0	4.0	4.2	3.7
Other drug[d]	12.2	11.8	17.9	10.0	11.9	11.0	8.0
Public-order[e]	10.7%	10.8%	8.9%	11.6%	9.5%	11.5%	11.5%
Other/unspecified[f]	0.8%	0.7%	1.2%	0.6%	0.3%	0.5%	0.7%
Total number of sentenced inmates	1,314,900	1,225,900	89,000	462,600	498,100	271,700	82,500

[a]Includes American Indians, Alaska Natives, Asians, Native Hawaiians, Pacific Islanders, persons of two or more races, or additional racial categories in reporting information systems.
[b]Excludes persons of Hispanic or Latino origin and persons of two or more races.
[c]Includes nonnegligent manslaughter.
[d]Includes trafficking and other drug offenses.
[e]Includes weapons, drunk driving, and court offenses; commercialized vice, morals, and decency offenses; and liquor law violations and other public-order offenses.
[f]Includes juvenile offenses and other unspecified offense categories.
Note: Estimates are based on state prisoners with a sentence of more than a year under the jurisdiction of state correctional officials. Detail may not sum to total due to rounding and missing offense data.

SOURCE: E. Ann Carson, "Table 13. Estimated Percent of Sentenced Prisoners under State Jurisdiction, by Offense and Sex, Race, and Hispanic Origin, December 31, 2012," in *Prisoners in 2013*, U.S. Department of Justice, Office of Justice Programs, Bureau of Justice Statistics, September 30, 2014, http://www.bjs.gov/content/pub/pdf/p13.pdf (accessed November 4, 2014)

HIV/AIDS

Maruschak reports in *HIV in Prisons, 2001–2010* (September 2012, http://www.bjs.gov/content/pub/pdf/hivp10.pdf) that the number of inmates with the human immunodeficiency virus (HIV) or confirmed cases of acquired immunodeficiency syndrome (AIDS) in state and federal prisons as of yearend 2010 was 20,093. The rate of HIV/AIDS among state and federal prisoners decreased from 194 cases per 10,000 prisoners in 2001 to 146 cases per 10,000 prisoners in 2010. Likewise, AIDS-related deaths among prisoners declined dramatically over the same period, from 24 deaths per 100,000 inmates in 2001 to 5 per 100,000 in 2010. In 2009 the AIDS mortality rate for state prison inmates aged 15 to 54 years (6 deaths per 100,000 state prisoners) fell below that for the general U.S. population in the same age group (7 deaths per 100,000 people).

Mental Health Problems of Inmates

A movement began during the 1970s to deinstitutionalize the mentally ill and reintegrate them into society. This widespread trend resulted in the closing of many large mental hospitals and treatment centers. With fewer options open to them, the mentally ill came into contact with law enforcement authorities much more often.

As of January 2015, the most recent comprehensive estimates of mental illness among prisoners were published in 2006. In *Mental Health Problems of Prison and Jail Inmates* (December 2006, http://bjs.ojp.usdoj.gov/content/pub/pdf/mhppji.pdf), Doris J. James and Lauren E. Glaze of the BJS estimated that more than half of all prison and jail inmates had a mental health problem at midyear 2005. Specifically, 705,600 inmates in state prisons (56.2% of all state prison inmates), 70,200 inmates in federal prisons (44.8% of all federal prison inmates), and 479,900 inmates in local jails (64.2% of all local jail inmates) were believed to have a mental health problem. For example, 35.1% of federal prisoners, 43.2% of state prisoners, and 54.5% of jail inmates reported symptoms of mania; 16% of federal prisoners, 23.5% of state prisoners, and 29.7% of jail inmates reported symptoms of major depression; and 10.2% of federal prisoners, 15.4% of state prisoners, and 23.9% of jail inmates reported symptoms of a psychotic disorder.

The Treatment Advocacy Center is a nonprofit organization devoted to issues related to the treatment of mental illness. In *The Treatment of Persons with Mental Illness in Prisons and Jails: A State Survey* (April 8, 2014, http://www.tacreports.org/storage/documents/treatment-behind-bars/treatment-behind-bars.pdf), E. Fuller Torrey et al. use percentages gleaned from James and Glaze's 2006 report to

TABLE 8.8

Percent of sentenced inmates under state jurisdiction, by most serious offense, yearend 1991, 2001, 2006, and 2011

Most serious offense	1991	2001	2006	2011
Total	**100%**	**100%**	**100%**	**100%**
Violent	**44.6%**	**50.6%**	**50.4%**	**53.5%**
Murder[a]	10.8	12.1	11.4	12.6
Negligent manslaughter	2.1	1.4	1.4	1.5
Rape/sexual assault	8.2	11.2	11.8	12.4
Robbery	13.9	13.5	13.2	13.7
Assault	7.9	9.7	9.9	10.3
Other violent	1.7	2.7	2.7	2.9
Property	**25.3%**	**20.6%**	**19.6%**	**18.6%**
Burglary	11.2	10.3	9.6	9.9
Larceny	5.8	4.0	3.4	3.2
Motor vehicle theft	1.9	1.4	1.6	1.1
Fraud	3.9	2.5	2.7	2.2
Other property	2.5	2.4	2.3	2.2
Drug	**23.0%**	**21.0%**	**20.0%**	**16.6%**
Possession	8.2	4.6	5.3	4.1
Other drug[b]	14.8	16.4	14.7	12.5
Public order[c]	**6.6%**	**7.2%**	**9.4%**	**10.6%**
Other/unspecified[d]	**0.4%**	**0.6%**	**0.6%**	**0.7%**
Number of sentenced prisoners	**732,916**	**1,208,708**	**1,331,065**	**1,341,797**

[a]Includes nonnegligent manslaughter.
[b]Includes drug trafficking.
[c]Includes weapons, drunk driving, and court offenses; habitual offender sanctions; commercialized vice, morals, and decency offenses; and liquor law violations and other public order offenses.
[d]Includes juvenile offenses and other unspecified offense categories.
Note: Counts based on prisoners under state jurisdiction on December 31 with a sentence of more than 1 year. Detail may not sum to total due to rounding and missing offense data. Estimates may vary from those previously published due to differences in methodology. Sentenced prisoner totals from National Prisoner Statistics Program. Offense distribution based on National Corrections Reporting Program administrative data.

SOURCE: E. Ann Carson and Daniela Golinelli, "Table 3. Estimated Percent of Sentenced Prisoners under State Jurisdiction, by Most Serious Offense, December 31, 1991, 2001, 2006, and 2011," in *Prisoners in 2012: Trends in Admissions and Releases, 1991–2012*, U.S. Department of Justice, Office of Justice Programs, Bureau of Justice Statistics, September 2, 2014, http://www.bjs.gov/content/pub/pdf/p12tar9112.pdf (accessed November 7, 2014)

TABLE 8.9

Inmates in local jails, by sex, age class, race, Hispanic origin, and conviction status, midyear 2013

Characteristic	2013
Sex	
Male	86.0%
Female	14.0
Adult	**99.4%**
Male	85.4
Female	13.9
Juvenile[a]	**0.6%**
Held as adult[b]	0.5
Held as juvenile	0.1
Race/Hispanic origin[c]	
White[d]	47.2%
Black/African American[d]	35.8
Hispanic/Latino	14.8
American Indian/Alaska Native[d, e]	1.4
Asian/Native Hawaiian/ other Pacific Islander[d, e]	0.7
Two or more races[d]	0.2
Conviction status[b, c]	
Convicted	38.0%
Male	—
Female	—
Unconvicted	62.0%
Male	—
Female	—

—Not collected. Starting in 2010, the annual survey of jails did not collect data on conviction status by sex.
[a]Persons age 17 or younger at midyear.
[b]Includes juveniles who were tried or awaiting trial as adults.
[c]Data adjusted for nonresponse.
[d]Excludes persons of Hispanic or Latino origin.
[e]Previous reports combined American Indians and Alaska Natives and Asians, Native Hawaiians, and other Pacific Islanders into an other race category.
Note: Percentages are based on the total number of inmates held on the last weekday in June. Detail may not sum to total due to rounding.

SOURCE: Adapted from Todd D. Minton and Daniela Golinelli, "Table 3. Percent of Inmates in Local Jails, by Characteristics, Midyear 2000 and 2005–2013," in *Jail Inmates at Midyear 2013 – Statistical Tables*, U.S. Department of Justice, Office of Justice Programs, Bureau of Justice Statistics, August 12, 2014, http://www.bjs.gov/content/pub/pdf/jim13st.pdf (accessed November 4, 2014)

estimate that in 2012 people with "severe mental illness" in the nation's state prisons and jails (356,268) far outnumbered similarly afflicted patients in state psychiatric hospitals (35,000). The researchers note that "prisons and jails have become America's 'new asylums.'" The incarceration of so many mentally ill inmates has had negative consequences, including high inmate suicide rates and "behavioral issues disturbing to other prisoners and correctional staff." According to Torrey et al., mentally ill prisoners tend to be incarcerated for longer periods than other prisoners. This contributes to overcrowding and increases taxpayer costs for the correctional system. Also, mentally ill prisoners are more likely than other prisoners to engage in physical attacks, be victimized while they are incarcerated, be put into solitary confinement (which typically worsens their symptoms), and be rearrested after being released.

The Treatment Advocacy Center, in collaboration with the National Sheriffs' Association, surveyed correctional officials around the country to obtain information about treatment policies for mentally ill inmates. Torrey et al. note that all states except Arkansas participated in the survey. One factor that greatly complicates treatment is that some mentally ill inmates "are unaware of their own illness" and refuse to take prescribed medications. The states have varying legal procedures for correctional officials to follow when they seek to provide treatment against inmate wishes. Torrey et al. complain that these procedures are "often grossly underutilized" or fail to provide desired outcomes. For example, they explain that "many jails require the inmate to be transferred to a state psychiatric hospital for treatment; since such hospitals are almost always full, such treatment does not take place in most cases." The researchers recommend reform measures for the nation's public mental health system to help prevent mentally ill people from being incarcerated in the first place. In addition, they advocate for changes to laws and policies to ensure that mentally ill inmates receive appropriate medical treatment while they are incarcerated.

SEXUAL VIOLENCE IN PRISONS AND JAILS

In response to concerns about sexual misconduct in prisons, President George W. Bush (1946–) signed into law the Prison Rape Elimination Act in September 2003. As part of this legislation, the BJS is charged with developing a national data collection on the incidence and prevalence of sexual assault within correctional facilities. As of January 2015, the most recent report on sexual violence involving inmates was by Allen J. Beck et al., in *Sexual Victimization in Prisons and Jails Reported by Inmates, 2011–12* (May 2013, http://www.bjs.gov/content/pub/pdf/svpjri1112.pdf).

The data are based on the third National Inmate Survey, which was conducted between February 2011 and May 2012 in 233 state and federal prisons, 358 jails, and 15 special confinement facilities that were operated by the U.S. Immigration and Customs Enforcement, the U.S. military, and correctional authorities on Native American tribal lands. More than 92,000 inmates participated in the survey. This number included some juveniles aged 16 or 17 years that were incarcerated in adult prisons and jails. During the survey the inmates were questioned about acts of nonconsensual sex between inmates and between inmates and facility staff. The results were extrapolated to provide estimates of sexual misconduct in the nation's entire inmate population.

According to Beck et al., the results indicate that an estimated 4% of state and federal inmates and 3.2% of jail inmates were sexually victimized in 2011–12. These rates were virtually unchanged from rates calculated in 2007. The data for 2011–12 for sexually victimized state and federal inmates indicate the following:

- 2.4% said they were sexually victimized by facility staff

- 2% said they were sexually victimized by another inmate

- 0.4% said they were sexually victimized by both facility staff and another inmate

Beck et al. note that for sexually victimized jail inmates the breakdown was as follows:

- 1.8% said they were sexually victimized by facility staff

- 1.6% said they were sexually victimized by another inmate

- 0.2% said they were sexually victimized by both facility staff and another inmate

INMATE DEATHS

The BJS initiated the Deaths in Custody Reporting Program in response to the Deaths in Custody Reporting Act of 2000. The program requires state prisons and local jails to report annually the cause of death and certain demographic data for all inmates who die in their custody. Data between 2000 and 2012 are summarized in Table 8.10 for state prison inmates and in Table 8.11 for local jail inmates. According to Margaret E. Noonan and Scott Ginder, in *Mortality in Local Jails and State Prisons, 2000–2012—Statistical Tables* (October 2014, http://www.bjs.gov/content/pub/pdf/mljsp0012st.pdf), a total of

TABLE 8.10

Percent of state prison inmate deaths in custody, by cause of death, 2001–12

Cause of death	2001	2002	2003	2004	2005	2006	2007[a]	2008	2009	2010	2011	2012
All causes	100%	100%	100%	100%	100%	100%	100%	100%	100%	100%	100%	100%
Illness	89.5%	89.1%	89.8%	89.1%	88.9%	87.5%	87.9%	87.9%	88.6%	88.7%	88.9%	88.1%
Cancer	24.1	23.2	25.7	23.5	25.4	24.9	22.8	25.3	28.5	28.7	30.7	30.5
Heart disease	25.9	27.3	25.4	27.0	26.4	26.4	24.8	24.0	24.7	25.7	25.5	23.9
Liver disease	10.7	10.1	9.7	9.1	10.0	9.4	9.3	9.2	9.8	8.8	10.1	9.0
Respiratory disease	4.8	5.3	6.2	6.3	6.7	6.0	6.0	7.3	5.7	6.4	5.9	6.4
AIDS-related	9.6	8.2	6.6	4.7	4.9	4.1	3.5	2.9	2.9	2.3	1.7	2.2
All other[b]	14.4	15.0	16.1	18.6	15.5	16.8	21.5	19.2	17.0	16.9	15.0	16.1
Suicide	5.9%	5.7%	6.3%	6.4%	6.7%	6.8%	6.3%	5.7%	5.9%	6.7%	5.5%	6.1%
Drug/alcohol intoxication	1.2%	1.3%	0.7%	0.7%	1.2%	1.7%	1.2%	1.7%	1.5%	1.2%	1.7%	1.0%
Accident	0.8%	1.0%	0.8%	1.1%	0.9%	1.0%	0.8%	0.8%	0.9%	1.0%	1.1%	1.5%
Homicide[c]	1.4%	1.6%	1.6%	1.6%	1.8%	1.7%	1.7%	1.2%	1.6%	2.2%	2.1%	2.5%
Other/unknown	0.0%	0.0%	0.8%	1.2%	0.5%	1.3%	0.5%	2.8%	0.5%	0.1%	0.3%	0.4%
Missing	1.3%	1.3%	0.0%	0.0%	0.0%	0.0%	1.5%	0.0%	1.0%	0.1%	0.3%	0.4%

[a]In 2007, a high number of illness cases were missing cause-of-death information and were classified as all other illnesses.
[b]Includes other specified illnesses, such as cerebrovascular disease, influenza, cirrhosis, and other nonleading natural causes of death, as well as unspecified illnesses.
[c]Includes homicides committed by other inmates, incidental to the staff use of force, and resulting from assaults sustained prior to incarceration.
Note: Data may have been revised from previously published statistics. Excludes executions.

SOURCE: Margaret E. Noonan and Scott Ginder, "Table 16. Percent of State Prisoner Deaths, by Cause of Death, 2001–2012," in *Mortality in Local Jails and State Prisons, 2000–2012 – Statistical Tables*, U.S. Department of Justice, Office of Justice Programs, Bureau of Justice Statistics, October 2014, http://www.bjs.gov/content/pub/pdf/mljsp0012st.pdf (accessed November 5, 2014)

TABLE 8.11

Percent of jail inmate deaths in custody, by cause of death, 2000–12

Cause of death	2000	2001	2002	2003	2004	2005	2006	2007	2008[a]	2009	2010	2011	2012
All causes	100%	100%	100%	100%	100%	100%	100%	100%	100%	100%	100%	100%	100%
Illness	57.1%	51.5%	52.4%	51.1%	51.8%	47.9%	55.2%	55.3%	46.4%	51.1%	52.0%	47.8%	55.2%
Heart disease	21.9	22.8	22.8	24.0	22.2	19.3	22.5	21.0	19.2	20.8	26.1	25.9	28.2
AIDS-related	6.3	6.3	5.4	5.5	5.1	3.8	4.9	3.9	3.3	2.8	2.8	1.5	2.2
Cancer	3.4	2.7	4.0	3.4	2.8	3.5	3.6	3.8	2.6	4.9	3.7	3.4	4.5
Liver disease	2.7	2.9	2.8	3.2	3.1	3.1	2.3	3.5	3.8	3.2	3.2	1.7	3.1
Respiratory disease	3.4	1.9	2.1	2.0	3.4	2.0	2.5	4.4	3.2	3.2	2.0	2.0	2.8
All other[b]	19.4	15.0	15.4	13.1	15.1	16.2	19.5	18.6	14.2	16.1	14.2	13.4	14.4
Suicide	32.0%	33.2%	32.4%	29.5%	29.3%	27.4%	25.4%	25.8%	23.8%	31.7%	33.2%	35.0%	31.3%
Drug/alcohol intoxication	4.1%	6.2%	5.6%	8.9%	7.4%	7.9%	8.0%	7.2%	4.5%	6.7%	5.9%	8.2%	5.9%
Accident	2.8%	3.8%	3.5%	2.8%	3.2%	2.3%	3.0%	1.6%	1.6%	2.7%	2.5%	3.0%	1.9%
Homicide[c]	1.9%	2.0%	1.9%	1.5%	2.4%	2.1%	3.3%	1.8%	1.7%	2.4%	2.2%	2.4%	2.3%
Other/unknown	1.9%	2.5%	3.6%	5.2%	4.9%	10.5%	4.8%	6.5%	0.8%	2.5%	1.4%	2.5%	2.5%
Missing	0.3%	0.7%	0.7%	1.0%	0.9%	1.8%	0.4%	1.8%	21.2%	2.9%	2.8%	1.1%	0.8%

[a]In 2008, a high number of illness cases were missing cause-of-death information and were classified as other or unknown.
[b]Includes other specified illnesses, such as cerebrovascular disease, influenza, cirrhosis, and other nonleading natural causes of death, as well as unspecified illnesses.
[c]Includes homicides committed by other inmates, incidental to the staff use of force, and resulting from assaults sustained prior to incarceration.
Note: Data may have been revised from previously published statistics. Cause-of-death rankings may differ from previously published estimates because cause of death was ranked on all deaths from 2000 to 2012.

SOURCE: Margaret E. Noonan and Scott Ginder, "Table 2. Percent of Local Jail Inmate Deaths, by Cause of Death, 2000–2012," in *Mortality in Local Jails and State Prisons, 2000–2012 – Statistical Tables*, U.S. Department of Justice, Office of Justice Programs, Bureau of Justice Statistics, October 2014, http://www.bjs.gov/content/pub/pdf/mljsp0012st.pdf (accessed November 5, 2014)

3,351 state prisoners died while incarcerated in 2012. The vast majority (88.1%) died of illnesses, primarily cancer (30.5%) and heart disease (23.9%). (See Table 8.10.) In addition, 6.1% of the state prisoners who died in custody committed suicide. Overall, 958 jail inmates died while incarcerated in 2012. Just over half (55.2%) died of illnesses, primarily heart disease (28.2%). (See Table 8.11.) Around one-third (31.3%) of jail inmate deaths were suicides.

PRISONERS' RIGHTS UNDER THE LAW

In 1871 a Virginia court, in *Ruffin v. Commonwealth* (62 Va. 790), commented that a prisoner "has, as a consequence of his crime, not only forfeited his liberty, but all his personal rights except those which the law in its humanity accords to him. He is for the time being the slave of the state." Eight decades later, in *Stroud v. Swope* (187 F. 2d. 850 [1951]), the U.S. Court of Appeals for the Ninth Circuit asserted that "it is well settled that it is not the function of the courts to superintend the treatment and discipline of prisoners in penitentiaries, but only to deliver from imprisonment those who are illegally confined." The American Correctional Association explains in *Legal Responsibility and Authority of Correctional Officers: A Handbook on Courts, Judicial Decisions, and Constitutional Requirements* (1987) that correctional administrators believed that prisoners lost all their constitutional rights after conviction. Prisoners had privileges, not rights, and privileges could be taken away arbitrarily.

A significant change in this legal view came during the 1960s. In *Cooper v. Pate* (378 U.S. 546 [1964]), the U.S. Supreme Court held that the Civil Rights Act of 1871 granted protection to prisoners. The U.S. Code states in Title 42, Chapter 21, Subchapter I, Section 1983 (which is part of the Civil Rights Act), that "every person who, under color of any statute, ordinance, regulation, custom, or usage, of any State or Territory or the District of Columbia, subjects, or causes to be subjected, any citizen of the United States or other person within the jurisdiction thereof to the deprivation of any rights, privileges, or immunities secured by the Constitution and laws, shall be liable to the party injured in an action at law, suit in equity, or other proper proceeding for redress."

With the *Cooper* decision, the court announced that prisoners had rights that were guaranteed by the U.S. Constitution and could ask the judicial system for help in challenging the conditions of their imprisonment.

THE CIVIL RIGHTS OF INSTITUTIONALIZED PERSONS ACT

Another safeguard for prisoners' rights came in 1980 with passage of the Civil Rights of Institutionalized Persons Act (CRIPA). CRIPA covers people in certain kinds of institutions that are owned, operated, or managed by or on the behalf of state or local governments. Examples include prisons, jails, juvenile correctional facilities, mental health facilities, and nursing homes. In "Rights of Persons Confined to Jails and Prisons" (2015, http://www.justice.gov/crt/about/spl/corrections.php), the DOJ's Special Litigation Section explains that CRIPA gives the U.S. attorney general the authority "to review conditions and practices" within the covered facilities. (Note that this authority does not apply to federal facilities, such as federal prisons.) The

DOJ does not act on behalf of individuals in regards to CRIPA, but rather on cases that indicate an institution has a systematic pattern or practice that causes harm. When it finds a problem, the agency works with the state or local governments that are involved to reach a solution. If an agreement cannot be reached, then the attorney general can file a lawsuit in federal court over the matter.

The Special Litigation Section maintains a database (http://www.justice.gov/crt/about/spl/findsettle.php#corrections) of cases that it has investigated and the legal documents associated with them. In addition, the DOJ is required by CRIPA to provide to Congress an annual report describing its enforcement efforts. In *Department of Justice Activities under the Civil Rights of Institutionalized Persons Act, Fiscal Year 2011* (March 2012, http://www.justice.gov/crt/about/spl/documents/split_cripa11.pdf), the most recent report available as of January 2015, the DOJ describes its activities for fiscal year 2011 (October 1, 2010, through September 30, 2011). The agency dealt with issues involving dozens of jails, prisons, and other types of correctional facilities in more than 20 states and U.S. territories.

HABEAS CORPUS REVIEW

In *Cooper v. Pate*, the Supreme Court relied on civil rights. Another source of prisoners' rights arose from the court's reliance on habeas corpus. This Latin phrase means "have the body" with the rest of the phrase "brought before me" implied. A writ of habeas corpus is therefore the command issued by one court to another court (or to a lesser authority) to produce a person and to explain why that person is being detained. Habeas corpus dates back to an act of the British Parliament passed in 1679. Congress enacted the Judiciary Act of 1789 and gave federal prisoners the right to habeas corpus review. The Habeas Corpus Act of 1867 later protected the rights of newly freed slaves and extended habeas corpus protection to state prisoners. The effective meaning of habeas corpus for prisoners is that it enables them to petition federal courts to review any aspect of their case.

FIRST AMENDMENT CASES

The First Amendment of the U.S. Constitution guarantees that "Congress shall make no law respecting an establishment of religion, or prohibiting the free exercise thereof; or abridging the freedom of speech, or of the press; or the right of the people peaceably to assemble, and to petition the government for a redress of grievances."

Censorship

In *Procunier v. Martinez* (416 U.S. 396 [1974]), the Supreme Court ruled that prison officials cannot censor inmate correspondence unless they "show that a regulation authorizing mail censorship furthers one or more of the substantial governmental interests of security, order, and rehabilitation. Second, the limitation of First Amendment freedoms must be no greater than is necessary or essential to the protection of the particular governmental interest involved."

Prison officials may refuse to send letters that detail escape plans or have encoded messages but may not censor inmate correspondence simply to "eliminate unflattering or unwelcome opinions or factually inaccurate statements." Because prisoners retain rights, "when a prison regulation or practice offends a fundamental constitutional guarantee, federal courts will discharge their duty to protect constitutional rights."

However, the court recognized that it was "ill equipped to deal with the increasingly urgent problems of prison administration and reform." Running a prison takes expertise and planning, all of which, the court explained, is part of the responsibility of the legislative and executive branches. According to the court, the task of the judiciary branch is to establish a standard of review for prisoners' constitutional claims that is responsive to both the need to protect inmates' rights and the policy of judicial restraint.

In *Pell v. Procunier* (417 U.S. 817 [1974]), the court ruled that federal prison officials could prohibit inmates from having face-to-face media interviews. The court reasoned that judgments regarding prison security "are peculiarly within the province and professional expertise of corrections officials, and, in the absence of substantial evidence in the record to indicate that the officials have exaggerated their response to these considerations, courts should ordinarily defer to their expert judgment in such matters."

The U.S. Court of Appeals for the First Circuit ruled in *Nolan v. Fitzpatrick* (451 F. 2d 545 [1985]) that inmates had the right to correspond with newspapers. The prisoners were limited only in that they could not write about escape plans or include contraband material in their letters.

The Missouri Division of Corrections permitted correspondence between immediate family members who were inmates at different institutions and between inmates writing about legal matters. It also allowed other inmate correspondence only if each prisoner's "classification/treatment team" thought it was in the best interests of the parties. Another Missouri regulation permitted an inmate to marry only with the superintendent's permission, which can be given only when there were "compelling reasons" to do so, such as a pregnancy. In *Turner v. Safley* (482 U.S. 78 [1987]), the Supreme Court found the first regulation constitutional and the second one unconstitutional.

The court held that the "constitutional right of prisoners to marry is impermissibly burdened by the Missouri marriage regulation." The court had ruled earlier in *Zablocki v. Redhail* (434 U.S. 374 [1978]) that prisoners had a constitutionally protected right to marry, subject to restrictions because of incarceration such as time and place and prior approval of a warden. However, the Missouri regulation practically banned all marriages.

The findings in *Turner v. Safley* have become a guide for prison regulations in the United States. In its decision, the court observed that:

> When a prison regulation impinges on inmates' constitutional rights, the regulation is valid if it is reasonably related to legitimate penological interests.... First, there must be a "valid, rational connection" between the prison regulation and the legitimate governmental interest put forward to justify it.... Moreover, the governmental objective must be a legitimate and neutral one.... A second factor relevant in determining the reasonableness of a prison restriction...is whether there are alternative means of exercising the right that remain open to prison inmates.... A third consideration is the impact accommodation of the asserted constitutional right will have on guards and other inmates, and on the allocation of prison resources generally.

Religious Beliefs

Although inmates retain their First Amendment right to practice their religion, the courts have upheld restrictions on religious freedom when corrections departments need to maintain security, when economic considerations are involved, and when the regulation is reasonable.

The Religious Land Use and Institutionalized Persons Act was signed into law in September 2000 by President Bill Clinton (1946–). Section 3 of the law indicates that prison officials are required to accommodate inmates' religious needs in certain cases, even if this means exempting the inmates from general prison rules. The state of Ohio challenged the act's constitutionality by arguing that it violates the First Amendment's prohibition on the establishment of religion. Because the law does not require prison officials to accommodate inmates' secular needs or desires in similar ways, Ohio claimed the statute impermissibly advances religion. The state also argued that the law creates incentives for prisoners to feign religious belief to gain privileges. The Supreme Court upheld the constitutionality of the act in *Cutter v. Wilkinson* (544 U.S. 709 [2005]), reversing a ruling by the U.S. Court of Appeals for the Sixth Circuit, which had agreed with Ohio's argument.

FOURTH AMENDMENT CASES

The Fourth Amendment guarantees the "right of the people to be secure...against unreasonable searches and seizures...and no warrants shall issue, but upon probable cause." The courts have not been as active in protecting prisoners under the Fourth Amendment as under the First and Eighth Amendments. In *Bell v. Wolfish* (441 U.S. 520 [1979]), the Supreme Court asserted that:

> simply because prison inmates retain certain constitutional rights does not mean that these rights are not subject to restrictions and limitations.... Maintaining institutional security and preserving internal order and discipline are essential goals that may require limitation or retraction of the retained constitutional rights of both convicted prisoners and pretrial detainees. Since problems that arise in the day-to-day operation of a corrections facility are not susceptible of easy solutions, prison administrators should be accorded wide-ranging deference in the adoption and execution of policies and practices that in their judgment are needed to preserve internal order and discipline and to maintain institutional security.

Based on this reasoning, the court ruled that body searches did not violate the Fourth Amendment: "Balancing the significant and legitimate security interests of the institution against the inmates' privacy interests, such searches can be conducted on less than probable cause and are not unreasonable."

In another Fourth Amendment case, *Hudson v. Palmer* (468 U.S. 517 [1984]), the court upheld the right of prison officials to search a prisoner's cell and seize property. The court explained that "the recognition of privacy rights for prisoners in their individual cells simply cannot be reconciled with the concept of incarceration and the needs and objectives of penal institutions." However, the fact that a prisoner does not have a reasonable expectation of privacy "does not mean that he is without a remedy for calculated harassment unrelated to prison needs. Nor does it mean that prison attendants can ride roughshod over inmates' property rights with impunity. The Eighth Amendment always stands as a protection against 'cruel and unusual punishments.'"

EIGHTH AMENDMENT CASES

The Eighth Amendment states that "excessive bail shall not be required, nor excessive fines imposed, nor cruel and unusual punishments inflicted." The prohibition against "cruel and unusual punishments" has been used to challenge numerous aspects of the criminal justice system, including the death penalty, three-strikes laws, crowded prisons, lack of health or safety in prisons, and excessive violence by the guards.

Prison Conditions and Medical Care

In *Rhodes v. Chapman* (452 U.S. 337 [1981]), the Supreme Court ruled that housing prisoners in double cells was not cruel and unusual punishment. The justices maintained that "conditions of confinement, as constituting the punishment at issue, must not involve the wanton and unnecessary infliction of pain, nor may they be grossly disproportionate to the severity of the crime warranting imprisonment. But conditions that cannot be said to be cruel and unusual under contemporary standards are not unconstitutional. To the extent such conditions are restrictive and even harsh, they are part of the penalty that criminals pay for their offenses against society."

The court concluded that the Constitution "does not mandate comfortable prisons" and that only those deprivations denying the "minimal civilized measure of life's necessities" violate the Eighth Amendment.

However, Judge Richard A. Enslen (1931–) of the U.S. District Court ruled in *Hadix v. Caruso* (461 F.Supp.2d 574 [2006]) that officials at the Southern Michigan Correctional Facility had to stop using non-medical restraints on prisoners because the "practice constitutes torture and violates the Eighth Amendment." In November 2006 Judge Enslen issued the opinion in the case of Timothy Souders, a mentally ill detainee who died after spending four days nude and shackled in an isolated cell. Judge Enslen ordered the prison to "immediately cease and desist from the practice of using any form of punitive mechanical restraints [and] shall timely develop practices, protocols and policies to enforce this limitation."

Chapter 7 details how a series of court decisions found that severe overcrowding and poor medical care in California's prison system constituted a violation of the Eighth Amendment.

Guards Using Force

The Supreme Court ruled in *Whitley v. Albers* (475 U.S. 312 [1986]) that guards, during prison disturbances or riots, must balance the need "to maintain or restore discipline" through force against the risk of injury to inmates. These situations require prison officials to act quickly and decisively and allow guards and administrators leeway in their actions. In *Whitley*, a prisoner was shot in the knee during an attempt to rescue a hostage. The court found that the injury suffered by the prisoner was not cruel and unusual punishment under the circumstances.

In 1983 Keith Hudson, an inmate at the state penitentiary in Angola, Louisiana, argued with Jack McMillian, a guard. McMillian placed the inmate in handcuffs and shackles to take him to the administrative lockdown area. On the way, according to Hudson, McMillian punched him in the mouth, eyes, chest, and stomach; another guard held him while the supervisor on duty watched. Hudson sued, accusing the guards of cruel and unusual punishment.

A magistrate found that the guards used "force when there was no need to do so" and that the supervisor allowed their conduct, thus violating the Eighth Amendment. However, the U.S. Court of Appeals for the Fifth Circuit reversed the decision, ruling in *Hudson v. McMillian* (929 F. 2d 1014 [1990]) that "inmates alleging use of excessive force in violation of the Eighth Amendment must prove: (1) significant injury; (2) resulting 'directly and only from the use of force that was clearly excessive to the need'; (3) the excessiveness of which was objectively unreasonable; and (4) that the action constituted an unnecessary and wanton infliction of pain."

The court agreed that the use of force was unreasonable and was a clearly excessive and unnecessary infliction of pain. However, the court found against Hudson because his injuries were "minor" and "required no medical attention."

DUE PROCESS COMPLAINTS

The Fifth Amendment provides that no person should "be deprived of life, liberty, or property" by the federal government "without due process of law." The 14th Amendment reaffirms this right and explicitly applies it to the states. Due process complaints brought by prisoners under the Fifth and 14th Amendments are generally centered on questions of procedural fairness. Most of the time disciplinary action in prison is taken on the word of the guard or the administrator, and the inmate has little opportunity to challenge the charges.

The Supreme Court, however, has affirmed that procedural fairness should be used in some institutional decisions. In *Wolff v. McDonnell* (418 U.S. 539 [1974]), the court declared that a Nebraska law providing for sentences to be shortened for good behavior created a "liberty interest." Thus, if an inmate met the requirements, prison officials could not deprive him of the shortened sentence without due process, according to the 14th Amendment.

At the Metropolitan Correctional Center, a federally operated short-term custodial facility in New York City that was designed mainly for pretrial detainees, inmates challenged the constitutionality of the facility's conditions. Because this was a pretrial detention center, the challenge was brought under the due process clause of the Fifth Amendment. The district court and the court of appeals found for the inmates, but the Supreme Court disagreed in *Bell v. Wolfish*.

EARLY RELEASE

Beginning in 1983 the Florida legislature enacted a series of laws authorizing the awarding of early release credits to prison inmates when the state prison population exceeded predetermined levels. In 1986 Kenneth Lynce received a 22-year prison sentence on a charge of attempted murder. He was released in 1992, based on the determination that he had accumulated five different types of early release credits totaling 5,668 days, including 1,860 days of provisional credits awarded as a result of prison overcrowding.

Shortly thereafter, the state attorney general issued an opinion interpreting a 1992 statute as having retroactively canceled all provisional credits awarded to inmates convicted of murder and attempted murder. Lynce was rearrested and returned to custody. He filed a habeas corpus petition alleging that the retroactive cancellation of provisional credits violated the ex post facto (from a thing done afterward) clause of the Constitution.

The Supreme Court agreed with Lynce. In *Lynce v. Mathis* (519 U.S. 443 [1997]), the court ruled that "to fall within the ex post facto prohibition, a law must be retrospective and 'disadvantage the offender affected by it.'" The 1992 statute was clearly retrospective and disadvantaged Lynce by increasing his punishment.

LIMITING FRIVOLOUS PRISONER LAWSUITS

In 1995 the Supreme Court made it harder for prisoners to bring constitutional suits that challenge due process rights. In *Sandin v. Conner* (515 U.S. 472), the majority asserted that it was frustrated with the number of due process cases, some of which, it believed, clogged the judiciary with unwarranted complaints, such as claiming a "liberty interest" in not being transferred to a cell without an electrical outlet for a television set.

Sandin concerned an inmate in Hawaii who was not allowed to call witnesses at a disciplinary hearing for misconduct that had placed him in solitary confinement for 30 days. The Court of Appeals for the Ninth Circuit had held in 1993 that the inmate, Demont Conner, had a liberty interest that allowed him a range of procedural protections in remaining free from solitary confinement. The Supreme Court overruled the court of appeals, stating that the inmate had no liberty interest. Due process protections play a role only if the state's action has infringed on some separate, substantive right that the inmate possesses. For example, in *Wolff v. McDonnell* the petitioner's loss of good-time credit was a substantive right that he possessed. The punishment Conner had received "was within the range of confinement to be normally expected for one serving an indeterminate term of 30 years to life" for a number of crimes, including murder.

The court noted that "states may under certain circumstances create liberty interests which are protected by the Due Process Clause," but these should be limited to actions that impose "atypical and significant hardship on the inmate in relation to the ordinary incidents of prison life." According to the court, being put in solitary confinement in a prison where most inmates are limited to their cells most of the day anyway is not a liberty-interest issue. Because there was no liberty interest involved, how the hearing was handled was irrelevant.

Based on this ruling, the court held that a federal court should consider a complaint to be a potential violation of a prisoner's due process rights only when prison staff impose "atypical and significant hardship on the inmate." Mismanaged disciplinary hearings or temporary placement in solitary confinement are just "ordinary incidents of prison life" and should not be considered violations of the Constitution.

Chief Justice William H. Rehnquist (1924–2005) asserted that past Supreme Court decisions have "led to the involvement . . . of federal courts in the day-to-day management of prisons, often squandering judicial resources with little offsetting benefit to anyone." Judges should allow prison administrators the flexibility to fine-tune the ordinary incidents of prison life.

In 1996 Congress passed the Prison Litigation Reform Act (PLRA) in an effort to limit so-called frivolous lawsuits by prisoners. The PLRA requires inmates to exhaust all possible internal prison grievance processes before filing civil rights lawsuits in federal courts. The law states that "no action shall be brought with respect to prison conditions under section 1983 of this title, or any other Federal law, by a prisoner confined in any jail, prison, or other correctional facility until such administrative remedies as are available are exhausted." After a few lower courts handed down controversial rulings on specific procedures that inmates must follow to exhaust administrative grievances, a case was brought before the U.S. Supreme Court. In the consolidated case of *Jones v. Bock* (No. 05-7058 [2007]) and *Williams v. Overton* (No. 05-7142 [2007]), the court overturned strict legal requirements that had been imposed by the Court of Appeals for the Sixth Circuit on Michigan inmates with grievances against their prison. Lorenzo Jones claimed that prison officials forced him to do "arduous" work even though he had been seriously injured in a car accident. Timothy Williams suffered a debilitating medical condition and claimed that his medical needs were not being properly met in prison. Instead of examining the merits of these claims, the Supreme Court chose to focus on specific legal issues associated with lawsuits that the prisoners had filed under the PLRA.

The court clarified that prisoners alleging federal civil rights violations under the PLRA do not have to prove they have exhausted all administrative remedies before filing lawsuits. The burden is on the defense to prove that administrative remedies were not exhausted. In addition, lower courts cannot dismiss lawsuits including multiple claims, even if some of the claims have not been exhausted. Finally, prisoners filing such lawsuits need not have named specific defendants in the administrative grievances to retain their rights to sue those defendants in court.

Complaints about the PLRA

The PLRA is roundly criticized by human rights groups, such as the ACLU and the Southern Center for Human Rights. The ACLU and dozens of other organizations formed the Stop Abuse and Violence Everywhere Coalition (2014, http://www.savecoalition.org/aboutus.html) to establish "proposed reforms to the law that do not interfere with its stated purpose: to reduce frivolous litigation by prisoners." The coalition complains that prisons have implemented complicated grievance systems with strict deadline requirements in order to thwart inmate efforts to file suits under the law. The coalition is also critical of the provision of the PLRA that specifies that inmates cannot bring federal civil action unless "physical injury" has occurred. Human rights advocates note that prisoners who have been raped or suffered degrading treatment at the hands of prison staff are barred from filing suits because of this provision.

INNOCENCE PROTECTION ACT

Deoxyribonucleic acid (DNA) testing has emerged as a powerful tool that is capable of establishing the innocence of a person in cases where organic matter from the perpetrator of a crime (e.g., blood, skin, or semen) has been obtained by law enforcement officials. This organic matter can be tested against DNA samples that have been taken from an accused or convicted person. If the two samples do not match, then they came from different people and the person being tested is innocent.

The Innocence Protection Act became law in 2004 as part of the Justice for All Act. The act enables people who are "convicted and imprisoned for federal offenses" and who claim to be innocent to have DNA testing on the biological evidence that was originally collected during the investigations of the crimes for which they were convicted. It mandates that the government has to preserve collected biological evidence so that it can be tested after the defendant is convicted. Finally, it provides funds to allow certain agencies to test evidence to identify perpetrators of unsolved crimes.

The Innocence Project is a private organization affiliated with the Benjamin N. Cardozo School of Law at Yeshiva University. The Innocence Project (2014, http://www.innocenceproject.org/Content/What_is_the_Innocence_Project_How_did_it_get_started.php) describes itself as "a national litigation and public policy organization dedicated to exonerating wrongfully convicted people through DNA testing and reforming the criminal justice system to prevent future injustice." In "DNA Exonerations Nationwide" (http://www.innocenceproject.org/Content/DNA_Exonerations_Nationwide.php), the organization claims that as of January 2015, 325 people in the United States had been exonerated by postconviction DNA testing, including 20 who had served time on death row. Furthermore, in "Access to Post-conviction DNA Testing" (2015, http://www.innocenceproject.org/Content/Access_To_PostConviction_DNA_Testing.php), the Innocence Project indicates that all 50 states have postconviction DNA testing access statutes, but notes that "many of these testing laws are limited in scope and substance." The Innocence Project claims that some state laws are deficient in that they do not include safeguards needed to properly preserve DNA evidence, do not include an appeals process for inmates denied postconviction DNA testing, and do not require "full, fair, and prompt" proceedings after inmates file DNA testing petitions.

CHAPTER 9
PROBATION AND PAROLE

Most of the correctional population of the United States—those under the supervision of correctional authorities—are walking about freely. They are people on probation or parole. A probationer is someone who has been convicted of a crime and sentenced—but the person's sentence has been suspended on condition that he or she behaves in a manner ordered by the court. Probation sometimes follows a brief period of incarceration; more often, it is granted by the court immediately. A parolee is an individual who has served a part of his or her sentence in jail or prison but, because of good behavior or legislative mandate, has been granted freedom before the sentence is fully served. The sentence remains in effect, however, and the parolee continues to be under the jurisdiction of a parole board. If the parolee fails to live up to the conditions of the release, he or she may be confined again. Probationers and parolees are still under official supervision and have to satisfy requirements placed on them as a condition of freedom or of early release from correctional facilities. They are sometimes referred to as being "under community supervision."

According to Erinn J. Herberman and Thomas P. Bonczar of the Bureau of Justice Statistics (BJS), in *Probation and Parole in the United States, 2013* (October 2014, http://www.bjs.gov/content/pub/pdf/ppus13.pdf), 4,751,400 adults (3.9 million on probation and 853,200 on parole) were under community supervision at yearend 2013. (See Figure 9.1 and Table 9.1.) The community supervision population grew, on average, by 0.4% annually between 2000 and 2012. It peaked in 2007 at 5.1 million before declining.

As shown in Table 9.2, at yearend 2013 the community supervision rate for adults was 1,950 per 100,000 adult U.S. residents. Approximately 1 out of every 51 adults in the United States was under community supervision (i.e., on probation or parole) at that time.

Table 9.3 provides a breakdown by jurisdiction for the community supervision population at yearend 2013. (Note that data were not available for Oklahoma.) In addition, Herberman and Bonczar include the District of Columbia when referring to *states* and *state jurisdiction*; thus, this chapter does likewise. As shown in Table 9.3, the vast majority (4.6 million or 97.2%) of people under community supervision were under state jurisdiction. Only 131,900 (2.8%) were under federal jurisdiction.

The 10 states with the largest numbers of adults under community supervision at yearend 2013 were:

- Georgia—536,200
- Texas—508,000
- California—381,600
- Pennsylvania—275,800
- Ohio—267,400
- Florida—237,800
- Michigan—195,200
- Illinois—153,400
- New York—151,400
- Indiana—134,000

According to Herberman and Bonczar, the number of adult probationers and parolees under state jurisdiction declined by 21,300 people, or 0.4%, between 2012 and 2013. Connecticut (down 10.3%), Kentucky (down 8.6%), and Missouri (down 7.8%) had the largest percentage declines. The states with the largest increases were Washington (up 10.7%), Pennsylvania (up 8.3%), and Wyoming (up 6.3%). Overall, there were 1,895 adults under state community supervision at yearend 2013 for every 100,000 adult residents of the United States. (See Table 9.3.)

FIGURE 9.1

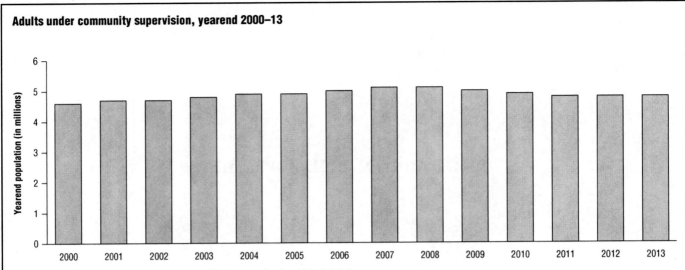

Adults under community supervision, yearend 2000–13

Note: Estimates based on most recent data and may differ from previously published statistics.

SOURCE: Erinn J. Herberman and Thomas P. Bonczar, "Figure 1. Adults under Community Supervision at Yearend, 2000–2013," in *Probation and Parole in the United States, 2013*, U.S. Department of Justice, Office of Justice Programs, Bureau of Justice Statistics, October 2014, http://www.bjs.gov/index .cfm?ty=pbdetail&iid=5135 (accessed November 5, 2014)

TABLE 9.1

Adults under community supervision, probation, and parole, 2000–13

Year	Community supervision population	Probation	Parole
2000	4,565,100	3,839,500	725,500
2001	4,665,900	3,934,700	731,100
2002	4,748,300	3,995,200	753,100
2003	4,847,500	4,074,000	773,500
2004	4,916,500	4,140,600	775,900
2005	4,946,800	4,162,500	784,400
2006	5,035,200	4,237,000	798,200
2007	5,119,300	4,293,200	826,100
2008	5,095,200	4,271,000	828,200
2009	5,017,900	4,198,200	824,100
2010	4,887,900	4,055,500	840,700
2011	4,814,200	3,971,300	853,900
2012	4,781,300	3,942,800	851,200
2013	4,751,400	3,910,600	853,200
Average annual percent change, 2000–2012	0.4%	0.2%	1.3%
Percent change, 2012–2013	−0.6	−0.8	0.2

Note: Counts rounded to the nearest 100. Detail may not sum to total due to rounding. Counts based on most recent data and may differ from previously published statistics. Reporting methods for some probation agencies changed over time.

SOURCE: Erinn J. Herberman and Thomas P. Bonczar, "Table 1. U.S. Adult Residents on Community Supervision, Probation, and Parole, 2000–2013," in *Probation and Parole in the United States, 2013*, U.S. Department of Justice, Office of Justice Programs, Bureau of Justice Statistics, October 2014, http://www.bjs.gov/index.cfm?ty=pbdetail&iid=5135 (accessed November 5, 2014)

Herberman and Bonczar indicate that the adult community supervision population under federal jurisdiction increased by 1.2% between 2012 and 2013. Overall, there were 54 adults under federal community supervision at yearend 2013 for every 100,000 adult residents of the United States. (See Table 9.3.)

PROBATION

Probation Population

In 2000 there were 3.8 million probationers. (See Table 9.1 and Figure 9.2). The number increased over subsequent years and peaked at nearly 4.3 million in 2007 before declining. According to Herberman and Bonczar, 2008 was the last year in which the number of entries to probation exceeded the number of exits from probation. Beginning in 2009 and continuing through 2013, the number of people entering the system was less each year than the number exiting the system.

Jurisdiction and Geographical Distribution of Probationers

As of yearend 2013, the 3.9 million people on probation represented a rate of 1,605 people on probation per 100,000 adult U.S. residents. (See Table 9.2.) In other words, 1 out of 62 adult U.S. residents were on probation. Table 9.4 provides a jurisdictional breakdown for the probationers. Nearly all of them (3.9 million or 99.5%) were under state jurisdiction. Only 20,676 (0.5) were under federal jurisdiction.

The 10 states with the highest probation populations at yearend 2013 were:

- Georgia—514,477
- Texas—399,655
- California—294,057
- Ohio—250,630
- Florida—233,128
- Michigan—176,795

TABLE 9.2

Adults under community supervision, on probation, or on parole, 2000 and 2005–13

Year	Number per 100,000 U.S. adult residents			U.S. adult residents on—		
	Community supervision[a]	Probation	Parole	Community supervision[b]	Probation	Parole
2000	2,162	1,818	344	1 in 46	1 in 55	1 in 291
2005	2,215	1,864	351	1 in 45	1 in 54	1 in 285
2006	2,228	1,875	353	1 in 45	1 in 53	1 in 283
2007	2,239	1,878	361	1 in 45	1 in 53	1 in 277
2008	2,203	1,846	358	1 in 45	1 in 54	1 in 279
2009	2,147	1,796	353	1 in 47	1 in 56	1 in 284
2010	2,067	1,715	355	1 in 48	1 in 58	1 in 281
2011	2,014	1,662	357	1 in 50	1 in 60	1 in 280
2012	1,980	1,633	353	1 in 50	1 in 61	1 in 284
2013	1,950	1,605	350	1 in 51	1 in 62	1 in 286

[a]Includes adults on probation and adults on parole. For 2008 to 2013, detail may not sum to total because the community supervision rate was adjusted to exclude parolees who were also on probation.

[b]Includes adults on probation and parole.

Note: Detail may not sum to total due to rounding. Rates based on most recent data and may differ from previously published statistics. Rates based on the community supervision, probation, and parole population counts as of December 31 of the reporting year and the estimated U.S. adult resident population on January 1 of each subsequent year.

SOURCE: Erinn J. Herberman and Thomas P. Bonczar, "Table 2. U.S. Adult Residents on Community Supervision, Probation, and Parole, 2000, 2005–2013," in *Probation and Parole in the United States, 2013*, U.S. Department of Justice, Office of Justice Programs, Bureau of Justice Statistics, October 2014, http://www.bjs.gov/index.cfm?ty=pbdetail&iid=5135 (accessed November 5, 2014)

- Pennsylvania—171,970
- Illinois—123,862
- Indiana—123,673
- New Jersey—113,231

According to Herberman and Bonczar, the number of adult probationers under state jurisdiction declined by 34,126 people, or 0.9%, between 2012 and 2013. Kentucky (down 11.6%), Connecticut (down 10.6%), and the District of Columbia (down 8.7%) had the largest percentage declines. The states with the largest increases were Washington (up 11.7%), Nevada (up 6.9%), and Wyoming (up 6.3%). Overall, there were 1,596 adults on state probation at yearend 2013 for every 100,000 adult residents of the United States. (See Table 9.4.)

Herberman and Bonczar indicate that the adult probationer population under federal jurisdiction decreased by 4.7% between 2012 and 2013. Overall, there were eight adults on federal probation at yearend 2013 for every 100,000 adult residents of the United States. (See Table 9.4.)

Probation Entries and Exits

Herberman and Bonczar note that probation entries generally climbed from 2000 through 2007 before declining sharply. Probation exits typically increased each year through 2009. After that time both entries and exits declined through 2012 and then grew slightly through 2013, when there were 2,094,100 entries and 2,131,300 exits.

Table 9.5 provides a breakdown of the probationers who exited supervision by type of exit between 2008 and 2013. In 2013 nearly two-thirds (66%) of those who left

the system did so because they had completed their probation terms successfully—that is, they either completed their full-term sentence or received an early discharge. The next largest group (15%) left probation because they were incarcerated. This includes probationers who were incarcerated because they violated the terms of their probation, as well as those who were incarcerated for another offense (or for other or unknown circumstances). Another 3% absconded—they escaped from supervision and had not yet been captured. The remaining probationers who left the system did so for a variety of reasons, including 11% who left for what are called "unsatisfactory" reasons. Unsatisfactory conclusions include those who did not successfully complete all the terms of their supervision, for example, those whose sentences expired before completion and those who failed to fulfill a financial requirement such as restitution.

Demographics of Probationers

Table 9.6 provides a breakdown of the adult probation population in 2000, 2012, and 2013 for which gender, race, ethnicity, type of probation and supervision, and type and seriousness of offense were identified. (Note that these statistics do not include probationers whose status for a given characteristic was not known.) The following conclusions are drawn from the data:

- Overall, 75% of the probationers in 2013 were male, while 25% were female. Between 2000 and 2013 the percentage of male probationers declined by three percentage points, and the percentage of female probationers increased by three percentage points.
- At yearend 2013 more than half (54%) of adult probationers were non-Hispanic white, 30% were non-Hispanic African American, and 14% were Hispanic.

TABLE 9.3

Adults under community supervision, by jurisdiction, yearend 2013

Jurisdiction	Community supervision population 12/31/2013[a]	Number under community supervision per 100,000 adult residents, 12/31/2013[b]
U.S. total	**4,751,400**	**1,950**
Federal	131,900	54
State	4,619,400	1,895
Alabama	70,800	1,896
Alaska[c]	9,500	1,728
Arizona	79,200	1,570
Arkansas	50,200	2,223
California	381,600	1,301
Colorado[c]	89,700	2,209
Connecticut	45,400	1,608
Delaware	16,700	2,299
District of Columbia	12,600	2,326
Florida[c]	237,800	1,521
Georgia[d]	536,200	7,117
Hawaii	23,300	2,116
Idaho	35,200	2,957
Illinois	153,400	1,552
Indiana	134,000	2,677
Iowa	34,700	1,462
Kansas	20,500	942
Kentucky[c]	65,900	1,943
Louisiana	70,700	2,006
Maine	6,700	631
Maryland	46,300	1,006
Massachusetts	70,000	1,313
Michigan[c]	195,200	2,545
Minnesota	107,800	2,590
Mississippi	38,600	1,707
Missouri	70,400	1,511
Montana	9,500	1,194
Nebraska	14,800	1,048
Nevada	17,600	823
New Hampshire	6,300	593
New Jersey	128,100	1,856
New Mexico[c]	18,700	1,184
New York	151,400	979
North Carolina	100,600	1,323
North Dakota	5,500	959
Ohio[c]	267,400	2,989
Oklahoma	—	—
Oregon	61,100	1,981
Pennsylvania	275,800	2,734
Rhode Island[c]	23,400	2,791
South Carolina	40,900	1,102
South Dakota	9,500	1,489
Tennessee	77,900	1,550
Texas	508,000	2,597
Utah	14,500	717
Vermont	6,900	1,365
Virginia	55,800	869
Washington[c]	111,100	2,056
West Virginia[c]	11,000	748
Wisconsin	65,300	1,468
Wyoming	6,000	1,338

Other races made up 2% of the total. This racial and ethnic breakdown was virtually unchanged from 2000.

- Nearly seven out of 10 (69%) probationers were under active supervision at yearend 2013. Much smaller percentages were classified as absconders (9%), under warrant status (9%), or inactive (6%). Overall, the percentage of probationers with active status declined by seven percentage points between 2000 and 2013.

TABLE 9.3

Adults under community supervision, by jurisdiction, yearend 2013 [CONTINUED]

—Not known.
[a]The January 1 population excludes 12,672 offenders and the December 31 population excludes 12,511 offenders under community supervision who were on both probation and parole.
[b]Computed using the estimated U.S. adult resident population in each jurisdiction on January 1, 2013.
[c]Data for entries and exits were estimated for nonreporting agencies.
[d]Probation counts include private agency cases and may overstate the number of persons under supervision.
Note: Counts rounded to the nearest 100. Detail may not sum to total due to rounding. Counts based on most recent data and may differ from previously published statistics. Due to nonresponse or incomplete data, the community supervision population for some jurisdictions on December 31, 2013, does not equal the population on January 1, 2013, plus entries, minus exits.

SOURCE: Adapted from Erinn J. Herberman and Thomas P. Bonczar, "Appendix Table 1. Adults under Community Supervision, 2013," in *Probation and Parole in the United States, 2013*, U.S. Department of Justice, Office of Justice Programs, Bureau of Justice Statistics, October 2014, http://www.bjs.gov/index.cfm?ty=pbdetail&iid=5135 (accessed November 5, 2014)

- More than half (55%) of the probationers at yearend 2013 had been convicted of a felony and 43% had been convicted of a misdemeanor. Another 2% had been convicted of other infractions, such as traffic offenses or tax crimes. The ratio of felony offenses to misdemeanor offenses in 2013 had changed little since 2000, when 52% of probationers had been convicted of a felony and 46% had been convicted of a misdemeanor.

- As of yearend 2013, the two largest contingents of probationers had been convicted of property offenses (29%) or drug law violations (25%) as their most serious crime. Another 19% were on probation for a violent crime and 14% were on probation for driving while intoxicated or driving under the influence.

PAROLE

Trends in Parole

There are two main types of parole. Discretionary parole is typically administered by parole boards. Their members examine prisoners' criminal histories and prison records and decide whether to release prisoners from incarceration. Since the mid-1990s several states have abolished discretionary parole in favor of mandatory parole. Mandatory parole is legislatively imposed at the state level and, with some exceptions, takes away parole boards' discretion. Mandatory parole provisions ensure that sentences for the same crime require incarceration for the same length of time. The prisoner can shorten his or her sentence only by good behavior—but time off for good behavior is also prohibited in some states. In some jurisdictions parole can only begin after prisoners have served 100% of their minimum incarceration time. Jeremy Travis and Sarah Lawrence of the

FIGURE 9.2

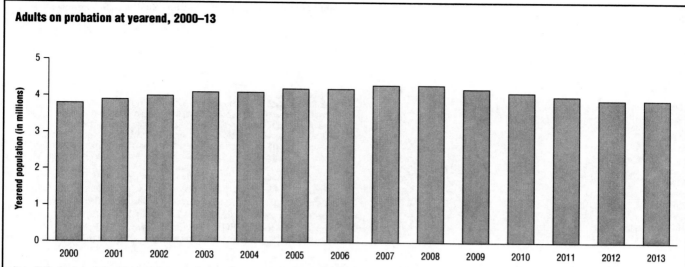

Adults on probation at yearend, 2000–13

Note: Estimates based on most recent data and may differ from previously published statistics. Reporting methods for some probation agencies changed over time, and probation coverage was expanded in 1998 and 1999.

SOURCE: Erinn J. Herberman and Thomas P. Bonczar, "Figure 2. Adults on Probation at Yearend, 2000–2013," in *Probation and Parole in the United States, 2013*, U.S. Department of Justice, Office of Justice Programs, Bureau of Justice Statistics, October 2014, http://www.bjs.gov/index.cfm?ty=pbdetail&iid=5135 (accessed November 5, 2014)

Urban Institute report in *Beyond the Prison Gates: The State of Parole in America* (November 2002, http://www.urban.org/UploadedPDF/310583_Beyond_prison_gates.pdf) that the share of discretionary prison releases decreased from 65% in 1976 to 24% in 1999.

The states have different prison release methods. Some states have cut back on parole supervision by releasing more prisoners directly to the community. Other states have aggressively enforced the conditions of parole, leading to the identification of more parole violations. States handle different types of offenses differently. Some allow victims or prosecutors to participate in release decisions, whereas others do not. Some states still rely heavily on parole boards to make release decisions, whereas others no longer use parole boards and have mandatory release policies for all their prisoners. Furthermore, parolees in some jurisdictions are required to wear electronic bracelets so that officials can monitor their movement.

For example, in 1983 Florida enacted sentencing guidelines that effectively eliminated the option of parole for most crimes that were committed on or after October 1, 1983. According to the Florida Parole Commission (2014, https://www.fcor.state.fl.us/release-types.shtml), the only exceptions to the parole ban are inmates who committed a capital felony murder between October 1, 1983, and May 25, 1994, and all inmates convicted of other capital felonies between October 1, 1983, and October 1, 1995.

Parole Population

In 2000 there were 725,500 parolees. (See Table 9.1 and Figure 9.3). The number fluctuated over subsequent years but has generally grown. According to Herberman and Bonczar, parolee entries and exits declined from 2009 through 2013.

Geographical Distribution of Parolees

As of yearend 2013, the parole rate was 350 people on parole per 100,000 adult U.S. residents. (See Table 9.2.) In other words, 1 out of 286 adult U.S. residents were on parole. Table 9.7 provides a jurisdictional breakdown for the parolees. The vast majority (741,989 or 87%) of them were under state jurisdiction. The other 111,226 parolees (13%) were under federal jurisdiction.

The 10 states with the highest parolee populations at yearend 2013 were:

- Texas—111,302

- Pennsylvania—103,802

- California—87,532

- New York—45,039

- Illinois—29,586

- Louisiana—28,744

- Georgia—26,611

- Oregon—23,246

- Arkansas—21,709

- Wisconsin—20,251

According to Herberman and Bonczar, the number of adult parolees under state jurisdiction increased by 11,117 people, or 1.5%, between 2012 and 2013. The states with the largest increases were North Carolina (up

TABLE 9.4

Adults on probation, by jurisdiction, yearend 2013

Jurisdiction	Probation population, 12/31/2013	Number on probation per 100,000 adult residents, 12/31/2013[a]
U.S. total	**3,910,647**	**1,605**
Federal	20,676	8
State	3,889,971	1,596
Alabama	61,801	1,655
Alaska[b]	7,167	1,308
Arizona	71,527	1,418
Arkansas	29,289	1,298
California	294,057	1,003
Colorado[b]	78,843	1,942
Connecticut	42,723	1,515
Delaware	16,039	2,209
District of Columbia	7,351	1,362
Florida[b]	233,128	1,491
Georgia[c]	514,477	6,829
Hawaii	21,576	1,958
Idaho	31,375	2,634
Illinois	123,862	1,253
Indiana	123,673	2,471
Iowa	29,301	1,233
Kansas	16,446	756
Kentucky[b]	51,027	1,505
Louisiana	42,046	1,192
Maine	6,719	629
Maryland	40,716	884
Massachusetts	67,784	1,273
Michigan[b]	176,795	2,305
Minnesota	101,762	2,446
Mississippi	31,675	1,402
Missouri	51,028	1,094
Montana	8,472	1,066
Nebraska	13,545	960
Nevada	12,102	565
New Hampshire	3,994	379
New Jersey	113,231	1,639
New Mexico[b]	16,696	1,057
New York	106,409	688
North Carolina	94,442	1,242
North Dakota	4,898	860
Ohio[b]	250,630	2,802
Oklahoma[b]	—	—
Oregon	37,891	1,228
Pennsylvania	171,970	1,705
Rhode Island[b]	22,988	2,737
South Carolina	35,825	964
South Dakota	6,952	1,084
Tennessee	64,216	1,278
Texas	399,655	2,043
Utah	11,203	554
Vermont	5,791	1,148
Virginia	54,020	841
Washington[b]	95,217	1,762
West Virginia[b]	8,465	574
Wisconsin	46,758	1,051
Wyoming	5,207	1,165

TABLE 9.4

Adults on probation, by jurisdiction, yearend 2013 [CONTINUED]

—Not known.
[a]Computed using the estimated U.S. adult resident population in each jurisdiction on January 1, 2013.
[b]Data for entries and exits were estimated for nonreporting agencies.
[c]Includes private agency cases and may overstate the number of persons under supervision.
Note: Counts based on most recent data and may differ from previously published statistics. Counts may not be actual, as reporting agencies may provide estimates on some or all detailed data. Due to nonresponse or incomplete data, the probation population for some jurisdictions on December 31, 2013, does not equal the population on January 1, 2013, plus entries, minus exits. Reporting methods for some probation agencies changed over time, and probation coverage was expanded in 1998 and 1999.

SOURCE: Adapted from Erinn J. Herberman and Thomas P. Bonczar, "Appendix Table 2. Adults on Probation, 2013," in *Probation and Parole in the United States, 2013*, U.S. Department of Justice, Office of Justice Programs, Bureau of Justice Statistics, October 2014, http://www.bjs.gov/index.cfm?ty=pbdetail&iid=5135 (accessed November 5, 2014)

Parole Entries and Exits

Herberman and Bonczar note that federal and state governments reported 465,500 entries to their parole systems in 2013. The type of entry was identified for 430,018 of these new parolees. They included 183,899 entries (42.8%) under discretionary parole and 109,768 entries (25.5%) under mandatory parole. In addition, 85,972 (20%) of the new parolees went into a term of supervised release in the community, including people who received a parole term as part of their original sentence. Another 13,060 (3%) of the new parolees in 2013 were reinstatement entries, meaning that they reentered parole after being incarcerated for a parole violation. The remaining new parolees were added to parole rolls for other reasons, for example, as part of release to a drug treatment program, or for reasons that were not reported.

In 2013 the federal and state governments reported that 457,500 parolees exited their parole systems. The type of exit was identified for 411,305 of the exiters. As shown in Table 9.8, 62% of them completed their obligation, meaning that they completed their full-term sentence or received an early discharge. Another 30% were returned to incarceration—18% whose parole was revoked, 9% who committed a new offense and received a new sentence, and 3% who were incarcerated for other or unknown reasons. An estimated 2% of parolees in 2013 absconded. Another 1% of parolees officially left the parole system, but under "unsatisfactory" conditions. For example, some still had financial obligations that they had not met. The remaining parolees who exited the system in 2013 included those who transferred to another state, died, or left for other or unknown reasons.

As can be seen in Table 9.8, the percentage of adult parolees completing their obligation increased from 49% in 2008 to 62% in 2013. Likewise, the percentage incarcerated declined from 36% in 2008 to 30% in 2013. The

64.5%), North Dakota (up 31.4%), and West Virginia (up 24.4%). Kansas (down 20.7%), New Mexico (down 18.6%), and Nebraska (down 9.9%) had the largest percentage declines. Overall, there were 304 adults on state parole at yearend 2013 for every 100,000 adult residents of the United States. (See Table 9.7.)

Herberman and Bonczar indicate that the adult parolee population under federal jurisdiction increased by 2.3% between 2012 and 2013. Overall, there were 46 adults on federal parole at yearend 2013 for every 100,000 adult residents of the United States. (See Table 9.7.)

TABLE 9.5

Probationers who exited supervision, by type of exit, 2008–13

Type of exit	2008	2009	2010	2011	2012	2013
Total	100%	100%	100%	100%	100%	100%
Completion	63%	65%	65%	66%	68%	66%
Incarceration[a]	17	16	16	16	15	15
Absconder	4	3	3	2	3	3
Discharged to custody, detainer, or warrant	1	1	1	1	1	—
Other unsatisfactory[b]	10	10	11	9	9	11
Transferred to another probation agency	1	—	1	1	1	1
Death	1	1	1	1	1	1
Other[c]	4	4	4	4	4	3
Estimated number[d]	2,320,100	2,327,800	2,261,300	2,189,100	2,089,800	2,131,300

— Less than 0.5%.

[a]Includes probationers who were incarcerated for a new offense and those who had their current probation sentence revoked (e.g. violating a condition of supervision).

[b]Includes probationers discharged from supervision who failed to meet all conditions of supervision, including some with only financial conditions remaining, some who had their probation sentence revoked but were not incarcerated because their sentence was immediately reinstated, and other types of unsatisfactory exits. Includes some early terminations and expirations of sentence.

[c]Includes, but not limited to, probationers who were discharged from supervision through a legislative mandate because they were deported or transferred to the jurisdiction of Immigration and Customs Enforcement; were transferred to another state through an interstate compact agreement; had their sentence dismissed or overturned by the court through an appeal; had their sentence administratively closed, deferred, or terminated by the court; were awaiting a hearing; and were released on bond.

[d]Counts rounded to the nearest 100. Calculated as the inverse of the exit rate times 12 months. Includes estimates for nonreporting agencies.

Note: Detail may not sum to total due to rounding. Percents based on most recent data and may differ from previously published statistics. Percents based on probationers with known type of exit. Reporting methods for some probation agencies changed over time.

SOURCE: Erinn J. Herberman and Thomas P. Bonczar, "Table 4. Probationers Who Exited Supervision, by Type of Exit, 2008–2013," in *Probation and Parole in the United States, 2013*, U.S. Department of Justice, Office of Justice Programs, Bureau of Justice Statistics, October 2014, http://www.bjs.gov/index.cfm?ty=pbdetail&iid=5135 (accessed November 5, 2014)

percentage of absconders also decreased from 11% in 2008 to 2% in 2013.

Characteristics of Parolees

A breakdown of adult parolees by gender, race, ethnicity, type of supervision, sentence length, and type of offense is provided in Table 9.9 for 2000, 2012, and 2013. (Note that these statistics do not include parolees whose status for a given characteristic was not known.)

The vast majority of the parolees in 2013 were men (88%), whereas 12% were women. As shown in Table 9.9, the ratio of males to females was unchanged from 2000.

At yearend 2013 the parolee population included 43% non-Hispanic whites and 38% non-Hispanic African Americans. (See Table 9.9.) Seventeen percent of the parolees were Hispanic. These values had changed only slightly from 2000, when 38% of parolees were non-Hispanic white, 40% were non-Hispanic African American, and 21% were Hispanic.

A large percentage (84%) of the adult parolees were under active supervision in 2013, up slightly from 83% in 2000. (See Table 9.9.) In 2013, 6% of the parole population had absconded, which was down slightly from 7% in 2000.

Sentence data shown in Table 9.9 indicate that 95% of the parolees in 2013 had served a sentence of at least one year and 5% had served less than a year.

As of yearend 2013, slightly less than one-third (32%) of parolees had been convicted of drug offenses as their most serious crime. (See Table 9.9.) Drug offenses were the largest single crime category. More than a quarter (29%) had served time for violent offenses, while 22% had served time for property offenses. Much smaller percentages had been convicted of other crimes (13%) and weapon offenses (4%).

IMPROVING PAROLE AND PROBATION OUTCOMES

One of the chief concerns associated with the community supervision population is recidivism. The U.S. Department of Justice's National Institute of Justice (June 17, 2014, http://www.nij.gov/topics/corrections/recidivism/Pages/welcome.aspx) defines recidivism as "a person's relapse into criminal behavior, often after the person receives sanctions or undergoes intervention for a previous crime." Recidivism is a serious problem. For example, the National Institute of Justice notes that a study begun in 2005 tracked 404,638 inmates after they were released from state prisons. More than half (56.7%) of the former inmates were rearrested within a year of their release; more than three-quarters (76.6%) were rearrested within five years of their release.

Various government and private programs are devoted to reducing the nation's recidivism rates. Many of these programs focus on enhancing the process of reentry into society when inmates are released from prison. In "Justice Department Announces More Than $62 Million to Strengthen Reentry, Probation and Parole Programs" (November 14, 2014, http://www.justice.gov/opa/pr/justice-department-announces-more-62-million-strengthen-reentry-probation-and-parole-programs), the

TABLE 9.6

Characteristics of adults on probation, 2000, 2012, and 2013

Characteristic	2000	2012	2013
Total	100%	100%	100%
Sex			
Male	78%	76%	75%
Female	22	24	25
Race/Hispanic origin[a]			
White	54%	54%	54%
Black/African American	31	30	30
Hispanic/Latino	13	13	14
American Indian/Alaska Native	1	1	1
Asian/Native Hawaiian/other Pacific Islander	1	1	1
Two or more races	—	—	*
Status of supervision			
Active	76%	72%	69%
Residential/other treatment program	—	1	1
Financial conditions remaining	—	1	1
Inactive	9	7	6
Absconder	9	10	9
Supervised out of jurisdiction	3	3	2
Warrant status	—	3	9
Other	3	3	3
Type of offense			
Felony	52%	53%	55%
Misdemeanor	46	45	43
Other infractions	2	2	2
Most serious offense			
Violent	—%	19%	19%
Domestic violence	—	4	4
Sex offense	—	3	3
Other violent offense	—	12	12
Property	—	28	29
Drug	24	25	25
Public order	24	17	17
DWI/DUI	18	15	14
Other traffic offense	6	2	2
Other[b]	52	11	10

*Less than 0.5%.
—Not available.
[a]Excludes persons of Hispanic or Latino origin, unless specified.
[b]Includes violent and property offenses in 2000 because those data were not collected separately.
Note: Detail may not sum to total due to rounding. Counts based on most recent data and may differ from previously published statistics. Characteristics based on probationers with known type of status.

SOURCE: Erinn J. Herberman and Thomas P. Bonczar, "Appendix Table 3. Characteristics of Adults on Probation, 2000, 2012, and 2013," in *Probation and Parole in the United States, 2013*, U.S. Department of Justice, Office of Justice Programs, Bureau of Justice Statistics, October 2014, http://www.bjs.gov/ index.cfm?ty=pbdetail&iid=5135 (accessed November 5, 2014)

Department of Justice indicates that in 2014 it awarded more than $62 million in grants to state, tribal, and local government and nonprofit organizations "to reduce recidivism, provide reentry services, conduct research and evaluate the impact of reentry programs."

The Department of Justice, in collaboration with the Council of State Governments, operates the National Reentry Resource Center (NRRC; http://csgjusticecenter .org/jc/category/reentry/nrrc), which is a clearinghouse for education, training, and technical assistance for government agencies and private organizations working on reentry projects. The NRRC notes in "States Ban the Box: Removing Barriers to Work for People with Criminal Records" (December 19, 2014, http://csgjusticecen ter.org/reentry/posts/states-ban-the-box-removing-barriers- to-work-for-people-with-criminal-records) that one of its initiatives is called "ban the box." This refers to the box that appears on many job applications in which applicants must place a check mark if they have a criminal record. According to the NRRC, around 65 million Americans have criminal records. The "ban the box" initiative seeks to encourage employers to cease including the box on job applications so as to give applicants with a criminal record a chance to present their qualifications before having to disclose their criminal record. According to the NRRC, as of December 2014, 13 states, the District of Columbia, and approximately 70 cities and counties had either legislatively or administratively banned the box on applications for public and, in some cases, private employment. In addition, Target and Walmart "have voluntarily removed questions about criminal history from their job applications nationwide."

REFORMING THE PROBATION AND PAROLE SYSTEMS

Chapter 6 discusses penalty reforms that have been implemented during the 21st century to reduce taxpayer spending on incarceration and relieve overcrowding in prisons. The federal government has encouraged the reform movement through programs such as the Justice Reinvestment Initiative, which helps state criminal justice systems generate cost savings that can be invested in public safety programs.

Many Justice Reinvestment Initiative reforms involve the probation and parole systems. Probationers and parolees are subject to certain technical requirements, such as mandatory interviews, appointments, or drug tests. Historically, the penalty for failing to meet such requirements has been incarceration, typically for many months. According to the editorial "New York's Broken Parole System" (NYTimes.com, February 16, 2014), technical violations account for nearly three-fourths of the parole revocations in New York. Reform-minded jurisdictions are taking new approaches to deal with technical violations by probationers and parolees. For example, Erik Eckholm indicates in "North Carolina Cuts Prison Time for Probation Violators, and Costs" (NYTimes.com, September 11, 2014) that North Carolina has implemented a "quick dip" penalty that sends some of the violators to jail for only a few days. This reduces incarceration costs and can prevent the violators from losing their job.

FIGURE 9.3

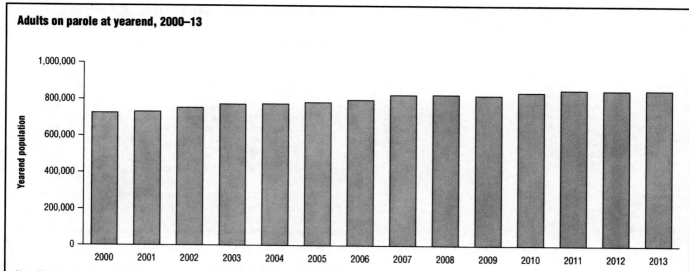

Adults on parole at yearend, 2000–13

Note: Estimates based on most recent data and may differ from previously published statistics.

SOURCE: Erinn J. Herberman and Thomas P. Bonczar, "Figure 3. Adults on Parole at Yearend, 2000–2013," in *Probation and Parole in the United States, 2013*, U.S. Department of Justice, Office of Justice Programs, Bureau of Justice Statistics, October 2014, http://www.bjs.gov/index.cfm?ty=pbdetail&iid=5135 (accessed November 5, 2014)

TABLE 9.7

Adults on parole by jurisdiction, yearend 2013

Jurisdiction	Parole population, 12/31/2013	Number on parole per 100,000 adult residents, 12/31/2013[a]
U.S. total	853,215	350
Federal	111,226	46
State	741,989	304
Alabama	8,982	241
Alaska	2,303	420
Arizona	7,636	151
Arkansas	21,709	962
California[b, c]	87,532	298
Colorado	10,846	267
Connecticut	2,640	94
Delaware	657	90
District of Columbia	5,623	1,042
Florida	4,683	30
Georgia	26,611	353
Hawaii	1,738	158
Idaho	3,851	323
Illinois	29,586	299
Indiana	10,340	207
Iowa	5,595	235
Kansas	4,065	187
Kentucky	14,922	440
Louisiana	28,744	815
Maine	21	2
Maryland	5,623	122
Massachusetts	2,166	41
Michigan	18,439	240
Minnesota	5,997	144
Mississippi	6,901	305
Missouri	19,401	416
Montana	1,021	128
Nebraska	1,246	88
Nevada	5,522	258
New Hampshire	2,256	214
New Jersey	14,918	216
New Mexico	2,010	127
New York	45,039	291
North Carolina	7,171	94
North Dakota	561	99
Ohio	16,797	188
Oklahoma	2,554	87
Oregon	23,246	753
Pennsylvania	103,802	1,029
Rhode Island	459	55
South Carolina	5,556	150
South Dakota	2,595	405
Tennessee	13,657	272
Texas	111,302	569
Utah	3,283	162
Vermont	1,095	217
Virginia	1,800	28
Washington	15,908	294
West Virginia	2,553	173
Wisconsin	20,251	455
Wyoming	776	174

TABLE 9.7

Adults on parole by jurisdiction, yearend 2013 [CONTINUED]

[a]Computed using the estimated U.S. adult resident population in each jurisdiction on January 1, 2014.
[b]Data for entries and exits were estimated when data were incomplete.
[c]Includes post-release community supervision and mandatory supervision parolees: 38,781 on January 1, 2013; and 24,559 entries, 21,393 exits, and 41,947 on December 31, 2013.
Note: Counts based on most recent data and may differ from previously published statistics. Counts may not be actual, as reporting agencies may provide estimates on some or all detailed data. Due to nonresponse or incomplete data, the parole population for some jurisdictions on December 31, 2013, does not equal the population on January 1, 2013, plus entries, minus exits.

SOURCE: Adapted from Erinn J. Herberman and Thomas P. Bonczar, "Appendix Table 4. Adults on Parole, 2013," in *Probation and Parole in the United States, 2013*, U.S. Department of Justice, Office of Justice Programs, Bureau of Justice Statistics, October 2014, http://www.bjs.gov/index.cfm?ty=pbdetail&iid=5135 (accessed November 5, 2014)

TABLE 9.8

Parolees who exited supervision, by type of exit, 2008–13

Type of exit	2008	2009	2010	2011	2012	2013
Total	**100%**	**100%**	**100%**	**100%**	**100%**	**100%**
Completion	49%	51%	52%	52%	58%	62%
Returned to incarceration	36%	34%	33%	32%	25%	30%
With new sentence	9	9	9	9	8	9
With revocation	25	24	23	21	14	18
Other/unknown	1	1	1	2	3	3
Absconder	11%	9%	9%	9%	11%	2%
Other unsatisfactory[a]	2%	2%	2%	2%	2%	1%
Transferred to another state	1%	1%	1%	1%	1%	1%
Death	1%	1%	1%	1%	1%	1%
Other[b]	1%	3%	1%	3%	3%	3%
Estimated number[c]	568,000	575,600	562,500	532,500	496,100	457,500

[a]Includes parolees discharged from supervision who failed to meet all conditions of supervision, including some who had their parole sentence revoked but were not incarcerated because their sentence was immediately reinstated, and other types of unsatisfactory exits. Includes some early terminations and expirations of sentence reported as unsatisfactory exits.
[b]Includes, but not limited to, parolees who were discharged from supervision through a legislative mandate because they were deported or transferred to the jurisdiction of Immigration and Customs Enforcement, had their sentence terminated by the court through an appeal, and were transferred to another state through an interstate compact agreement or discharged to probation supervision.
[c]Estimates rounded to the nearest 100. Includes estimates for nonreporting agencies.
Note: Detail may not sum to total due to rounding. Counts based on most recent data and may differ from previously published statistics. Percents based on parolees with known type of exit.

SOURCE: Erinn J. Herberman and Thomas P. Bonczar, "Appendix Table 8. Percent of Parole Exits, by Type of Exit, 2008–2013," in *Probation and Parole in the United States, 2013*, U.S. Department of Justice, Office of Justice Programs, Bureau of Justice Statistics, October 2014, http://www.bjs.gov/index.cfm?ty=pbdetail&iid=5135 (accessed November 5, 2014)

TABLE 9.9

Characteristics of adults on parole, 2000, 2012, and 2013

Characteristic	2000	2012	2013
Total	100%	100%	100%
Sex			
Male	88%	89%	88%
Female	12	11	12
Race/Hispanic origin[a]			
White	38%	41%	43%
Black/African American	40	40	38
Hispanic/Latino	21	17	17
American Indian/Alaska Native	1	1	1
Asian/Native Hawaiian/other Pacific Islander	*	1	1
Two or more races	—	*	*
Status of supervision			
Active	83%	82%	84%
Inactive	4	5	5
Absconder	7	6	6
Supervised out of state	5	4	4
Financial conditions remaining	—	*	*
Other	1	3	1
Maximum sentence to incarceration			
Less than 1 year	3%	5%	5%
1 year or more	97	95	95
Most serious offense			
Violent	—%	29%	29%
Sex offense	—	9	10
Other violent	—	20	20
Property	—	22	22
Drug	—	33	32
Weapon	—	4	4
Other[b]	—	13	13

*Less than 0.5%.
—Not available.
[a]Excludes persons of Hispanic or Latino origin, unless specified.
[b]Includes public order offenses.
Note: Detail may not sum to total due to rounding. Counts based on most recent data and may differ from previously published statistics. Characteristics based on parolees with known type of status.

SOURCE: Erinn J. Herberman and Thomas P. Bonczar, "Appendix Table 6. Characteristics of Adults on Parole, 2000, 2012, and 2013," in *Probation and Parole in the United States, 2013*, U.S. Department of Justice, Office of Justice Programs, Bureau of Justice Statistics, October 2014, http://www.bjs.gov/index.cfm?ty=pbdetail&iid=5135 (accessed November 5, 2014)

CHAPTER 10
JUVENILE CRIME

WHO IS A JUVENILE?

Juvenile courts date to the late 19th century, when Cook County, Illinois, established the first juvenile court under the Juvenile Court Act of 1899. The underlying concept was that if parents failed to provide children with proper care and supervision, then the state had the right to intervene benevolently. Other states followed Illinois, and by 1925 juvenile courts were in operation in most states. Juvenile courts favored a rehabilitative philosophy rather than a punitive philosophy and evolved less formal approaches than those in place in adult courts.

In modern law, juvenile offenses fall into two main categories: delinquency offenses and status offenses. Delinquency offenses are acts that are illegal regardless of the age of the perpetrator. Status offenses are acts that are illegal only for minors, such as truancy (failure to attend school), running away, or curfew violations. Each state defines by legislation the oldest age at which a youth falls under jurisdiction of its juvenile court. As of January 2015, that age was 17 in the vast majority of states. The upper age was set at 16 in eight states (Georgia, Louisiana, Michigan, Missouri, New Hampshire, South Carolina, Texas, and Wisconsin).

New York and North Carolina use an upper age of 15. This means that youths aged 16 and 17 years fall under the jurisdiction of adult courts in these two states. However, New York provides for a "youthful offender" sentence that can be given to certain youths who are tried in adult courts. A "youthful offender" finding results in a shorter sentence than would have been imposed otherwise and no criminal record for the offender.

Many states place certain young offenders in the jurisdiction of the criminal (adult) court rather than the juvenile court based on the youth's age, offense, or previous court history.

PARENTAL RESPONSIBILITY

One issue associated with juvenile crime is parental responsibility. Societies expect parents to provide moral guidance to their children and to supervise their behavior at least to some degree. "Where were the parents?" is a popular media question after particularly shocking juvenile crimes occur. Parental responsibility was a topic of focus in a 2013 case in which Ethan Couch (1997–), a 16-year-old Texas youth, was charged with driving under the influence and crashing into a disabled car. Four people were killed and two were critically injured in the incident. At his trial, a defense witness testified that the teenager suffered from "affluenza" (a combination of the words *affluence*, meaning wealth, and *influenza*, that is, the flu). The implication was that the juvenile's parents had allowed him too much freedom and given him the notion that their wealth absolved him from behaving in a socially responsible manner. The so-called affluenza case attracted widespread public attention after Couch pleaded guilty and was sentenced to probation rather than incarceration.

Parental supervision (or lack thereof) was also an issue in a crime that occurred in 2012 in Steubenville, Ohio. Teenaged partygoers shared photos, tweets, and text messages about a very intoxicated 16-year-old girl who was stripped naked and sexually abused. One shocking aspect of the case was the apparently callous and nonchalant attitude of the teens who corresponded about the incident via social media. Critics also decried the lack of parental involvement in the lives of the victim and the perpetrators. In 2013 two male teens were tried in juvenile court and found delinquent in the case.

JUVENILE ARREST STATISTICS

The report *Crime in the United States, 2013* (November 10, 2014, http://www.fbi.gov/about-us/cjis/ucr/crime-in-the-u.s/2013/crime-in-the-u.s.-2013) includes Uniform

Crime Reporting (UCR) statistics on crimes reported to law enforcement, arrests, and crimes cleared by arrest or exceptional means through 2013. Crimes cleared by exceptional means are those for which there can be no arrest, such as a murder-suicide, when the perpetrator is known to be deceased. In this report the Federal Bureau of Investigation (FBI) provides a partial breakdown of arrest statistics by age, that is, the age of the arrested offender. Because the upper age classification for juveniles differs between states, the FBI does not categorize arrested individuals as adults or juveniles. However, for ease of terminology offenders under the age of 18 years will be referred to as juveniles in this chapter.

Juvenile Arrests in 2013

As shown in Table 10.1, 875,262 people under the age of 18 years were arrested in 2013 based on UCR data from 11,951 law enforcement agencies around the country. The 10 most common offenses were:

- Larceny-theft—151,427 arrests
- Assaults other than aggravated assaults—118,253 arrests
- Drug abuse violations—94,187 arrests
- Disorderly conduct—76,318 arrests
- Liquor laws—48,126 arrests
- Curfew and loitering law violations—47,934 arrests
- Vandalism—37,678 arrests
- Burglary—34,760 arrests
- Aggravated assault—25,016 arrests
- Weapons offenses—16,683

TABLE 10.1

Arrests of persons under 18 years of age, by age and offense, 2013

[11,951 agencies. 2013 estimated population 245,741,701.]

Offense charged	Ages under 18	Under 10	10–12	13–14	15	16	17
Total	875,262	6,394	53,316	184,978	165,481	209,804	255,289
Total percent distribution[a]	9.7	0.1	0.6	2.0	1.8	2.3	2.8
Murder and nonnegligent manslaughter	614	0	9	62	91	163	289
Rape[b]	2,089	17	205	568	369	413	517
Robbery	15,932	14	412	2,783	3,268	4,397	5,058
Aggravated assault	25,016	243	2,080	5,898	4,713	5,725	6,357
Burglary	34,760	241	1,945	7,323	6,792	8,669	9,790
Larceny-theft	151,427	692	9,380	32,734	28,896	36,858	42,867
Motor vehicle theft	9,469	19	223	1,898	2,145	2,620	2,564
Arson	2,943	170	539	974	493	406	361
Violent crime[c]	43,651	274	2,706	9,311	8,441	10,698	12,221
Violent crime percent distribution[a]	11.1	0.1	0.7	2.4	2.1	2.7	3.1
Property crime[c]	198,599	1,122	12,087	42,929	38,326	48,553	55,582
Property crime percent distribution[a]	15.7	0.1	1.0	3.4	3.0	3.8	4.4
Other assaults	118,253	1,415	12,238	32,712	22,928	24,818	24,142
Forgery and counterfeiting	850	3	20	71	90	189	477
Fraud	3,542	10	140	547	539	918	1,388
Embezzlement	318	1	6	28	27	78	178
Stolen property; buying, receiving, possessing	8,388	19	281	1,653	1,699	2,187	2,549
Vandalism	37,678	689	4,129	9,508	7,145	7,843	8,364
Weapons; carrying, possessing, etc.	16,683	320	1,516	3,837	3,007	3,627	4,376
Prostitution and commercialized vice	655	1	5	55	80	180	334
Sex offenses (except rape and prostitution)	8,389	149	1,188	2,808	1,461	1,391	1,392
Drug abuse violations	94,187	85	2,209	13,781	15,648	24,490	37,974
Gambling	615	0	14	90	87	170	254
Offenses against the family and children	2,224	39	156	546	504	439	540
Driving under the influence	5,963	11	9	97	249	1,320	4,277
Liquor laws	48,126	35	316	4,211	7,192	13,456	22,916
Drunkenness	5,902	18	56	622	932	1,389	2,885
Disorderly conduct	76,318	651	6,734	21,977	15,680	15,812	15,464
Vagrancy	733	3	28	145	158	175	224
All other offenses (except traffic)	156,079	1,173	6,560	29,149	30,491	39,573	49,133
Suspicion	175	9	20	54	32	37	23
Curfew and loitering law violations	47,934	367	2,898	10,847	10,765	12,461	10,596

[a]Because of rounding, the percentages may not add to 100.0.
[b]The rape figures in this table are an aggregate total of the data submitted using both the revised and legacy Uniform Crime Reporting definitions.
[c]Violent crimes in this table are offenses of murder and nonnegligent manslaughter, rape (revised and legacy definitions), robbery, and aggravated assault. Property crimes are offenses of burglary, larceny-theft, motor vehicle theft, and arson.

SOURCE: Adapted from "Table 38. Arrests by Age, 2013," in Crime in the United States 2013, U.S. Department of Justice, Federal Bureau of Investigation, November 10, 2014, http://www.fbi.gov/about-us/cjis/ucr/crime-in-the-u.s/2013/crime-in-the-u.s.-2013/tables/table-38/table_38_arrests_by_age_2013.xls (accessed November 12, 2014)

Overall, the arrests of people under the age of 18 years in 2013 totaled 43,651 for violent crimes and 198,599 for property crimes. (See Table 10.1.) The FBI includes four offenses in its definition of violent crimes: murder and nonnegligent manslaughter, rape, robbery, and aggravated assault. All these offenses involve the use or threat of violence by the perpetrator. Property crimes include burglary, larceny-theft, motor vehicle theft, and arson. The FBI counts only the most serious charge for which a single offender is arrested. Violent crimes are considered more serious than property crimes. Thus, a person arrested for rape and burglary would be counted only once in Table 10.1 (for the rape offense).

In 2013 people under the age of 18 years accounted for 11.1% of total arrests for violent crimes and 15.7% of total arrests for property crimes. (See Table 10.1.)

JUVENILE ARRESTS BY AGE AND SEX. As shown in Table 10.2, 622,630 (71.1%) of total juvenile arrestees

(875,262) in 2013 were male. (See Table 10.1.) More than half (54.1%) of the male arrests were of youths aged 17 years (187,188) or 16 years (149,571). Youths aged 15 years accounted for 115,270 of the male total, and those aged 13 to 14 years made up 126,884 of the male total. Younger male juveniles had much smaller numbers of arrests.

Female juvenile arrestees numbered 252,632 in 2013. (See Table 10.3.) Females accounted for 28.9% of the 875,262 total juvenile arrests that year. (See Table 10.1.) Just over half (50.8%) of the female arrests were of youths aged 17 years (68,101) or 16 years (60,233). Youths aged 15 years accounted for 50,211 of the female total, and those aged 13 to 14 years made up 58,094 of the female total. Younger female juveniles had much smaller numbers of arrests.

JUVENILE ARRESTS BY RACE. Table 10.4 provides a racial breakdown of the 868,693 juvenile arrestees in

TABLE 10.2

Arrests of males under 18 years of age, by age and offense, 2013

[11,951 agencies. 2013 estimated population 245,741,701.]

Offense charged	Ages under 18	Under 10	10–12	13–14	15	16	17
Total	622,630	5,246	38,471	126,884	115,270	149,571	187,188
Murder and nonnegligent manslaughter	541	0	8	45	79	143	266
Rape[b]	2,014	17	198	536	355	399	509
Robbery	14,403	13	372	2,467	2,918	3,974	4,659
Aggravated assault	18,530	204	1,573	4,185	3,417	4,252	4,899
Burglary	30,740	206	1,712	6,445	5,967	7,754	8,656
Larceny-theft	89,780	515	5,954	20,015	17,392	21,331	24,573
Motor vehicle theft	7,825	15	178	1,491	1,748	2,173	2,220
Arson	2,491	146	468	819	413	343	302
Violent crime[c]	35,488	234	2,151	7,233	6,769	8,768	10,333
Violent crime percent distribution[a]	11.3	0.1	0.7	2.3	2.2	2.8	3.3
Property crime[c]	130,836	882	8,312	28,770	25,520	31,601	35,751
Property crime percent distribution[a]	16.7	0.1	1.1	3.7	3.3	4.0	4.6
Other assaults	75,173	1,180	8,349	20,006	13,979	15,770	15,889
Forgery and counterfeiting	607	3	11	56	70	133	334
Fraud	2,390	9	109	399	363	615	895
Embezzlement	207	1	6	20	19	54	107
Stolen property; buying, receiving, possessing	7,034	15	218	1,367	1,385	1,848	2,201
Vandalism	31,727	602	3,488	7,978	6,007	6,599	7,053
Weapons; carrying, possessing, etc.	14,944	284	1,305	3,348	2,674	3,284	4,049
Prostitution and commercialized vice	132	1	3	15	13	32	68
Sex offenses (except rape and prostitution)	7,433	129	1,053	2,496	1,256	1,229	1,270
Drug abuse violations	77,022	72	1,733	10,592	12,540	20,238	31,847
Gambling	570	0	10	76	82	163	239
Offenses against the family and children	1,366	27	101	319	299	257	363
Driving under the influence	4,496	10	6	68	188	992	3,232
Liquor laws	29,321	21	173	2,192	4,007	8,185	14,743
Drunkenness	4,313	14	31	387	640	1,007	2,234
Disorderly conduct	49,973	532	4,447	13,698	9,979	10,475	10,842
Vagrancy	569	2	16	102	124	147	178
All other offenses (except traffic)	114,554	913	4,767	20,126	21,785	29,198	37,765
Suspicion	125	7	12	38	26	26	16
Curfew and loitering law violations	34,350	308	2,170	7,598	7,545	8,950	7,779

[a]Because of rounding, the percentages may not add to 100.0.
[b]The rape figures in this table are an aggregate total of the data submitted using both the revised and legacy Uniform Crime Reporting definitions.
[c]Violent crimes in this table are offenses of murder and nonnegligent manslaughter, rape (revised and legacy definitions), robbery, and aggravated assault. Property crimes are offenses of burglary, larceny-theft, motor vehicle theft, and arson.

SOURCE: Adapted from "Table 39. Arrests: Males, by Age, 2013," in *Crime in the United States 2013*, U.S. Department of Justice, Federal Bureau of Investigation, November 10, 2014, http://www.fbi.gov/about-us/cjis/ucr/crime-in-the-u.s/2013/crime-in-the-u.s.-2013/tables/table-39/table_39_arrests_males_by_age_2013.xls (accessed November 12, 2014)

TABLE 10.3

Arrests of females under 18 years of age, by age and offense, 2013

[11,951 agencies. 2013 estimated population 245,741,701.]

Offense charged	Ages under 18	Under 10	10–12	13–14	15	16	17
Total	252,632	1,148	14,845	58,094	50,211	60,233	68,101
Murder and nonnegligent manslaughter	73	0	1	17	12	20	23
Rape[a]	75	0	7	32	14	14	8
Robbery	1,529	1	40	316	350	423	399
Aggravated assault	6,486	39	507	1,713	1,296	1,473	1,458
Burglary	4,020	35	233	878	825	915	1,134
Larceny-theft	61,647	177	3,426	12,719	11,504	15,527	18,294
Motor vehicle theft	1,644	4	45	407	397	447	344
Arson	452	24	71	155	80	63	59
Violent crime[b]	8,163	40	555	2,078	1,672	1,930	1,888
Violent crime percent distribution[c]	10.3	0.1	0.7	2.6	2.1	2.4	2.4
Property crime[b]	67,763	240	3,775	14,159	12,806	16,952	19,831
Property crime percent distribution[c]	14.2	0.1	0.8	3.0	2.7	3.6	4.2
Other assaults	43,080	235	3,889	12,706	8,949	9,048	8,253
Forgery and counterfeiting	243	0	9	15	20	56	143
Fraud	1,152	1	31	148	176	303	493
Embezzlement	111	0	0	8	8	24	71
Stolen property; buying, receiving, possessing	1,354	4	63	286	314	339	348
Vandalism	5,951	87	641	1,530	1,138	1,244	1,311
Weapons; carrying, possessing, etc.	1,739	36	211	489	333	343	327
Prostitution and commercialized vice	523	0	2	40	67	148	266
Sex offenses (except rape and prostitution)	956	20	135	312	205	162	122
Drug abuse violations	17,165	13	476	3,189	3,108	4,252	6,127
Gambling	45	0	4	14	5	7	15
Offenses against the family and children	858	12	55	227	205	182	177
Driving under the influence	1,467	1	3	29	61	328	1,045
Liquor laws	18,805	14	143	2,019	3,185	5,271	8,173
Drunkenness	1,589	4	25	235	292	382	651
Disorderly conduct	26,345	119	2,287	8,279	5,701	5,337	4,622
Vagrancy	164	1	12	43	34	28	46
All other offenses (except traffic)	41,525	260	1,793	9,023	8,706	10,375	11,368
Suspicion	50	2	8	16	6	11	7
Curfew and loitering law violations	13,584	59	728	3,249	3,220	3,511	2,817

[a]The rape figures in this table are an aggregate total of the data submitted using both the revised and legacy Uniform Crime Reporting definitions.
[b]Violent crimes in this table are offenses of murder and nonnegligent manslaughter, rape (revised and legacy definitions), robbery, and aggravated assault. Property crimes are offenses of burglary, larceny-theft, motor vehicle theft, and arson.
[c]Because of rounding, the percentages may not add to 100.0.

SOURCE: Adapted from "Table 40. Arrests: Females, by Age, 2013," in *Crime in the United States 2013*, U.S. Department of Justice, Federal Bureau of Investigation, November 10, 2014, http://www.fbi.gov/about-us/cjis/ucr/crime-in-the-u.s/2013/crime-in-the-u.s.-2013/tables/table-40/table_40_arrests_females_by_age_2013.xls (accessed November 12, 2014)

2013. Whites accounted for 547,395 (63%) of the total. There were 298,425 African American youths arrested, making up 34.4% of the total. The number of arrests for Native Americans or Alaskan Natives (12,601 or 1.5%), Asian Americans (9,716 or 1.1%), and Hawaiians or other Pacific Islanders (556 or 0.1%) were much lower. Whites made up the majority of juvenile arrestees for most offenses, particularly driving under the influence (91.3%), liquor laws (87.6%), drunkenness (86.7%), suspicion (83.4%), and vandalism (73.8%). African Americans accounted for the majority of juvenile arrests for four offenses: gambling (89.4%), robbery (71.4%), prostitution and commercialized vice (61.9%), and murder (54.3%).

In 2013, 53.3% of juveniles arrested for violent crimes were African American and 44.8% were white. (See Table 10.4.) In contrast, the breakdown of arrests for property crimes was 59.7% white and 37.2% African American.

Juvenile Arrest Trends between 2004 and 2013

In *Crime in the United States, 2013*, the FBI uses age data from 7,858 law enforcement agencies to compile 10-year trends in arrests of people under the age of 18 years. As shown in Table 10.5, overall juvenile arrests declined by 45.7%, from 1.2 million in 2004 to 666,263 in 2013. Juvenile arrests decreased for all offenses, particularly suspicion (down 92.9%), vagrancy (down 82.6%), and forgery and counterfeiting (down 78.3%). The number of juvenile arrests for all violent crimes decreased by 37.5% between 2004 and 2013. Juvenile arrests for property crimes declined by 43.7% over the same period.

Table 10.6 provides a breakdown by sex for the 10-year arrest trends. Arrests of male juvenile offenders decreased by 46.1% between 2004 and 2013 and were down for all offenses. The number of male juveniles who were arrested for violent crimes decreased by 37.7% and for property crimes by 43.7%. Overall, female juvenile

TABLE 10.4

Arrests of persons under 18 years of age, by race and offense, 2013

[11,951 agencies. 2013 estimated population 245,741,701.]

| | Arrests under 18 | | | | | | Percent distribution[a] | | | | | |
| | Race | | | | | | | | | | | |
Offense charged	Total	White	Black or African American	American Indian or Alaska Native	Asian	Native Hawaiian or other Pacific Islander	Total	White	Black or African American	American Indian or Alaska Native	Asian	Native Hawaiian or other Pacific Islander
Total	868,693	547,395	298,425	12,601	9,716	556	100.0	63.0	34.4	1.5	1.1	0.1
Murder and nonnegligent manslaughter	613	263	333	10	6	1	100.0	42.9	54.3	1.6	1.0	0.2
Rape[b]	2,065	1,316	709	21	18	1	100.0	63.7	34.3	1.0	0.9	*
Robbery	15,903	4,356	11,351	63	111	22	100.0	27.4	71.4	0.4	0.7	0.1
Aggravated assault	24,914	13,544	10,802	295	251	22	100.0	54.4	43.4	1.2	1.0	0.1
Burglary	34,610	19,948	13,913	331	385	33	100.0	57.6	40.2	1.0	1.1	0.1
Larceny-theft	150,213	90,606	54,725	2,368	2,431	83	100.0	60.3	36.4	1.6	1.6	0.1
Motor vehicle theft	9,428	5,090	4,111	135	81	11	100.0	54.0	43.6	1.4	0.9	0.1
Arson	2,928	2,157	694	43	32	2	100.0	73.7	23.7	1.5	1.1	0.1
Violent crime[c]	43,495	19,479	23,195	389	386	46	100.0	44.8	53.3	0.9	0.9	0.1
Property crime[c]	197,179	117,801	73,443	2,877	2,929	129	100.0	59.7	37.2	1.5	1.5	0.1
Other assaults	117,546	67,130	47,948	1,459	937	72	100.0	57.1	40.8	1.2	0.8	0.1
Forgery and counterfeiting	847	521	302	6	17	1	100.0	61.5	35.7	0.7	2.0	0.1
Fraud	3,517	2,045	1,352	71	49	0	100.0	58.1	38.4	2.0	1.4	0.0
Embezzlement	316	191	110	8	7	0	100.0	60.4	34.8	2.5	2.2	0.0
Stolen property; buying, receiving, possessing	8,349	4,222	3,952	81	85	9	100.0	50.6	47.3	1.0	1.0	0.1
Vandalism	37,364	27,564	8,968	511	304	17	100.0	73.8	24.0	1.4	0.8	*
Weapons; carrying, possessing, etc.	16,598	9,867	6,322	139	246	24	100.0	59.4	38.1	0.8	1.5	0.1
Prostitution and commercialized vice	654	242	405	4	3	0	100.0	37.0	61.9	0.6	0.5	0.0
Sex offenses (except rape and prostitution)	8,298	5,925	2,202	65	102	4	100.0	71.4	26.5	0.8	1.2	*
Drug abuse violations	93,579	68,322	22,819	1,234	1,161	43	100.0	73.0	24.4	1.3	1.2	*
Gambling	622	59	556	0	7	0	100.0	9.5	89.4	0.0	1.1	0.0
Offenses against the family and children	2,210	1,462	648	88	12	0	100.0	66.2	29.3	4.0	0.5	0.0
Driving under the influence	5,908	5,395	313	112	85	3	100.0	91.3	5.3	1.9	1.4	0.1
Liquor laws	47,594	41,710	3,554	1,713	603	14	100.0	87.6	7.5	3.6	1.3	*
Drunkenness	5,863	5,081	549	141	81	11	100.0	86.7	9.4	2.4	1.4	0.2
Disorderly conduct	75,705	40,394	33,859	894	526	32	100.0	53.4	44.7	1.2	0.7	*
Vagrancy	729	509	214	2	3	1	100.0	69.8	29.4	0.3	0.4	0.1
All other offenses (except traffic)	154,523	104,323	46,334	2,197	1,543	126	100.0	67.5	30.0	1.4	1.0	0.1
Suspicion	175	146	29	0	0	0	100.0	83.4	16.6	0.0	0.0	0.0
Curfew and loitering law violations	47,622	25,007	21,351	610	630	24	100.0	52.5	44.8	1.3	1.3	0.1

[a]Because of rounding, the percentages may not add to 100.0.
[b]The rape figures in this table are an aggregate total of the data submitted using both the revised and legacy Uniform Crime Reporting definitions.
[c]Violent crimes in this table are offenses of murder and nonnegligent manslaughter, rape (revised and legacy definitions), robbery, and aggravated assault. Property crimes are offenses of burglary, larceny-theft, motor vehicle theft, and arson.

SOURCE: Adapted from "Table 43B. Arrests by Race, 2013," in *Crime in the United States 2013*, U.S. Department of Justice, Federal Bureau of Investigation, November 10, 2014, http://www.fbi.gov/about-us/cjis/ucr/crime-in-the-u.s/2013/crime-in-the-u.s.-2013/tables/table-43 (accessed November 12, 2014)

arrests decreased by 44.6% and were down for all offenses except one: murder, which saw a 3.1% rise. However, the number of arrests involved (66 in 2013) is small. Among female juveniles, violent crime arrests declined by 36.8%, while property crime arrests decreased by 43.7% between 2004 and 2013.

Murder: Juvenile Offenders and Victims

Table 2.2 in Chapter 2 provides demographic information about the 14,132 people arrested for murder in 2013. There were 595 people under 18 years of age arrested for murder that year, accounting for 4.2% of arrests for murder. The vast majority of these juvenile arrestees (558 or 93.8%) were male. Concerning the racial breakdown, 370 (62.2%) were African American and 209 (35.1%) were white.

The FBI also provides demographic data about murder victims in *Crime in the United States, 2013*. (See Table 2.3 in Chapter 2.) Of the 12,253 total victims in 2013, 1,027 (8.4%) were under the age of 18 years. Over two-thirds (715 or 69.6%) of the juvenile victims were male. The racial makeup of the juvenile victims was 47.9% (492) white and 46.9% (482) African American.

Howard N. Snyder and Melissa Sickmund of the National Center for Juvenile Justice report in *Juvenile Offenders and Victims: 2006 National Report* (March 2006, http://www.ojjdp.gov/ojstatbb/nr2006/downloads/NR2006.pdf) that murders involving a juvenile offender increased dramatically from the early 1980s to the early 1990s. In 1984 just over 1,000 murders involved a juvenile

TABLE 10.5

Ten-year arrest trends for persons under 18 years of age, by offense, 2004–13

[7,858 agencies. 2013 estimated population 192,473,854; 2004 estimated population 178,805,123.]

Offense charged	Under 18 years of age		
	2004	2013	Percent change
Total[a]	1,226,865	666,263	−45.7
Murder and nonnegligent manslaughter	643	492	−23.5
Rape[b]	2,414	1,484	−38.5
Robbery	14,936	12,340	−17.4
Aggravated assault	35,912	19,351	−46.1
Burglary	49,721	27,960	−43.8
Larceny-theft	198,071	117,141	−40.9
Motor vehicle theft	22,784	7,367	−67.7
Arson	4,593	2,370	−48.4
Violent crime[c]	53,905	33,667	−37.5
Property crime[c]	275,169	154,838	−43.7
Other assaults	148,743	91,436	−38.5
Forgery and counterfeiting	2,988	649	−78.3
Fraud	4,622	2,755	−40.4
Embezzlement	698	233	−66.6
Stolen property; buying, receiving, possessing	13,879	6,354	−54.2
Vandalism	61,262	29,676	−51.6
Weapons; carrying, possessing, etc.	25,478	12,771	−49.9
Prostitution and commercialized vice	1,157	550	−52.5
Sex offenses (except rape and prostitution)	10,923	6,249	−42.8
Drug abuse violations	118,392	75,767	−36.0
Gambling	1,099	569	−48.2
Offenses against the family and children	3,608	1,668	−53.8
Driving under the influence	11,212	4,315	−61.5
Liquor laws	71,976	34,283	−52.4
Drunkenness	11,117	5,107	−54.1
Disorderly conduct	110,374	53,471	−51.6
Vagrancy	3,138	545	−82.6
All other offenses (except traffic)	230,539	125,976	−45.4
Suspicion	535	38	−92.9
Curfew and loitering law violations	66,586	25,384	−61.9

[a]Does not include suspicion.
[b]The rape figures in this table are based on the legacy definition of rape only. The rape figures shown include converted National Incident-Based Reporting System rape data and those states/agencies that reported the legacy definition of rape for both years.
[c]Violent crimes in this table are offenses of murder and nonnegligent manslaughter, rape (legacy definition), robbery, and aggravated assault. Property crimes are offenses of burglary, larceny-theft, motor vehicle theft, and arson.

SOURCE: Adapted from "Table 32. Ten-Year Arrest Trends: Totals, 2004–2013," in *Crime in the United States 2013*, U.S. Department of Justice, Federal Bureau of Investigation, November 10, 2014, http://www.fbi.gov/about-us/cjis/ucr/crime-in-the-u.s/2013/crime-in-the-u.s.-2013/tables/table-32/table_32_ten_year_arrest_trends_totals_2013.xls (accessed November 12, 2014)

offender. By 1994 that number had climbed to more than 3,500. Then, murders by juveniles underwent a steep decline.

SCHOOL CRIME

A comprehensive examination of school crime was conducted for the National Center for Education Statistics and the Bureau of Justice Statistics (BJS) by Simone Robers et al. in *Indicators of School Crime and Safety: 2013* (June 2014, http://www.bjs.gov/content/pub/pdf/iscs13.pdf). According to the researchers, approximately 1.4 million students aged 12 to 18 years were the victims of nonfatal crimes at school in 2012. There were 749,200

violent crimes, including rape, sexual assault, robbery, aggravated assault, and simple assault. Another 615,600 crimes were thefts.

School Shootings

Despite the relative safety of schools, several school shootings by juveniles have received national media attention in the past several years:

- April 20, 1999: 12 students and a teacher were fatally shot at Columbine High School in Littleton, Colorado, by students Eric Harris (1981–1999) and Dylan Klebold (1982–1999), who eventually killed themselves after an hour-long rampage.

- February 29, 2000: a six-year-old student was killed at Theo J. Buell Elementary School near Flint, Michigan, by Dedrick Owens (1993–), a fellow six-year-old student who brought a handgun to school.

- March 5, 2001: two students were killed and 13 wounded at Santee High School in Santana, California, when Charles A. Williams (1986–), a 15-year-old student at the school, opened fire from a school bathroom.

- April 14, 2003: one 15-year-old student was killed and three were wounded at John McDonogh High School in New Orleans, Louisiana, by gunfire from four teenagers who attended a different school.

- March 21, 2005: 16-year-old Jeff Weise (1988–2005) killed his grandfather and a companion. He then went to Red Lake High School in Red Lake, Minnesota, and killed five students, a security guard, a teacher, and finally himself.

- February 27, 2012: 17-year-old Thomas "T. J." Lane (1994–) used a firearm to kill three students in the cafeteria at Chardon High School in Chardon, Ohio. Lane attended another school and gave no reason for the killings after his capture.

- October 24, 2014: 15-year-old Jaylen Fryberg used a firearm to kill four students and wound another one in the cafeteria at Marysville High School near Seattle, Washington. He then committed suicide.

YOUTH GANGS

Although gangs have been a part of American life since the early 18th century, modern street gangs pose a greater threat to public safety and order than ever before. Many gangs originated as social clubs. In the early 20th century most were small groups who engaged in delinquent acts or minor crimes, such as fighting with other gangs. By the late 20th century, however, they were frequently involved in violence, intimidation, and the illegal trafficking of drugs and weapons. An increasing number supported themselves by the sale of crack

TABLE 10.6

Ten-year arrest trends for persons under 18 years of age, by sex and offense, 2004–13

[7,858 agencies. 2013 estimated population 192,473,854; 2004 estimated population 178,805,123.]

	Male Under 18			Female Under 18		
Offense charged	2004	2013	Percent change	2004	2013	Percent change
Total[a]	880,360	474,379	−46.1	346,505	191,884	−44.6
Murder and nonnegligent manslaughter	579	426	−26.4	64	66	+3.1
Rape[b]	2,350	1,431	−39.1	64	53	−17.2
Robbery	13,493	11,146	−17.4	1,443	1,194	−17.3
Aggravated assault	27,713	14,486	−47.7	8,199	4,865	−40.7
Burglary	43,716	24,592	−43.7	6,005	3,368	−43.9
Larceny-theft	114,914	69,383	−39.6	83,157	47,758	−42.6
Motor vehicle theft	18,772	6,058	−67.7	4,012	1,309	−67.4
Arson	3,959	2,009	−49.3	634	361	−43.1
Violent crime[c]	44,135	27,489	−37.7	9,770	6,178	−36.8
Property crime[c]	181,361	102,042	−43.7	93,808	52,796	−43.7
Other assaults	98,809	57,829	−41.5	49,934	33,607	−32.7
Forgery and counterfeiting	1,965	462	−76.5	1,023	187	−81.7
Fraud	2,919	1,838	−37.0	1,703	917	−46.2
Embezzlement	424	161	−62.0	274	72	−73.7
Stolen property; buying, receiving, possessing	11,674	5,361	−54.1	2,205	993	−55.0
Vandalism	52,463	25,044	−52.3	8,799	4,632	−47.4
Weapons; carrying, possessing, etc.	22,772	11,539	−49.3	2,706	1,232	−54.5
Prostitution and commercialized vice	311	104	−66.6	846	446	−47.3
Sex offenses (except rape and prostitution)	9,896	5,601	−43.4	1,027	648	−36.9
Drug abuse violations	97,947	62,043	−36.7	20,445	13,724	−32.9
Gambling	1,073	545	−49.2	26	24	−7.7
Offenses against the family and children	2,269	1,034	−54.4	1,339	634	−52.7
Driving under the influence	8,862	3,283	−63.0	2,350	1,032	−56.1
Liquor laws	46,834	21,047	−55.1	25,142	13,236	−47.4
Drunkenness	8,558	3,754	−56.1	2,559	1,353	−47.1
Disorderly conduct	74,220	35,078	−52.7	36,154	18,393	−49.1
Vagrancy	2,221	419	−81.1	917	126	−86.3
All other offenses (except traffic)	166,822	92,400	−44.6	63,717	33,576	−47.3
Suspicion	380	31	−91.8	155	7	−95.5
Curfew and loitering law violations	44,825	17,306	−61.4	21,761	8,078	−62.9

[a]Does not include suspicion.
[b]The rape figures in this table are based on the legacy definition of rape only. The rape figures shown include converted National Incident-Based Reporting System rape data and those states/agencies that reported the legacy definition of rape for both years.
[c]Violent crimes in this table are offenses of murder and nonnegligent manslaughter, rape (legacy definition), robbery, and aggravated assault. Property crimes are offenses of burglary, larceny-theft, motor vehicle theft, and arson.

SOURCE: Adapted from "Table 33. Ten-Year Arrest Trends by Sex, 2004–2013," in *Crime in the United States 2013*, U.S. Department of Justice, Federal Bureau of Investigation, November 10, 2014, http://www.fbi.gov/about-us/cjis/ucr/crime-in-the-u.s/2013/crime-in-the-u.s.-2013/tables/table-33/table_33_ten_year_arrest_trends_by_sex_2013.xls (accessed November 12, 2014)

cocaine, heroin, and other illegal drugs, and had easy access to high-powered guns and rifles.

In the fact sheet "Highlights of the 2011 National Youth Gang Survey" (September 2013, http://www.ojjdp.gov/pubs/242884.pdf), Arlen Egley Jr. and James C. Howell of the National Gang Center summarize results from a 2011 survey of more than 2,000 police and sheriff's departments around the country. According to the researchers, the results indicate that there were approximately 782,500 gang members and 29,900 gangs in the United States in 2011. It should be noted that exact statistics on national gang activity are difficult to compile because local law enforcement agencies may not be aware of gang connections in some cases or may not regularly record offenses as gang related. Egley and Howell note that approximately 1,824 gang-related homicides occurred in 2011. This value was down from 2,020 in 2010.

CRIMINAL VICTIMIZATIONS BY JUVENILES

As described in Chapter 3, the BJS conducts an annual survey called the National Crime Victimization Survey (NCVS), in which a national representative sample of U.S. households is surveyed about criminal victimization. U.S. residents aged 12 years and older are questioned to determine if they have been crime victims during the previous year. If so, information is collected about the circumstances of the crime(s) and the perpetrators involved. Figure 10.1 provides NCVS data for serious violent crimes in which the victims "perceived" that the perpetrators were 12 to 17 years of age. The BJS definition of serious violent crimes includes aggravated assault, rape, and robbery (e.g., stealing that involves the use or threat of force or violence). The data graphed in Figure 10.1 also cover homicides that are believed to have involved one or more juvenile offenders. These homicides were reported to law enforcement agencies.

FIGURE 10.1

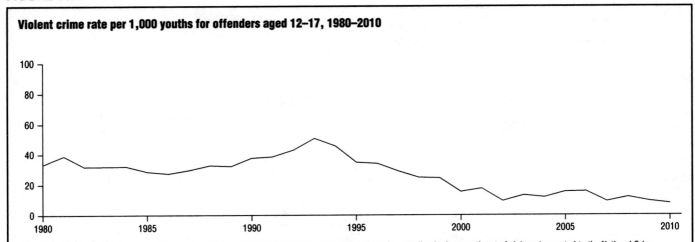

Violent crime rate per 1,000 youths for offenders aged 12–17, 1980–2010

Note: The offending rate is the ratio of the number of crimes (aggravated assault, rape, and robbery, i.e., stealing by force or threat of violence) reported to the National Crime Victimization Survey (NCVS) that involved at least one offender perceived by the victim to be 12–17 years of age, plus the number of homicides reported to the police that involved at least one juvenile offender, to the number of juveniles in the population. Homicide data were not available for 2010 at the time of publication. The number of homicides for 2009 is included in the overall total for 2010. In 2009, homicides represented about 1 percent of serious violent crime, and the total number of homicides by juveniles has been relatively stable over the last decade. Because of changes made in the victimization survey, data prior to 1992 are adjusted to make them comparable with data collected under the redesigned methodology. Due to further methodological changes in the 2006 NCVS, use caution when comparing 2006 criminal perpetration estimates to those for other years. Estimates may vary from previous publications due to updating of more recent homicide numbers.

SOURCE: "Figure 11. Rate of Serious Violent Crimes by Youth Perpetrators Ages 12–17, 1980–2010," in *America's Children in Brief: Key National Indicators of Well-Being, 2012*, Federal Interagency Forum on Child and Family Statistics, July 2012, http://www.childstats.gov/pdf/ac2012/ac_12.pdf (accessed November 9, 2014)

Homicide data are collected and published by the FBI as part of its UCR Program, which is described in Chapter 2.

As shown in Figure 10.1, the rate of serious violent crimes attributed to juvenile offenders aged 12 to 17 years peaked during the early 1990s at around 50 crimes per 1,000 U.S. youth aged 12 to 17 years. The rate plummeted over the following decade, dropping to less than 20 crimes per 1,000 youth. In 2010 the rate was 9 crimes per 1,000 youth. (Note that homicide data were not available for 2010, so the 2010 rate is based on 2009 homicide data.)

JUVENILE COURT CASES

Each state and the District of Columbia has its own juvenile justice system. Although no nationwide uniform procedure exists for processing juvenile cases, the cases do follow similar paths. An intake department first screens cases. The intake department can be the court itself, a state department of social services, or a prosecutor's office. The intake officer may decide that the case will be dismissed for lack of evidence, handled formally (petitioned), or resolved informally (nonpetitioned). Formal processing can include placement outside the home, probation, a trial in juvenile court, or transfer to an adult court. Informal processing may consist of referral to a social services agency, a fine, some form of restitution, or informal probation. Both formal and informal processing can result in dismissal of the charges and release of the juvenile.

There are two broad types of cases within juvenile court: petitioned and nonpetitioned. Petitioned cases are those in which a petition is filed requesting a hearing. Nonpetitioned cases do not include such a petition and are handled more informally by the courts.

Juvenile courts may place youths in a detention facility during court processing. Detention may be needed to protect the community from the juvenile, to protect the juvenile, or both. In addition, detention is sometimes necessary to ensure a youth's appearance at scheduled hearings or evaluations.

All states allow certain juveniles to be tried in adult criminal court under some circumstances. These circumstances include the use of firearms or other weapons and a history of criminality. In some states juvenile court judges are allowed to determine whether individual suspects will be prosecuted in juvenile or adult criminal court; some states allow prosecutors to determine whether to file cases in juvenile or adult criminal court; and some states have laws that determine which court holds jurisdiction over cases, depending on the age of the suspect and the crime committed.

Although juvenile justice is governed by state laws, the federal government plays a role by setting standards for juvenile courts and providing funding to state agencies that deal with juvenile crime. In 1968 Congress passed the Juvenile Delinquency Prevention and Control Act; in 1972 it was amended and renamed the Juvenile Delinquency Prevention Act. According to the Cornell

University Law School's Legal Information Institute, in "Juvenile Justice" (2014, http://www.law.cornell.edu/wex/juvenile_justice), "The stated purpose of the act is to assist states and local communities in providing community based preventative services to youths in danger of becoming delinquent, to help train individuals in occupations providing such services, and to provide technical assistance in the field." It also sets standards and rules for state juvenile court "procedures and punishments."

The Juvenile Justice and Delinquency Prevention Act was passed in 1974 and has been amended several times. It provides grant funding to states that comply with its requirements. As explained by Snyder and Sickmund, in *Juvenile Offenders and Victims: 1999 National Report* (September 1999, http://www.ncjrs.gov/html/ojjdp/national report99/toc.html), the act establishes four primary or "core" requirements for the grants:

- Status offenders (e.g., offenders who commit acts such as running away from home, failing to attend school, or violating curfew) should not be placed in secure detention or correctional facilities.

- Detained or confined juveniles cannot have "sight or sound" contact with incarcerated adults.

- Juveniles cannot be detained or confined in adult jails or lockups except under certain circumstances.

- States must determine if they are confining minority juveniles disproportionately to nonminority juveniles and, if so, demonstrate efforts to reduce the disproportionality.

CHANGING APPROACHES TO JUVENILE DELINQUENCY

Before the 1950s the U.S. juvenile justice system was heavily focused on rehabilitation. This approach began to change as the public judged rehabilitation techniques to be ineffective. A growing number of juveniles were being institutionalized until they reached adulthood because the medical treatment they received did not seem to modify their behavior. Under the impetus of a number of U.S. Supreme Court decisions, juvenile courts became more formal to protect juveniles' rights when they were transferred to adult courts or if they were to be confined. During the 1970s the national policy became community-based management of juvenile delinquents.

Public perception changed again during the 1980s. Juvenile crime was growing, and the systems in place were perceived as being too lenient in dealing with delinquents. This spurred a nationwide movement toward tougher treatment of juveniles. In *Juvenile Offenders and Victims: 1999 National Report*, Snyder and Sickmund note that between 1992 and 1997 nearly all the states passed laws making their juvenile justice system more punitive (punishment oriented).

Laurence Steinberg argues in "Introducing the Issue" (*Future of Children*, vol. 18, no. 2, Fall 2008) that during the 1990s Americans experienced a "moral panic" about juvenile crime that fueled "get tough" on crime policies that treated many juvenile offenders as adults. However, Steinberg suggests that by the end of the first decade of the 21st century get-tough policies were softening "as politicians and the public come to regret the high economic costs and ineffectiveness of the punitive reforms and the harshness of the sanctions."

JUVENILE CRIMES: COURT STATISTICS

As noted earlier, juvenile offenses are either status offenses or delinquency offenses. Status offenses apply only to minors, not to adults. They include acts such as running away from home, truancy (failure to attend school), or violating curfew. Delinquency offenses include murder, rape and other sexual offenses, robbery, burglary, larceny-theft, and other criminal acts for which adults can also be charged.

The Office of Juvenile Justice and Delinquency Prevention (OJJDP) is an agency within the U.S. Department of Justice that compiles statistics on the nation's juvenile courts. As shown in Figure 10.2, the number of delinquency cases handled in U.S. juvenile courts increased from around 400,000 cases in 1960 to more than 1.8 million cases per year during the late 1990s. By 2010 the number had declined to nearly 1.4 million cases.

Table 10.7 provides detailed data about the nearly 1.4 million delinquency cases that were handled by juvenile courts in 2010. The number of person offense cases decreased by 15% between 2001 and 2010. Property offenses declined by 24%, while drug law violations decreased by 15% and public order offenses fell by 16%.

Charles Puzzanchera and Crystal Robson of the OJJDP report in "Delinquency Cases in Juvenile Court, 2010" (February 2014, http://www.ojjdp.gov/pubs/243041.pdf) that male juveniles accounted for 986,700 cases or 72.1% of the total delinquency caseload in 2010. In contrast, female juveniles were involved in 27.9% of the total delinquency caseload. This value was up from 26% in 2001. The racial and ethnic breakdown of juvenile delinquency cases in 2010 is shown in Table 10.8. Overall, whites (64%) accounted for the largest share of juvenile delinquents, followed by African Americans (33%), Native Americans (1%), and Asian Americans (1%). At that time whites accounted for 76% of the overall U.S juvenile population and African Americans accounted for 16%. Thus, African American youths were highly overrepresented within the juvenile delinquent population. Table 10.8 also provides a racial breakdown of juvenile delinquents by offense type. In all offense categories, white offenders outnumbered African

FIGURE 10.2

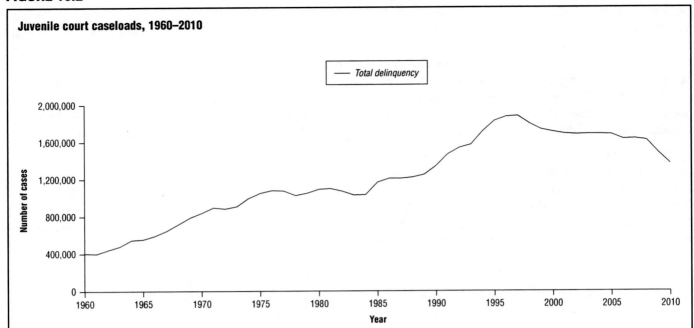

Juvenile court caseloads, 1960–2010

—— Total delinquency

SOURCE: Charles Puzzanchera and Crystal Robson, "The decline in juvenile court caseloads since the mid-1990s is the most substantial decline since 1960," in *Delinquency Cases in Juvenile Court, 2010*, U.S. Department of Justice, Office of Justice Programs, Office of Juvenile Justice and Delinquency Prevention, February 2014, http://www.ojjdp.gov/pubs/243041.pdf (accessed November 5, 2014)

TABLE 10.7

Juvenile delinquency cases disposed, by most serious offense, 2010

Most serious offense	Number of cases	10 year 2001–2010	5 year 2006–2010	1 year 2009–2010
Total delinquency	**1,368,200**	**−19%**	**−16%**	**−8%**
Person offenses	346,800	−15	−17	−5
Criminal homicide	1,000	−23	−27	−20
Forcible rape	3,900	−15	−12	−3
Robbery	26,300	22	−12	−10
Aggravated assault	39,900	−21	−20	−6
Simple assault	237,100	−17	−16	−4
Other violent sex offenses	12,700	−2	−12	−1
Other person offenses	26,000	−19	−23	−7
Property offenses	502,400	−24	−15	−11
Burglary	90,100	−21	−14	−8
Larceny-theft	243,800	−19	−2	−11
Motor vehicle theft	16,100	−58	−45	−16
Arson	5,500	−41	−35	−18
Vandalism	79,400	−19	−26	−14
Trespassing	42,500	−21	−20	−10
Stolen property offenses	14,000	−42	−28	−10
Other property offenses	11,100	−55	−40	−15
Drug law violations	164,100	−15	−10	−1
Public order offenses	354,800	−16	−20	−9
Obstruction of justice	166,200	−20	−15	−9
Disorderly conduct	101,200	−6	−22	−8
Weapons offenses	29,700	−12	−33	−9
Liquor law violations	16,400	3	−18	−5
Nonviolent sex offenses	11,200	−21	−9	0
Other public order offenses	30,000	−26	−29	−12

Notes: Data may not add to totals because of rounding. Percent change calculations are based on unrounded numbers.

SOURCE: Charles Puzzanchera and Crystal Robson, "Delinquency Cases Disposed, by Most Serious Offense, 2010," in *Delinquency Cases in Juvenile Court, 2010*, U.S. Department of Justice, Office of Justice Programs, Office of Juvenile Justice and Delinquency Prevention, February 2014, http://www.ojjdp.gov/pubs/243041.pdf (accessed November 5, 2014)

American offenders, but African American youth were overrepresented compared with their share of the overall population.

Figure 10.3 shows the outcome of the delinquency cases in 2010. Just over half (54%) were petitioned and 46% were not petitioned. In more than half (58%) of the petitioned cases the juvenile was adjudicated delinquent (found responsible by a judge for the alleged act). This is procedurally similar to a conviction in criminal court. In another 41% of the petitioned cases the juvenile was not adjudicated delinquent. Approximately 1% of the petitioned cases were waived to adult criminal court.

Most (60%) of the juveniles whose cases were petitioned but were not adjudicated delinquent had their

TABLE 10.8

Breakdown of juvenile delinquency cases, by most serious offense and race, 2010

Most serious offense	Total	White	Black	American Indian	Asian
Total delinquency	**100%**	**64%**	**33%**	**1%**	**1%**
Person	100	57	40	1	1
Property	100	66	31	2	2
Drugs	100	76	21	2	1
Public order	100	63	34	2	1

Note: Detail may not add to totals because of rounding.

SOURCE: Charles Puzzanchera and Crystal Robson, "Race Profile of Cases, 2010," in *Delinquency Cases in Juvenile Court, 2010*, U.S. Department of Justice, Office of Justice Programs, Office of Juvenile Justice and Delinquency Prevention, February 2014, http://www.ojjdp.gov/pubs/243041.pdf (accessed November 5, 2014)

cases dismissed. (See Figure 10.3.) In the remainder the juveniles either received probation (25%) or some other sanction (14%). Probation was given in 61% of the petitioned cases where juveniles were adjudicated delinquent. Over one-fourth (26%) of the juveniles who were adjudicated delinquent went into residential placement and 13% received some other sanction.

For 2010 there were 635,000 juvenile delinquency cases that were not petitioned. (See Figure 10.3.) Among these juveniles, 267,600 (42%) had their case dismissed, while 155,500 (24%) were put in probation and 211,800 (33%) received other sanctions.

STATUS OFFENSE CASES

Status offenses are acts that are against the law only because the people who commit them are juveniles. In many communities social service agencies rather than juvenile courts are responsible for accused status offenders. Because of the differences in screening procedures, national estimates of informally handled status offense cases are not calculated. Therefore, the statistics presented in this chapter report only on status offense cases that are formally handled (petitioned) through the juvenile justice system.

FIGURE 10.3

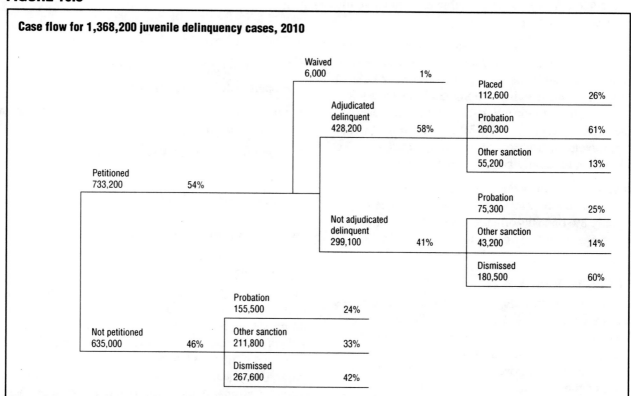

Case flow for 1,368,200 juvenile delinquency cases, 2010

Waived 6,000 — 1%

Adjudicated delinquent 428,200 — 58%
Placed 112,600 — 26%
Probation 260,300 — 61%
Other sanction 55,200 — 13%

Petitioned 733,200 — 54%

Not adjudicated delinquent 299,100 — 41%
Probation 75,300 — 25%
Other sanction 43,200 — 14%
Dismissed 180,500 — 60%

Not petitioned 635,000 — 46%
Probation 155,500 — 24%
Other sanction 211,800 — 33%
Dismissed 267,600 — 42%

Notes: Cases are categorized by their most severe or restrictive sanction. Detail may not add to totals because of rounding.

SOURCE: Charles Puzzanchera and Crystal Robson, "Case Flow for 1,368,200 Delinquency Cases in 2010," in *Delinquency Cases in Juvenile Court, 2010*, U.S. Department of Justice, Office of Justice Programs, Office of Juvenile Justice and Delinquency Prevention, February 2014, http://www.ojjdp.gov/pubs/243041.pdf (accessed November 5, 2014)

According to Sarah Hockenberry and Charles Puzzanchera of the National Center for Juvenile Justice, in *Juvenile Court Statistics 2011* (July 2014, http://ojjdp .gov/ojstatbb/njcda/pdf/jcs2011.pdf), the OJJDP uses five major status offense categories: running away, truancy, liquor law violations, curfew violations, and ungovernability (also known as incorrigibility or being beyond parental control). The researchers report that 116,200 status offense cases were petitioned to juvenile courts in 2011. This number was down 7% from 1995. The following is a breakdown by offenses for 2011:

- Truancy—40% of cases

- Liquor law violations—20% of cases

- Ungovernability—12% of cases

- Curfew violations—10% of cases

- Running away—9% of cases

- Miscellaneous—9% of cases

Detention and Case Processing

The handling of status crimes has changed considerably since the mid-1980s. The Juvenile Justice and Delinquency Prevention Act of 1974 offered substantial federal funds to states that tried to reduce the detention of status offenders. The primary responsibility for status offenders was often transferred from the juvenile courts to child welfare agencies. As a result, the character of the juvenile courts' activities changed.

Before this change many juvenile detention centers held a substantial number of young people whose only offense was that their parents could no longer control them. By not routinely institutionalizing these adolescents, the courts demonstrated that children deserved the same rights as adults. A logical extension of this has been that juveniles accused of violent crimes are also now being treated legally as if they are adults.

Those involved in petitioned status offense cases are rarely held in detention. Hockenberry and Puzzanchera indicate that only 8% of status offenders were detained in 2011. This percentage is virtually unchanged from 7% in 1995.

JUVENILES IN RESIDENTIAL PLACEMENT

Accused juveniles, delinquency offenders, and status offenders may be housed in residential placement facilities. These institutions may be under the administration of the state or be operated by private nonprofit or for-profit corporations or organizations and staffed by employees of the corporation or organization.

In *Juveniles in Residential Placement, 1997–2008* (February 2010, http://www.ncjrs.gov/pdffiles1/ojjdp/ 229379.pdf), Sickmund notes that juvenile residential placement facilities are also known as "detention centers,

juvenile halls, shelters, reception and diagnostic centers, group homes, wilderness camps, ranches, farms, youth development centers, residential treatment centers, training or reform schools, and juvenile correctional institutions."

Every two to three years the OJJDP conducts the Census of Juveniles in Residential Placement, a one-day count of the juvenile offenders who are held nationwide. The data collected include juvenile offender demographics, such as gender, race, ethnicity, and most serious offense. As of January 2015, the most recent census was conducted in 2011. The results are presented by Hockenberry, in *Juveniles in Residential Placement, 2011* (August 2014, http://www.ojjdp.gov/pubs/246826.pdf). According to Hockenberry, 61,423 juvenile offenders were housed in public and private residential placement facilities around the country in 2011. (See Figure 10.4.) This was down considerably from 1997, when the number was 105,055. The gender split in 2011 was 86% male and 14% female. The racial and ethnic breakdown was as follows:

- African American—40% of the total

- White—32% of the total

- Hispanic—23% of the total

- Native American—2% of the total

- Asian American—1% of the total

- Other—2% of the total

The breakdown by offense was as follows:

- Person offense—36% of the total

- Property offense—22% of the total

- Technical violation of probation or parole or a violation of a valid court order—22% of the total

- Public order offense—12% of the total

- Drug offense—6% of the total

- Status offense—3% of the total

Sexual Victimization of Juvenile Inmates

As noted in Chapter 8, the Prison Rape Elimination Act of 2003 requires the BJS to collect data on the incidence and prevalence of sexual assault within correctional facilities. Allen J. Beck et al. report on sexual victimization involving juvenile inmates in *Sexual Victimization in Juvenile Facilities Reported by Youth, 2012* (June 2013, http://www.bjs.gov/content/pub/pdf/svjfry12 .pdf). The researchers note that the BJS conducted its second National Survey of Youth in Custody between February and September 2012. The survey covered 326 public and private juvenile facilities that held adjudicated juveniles for at least 90 days. National-level estimates of sexual victimization for all adjudicated juvenile inmates

FIGURE 10.4

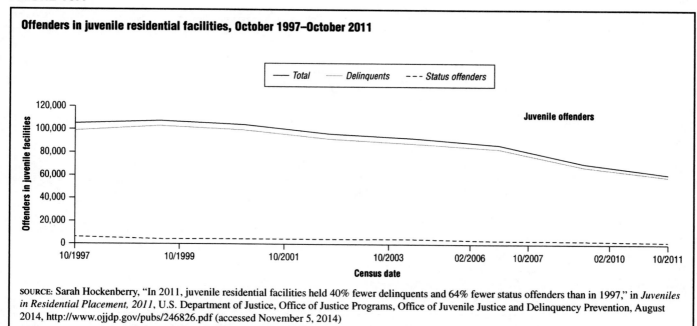

Offenders in juvenile residential facilities, October 1997–October 2011

— Total   ······ Delinquents   - - - Status offenders

Juvenile offenders

Offenders in juvenile facilities

120,000
100,000
80,000
60,000
40,000
20,000
0

10/1997   10/1999   10/2001   10/2003   02/2006   10/2007   02/2010   10/2011

Census date

SOURCE: Sarah Hockenberry, "In 2011, juvenile residential facilities held 40% fewer delinquents and 64% fewer status offenders than in 1997," in *Juveniles in Residential Placement, 2011*, U.S. Department of Justice, Office of Justice Programs, Office of Juvenile Justice and Delinquency Prevention, August 2014, http://www.ojjdp.gov/pubs/246826.pdf (accessed November 5, 2014)

were developed based on the results of the survey. Overall, Beck et al. estimate that 9.5% of adjudicated juvenile inmates experienced sexual victimization by another youth or staff within the previous 12 months or since their time of admission if admission occurred less than 12 months prior to the time of the survey. Any type of sexual activity involving staff was considered sexual victimization, and 7.7% of adjudicated juvenile inmates were estimated to have experienced such victimization.

JUVENILE DELINQUENCY PREVENTION

The criminal justice system also focuses resources on preventing juveniles from becoming delinquents in the first place and on helping delinquents to reform. For example, as of January 2015 the OJJDP (http://www.ojjdp.gov) noted that it had programs devoted to preventing gang involvement, girls' delinquency, and underage drinking. In "Comprehensive Anti-gang Initiative" (2014, http://www.ojjdp.gov/programs/antigang), the agency describes its role in developing, funding, and evaluating "community-based anti-gang programs that coordinate prevention, intervention, enforcement, and reentry strategies."

In accordance with the Juvenile Justice and Delinquency Prevention Act of 1974, as amended, the OJJDP provides funding for state programs that are devoted to delinquency prevention. These programs typically provide a variety of services to youths, such as mentoring, substance abuse education and treatment, and educational support. For example, the New York State Division of Criminal Justice Services (2014, http://www.criminaljustice.ny.gov/ofpa/juvdelprevfactsheet.htm) operates the state's Delinquency Prevention Grant Program with funding provided by the federal government. The program

provides grants to local communities to fund delinquency prevention activities. The agency notes that "prevention strategies succeed when they are positive in orientation and comprehensive in scope. Successful community strategies create opportunities for healthy physical, social, and mental development of juveniles. Programs consider the influence of family, peer group, school, and the community on a child's development." The North Carolina Department of Public Safety's Division of Juvenile Justice is also active in juvenile delinquency prevention and notes in "Community Programs" (2014, https://www.ncdps.gov/Index2.cfm?a=000003,002476,002483) that its goals are "to strengthen families, promote delinquency prevention, support core social institutions, intervene immediately and effectively when delinquent behavior occurs, and to identify and control the small group of serious, violent, and chronic juvenile offenders in the local communities."

Besides government resources, many private organizations devote themselves to juvenile delinquency prevention. For example, the Prevent Delinquency Project (2015, http://preventdelinquency.org) was founded in New York in 2003 and advocates "proactive parenting techniques." The organization's founder, Carl A. Bartol, is a former prosecutor and focuses on educating parents about the nature of juvenile crime and the measures they can take to help prevent their children from becoming juvenile delinquents.

JUVENILES IN THE ADULT JUSTICE SYSTEM

As noted earlier and shown in Figure 10.5, 6,000 juvenile cases were waived to adult criminal court in 2010. In "Delinquency Cases Waived to Criminal Court,

FIGURE 10.5

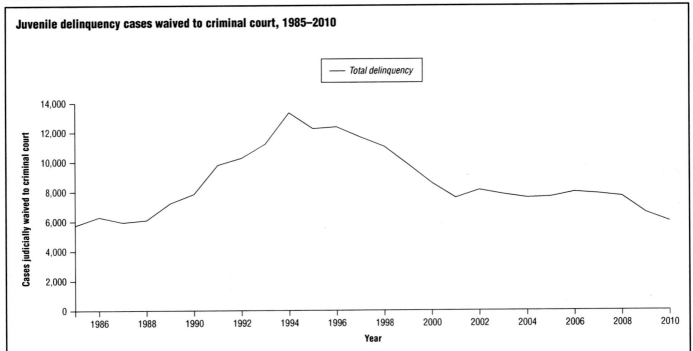

Juvenile delinquency cases waived to criminal court, 1985–2010

SOURCE: Charles Puzzanchera and Sean Addie, "The number of cases judicially waived to criminal court in 2010 was 55% less than in 1994, the peak year," in *Delinquency Cases Waived to Criminal Court, 2010*, U.S. Department of Justice, Office of Justice Programs, Office of Juvenile Justice and Delinquency Prevention, February 2014, http://www.ojjdp.gov/pubs/243042.pdf (accessed November 5, 2014)

2010" (February 2014, http://www.ojjdp.gov/pubs/243042.pdf), Charles Puzzanchera and Sean Addie of the OJJDP indicate that this number was down substantially from the 1990s, when more than 12,000 waivers were issued per year. They explain that this decline was driven by an overall drop in the juvenile violent crime rate as well as by more widespread use of nonjudicial transfer laws. These laws allow prosecutors to directly file charges against juveniles in adult criminal court, bypassing the juvenile justice system entirely.

Figure 10.6 shows the number of inmates aged 17 years or younger held in adult state and federal prisons between 2000 and 2013. According to E. Ann Carson of the BJS, in *Prisoners in 2013* (September 30, 2014, http://www.bjs.gov/content/pub/pdf/p13.pdf), state prisons held 1,188 youths in 2013. This number was down significantly from nearly 4,000 youth in 2000. Florida had the most youth inmates (144) at yearend 2013, followed by New York (131) and Connecticut (88). The federal prison system held only 89 inmates aged 17 years or younger at yearend 2013. Carson notes that these youths were incarcerated in private contract facilities rather than in regular federal prisons.

Until 2005 convicted criminals could be executed for crimes they committed as juveniles. Victor L. Streib of Ohio Northern University reports in *The Juvenile Death Penalty Today: Death Sentences and Executions for Juvenile Crimes, January 1, 1973–February 28, 2005*

(October 7, 2005, http://www.deathpenaltyinfo.org/documents/StreibJuvDP2005.pdf) that between 1973 and 2005, 22 offenders were executed for crimes they committed when they were younger than 18 years old. The U.S. Supreme Court has considered many cases that address the practice of executing offenders for crimes they committed as juveniles. For example, in *Eddings v. Oklahoma* (455 U.S. 104 [1982]), the court found that a juvenile's mental and emotional development should be considered as a mitigating factor when deciding whether to apply the death penalty, noting that adolescents are less mature and responsible than adults and not as able to consider long-range consequences of their actions. In this case, the court reversed the death sentence of a 16-year-old who had been tried as an adult.

Subsequent Supreme Court rulings have further limited the application of the death penalty in cases involving juveniles. In *Thompson v. Oklahoma* (487 U.S. 815 [1988]), the court found that applying the death sentence to an offender who had been 15 years old at the time of the murder was cruel and unusual punishment, concluding that the death penalty could not be applied to offenders who were younger than 16 years old. The following year the court found in *Stanford v. Kentucky* (492 U.S. 361 [1989]) that applying the death penalty to offenders who were aged 16 or 17 years at the time of the crime was not cruel and unusual punishment.

The court was asked to reconsider this decision in 2005. In *Roper v. Simmons* (543 U.S. 551), the court set

FIGURE 10.6

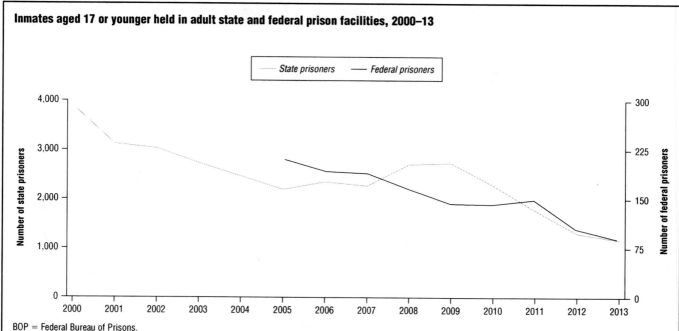

Inmates aged 17 or younger held in adult state and federal prison facilities, 2000–13

BOP = Federal Bureau of Prisons.

Note: Counts based on inmates age 17 or younger in custody of state and federal correctional authorities, regardless of sentence length. The Federal Bureau of Prisons holds inmates age 17 or younger in private contract facilities. Counts for BOP may include some inmates under the jurisdiction of U.S. probation being held by the BOP in private contract facilities.

SOURCE: E. Ann Carson, "Figure 2. Inmates Age 17 or Younger Held in Adult State and Federal Prison Facilities, 2000–2013," in *Prisoners in 2013*, U.S. Department of Justice, Office of Justice Programs, Bureau of Justice Statistics, September 30, 2014, http://www.bjs.gov/content/pub/pdf/p13.pdf (accessed November 4, 2014)

aside the death sentence of Christopher Simmons, concluding that the "Eighth and Fourteenth Amendments forbid imposition of the death penalty on offenders who were under the age of 18 when their crimes were committed." Snyder and Sickmund note in *Juvenile Offenders and Victims: 2006 National Report* that few states applied death penalty provisions to juveniles at the time of the *Roper* decision, even though 20 states allowed juveniles to be sentenced to death under the law.

After the 2005 *Roper* ruling, the most severe punishment for juveniles convicted of committing serious crimes was a sentence of life in prison without the possibility of parole. However, this sentence was also challenged on constitutional grounds. In May 2010 the Supreme Court ruled in *Graham v. Florida* (No. 08-7412) that juveniles convicted of crimes in which nobody is killed cannot be sentenced to life in prison without the possibility of parole. The case involved Terrance Graham, a Florida juvenile who was convicted of several armed robberies when he was 16 and 17 years old. In 2005 Graham was sentenced to life in prison without the possibility of parole. Jeff Kunerth notes in "Life without Parole Becomes 25 Years for Terrance Graham, Subject of U.S. Supreme Court Case" (OrlandoSentinel.com, February 24, 2012) that in February 2012 Graham's sentence was converted to a 25-year term.

In June 2012 the U.S. Supreme Court ruled in *Miller v. Alabama* (No. 10-9646) and *Jackson v. Hobbs* (No. 10-9647) that juveniles cannot be subject to mandatory life sentences without the possibility of parole, even if they have committed murder. The subjects of both cases were 14 years old at the time their crimes were committed. Evan Miller was convicted of arson and murder for the 2003 death of a man in Alabama, while Kuntrell Jackson of Arkansas was convicted for participating in a 1999 robbery in which an accomplice killed a store clerk. In giving the opinion of the court, Justice Elena Kagan (1960–) cited the precedents set in *Roper* and *Graham* and stated "mandatory life without parole for those under the age of 18 at the time of their crimes violates the Eighth Amendment's prohibition on 'cruel and unusual punishments.'"

IMPORTANT NAMES
AND ADDRESSES

American Bar Association
321 N. Clark St.
Chicago, IL 60654
(312) 988-5000
1-800-285-2221
URL: http://www.americanbar.org/
aba.html

American Civil Liberties Union
125 Broad St., 18th Floor
New York, NY 10004
(212) 549-2500
URL: http://www.aclu.org/

American Correctional Association
206 N. Washington St.
Alexandria, VA 22314
(703) 224-0000
FAX: (703) 224-0179
URL: http://www.aca.org/

American Jail Association
1135 Professional Ct.
Hagerstown, MD 21740-5853
(301) 790-3930
FAX: (301) 790-2941
URL: http://www.americanjail.org/

**Bureau of Alcohol, Tobacco,
Firearms, and Explosives
Office of Public and Governmental
Affairs**
99 New York Ave. NE, Rm. 5S 144
Washington, DC 20226
(202) 648-8500
1-800-800-3855
URL: http://www.atf.gov/

**Bureau of Engraving and Printing
U.S. Department of the Treasury**
14th St. and C St. SW
Washington, DC 20228
(202) 874-4000
E-mail: moneyfactory.info@bep.gov
URL: http://www.moneyfactory.gov/

**Bureau of Justice Statistics
U.S. Department of Justice**
810 Seventh St. NW
Washington, DC 20531
(202) 307-0765
E-mail: askbjs@usdoj.gov
URL: http://www.bjs.gov/

**Congressional Research Service
Library of Congress**
101 Independence Ave. SE
Washington, DC 20540
(202) 707-5000
URL: http://www.loc.gov/crsinfo/

Federal Bureau of Investigation
J. Edgar Hoover Bldg.
935 Pennsylvania Ave. NW
Washington, DC 20535-0001
(202) 324-3000
URL: http://www.fbi.gov/

Federal Bureau of Prisons
320 First St. NW
Washington, DC 20534
(202) 307-3198
URL: http://www.bop.gov/

Federal Trade Commission
600 Pennsylvania Ave. NW
Washington, DC 20580
(202) 326-2222
URL: http://www.ftc.gov/

National Center for Juvenile Justice
3700 S. Water St., Ste. 200
Pittsburgh, PA 15203
(412) 227-6950
FAX: (412) 227-6955
E-mail: ncjj@ncjfcj.org
URL: http://www.ncjj.org/

National Center for Victims of Crime
2000 M St. NW, Ste. 480
Washington, DC 20036
(202) 467-8700

FAX: (202) 467-8701
URL: http://www.victimsofcrime.org/

National Conference of State Legislatures
7700 E. First Place
Denver, CO 80230
(303) 364-7700
FAX: (303) 364-7800
URL: http://www.ncsl.org/

**National Correctional Industries
Association**
800 N. Charles St., Ste. 550B
Baltimore, MD 21201
(410) 230-3972
FAX: (410) 230-3981
URL: http://www.nationalcia.org/

National Crime Prevention Council
2001 Jefferson Davis Hwy., Ste. 901
Arlington, VA 22202-4801
(202) 466-6272
FAX: (202) 296-1356
URL: http://www.ncpc.org/

**National Gang Center
Institute for Intergovernmental Research**
PO Box 12729
Tallahassee, FL 32317
(850) 385-0600
FAX: (850) 386-5356
E-mail: information@nationalgangcenter.gov
URL: http://www.nationalgangcenter.gov/

National Institute of Corrections
320 First St. NW
Washington, DC 20543
(202) 307-3106
1-800-995-6423
URL: http://www.nicic.org/

National Institute of Justice
810 Seventh St. NW
Washington, DC 20531
(202) 307-2942
URL: http://www.nij.gov/

National Organization for Victim Assistance
510 King St., Ste. 424
Alexandria, VA 22314
(703) 535-6682
1-800-879-6682 (victim assistance hotline)
FAX: (703) 535-5500
URL: http://www.trynova.org/

National White Collar Crime Center
10900 Nuckols Rd., Ste. 325
Glen Allen, VA 23060
(804) 273-6932
1-800-221-4424
FAX: (804) 273-1234
E-mail: contact@nw3c.org
URL: http://www.nw3c.org/

Office for Victims of Crime
U.S. Department of Justice
810 Seventh St. NW, Eighth Floor
Washington, DC 20531
(202) 307-5983
FAX: (202) 514-6383
URL: http://www.ojp.usdoj.gov/ovc/

Office of Juvenile Justice and Delinquency Prevention
810 Seventh St. NW
Washington, DC 20531
(202) 307-5911
URL: http://www.ojjdp.gov/

Office of National Drug Control Policy
URL: http://www.whitehouse.gov/ondcp

Rape, Abuse, and Incest National Network
1220 L St. NW, Ste. 505
Washington, DC 20005
(202) 544-3064
1-800-656-4673
FAX: (202) 544-3556

E-mail: info@rainn.org
URL: https://www.rainn.org/

Sentencing Project
1705 DeSales St. NW, Eighth Floor
Washington, DC 20036
(202) 628-0871
FAX: (202) 628-1091
E-mail: staff@sentencingproject.org
URL: http://www.sentencingproject.org/

Southern Poverty Law Center
400 Washington Ave.
Montgomery, AL 36104
(334) 956-8200
1-888-414-7752
URL: http://www.splcenter.org/

Substance Abuse and Mental Health Services Administration
One Choke Cherry Rd.
Rockville, MD 20857
1-877-726-4727
URL: http://www.samhsa.gov/

Supreme Court of the United States
One First St. NE
Washington, DC 20543
(202) 479-3000
URL: http://www.supremecourt.gov/

UNICOR
Federal Prison Industries, Inc.
PO Box 13640
Lexington, KY 40583-3640
1-800-827-3168
FAX: (859) 254-9626
E-mail: UNICOR.CUSTOMER.SERVICE
@usdoj.gov
URL: http://www.unicor.gov/

Urban Institute
2100 M St. NW
Washington, DC 20037

(202) 833-7200
URL: http://urban.org/

U.S. Census Bureau
4600 Silver Hill Rd.
Washington, DC 20233
(301) 763-4636
1-800-923-8282
URL: http://www.census.gov/

U.S. Department of Justice
950 Pennsylvania Ave. NW
Washington, DC 20530-0001
(202) 514-2000
E-mail: askdoj@usdoj.gov
URL: http://www.justice.gov/

U.S. Drug Enforcement Administration
U.S. Department of Justice
8701 Morrissette Dr.
Springfield, VA 22152
(202) 307-1000
URL: http://www.usdoj.gov/dea/index.htm

U.S. Parole Commission
90 K St. NE, Third Floor
Washington, DC 20530
(202) 346-7000
E-mail: public.inquiries@usdoj.gov
URL: http://www.justice.gov/uspc/

U.S. Securities and Exchange Commission
100 F St. NE
Washington, DC 20549
(202) 942-8088
E-mail: help@sec.gov
URL: http://www.sec.gov/

U.S. Sentencing Commission
Office of Public Affairs
One Columbus Circle NE, Ste. 2-500
Washington, DC 20002-8002
(202) 502-4500
E-mail: pubaffairs@ussc.gov
URL: http://www.ussc.gov/

RESOURCES

The various agencies of the U.S. Department of Justice (DOJ) are the major sources of crime and justice data in the United States. The Bureau of Justice Statistics (BJS) compiles statistics on virtually every area of crime and reports these data in a number of publications. The annual BJS National Crime Victimization Survey provides data for several studies, the most important of which is *Criminal Victimization*. The BJS also publishes data about the nation's corrections systems, including detailed counts and information about facilities and inmates, courts and sentencing, types of crime, the population of probationers and parolees, and justice system employment and expenditures.

The Federal Bureau of Investigation (FBI) collects crime data from state and local law enforcement agencies through its Uniform Crime Reporting Program. The FBI's annual *Crime in the United States* is the most important source of information on crime that is reported to law enforcement agencies. The FBI also publishes the annual *Financial Crimes Report to the Public*, which provides statistical data regarding white-collar crime. Other major resources for white-collar crime information include the National White Collar Crime Center, the DOJ's Computer Crime and Intellectual Property Section,

and the Federal Trade Commission's Consumer Sentinel Network and Identity Theft Clearinghouse.

The FBI's annual report *Hate Crime Statistics* provided valuable data about hate crimes, as did private organizations, such as the Southern Poverty Law Center.

The Office of Juvenile Justice and Delinquency Prevention within the DOJ publishes numerous helpful resources about juvenile crime and justice issues, particularly its annual series *Juvenile Arrests*, *Juvenile Court Statistics*, and *Juvenile Offenders and Victims*.

Other important government resources included the U.S. Sentencing Commission's *U.S. Sentencing Commission Guidelines Manual* (November 2014); the Office of National Drug Control Policy of the Executive Office of the President; the Substance Abuse and Mental Health Services Administration of the U.S. Department of Health and Human Services; the U.S. Drug Enforcement Administration; the Federal Interagency Forum on Child and Family Statistics; the U.S. Government Accountability Office; and the Congressional Research Service.

Key information was also acquired from polling results reported by the Gallup Organization.

INDEX

M

Madoff, Bernard, 69–70
Mail censorship, 118
Mala in se crimes, 1, 2
Mala prohibita crimes, 1–2
Malware, 66–67
Mandatory parole, 126
Mandatory sentencing, 53–54, 89, 90–91, 93, 149
Manslaughter, 2–3, 14, 16, 26*f*
Manson, Charles, 12
Marijuana, 52, 54–57, 55*f*, 58*t*
Marriage rights of inmates, 118–119
Martinez, Procunier v., 118
Maryland, Booth v., 43–44
Marysville High School (WA), 140
Mass murderers, 12
Mathis, Lynce v., 121
McDonnell, Wolff v., 120, 121
McDonogh High School, 140
McMillian, Hudson v., 120
McVeigh, Timothy, 5
Mechanical restraints, 120
Mediation, 93
Medical issues among inmates, 113–116, 119–120
Medicare fraud, 61
Medicinal marijuana, 56
Medium-security federal correctional institutions, 97
Mental health issues among inmates, 114–116
Methamphetamine Trafficking Penalty Enhancement Act, 58
Methamphetamines, 58
Militarization of the police, 80–81
Miller, Evan, 149
Miller v. Alabama, 149
Minimum security federal prisons, 97
Miranda v. Arizona, 86
Misdemeanors, 2
Mitchell, Wisconsin v., 25
Money counterfeiting, 68–69
Motor vehicle theft, 23, 28–29, 28(*f*2.11), 32, 39(*t*3.9)
Muhammad, John Allen, 5
Murder
　circumstances and weapons, 17, 19*t*
　crime types, 2–3
　juvenile offenders and victims, 139–140
　notorious criminals, 12
　offenders, 16*t*
　offenders and victims, data on, 16–17
　rates, 14, 16, 26, 26*f*
　victim-offender relationship, 18*t*
　victims, 17*t*

N

National Center for Victims of Crime, 44
National Crime Victimization Survey, 31–33, 71–73
National Crime Victims' Rights Week, 44, 45
National Defense Authorization Act, 81
National Instant Criminal Background Check System, 24
National Organization for Victim Assistance, 42
National White Collar Crime Center, 71
Nelson, Baby Face, 12
New Jersey, Apprendi v., 89, 90
New York City Police Department, 80
Newtown, CT, 12
Nichols, Terry L., 5
Nixon, Richard M., 47
Nolan v. Fitzpatrick, 118
North Carolina, Woodson v., 93
Notorious criminals, 11–12

O

Obama, Barack, 53, 81
Offenders
　juvenile murder offenders, 139–140
　juveniles, 141–142
　murder, 16
　restitution programs, 45
　See also Victim-offender relationship
Office for Victims of Crime, Department of Justice, 43, 44, 45
Ohio, Brandenburg v., 25
Oklahoma, Eddings v., 148
Oklahoma, Thompson v., 148
Oklahoma City bombing, 6
Olympic Park (Atlanta) bombing, 6
Outlaws, 12
Overcrowding, prison, 99–104
Overton, Williams v., 121
Owens, Dedrick, 140

P

Palmer, Hudson v., 119
Parental responsibility, 135
Parker, Bonnie, 12
Parole, 124*t*, 125*t*, 126–130, 126*t*, 131*f*, 132*t*–134*t*
Pataki, George, 6
Pate, Cooper v., 117
PATRIOT Act, 67
Payne v. Tennessee, 44
Pell v. Procunier, 118
Penalties. *See* Sentencing
Penn, William, 95
Personal larceny, 32, 36
Phishing, 66
Physical injuries of victims, 39, 42(*t*3.12)
Plata, Brown v., 102
Plea bargains, 87

Police. *See* Law enforcement
Ponzi schemes, 69–70
Post-conviction DNA testing, 122
Pregnant prisoners, 113
Prevention, delinquency, 147
Prison Litigation Reform Act, 121–122
Prisons
　admissions and releases, 98, 98*f*, 99*t*, 100*t*
　California prison population, 104*t*
　death row inmates, 110–111, 113
　federal, 97–98, 113(*t*8.5), 113(*t*8.6)
　incarceration costs, 106–107
　inmate characteristics, 109–110, 110*t*
　inmate deaths, 116–117, 116*t*
　inmate population numbers and rates, 98–104, 101*f*, 102*t*
　inmates, by offense, 112*t*, 115(*t*8.8)
　inmates' rights, 117–122
　jails compared to, 96–97
　juveniles in adult facilities, 148, 149*f*
　medical issues among inmates, 113–116
　sexual violence in, 116
　state inmate characteristics, 114*t*
Prisons inmate characteristics, 111*t*
Privacy Rights Clearinghouse, 64
Private correctional facilities, 97
Proactive policing, 79
Probation
　alternative sentencing, 92–93
　exits, 129*t*
　probation and parole, adults under, 125*t*, 126*t*
　recidivism rate reduction efforts, 129–130
　reform, 130
　statistics and demographics, 124–126, 124*t*, 127*f*, 128*t*, 130*t*
Procunier, Pell v., 118
Procunier v. Martinez, 118
Property crimes
　economic losses of victims, 41
　rate trends, 15*t*
　reasons for not reporting crimes, 38–39
　reporting rates, 37
　types, 20, 22
　types and circumstances, 21*t*
　victimization rates, 36, 37(*f*3.3)
　victimizations, by crime type, 39(*t*3.9)
　See also specific crimes
Prosecutors, 87
Public opinion. *See* Surveys and public opinion
Public *vs.* private correctional facilities, 97
Punishment categories, 2

Q

Quakers, 95
Quinn, Pat, 107

robbery, 20
violent victimizations, 36t
Weekender programs, 92
Weise, Jeff, 140
White-collar crime
Consumer Sentinel Network, 73–74,
74(t5.5), 75t, 76t
corporate and securities fraud, 69–70
counterfeiting money, 68–69
crime types, 4, 62t–63t
cybercrime, 66–68
identity theft, 64, 66, 72t, 73f, 74(t5.4)
intellectual property crimes, 68

Internet Crime Complain Center, 74–75
National White Collar Crime Center, 71
offenses and arrests, 61–64
public corruption, 70–71
victimization surveys, 71–73
Whitley v. Albers, 120
Wilkinson, Cutter v., 119
Williams, Charles A., 140
Williams v. Overton, 121
Wisconsin v. Mitchell, 25
Wolff v. McDonnell, 120, 121
Wolfish, Bell v., 119, 120

Women prisoners, 113
Woodson v. North Carolina, 93
Work programs, prisoner, 107–108
Work release programs, 92
World Intellectual Property Organization, 68

Y

Youth gangs, 140–141

Z

Zablocki v. Redhail, 119